Linux® Socket Programming

Sean Walton

201 West 103rd St., Indianapolis, Indiana, 46290 USA

Linux® Socket Programming

Trademarks

Warning and Disclaimer

ASSOCIATE PUBLISHERS
Jeff Koch
Michael Stephens

ACQUISITIONS EDITOR
William E. Brown

DEVELOPMENT EDITOR
Tony Amico

MANAGING EDITOR
Matt Purcell

PROJECT EDITOR
Andy Beaster

COPY EDITORS
Pat Kinyon
Gene Redding

INDEXER
Eric Schroeder

PROOFREADERS
Ben Berg
Candice Hightower
Daniel Ponder
Matt Wynalda

TECHNICAL EDITOR
Stephen Heaven

TEAM COORDINATOR
Pamalee Nelson

MEDIA DEVELOPER
Dan Scherf

INTERIOR DESIGNER
Anne Jones

COVER DESIGNER
Aren Howell

LAYOUT TECHNICIANS
Ayanna Lacey
Heather Hiatt Miller
Stacey Richwine-DeRome

Overview

Contents

PART II The Server Perspective and Load Control

6 A Server Primer 115

7 Dividing the Load: Multitasking 133

About the Author

Sean Walton received his master of science degree in computer science in 1990 from Brigham Young University, specializing in merging language and multitasking theory. In 1988 he was hired by the BYU computer science department as a consultant in developing theory and methods for transputer process management, migration, and communication. He began working with BSD sockets while he was an administrator for the computer science department. While he worked for Hewlett-Packard, he developed the automatic language detection (between PostScript and PCL) feature found on LaserJet 4 and later. He also developed a real-time micro operating system for the 8052 microcontroller for emulating printer engines.

Sean has years of professional experience in several types of UNIX programming and administration, including Linux, HPUX, Ultrix, SunOS, and System V. Because he works on so many different systems, he focuses on system-independent programming styles to allow easy porting.

In the last few years, Sean has worked as a professional facilitator, course designer/writer, and instructor in computer fundamentals, requirements gathering, OOA/D, Java, and C++. Early in 1998 he began working with Java sockets and integrated the information into his Java course. He has been a highly sought instructor. While he worked on the Nationwide Financial Process Improvement team, he defined the analysis and design processes to integrate new development with legacy work. He lead and designed the Nationwide Insurance Authentication product, which included split authentication and policies.

Dedication

To the Giver of all Good and Prince of perfect Peace.

Acknowledgments

I know that this book would not have been possible except for several people. First, my beloved wife, Susan, patiently encouraged me and gave me time and coaxing. Second, Wendel, my father, tried to teach me good organization and presentation. Third, the Linux movement selflessly provided me an effective, reliable operating system upon which I could do this work. Fourth, Beverly Scherf opened my eyes and showed me an effective way to communicate. Lastly, I did not realize how important this work was for me professionally until my friends Charles Knutson and Mike Holstein provided input and encouragement.

Tell Us What You Think!

As the reader of this book, *you* are our most important critic and commentator. We value your opinion and want to know what we're doing right, what we could do better, what areas you'd like to see us publish in, and any other words of wisdom you're willing to pass our way.

As an Associate Publisher for Sams, I welcome your comments. You can fax, email, or write me directly to let me know what you did or didn't like about this book—as well as what we can do to make our books stronger.

Please note that I cannot help you with technical problems related to the topic of this book, and that due to the high volume of mail I receive, I might not be able to reply to every message.

When you write, please be sure to include this book's title and author as well as your name and phone or fax number. I will carefully review your comments and share them with the author and editors who worked on the book.

Fax:	317-581-4770
Email:	Samsfeedback@macmillanusa.com
Mail:	Associate Publisher
	Sams
	201 West 103rd Street
	Indianapolis, IN 46290 USA

Introduction

Expanding the Programming Challenge

Most programming targets immediate functions or tasks on your desktop or laptop. These tasks rarely communicate with more than just the mouse, keyboard, display, and file system. A greater programming challenge involves several programs on different computers connected through a network channel. Network programming expands the challenge, because you have to coordinate tasks and send assignments.

The fundamental unit of all network programming in Linux (and most other operating systems) is the socket. In the same way that file I/O connects you to the file system, the socket connects you to the network. The socket is a junction that your program uses to address, send, and receive messages.

Network or socket programming is more challenging than single-task or even multitask programming because true multiprocessing introduces more power and issues. The power is obvious: Parallel Virtual Machines (PMVs) like Beowolf can do much more processing by organizing blocks of tasks and distributing them to networked computers. The issues arise through getting the best throughput, coordinating transfers, and managing I/O.

This book describes and offers several solutions to these issues. It is geared to meet the immediate and long-term needs of the professional network programmer.

Book Organization

This book delves into many particulars of network programming. It is organized into five specific parts, each part building upon earlier parts:

- Part I: Network Programming from the Client Perspective

  This part introduces sockets and defines terms. It describes the different types of sockets, addressing schemes, and network theory.

- Part II: The Server Perspective and Load Control

  Part II expands socket programming with servers, multitasking techniques, I/O control, and socket options.

- Part III: Looking at Sockets Objectively

  C is not the only programming language that provides access to sockets. This part presents some object-oriented approaches and describes the advantages and limitations of object technology in general.

- Part IV: Advanced Sockets—Adding Value

  This part introduces the large realm of advanced network programming techniques, including security, broadcast and multicasting, IPv6, and raw sockets.
- Part V: Appendixes

  The appendixes consolidate much of the resource material relevant to sockets. The first appendix includes tables and listings too large for the chapters. The second and third appendixes describe the Socket and Kernel APIs.

The companion Web site contains all the source code for the book examples, the book appendixes in HTML and Adobe's Portable Document Format (PDF), and socket programming–related RFCs in HTML format.

Professional Reader's Styles

This book is designed for the professional programmer. Typically, the professional wants to do one of three things: learn a new technology, solve a particular problem, or look up some example or definition. The chapters and appendixes attempt to meet each of these criteria.

- *Linear reading front-to-back*   This is for those who want to be exposed to one topic at a time. Each section and chapter builds on previous knowledge. This text is organized to build complexity. Sockets programming may seem rather intuitive at first. However, the programming gives rise to several caveats and issues with regard to timing, exceptions, performance, and so on that can corrupt a great design. Reading linearly helps you build concept upon concept to know how to do it right.
- *Browsing*   The browser gets the needed information without wading through too much unnecessary detail. He knows more about the topic and wants to skip to the good stuff. Like navigating a Web site, the browser skips around the topics until he finds all the needed pieces of information.
- *Referencing*   The expert typically wants to find information (tables, program fragments, APIs) quickly. The information needs to be succinct and easy to find.

This book is laid out with the fundamental information to accomplish what is typically needed or wanted. Additionally, many chapters have passages set apart from the text. These passages provide additional information, detail, expert notes, and opinions.

Audience and Expected Interaction

The book and Web site contain many code examples that illustrate the current topic. Read the section and try the program. You will need to know how to do the following:

1. Create a C or Java source file (in whatever editor you desire).
2. Compile it using a C or Java compiler.
3. Run the program.

Some examples may require changing the kernel (broadcasting and multicasting). Most Linux distributions install and run the network even if you are not connected to a physical network. To run all programs in this book, you must

- Be able to program and compile C, C++, and Java code.
- Have all the compilers installed.
- Be able to configure the kernel for networking, broadcasting, and multicasting.
- Compile and install the new kernel. ✓

Disclaimers and Limits

While all the programs listed in this text have been tested, they may not always work out of the box, because the system configurations change over time. Most of the time, if something does not work, the distribution may have changed the includes to some extent.

Also, testers have verified some of the programs on other UNIX operating systems. This helps to iron out some portability problems. However, if there is a discrepancy between Linux and some other implementation, the book lists the Linux version (and includes a note describing the issue). This book is primarily focused on Linux.

Lastly, this book does not cover other operating systems (Microsoft Windows or Macintosh). Some chapters note comparisons, but all algorithms support Linux/UNIX.

Conventions Used in This Book

The following typographic conventions are used in this book:

- Code lines, commands, statements, variables, and any text you type or see onscreen appears in a mono typeface. **Bold mono** typeface is often used to represent the user's input.
- Placeholders in syntax descriptions appear in an *italic mono* typeface. Replace the placeholder with the actual filename, parameter, or whatever element it represents.
- *Italic* highlights technical terms when they're being defined.
- The ➥ icon is used before a line of code that is really a continuation of the preceding line. Sometimes a line of code is too long to fit as a single line on the page. If you see ➥ before a line of code, remember that it's part of the line immediately above it.
- The text also includes references to the Internet standards documents called Requests For Comment (RFCs). The reference citations are enclosed in brackets with the RFC number, for example [RFC875].

Network Programming from the Client Perspective

IN THIS PART

Introducing the Cookbook Network Client

IN THIS CHAPTER

That blasted CMOS RAM battery! Okay, what time is it? No clocks visible, I'll just call Time. 1-614-281-8211. Ring. "...The time is eight twenty-three and forty seconds." Click. Hurrumph! a.m. or p.m.? Do they expect me to look outside?

The computer you use probably is connected to a network of some kind. It could be a full corporate intranet with firewalls into the Internet; it could be a couple of computers you connected in your spare time. The network connects workstations, servers, printers, disk arrays, faxes, modems, and so forth. And each network connection uses or provides a service. Some services provide information without any interaction. Just as in our example of calling Time, a basic network client connects with and listens to a server.

What kinds of services do servers provide? Many. All services fit into four resource categories: common, limited or expensive, shared, and delegated. Here are some examples of each:

Common	Disk space (centrally backed up)
Limited	Printers, modems, disk arrays
Shared	Databases, project control, documentation
Delegated	Remote programs, distributed queries

This chapter steps you through writing a basic client that connects to some server. This process helps you understand all that is involved in writing network programs. The client initially connects to the server's correct time service (or some other service that does not expect input first). Along the way, the chapter explains the different calls, their parameters, and common errors.

 The client program needs a send/receive interface and an address to connect to a server. Both clients and servers use sockets to connect and send messages independently of location. Consider the telephone example again: The handset has two parts, a microphone (transmission) and a speaker (reception). Sockets also have these two channels. In addition, the telephone number is essentially the unique address for the phone.

The socket likewise has two parts or channels: one for listening and one for sending (like the read/write mode for file I/O). The client (or caller) connects with the server (or answerer) to start a network conversation. Each host offers several standard services (see `/etc/services` on the file system), like the correct time telephone number.

> ## Running the Book's Examples
>
> You can run most of the book's program examples without being connected to a network, if you have networking enabled in the kernel and the inetd network server daemon running. In fact, many examples use the local (or *loopback*) address of `127.0.0.1`. If you do not have the network drivers up and running, most Linux distributions include everything you need for at least loopback networking.

Your client program must take several steps to communicate with a peer or server. These steps have to follow a particular sequence. Of course, you could ask: "Why not replace all the steps with fewer calls?" Between each step, your program can select from many options. Still, some steps are optional. If your client skips some steps, usually the operating system fills in the blanks for you with default settings.

You can follow a few basic steps to create a socket, set up the destination host, establish the channel to another network program, and shut down. Figure 1.1 graphically shows the steps the client takes to connect to a server.

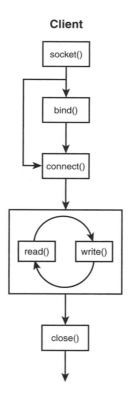

FIGURE 1.1

Each client interfaces with the operating system by making several calls in succession.

The following list describes each step:

1. Create a socket. Select from the various network domains (such as the Internet) and socket types (stream).
2. Set socket options (optional). You have many options that affect the behavior of the socket. The program can change these options anytime the socket is open. (See Chapter 9, "Breaking Performance Barriers," for more detail.)

3. Bind to address/port (optional). Accept connections from all or a single IP address, and establish port service. If you skip this, the operating system assumes any IP address and assigns a random port number. (Chapter 2, "TCP/IP Network Language Fluency," discusses addresses and ports in much greater detail.)

4. Connect to peer/server (optional). Reach out and establish a bidirectional channel between your program and another network program. If you skip this, your program uses directed or *connectionless* communication.

5. Partially close the connection (optional). Limit the channel to either sending or receiving. You may want to use this step after duplicating the channel.

6. Send/receive messages (optional). One reason to opt out of any I/O might include checking host availability.

7. Close the connection. Of course this step is important: Long-running programs may eventually run out of available file descriptors if the programs do not close defunct connections.

The following sections describe some of these steps, defining the system calls and providing examples.

Connecting the World with Sockets

Several years ago, networking involved a dedicated serial line from one computer to another. No other computers shared the same circuit, and UNIX used UUCP (UNIX-to-UNIX Copy) to move files around. As line transmission technology improved, the concept of sharing the transmission line became feasible. This meant that each computer needed to identify itself uniquely and take turns transmitting. There are several different methods for sharing time on the network, and many work rather well. At times, computers transmit simultaneously, causing a packet collision.

The hardware and low-level drivers handle issues such as collisions and retransmission, now an artifact of past programming. This frees up your design to focus on transmission and reception of messages. The Socket API (Application Programming Interface) provides designers the conduit to receive or send messages.

Socket programming differs from typical application or tool programming, because you work with concurrently running programs and systems. This means that you need to consider synchronization, timing, and resource management.

Sockets link asynchronous tasks with a single bidirectional channel. This could lead to problems like deadlock and starvation. With awareness and planning, you can avoid most of these problems. You can read how to handle multitasking issues in Chapter 7, "Dividing the Load: Multitasking," and building robust sockets in Chapter 10, "Designing Robust Linux Sockets."

Typically, an overloaded server slows down the Internet's perceived responsiveness. Timing and resource management reduce the server's burden, increasing network performance. You can find many ideas for improving performance in Part II, "The Server Perspective and Load Control."

The Internet was designed to be entirely *packet switched*. Each and every packet has to have all the necessary information it needs to get to the destination. Like a letter, a packet must include source and destination addresses. The packet switches from one computer to the next along the connections (or *links*). If the network loses a link while passing a message, the packet finds another route (packet switching), or the router bounces an error back to the originator if it fails to reach the host. This ensures a form of data reliability. Broken paths in the network result in network outages. You probably have encountered a few network outages yourself.

Talking the Talk: TCP/IP Addressing Overview

Networks support many different types of protocols. Programmers have geared some protocols to address specific issues such as radio/microwave; others attempt to solve the network reliability problems. TCP/IP (Transmission Control Protocol/Internet Protocol) focuses on the packet and the potential of lost communication channels. At any time, the protocol attempts to find a new route when a network segment fails.

Packet tracking, loss detection, and retransmission are difficult algorithms, because timing is not the only indicator. Luckily, industry experience has proven the algorithms used in the protocol. Usually, you can ignore those issues during design, because the solutions are hidden deep in the protocol.

TCP/IP is layered: Higher-level protocols provide more reliability but less flexibility, and lower levels offer greater flexibility but sacrifice reliability. With all the different levels of flexibility and reliability, the Socket API offers all the needed interfaces. This is a departure from the standard UNIX approach of every level having its own set of calls.

The standard file I/O likewise uses a layered approach. Computers connected via TCP/IP use sockets predominantly to communicate with each other. This may seem strange, considering all the different protocol layers available to a program and having been taught that open() (which yields a file descriptor) and fopen() (which yields a file reference) are different and almost incompatible. All protocol layers are available through one call: socket(). This single call abstracts away all the implementation details of the different networks (TCP/IP, IPX, Rose).

Fundamentally, each packet has the data, the originator address, and the destination address. Every layer in the protocol adds its own signature and other data (wrapper) to the transmission packet. When transmitted, the wrapper helps the receiver forward the message to the appropriate layer to await reading.

Every computer connected to the Internet has an Internet Protocol (IP) address, a unique 32-bit number. Without the uniqueness, there is no way to know the proper destination for packets.

TCP/IP takes the addressing one step further with the concept of *ports*. Like the 3- to 5-digit telephone extensions, each computer address has several ports through which the computers communicate. These are not physical; rather, they are abstractions of the system. All information still goes through the network address like the primary telephone number.

The standard written format for IP addresses is [0-255].[0-255].[0-255].[0-255]—for example, 123.45.6.78. Note that zero and 255 are special numbers used in network masks and broadcasting, so be careful how you use them (Chapter 2 discusses IP numbering in greater detail). Internet ports usually separate these numbers with either a colon or a period:

```
[0-255].[0-255].[0-255].[0-255]:[0-65535]
```

For example, 128.34.26.101:9090 (IP=128.34.26.101, port=9090).

```
[0-255].[0-255].[0-255].[0-255].[0-65535]
```

For example, 64.3.24.24.9999 (IP=64.3.24.24, port=9999).

Colon Versus Period Ports
The colon notation is more common for ports than the period notation.

Each IP address effectively offers about 65,000 port numbers that a socket may connect to. See Chapter 2 for more information.

Hearing the Server: The Client's Basic Algorithm

The simplest client-socket connection is one that opens a connection to a server, sends a request, and accepts the response. Some of the standard services don't even expect any prompting. One example is the time-of-day service found on port 13. Unfortunately, many Linux distributions do not have that service open without revising the /etc/inetd.conf file. If you have access to a BSD, HP-UX, or Solaris machine, you can try that port.

There are several services available to play with safely. You may try running Telnet on your machine to connect to the FTP port (21):

```
% telnet 127.0.0.1 21
```

After connecting, the program gets the welcome message from the server. Using Telnet to connect with the FTP server does not work very well, but you can see the basic interaction. The simple client example in Listing 1.1 connects to the server, reads the welcome, and then disconnects.

LISTING 1.1   A Basic TCP Client Algorithm

```
/**********************************************************/
/*** A basic client algorithm.                       ***/
/**********************************************************/
Create a socket
Create a destination address for server
Connect to server
Read & display any messages
Close connection.
```

The algorithm in Listing 1.1 may seem overly simplified, and perhaps it is. However, connecting to and communicating with a server is really that simple. The following sections describe each of these steps. You can find the complete source for this program at the end of the book and on the accompanying CD-ROM.

The Socket System Call: Procedures and Caveats

The single tool that creates your effective message receiver and starts the whole process of sending and receiving messages from other computers is the socket() system call. This call is the common interface between all protocols available on a Linux/UNIX operating system. Just like the system call open() creates a file descriptor to access files and devices on your system, socket() creates a descriptor to access computers on your network. It requires information that determines what layers you want to access. The syntax is as follows:

```
#include <sys/socket.h>
#include <resolv.h>
int socket(int domain, int type, int protocol);
```

The socket() system call accepts several different values. For a complete list, see Appendix A, "Data Tables." For now, you'll find a few in Table 1.1.

TABLE 1.1   Selected socket() System Call Parameter Values

Parameter	Value	Description
domain	PF_INET	Internet IPv4 protocols; TCP/IP stack.
	PF_LOCAL	BSD-style locally named pipes. Typically used in the system logger or a print queue.
	PF_IPX	Novell protocols.
	PF_INET6	Internet IPv6 protocols; TCP/IP stack.
type	SOCK_STREAM	Reliable, sequential data flow (byte stream) [Transaction Control Protocol (TCP)].
	SOCK_RDM	Reliable, packetized data (not yet implemented in most operating systems).

TABLE 1.1 Continued

Parameter	Value	Description
	SOCK_DGRAM	Unreliable, packetized data (datagram) [User Datagram Protocol (UDP)].
	SOCK_RAW	Unreliable, low-level packetized data.
protocol		This is a 32-bit integer in network byte order (see the section on network byte-ordering in Chapter 2). Most connection types support only protocol = 0 (zero). The SOCK_RAW requires specifying a protocol value between 0 and 255.

For now, the only parameters the example uses are domain=PF_INET, type=SOCK_STREAM, and protocol=0 (zero).

PF Values Versus AF Values

This book uses the PF_* (*protocol family*) domains in the socket call, because PF_* domain constants are the proper form. However, most programs use the AF_* (*address family*) constants interchangeably. Be careful not to get confused when you see source code that uses the AF style. (The C-header files define the AF_* constants as PF_*.) If you want, using AF_* works just as well. However, this may cause incompatibilities in the future.

An example for a streaming TCP/IP call looks like this:

```
int sd;
sd = socket(PF_INET, SOCK_STREAM, 0);
```

The sd is the socket descriptor. It functions the same way as the file descriptor fd:

```
int fd;
fd = open(...);
```

The call returns a negative value when an error occurs and places the error code in errno (the standard global variable for library errors). Here are some common errors you can get:

- EPROTONOSUPPORT   The protocol type or the specified protocol is not supported within this domain. This occurs when the domain does not support the requested protocol. Except for SOCK_RAW, most domain types support only a protocol of zero.

*Handwritten at top: Protocol / Address (Family (PF → * / AF → *)*

- EACCES   Permission to create a socket of the specified type or protocol is denied. Your program may not have adequate privileges to create a socket. SOCK_RAW and PF_PACKET require root privileges.

- EINVAL   Unknown protocol, or protocol family not available. This occurs when a value in either the domain or type field is invalid. For a complete list of valid values, refer to Appendix A.

Of course, you need to know the important header files to include. For Linux, these are

```
#include <sys/socket.h>      /* defines function prototypes */
#include <sys/types.h>       /* standard system data types */
#include <resolv.h>          /* defines needed data types */
```

The sys/socket.h file has the needed function definitions for the Socket API (including socket(), of course). sys/types.h carries many of the data types you use for sockets.

Using resolv.h Versus sys/types.h

This book uses the resolv.h file for defining the data types. Please note that other Linux distributions or UNIX versions may use the more standard include file sys/types.h. During the writing of this book, the examples were tested on Mandrake 6.0–7.0, which use the odd includes. (It appears that these distribution versions have a bad sys/types.h file that does not include the netinet/in.h file needed for the address types.)

The socket() system call does nothing more than create the queues for sending and receiving data, unlike the system call for opening files, which actually opens the file and reads the first block. Only when your program executes a bind() system call does the operating system connect the queue to the network.

Using the telephone example again, the socket is just the handset with no telephone or network connection. Executing bind(), connect(), or some I/O attaches the handset to a telephone and the telephone to the network. (If your program does not explicitly call bind(), the operating system implicitly makes the call for you. For more information, see Chapter 4, "Sending Messages Between Peers.")

Making the Call: Connecting to the Server

After creating the socket, you can get the first "hello?" by connecting to the server. The connect() system call is similar in several ways to calling someone on the telephone:

- You identify the destination using a phone number. When you dial a phone number, you're identifying a specific telephone found on the telephone network anywhere in the world. The IP address likewise identifies the computer. Just as telephone numbers have a specific format, the connection requires a specific format to define which computer and how to connect.

- The connection provides the channel for messages. Once the telephone is answered, there is a channel through which two or more people may converse. Your telephone number is not important unless the person has to call you back.

- The path back to your handset is hidden inside the telephone system. The telephone network has several shared paths, like a computer network. So having a reverse path is important for getting the messages back to your handset. The destination peer or server gets the address and port of your program so that it can reply using a similar path.

  Your telephone number has to be published for others to call you. If your program is going to accept calls, you must specify a unique channel (or port) and publish it to your clients.

The connect() system call's definition follows:

```
#include <sys/socket.h>
#include <resolv.h>
int connect(int sd, struct sockaddr *server, int addr_len);
```

The first parameter (sd) is the socket descriptor that you created with the socket() call. The last parameter is the length of the sockaddr structure. The second parameter points to different types and sizes of structures. This is important, because this is what makes the socket() calls different from the file I/O calls.

Recall that the socket() system call supports at least two different domains (PF_INET and PF_IPX). Each network domain (PF_*) has its own structure to describe the address. They all have one common parent—the one you see in the connect() definition—struct sockaddr. For a complete list of all the structure declarations, see Appendix A.

Sockaddr Data Abstraction

The sockaddr interface uses data abstraction. Data abstraction simplifies interfaces by asserting that while the data types may change, the algorithms remain the same. For example, a stack can contain different data types, but the function of the stack remains the same: push, pop, and so forth. To use an abstract interface, the first field of the sockaddr structure must have the same meaning. All structures have one common field: ..._family. The field's type is an unsigned 16-bit integer. The value this field holds determines what kind of network domain to use.

Matching the Socket Type with sockaddr Family Field

The domain type you had set in the socket() system call must be the same value as the first field in the sockaddr family. For example, if your program created a ✓ PF_INET6 socket, the structure field must be AF_INET6 in order for the program to work correctly.

For now, here is the generic record and the INET record for comparison (from the header files):

```
struct sockaddr {                        struct sockaddr_in {
    unsigned short int sa_family;            sa_family_t         sin_family;
    unsigned char  sa_data[14];              unsigned short int sin_port;
};                                 ———▸ struct in_addr        sin_addr;
                                           unsigned char       __pad[];
                                       };
```

Note that sa_family and sin_family are common between the two structures. The task every procedure call executes when it receives this record is to check the first field. Please notice that ✓ this is the only field that is in *host byte ordering* (see Chapter 2). The padding field (named sa_data and __pad) may be common for each in the sockaddr family. By convention, the generic sockaddr structure and the INET sockaddr_in structure have to be 16 bytes long (the IPv6 structure, sockaddr_in6, is 24 bytes). So, the padding field fills out the structure with any unused bytes.

You may notice that the length of the padding field in sockaddr_in is missing. This is merely a convention. Since the padding has to be set to zero, the actual size is not important. (In the case of this sockaddr_in definition, it is 8 bytes wide.) Some implementations may define additional fields for internal computations. Don't worry about them—and don't use them, because you can't guarantee the field's availability from system to system and version to version. Any changes may break your code when you use nonstandard fields. In all cases, initial- ✓ izing the entire structure instance to zero is best.

The following table describes each field. It also gives examples of possible values.

Field Name	Description	Byte Ordering	Example
sin_family	The protocol family	Host, Native	AF_
sin_port	The server's port number	Network	13 (time of day)
sin_addr	The server's numeric IP address	Network	127.0.0.1 (localhost)

Before calling the connect() system call, the program fills each field. Linux has masked the system call slightly, so it is not necessary to cast sockaddr_in to be a sockaddr. For portability, you may still want to follow conventions and add the casts.

Casting sockaddr Types

With other UNIX-compatible OSs, you can cast any of the sockaddr_* family members to sockaddr to avoid warnings. The examples here don't use any casting merely for space (and because Linux allows it).

The code may look like Listing 1.2.

LISTING 1.2 Connect() Example

```
/****************************************************************/
/*** Code snippet showing initialization and calling of    ***/
/*** the connect() system call.                            ***/
/****************************************************************/
#define PORT_TIME    13
struct sockaddr_in dest;
char *host = "127.0.0.1";
int sd;
/**** Create the socket & do other work ****/

bzero(&dest, sizeof(dest));       /* start with a clean slate */
dest.sin_family = AF_INET;        /* select the desired network */
dest.sin_port = htons(PORT_TIME);        /* select the port */
inet_aton(host, &dest.sin_addr);         /* remote address */

if ( connect(sd, &dest, sizeof(dest)) == 0 )    /* connect! */
{
    perror("Socket connection");
    abort();
}
...
```

The connect() system call in this code requires several preparatory steps before you connect the socket to the server. First, create a sockaddr_in structure. Use the server address for the second line. If you want to connect to a different server, place the appropriate IP address in this string. The program proceeds with other initializations, including the socket() system call. When you start working with the structure, zero it out with bzero(). The program sets the family to AF_INET. Next, the program sets the port and the IP address. The htons() and inet_aton() conversion tools used here are covered in Chapter 2.

The next call is the connection to the server. Please note that the code fragment checks the return values for every procedure call. That policy is one of many keys to making your network programs robust.

After the program establishes the connection, the socket descriptor, sd, becomes a read/write channel between the two programs. Most servers we are accustomed to offer single transactions and then hang up (for example, an HTTP 1.0 server sends the requested file, then closes the connection). To interface with these types of server, your program has to send the request, get the reply, and close the connection.

Getting the Server's Reply

The socket is open and the channel is established. Now, you can get the first "hello." Some servers initiate the conversion like the person answering the phone. This message may include the server's name and some instructions for connection. Once your connection is open, you can use the standard library low-level I/O calls for communication. Here is the read() system call:

```
#include <unistd.h>
ssize_t read(int fd, void *buf, size_t count);
```

You're probably familiar with this call. Other than its special capability to use the socket descriptor (sd) instead of the file descriptor (fd), everything else is almost the same as reading from a file. You can even use the read() system call as in the following code fragment:

```
...
int sd, bytes_read;
sd = socket(PF_INET, SOCK_STREAM, 0);      /* create socket */

/**** Connect to host ****/

bytes_read = read(sd, buffer, MAXBUF);   /* read the message */
if ( bytes_read < 0 )
    /* report connection error; exit routine */
...
```

In fact, you could convert the socket descriptor into a FILE* for higher-level I/O. For example, to use fscanf(), you could follow the example below. (The lines in **bold** indicate the changes from the previous listing.)

```
char Name[NAME], Address[ADDRESS], Phone[PHONE];
FILE *sp;
int sd;
sd = socket(PF_INET, SOCK_STREAM, 0);        /* create socket */

/**** Connect to host ****/

if ( (sp = fdopen(sd, "r")) == NULL )   /* convert to FILE* */
    perror("FILE* conversion failed");
else if ( fscanf(sp, "%*s, %*s, %*s\n",       /* use as usual */
    NAME, Name, ADDRESS, Address, PHONE, Phone) < 0 )
{
    perror("FScanf");
...
```

Only stream-style sockets can be converted reliably into a FILE* stream. The reason is simple: Datagram sockets are typically connectionless—a message is sent and that's it. Also, streaming sockets provide data integrity and message reliability, whereas datagrams are unreliable. Datagrams are similar to putting a message in an addressed and stamped envelope that you send through the postal system: The message may not arrive at all. A FILE* connection must be an open channel. If you try to convert a datagram, you may lose critical data. For more information about streams versus datagrams, see Chapter 3, "Different Types of Internet Packets."

FILE* socket connections provide excellent scanning and parsing resources for the network programmer. However, when you use them, you must check *all* return values, including *printf() and *scanf(). Note the preceding example: If the return value of fscanf() is less than zero, there was an error.

Network Security and Reliability

Security and reliability are of the utmost importance when you create network programs. At the time of writing this book, Microsoft operating systems have faced several fundamental security problems, several involving network connections. When you write your programs, make sure that buffers cannot be overflowed and all return values are checked. In a software bazaar setting, you can solicit input from others on your source code. The peer review of the software bazaar is a vast resource of knowledge and experience—use it.

Referring back to the read() system call, you may get the following common errors:

- **EAGAIN**   Nonblocking I/O is selected, and no data is available. This error instructs the program to try the call again.
- **EBADF**   *fd* is not a valid file descriptor or is not open for reading. This can occur if the socket call was unsuccessful or the program closed the input pipe (making it write-only).
- **EINVAL**   *fd* is attached to an object that is unsuitable for reading.

The read() system call provides no special control over the way it uses the socket. Linux offers another standard system call, recv(). You can use recv() directly with the socket descriptor for getting information while providing you with more control:

```
#include <sys/socket.h>
#include <resolv.h>
int recv(int sd, void *buf, int len, unsigned int flags);
```

The recv() call is no different from the read() call except for the flags. The flags give you more control over what you get or even flow control. These values can be arithmetically ORed together (FLAG1 | FLAG2 | ...). Under normal circumstances, the parameter is set to zero. You may wonder why not use the read call if it's no different than read() when the flags are zero. Just as a suggestion, use recv() instead of read()—it may help you later as your program becomes more complex. Also, generally speaking, it's better to use one tool set rather than mixing tools. Finally, read() checks what kind of I/O descriptor you sent and executes the appropriate system call.

Here are a few useful flags you can use to control the recv() system call. You can find a more complete listing in Appendix B, "Networking API."

- **MSG_OOB**   Process out-of-band data. Used for higher priority messages. Some protocols allow you to choose between a normal and a high priority when you send a message. Set this flag to have the queue manager look for and return out-of-band messages instead of normal data. See Chapter 10 for more information.
- **MSG_PEEK**   Read nondestructively. Used to tell the queue manager to read the message queue without moving the read-index pointer. (In other words, a subsequent read yields at least the same data each time. See the box on the next page.)
- **MSG_WAITALL**   Used so that your message doesn't return until the supplied buffer is filled. Sometimes you get only a partially filled buffer, because the remaining data is in transit. If you know how much information the server is sending and you don't want to reassemble it yourself, use this flag to fill the buffer (or wait forever).

- MSG_DONTWAIT   Used so that your message doesn't block if the queue is empty. Similar to setting the nonblocking feature on the socket, only requiring this option on this recv() system call exclusively. Normally, if no message data is available, the process waits (blocks) until some data arrives. If you use this flag and the queue has no data available at the time of the call, the system call returns immediately with an EWOULDBLOCK error code. (Linux does not currently support this option in the recv() call. You can use O_NOBLOCK with the fcntl() system call. This makes the socket always nonblocking.)

Getting Fragmented Packets

Your programs are going to execute much faster than the network does. Sometimes a packet arrives at the computer in pieces, because the network routers fragmented it to fit more limited networks. If you call recv() when this occurs, you may get an incomplete message. This is one reason why MSG_PEEK could give you different results with consecutive calls: The first call may yield 500 bytes, and the second could be 750 bytes. Likewise, this is why there's a MSG_WAITALL flag.

The recv() system call is more flexible than read(), letting you use the different flags to modify behavior. Do a normal read from socket pipe (equivalent to read()):

```
int bytes_read;
bytes_read = recv(sd, buffer, MAXBUF, 0);
...
```

Read *nondestructively* from socket pipe:

```
int bytes_read;
bytes_read = recv(sd, buffer, MAXBUF, MSG_PEEK);
...
```

Read nondestructively out of band data from socket:

```
int bytes_read;
bytes_read = recv(sd, buffer, MAXBUF, MSG_OOB | MSG_PEEK);
...
```

The first statement gets the information from the server supplying a buffer, length, and no flags. The next statement displays the information. There is an intentional flaw here: What if the server sends more information than the buffer can accept? This is not a critical defect; nothing is going to crash. The algorithm simply may lose the data it doesn't read.

The recv() system call yields similar error codes to read() along with the following extensions:

- ENOTCONN   sd not connected. The supplied socket descriptor is not connected to the peer or server.
- ENOTSOCK   sd not a socket. The supplied socket descriptor does not have the signatures indicating that it came from a socket() system call.

Note that if you use the read() system call, you can still get these error codes when using a socket descriptor, because the read() call is just a portal to the recv() call.

Closing the Connection

You have the information you need from the server, everything went well, and now you want to close the connection. There are again two ways you can close the connection. Most programs use the standard I/O close() system call:

```
#include <unistd.h>
int close(int fd);
```

Again, the socket descriptor (sd) may substitute for the file descriptor (fd). It works the same. If successful, the return value is zero.

Always Close Socket Descriptors

Make it a point always to close descriptors manually, particularly sockets. By default, the operating system closes all descriptors and flushes buffers for you. If the descriptor refers to a file, the process works without affecting other systems. Sockets, on the other hand, can linger longer than necessary, tying up resources and making it difficult for other clients to connect.

This call yields only one error:

- EBADF   fd isn't a valid open file descriptor.

The shutdown() system call gives you more control over closing the channels, because you can close either the incoming or outgoing channels. This call is especially helpful when using sockets to replace stdin or stdout.

Confusing Shutdown Commands

The shutdown() system call is different from the shutdown command (section 8 of online UNIX manuals) for bringing down the operating system.

With the `shutdown()` system call, you can close different directions of data flow in the communication path, making the path read-only or write-only:

```
#include <sys/socket.h>
int shutdown(int s, int how);
```

The `how` parameter can have three values:

Value	Function
0 (zero)	✓ Write only (think of "O" in "output")
1 (one)	Read only (think of "I" in "input")
2	Close both input and output

Summary: What's Going On Behind the Scenes?

Several things occur behind the scenes when the program opens a socket and connects to a TCP server. All the socket call does is create a message queue. Things really happen when the program connects. (You can get the complete program listing on the companion CD.) Table 1.2 shows what happens on the client and server sides.

TABLE 1.2   Steps of Creating a Socket and Connecting

Client's Actions	Server's Actions
1. Calls `socket()`: Creates a queue; sets flags for communication protocols.	(Waiting for connection)
2. Calls `connect()`: The operating system assigns a temporary port number if the socket doesn't have an assigned port number through `bind()`.	(Waiting)
3. Sends a message to the server requesting a connection, telling the server which port the client is using.	
(Waiting for server)	4. Places the connection request on the listening queue.
(Waiting)	5. Reads the connection queue, accepts a connection, and creates a unique socket channel.

TABLE 1.2   Continued

Client's Actions	Server's Actions
(Waiting)	6. Creates (sometimes) a unique task or thread to inter-act with your program.
(Waiting)	7. Sends back a confirmation that the connection is accepted. Either sends a message to your port or awaits a request from your program. The server may close the channel after sending the data, if it provides simple bulletin messages (like time-of-day).
8. Begins data correspondence.	

That's quite a bit for a simple `connect()` call. This process could get much more complicated, especially for the routing computers in between (such as routing management, packet verification, fragmentation and defragmentation, protocol translation, tunneling, and so on). The Socket API considerably simplifies network communication.

The network requires a particular language and algorithm in order to establish a connection. First and foremost, the `socket()` system call starts the ball rolling by creating the telephone handset. This handset allows a program to send and receive messages it is connected to. The program may use regular `read()` and `write()` as used in pipes and file descriptors. Alternatively, you can use the more specialized system calls like `recv()`.

The IP network has several features that require further explanation. The next chapter expands IP numbering, ports, and byte ordering. It explains very useful tools to convert the information, simplifying your programming efforts.

TCP/IP Network Language Fluency

IN THIS CHAPTER

Working with the Internet requires you to know how to address messages so that they arrive correctly. Addressing is an important part of creating messages. Like the telephone, a computer must have an address or ID so that it can get the right messages and other computers can direct the traffic accordingly.

The previous chapter introduced you to the socket. This chapter expands the topic with more of the Socket API. First it discusses the IP numbering system, how routing works at an abstract level, correct binary formats, and different socket types.

An IP Numbering Overview

The IP numbering uses a fixed-length address. This restriction required a great deal of planning when the protocol was designed. The protocol provided solutions to several issues during its lifetime: computer identification, network organization, routing, and address resolution. Now it faces new issues such as explosive growth and address loss.

Computer Identification

Networks involve sharing a single resource (the network cable) with several computers. Because of all the information that could flow on a network medium, each computer must accept the information. However, if every computer on your network were named Bert or Ernie, other hosts would not be able to determine the actual destination. Every network computer requires a unique identification (ID). But that is not all.

Facing Address Collision

A workstation does not work very well with the network when it shares an address (*address collision*). Anyone who has tried to track down an address collision can attest that it is pretty hard to fix. It's even worse when one of the computers is supposed to be using some dynamic address-allocation (like DHCP). The most obvious (and laborious) way to solve this problem is to look at each computer in the area.

Networks are dynamic and tend to increase in complexity. The computer has to be easily locatable by its ID as the network expands. All information placed on the network consumes a portion of that valuable real estate, so no unnecessary information should be included in the message.

Some networking systems include a routing map in the message. Each server in the list gets the message and passes it on to the next server. This approach reduces the throughput of the network by lowering the ratio of header to real data. If you encode the directions to the destination in the address itself, the routing map becomes unnecessary.

Network-connected computers already have a unique ID called the *Media Access Control (MAC)*; one example is the ethernet ID. Your computer uses this ID to do network booting (diskless systems that only have RAM and all permanent storage is on a server). The ethernet ID is six bytes long, and you usually see it written in hexadecimal: 00:20:45:FE:A9:0B. Every ethernet card has one, and it is unique.

Unfortunately, you cannot use that ID for identifying your computer exclusively. It has two fundamental problems. First, every routing server must acquire every ID on the network. The database of IDs could get very large and could significantly slow the routing time for each message. Second, not every interface has a MAC (PPP, for example).

The computer ID could have a built-in mechanism for routing the message. This mechanism is like addressing a letter: most general to most specific. Internet IDs solve the uniqueness issues while providing hints for the routing issues.

IP addresses provide several advantages over the hardware-supplied MAC. First the number can change (it is not fixed), so deploying consistent clusters of addresses is easier, and laptops don't run into problems. The network can map the IP to the hardware MAC using the *Address Resolution Protocol (ARP)*. See the Request For Comment #826 [RFC826] on the accompanying CD-ROM.

Address Resolution Protocol (ARP)

The ARP is a simple translation table that takes the IP and fills in the associated MAC. All messages on the network must have a MAC so that the adaptor (or drivers) can pick up the message. The source may not know the MAC of the destination host, which hides deeply behind several routers. The router instead sends the message to routers that control the sub-networks (or subnets) defined in the IP address. When the message gets to a router with ARP, it checks the tables. If the router find the IP address, the packet's MAC gets the correct destination. Otherwise, the router sends a broadcast into the subnet to resolve the IP address.

Internet ID Organization

The Internet ID uses a most-to-least–specific addressing scheme. Each ID is a four-byte number, like the ethernet ID. The first number, reading from left to right, is the network *class*. Look at Figure 2.1.

The IP address acts as a general roadmap to the routers. Each part of the address provides more specific information about where the destination is. Beginning with the network class, the address ends with the host number. You could easily compare it to an address on an envelope: The first line is the addressee, then the street address or box number. The detail decreases in the address until the state or country.

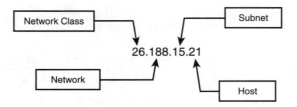

FIGURE 2.1

The IP address has several parts that identify network granularity.

Internet addressing has five basic address classes. Each class is a block of allocations for very large to small networks. The Internet addressing plan is organized so that companies may buy segments from the addressing space. The classes are labeled A–E:

Class	Address	Address Range, Description
	0.0.0.0 to 0.255.255.255	(Reserved)
A	1.0.0.0 to 126.255.255.255	2^{24}–2 or 16,777,214 nodes for each allocation segment. This class has 126 segments.
		Used in very large organizations that subnet as needed, such as Internet service providers (ISPs).
	127.0.0.0 to 127.255.255.255	(Reserved for loopback interface)
B	128.XXX.0.0 to 191.XXX.255.255	2^{16}–2 or 65,534 nodes for each allocation segment. This class has 64×256 available segments.
		Used in large organizations such as companies and universities. They may create subnets. The XXX is the allocated and assigned subnet (for example, 129.5.0.0 is an allocated subnet). Note: This address space is almost used up.
C	192.XXX.XXX.0 to 223.XXX.XXX.255	2^{8}–2 or 254 nodes for each allocation segment. This class has 32×65,536 available segments.
		Small companies or individual. The address has several slots available here.

Class	Address	Address Range, Description
D	224.0.0.0 to 239.255.255.255	$2^{28}-2$ or 268,435,454 nodes.
		These addresses are not allocated but are reserved for multicasting addresses.
E	240.0.0.0 to 255.255.255.255	$2^{28}-2$ or 268,435,454 nodes.
		These are reserved for future use. Please note that 255.255.255.255 is a general broadcast IP address. It is never a legal address.

The network classes are numbered peculiarly, because the addressing uses the first bits of the address to determine the class. For example, the Class A network has a zero in the first bit of the address. Likewise, the Class B has a one in the first bit and a zero in the second bit:

Class A: 0 (**0**000,0000) to 126 (**0**111,1110)

Class B: 128 (**10**00,0000) to 191 (**10**11,1111)

Class C: 192 (**110**0,0000) to 223 (**110**1,1111)

Class D: 224 (**1110**,0000) to 239 (**1110**,1111)

Class E: 240 (**1111**,0000) to 255 (**1111**,1111)

Using this approach historically, the routers on the network can quickly determine (within four bits) whether to let the message enter the gate. Today the routing is more efficient, using Classless Internet Domain Routing (CIDR). These new definitions (found in RFCs 1517–1519) identify the location and route of a host using the upper bits of the address.

The IP protocol introduced this numbering scheme for computer identification to cluster these computers in an efficient way. With it, a router can quickly determine whether to block a packet or move it to the interface that leads to the destination subnet. Propagation is very important: Simply receiving a packet, checking it, and passing it on is not acceptable. Each bit that the router accepts means a delay on the network. The router must delay no more bits than necessary to determine the relevance. In other words, it must be invisible to propagation delays. For example, typical telephone switching in the United States of America does not try to resolve the whole phone number at once; the first three digits indicate an area or region, and the next three digits indicate the station.

Subnetwork Masks

Some of the classes require more filtering. A network with 16 million nodes is excessive if all are clumped in one space. As you set up your Linux computer and configured the network, you may have noticed the term *subnet mask*. The introduction of CIDR has helped to simplify the complexity of large subnets [RFC950].

The network subnet mask is specifically for identifying the group of contiguous addresses an interface can reach. It provides an additional filter that permits only specific messages to pass through. When a message arrives, the router uses the subnet mask on the message's destination address. If it matches, the router passes the message on. You may build mask any way you wish, but the least significant set bit specifies the subnetwork.

For example, if you had a small network of eight machines, and you expected the group to grow by no more than five machines, you could set your router subnet mask to 187.35.209.176. The last bit in the address is in the 176 (1101,0000). The address range is in 'X' part (*active subnet*) of 1101,XXXX. From here, you can dole out the addresses: 187.35.209.176 (router), 187.35.209.177 (host #1), up to 187.35.209.222. You can have any combination, but the least significant set bit is the marker.

Subnetwork Masks and Default Addresses

Using the network mask as a host address may cause conflict and lose packets. This is due to the special address 0 (zero). The example, 187.35.209.0, has the last eight bits as zeros. If the address matches the network mask, it is the *zeroth* address. You should always reserve the zeroth address for the network address mask. Likewise, you may have noticed that the example omits 187.35.209.223. If you were to use that ID, that host may never see a message. The number 223 has the active subnet as all ones: 1101,1111. This is a *broadcast* address. You should not use that as a host address.

In most cases you do not need to worry about setting up routers, and the configuration is beyond the scope of this book. Usually, when you see the subnetwork mask in the network configuration, you can accept the mask that the script offers you.

Routers and Address Resolution

Local area networks (LANs) can become very burdened by all the messages between hosts. Every computer on the Internet potentially could hear every message. But with all the traffic, the networks become very cluttered, packets collide with others (simultaneous transmissions), and throughput drops to near nothing.

LANs use addressing and submasking to limit the traffic within groups (or *clusters*) of computers. Beyond passing messages to the appropriate interfaces, routers act as information control gates that localize the traffic. Local traffic stays inside the cluster, and external traffic passes through.

The host uses the subnet mask to determine if it must pass a message to the router. All messages destined for the outside pass through the router, and local messages remain inside the subnetwork. This process reduces congestion on the network backbone.

Routers also direct messages toward the destination using their routing tables. Each router tells others on the network what it can accept for directing traffic. Wide area networks (WANs) use this feature to deliver messages.

Each step along the way between the source and the destination looks at the IP address, comparing the networks with the routing tables. The routers move your message toward a more and more specific destination. The first hop tries to resolve it in the cluster, the second moves the message up to resolve in the subnetwork, and so on, until it resolves the class.

As soon as a router finds a match (either general or specific), it moves your message in that direction, using the MAC address to send the message to the next router. Eventually the matched cluster gets the message, and the router's ARP replaces the router MAC with the destination MAC.

An ethernet network adapter accepts only messages with its ID. As soon as the host boots up and stabilizes, it tells everyone else on the subnetwork its ethernet ID and IP address. This is the function of ARP, as mentioned previously.

Special and Dwindling Addresses

As mentioned earlier, there are some reserved addresses. The active subnet of a subnetwork mask has two reserved addresses: all zeros (network) and all ones (broadcast). This means that when you count how many address you have at your disposal, you must subtract 2 from that number. Consider this: If you create 100 subnetworks, you effectively lose 200 addresses.

This loss is just the beginning. Two large blocks of addresses are reserved for internal use: 0.0.0.0 to 0.255.255.255 and 127.0.0.0 to 127.255.255.255. The first address group means "this network" in IP shorthand (see the shaded note that follows). If you have a network address of 128.187.0.0, using 0.0.25.31 in a message results in 128.187.25.31, implicitly.

In 1992, the Internet Activities Board (IAB—see RFC1160 for the design, engineering, and management of the Internet), became very concerned with the explosive growth of the Internet—even with all the addressing techniques and careful planning. The allocation of addresses exceeded 450 million nodes. The Board saw increased allocations chewing up the available address space. However, only about 2% of the allocations were actually used. Where were all the remaining addresses?

IAB allocates address ranges to companies in whole blocks. The companies, in anticipation of additional use and to keep their addresses as contiguous as possible, buy larger ranges than they need.

Allocation Inflation

One small place I worked showed me its allocation of 128 addresses; only 30 were in use at the time. They carved out 10 slots for me. I never used more than 2. To this day, I think those addresses may still be allocated to me, even though I left the company about four years ago.

In all, address exceptions and squandered allocations have eaten up most of the address space. Recent estimates indicate that Class B and Class C networks are full. ISPs are using more of Class A. Before long, the demand may use up all the addresses.

What is the Internet going to do with the lost address space? How can the current IP addressing be better used? The IAB, now called Internet Corporation for Assigned Names and Numbers (ICANN), cannot easily reclaim the unused slots sold to companies, because the companies' IT departments have already allocated those addresses within the organization.

Many companies now use *Dynamic Host Configuration Protocol (DHCP)* [RFC2131], which allocates an IP address upon bootup. No host owns an IP address permanently. DHCP also helps with security: Computer crackers love fixed IP addresses. If you recall, bootp sends out a broadcast message to find a bootp server. When found, the server issues an IP address. Similarly, a normal host loads its DHCP requestor during bootup. The requestor sends a broadcast message to find a responsive DHCP server. When found, the server allocates an address from its pool of available addresses and passes it (along with the appropriate network mask) to the requestor.

The DHCP requestor accepts the information and configures the local host's network protocols. In some cases this can take several seconds, due to network congestion. Until the local host is properly configured, it may suffer from *IP amnesia* (the host won't know its own address).

Host or IP Amnesia

Host or IP amnesia also occurs when network and host naming are not properly set up. This can be a significant problem. Even ping 127.0.0.1 may not work. If your host has amnesia, check your distribution. The RedHat Distribution (and derivatives) use /etc/sysconfig/network and /etc/sysconfig/network-scripts/ifcfg-* to define and set the values.

Another solution is to lengthen the IP address size itself. Introducing: IPv6 [RFC2460]! IPv6 in a nutshell is four times the size of an IP address: 128 bits versus 32 bits. IPv6 changed the appearance dramatically as well:

```
8008:4523:F0E1:23:830:CF09:1:385
```

The result is a not-so-memorable address.

The primary advantage of IPv6 is that it has a much larger address space to work with. More than 3×10^{38} addresses probably removes any problem of address limitations for a very long time. See Chapter 17, "Sharing Messages with Multicast, Broadcast, and Mbone," for more information.

IP Host Port Numbers

All messages arrive at one or more recognized address. If a program accepts these messages, it may receive information destined for other running programs. The operating system has little regard for where the message goes, as long as it delivers. The TCP/IP stack adds the concept of a port. One system can have several ports available, all associated with the same address.

The TCP/IP stack adds the ports to abstract the network and ease programming for you. These are not real, physical ports. They are channels that the networking subsystem uses to redirect information to the appropriate program. All network programs no longer receive all messages; they receive only the messages for their port.

Every typical IP data packet on your Internet-based network has the address of the host and the port number. When a packet arrives from the network, the 16-bit field in the packet header indicates the destined port number. The operating system reads this field and places the new packet on the port's queue. From there, the program reads the socket (with either the `read()` or `recv()` system call). Likewise, when the program transmits a message (via the `write()` or `send()` system call), the operating system places the data in the port's outgoing queue.

By default, only one program owns a port. In fact, if you attempt to run two programs that allocate the same port number on the same computer, the system call returns an `EINVAL` error code. You can elect to share a port using `SO_REUSEADDR` (see Chapter 9, "Breaking Performance Barriers").

Sharing Ports on SMPs

The rule that no two sockets can share the same port applies to symmetric processors as well. The reason is simple: The processors, like resources, share the memory and operating system. If you were to have two operating systems running, you could theoretically have two sockets in separately running programs with the same port number, as long as they reside in different operating system spaces.

All the standard services have assigned port numbers. You can see the complete list in /etc/services, in Appendix A, "Data Tables," and on your Linux workstation. Here are a few standard ports:

Port	Service Name, Alias	Description
1	tcpmux	TCP port service multiplexer
7	echo	Echo server
9	discard	Like /dev/null
13	daytime	System's date/time
20	ftp-data	FTP data port
21	ftp	Main FTP connection
23	telnet	Telnet connection
25	smtp, mail	UNIX mail
37	time, timeserver	Time server
42	nameserver	Name resolution (DNS)
70	gopher	Text/menu information
79	finger	Current users
80	www, http	Web server

You can find a more complete list in Appendix A.

You probably recognize a few of these services. The file's format is clear: Port Number, Service Name, Alias, and Description. You can interact with many of them using Telnet or the program listed earlier. Note that even though /etc/services may list a server, the computer may not have the associated server running (for example, the Mandrake distribution does not enable the time services). All the ports listed in the /etc/services file are reserved, so any use may cause conflicts.

Your sockets-based program uses some local port for all communication: This is bind()'s primary responsibility. Even if you do not use the bind() system call, as soon as your program uses the socket for any I/O, the operating system assigns an available local port to the socket.

Privileged Ports

As part of the kernel's security, ports with values less than 1024 require root or privileged access. For example, if you wanted to create a time server (port 13), root would have to run that program (or *SUID root*). SUID is an acronym for "set user ID." Each program in the file system can allow users to run it as if the owner were running it.

> Normally, when a user runs a program, the program has the same rights as the user. Sometimes the program needs different or extra rights. By switching the user ID, the program can run as if the owner were running the program. For example, /usr/bin/at requires accessing the cron tables (owned by root). For this to occur, /usr/bin/at must switch automatically to root access. For more information, refer to standard UNIX documentation. Warning: SUID root is a potential source of security risks. Never create or set the SUID while you are root, unless you know the program very well and know all the risks.

As noted previously, if you do not assign a port to a socket, the operating system assigns one for you. These automatically or dynamically assigned ports are called *ephemeral ports*. Linux appears to follow the BSD style in port assignment: It assigns port 1024 and greater to ephemeral ports.

> ## Secure Debugging
>
> When experimenting with different ports, you may want to follow these simple rules:
>
> Program, run, and debug as a regular user (not as root).
>
> Use ports and addresses that do not affect others or cause security risks.
>
> Log the source of all incoming messages.

Network Byte Ordering

Many different types of computers may reside on a network, but they may not all use the same processor. Not all processors store their binary numbers in the same way. Computers use two basic types of binary number storage: *big-endian* and *little-endian*. Simply, big-endian numbers read from left to right; little-endian numbers read from right to left. For example, consider the number 214,259,635. In hexadecimal, the number reads as #0CC557B3. A big-endian processor stores this value like this:

```
Address:    00    01    02    03    04
Data:       0C    C5    57    B3    ...
```

Note that the most significant byte (0C) is listed first. The little-endian processor stores it in reverse:

```
Address:    00    01    02    03    04
Data:       B3    57    C5    0C    ...
```

Note that the least significant byte (B3) is listed first.

Usefulness of the different endianness is a long-debated topic. This is not to resurrect these discussions, only to point out the important uses and differences. Of course, why couldn't you just use hexadecimal ASCII? The representation is inefficient, essentially doubling the number of needed bytes. For computers on a heterogeneous network to communicate efficiently, they have to use binary and must settle on one endianness. The endianness of the computer or host is the *host-byte order*. Likewise, the endianness of the network is called *network-byte order*. The network byte order is always big-endian.

Using Internet Conversion Tools

Many years ago, the network protocol chose to speak big-endian. That's just fine for big-endian processors, but what about little-endian ones? Several tools are available that help do the conversion. Network programs use these tools all the time for filling the `struct sockaddr_*` structure, regardless of the process's endianness. Now, for another hitch: Not all fields in the structure are network ordered. Some are host ordered. Consider the code excerpt from Chapter 1, "Introducing the Cookbook Network Client":

```
/*************************************************************/
/*** Conversion tools example: filling sockaddr_in      ***/
/*************************************************************/
struct sockaddr_in dest;
char *dest_addr = "127.0.0.1";
...
dest.sin_family = AF_INET;
dest.sin_port = htons(13);    /* port #13 (time server) */
if ( inet_aton(dest_addr, &dest.sin_addr) == 1 ) {
...
```

The code is filling three fields: sin_family, sin_port, and sin_addr. sin_family is a host-ordered field, so it does not need conversion. The other two are network ordered. The two-byte field sin_port converts port 13 using htons(). There are several converters like this:

Call	Meaning	Description
htons	Host to Network Short	Converts 16-bit binary to big-endian.
htonl	Host to Network Long	Converts 32-bit binary to big-endian.
ntohs	Network to Host Short	Converts 16-bit to host format.
ntohl	Network to Host Long	Converts 32-bit to host format.

Appendix B, "Networking API," lists these functions with greater detail. You may be interested to know that using these tools does not cost anything in CPU time if your computer is already big-endian (network-byte ordered).

The next call in the example, inet_aton(), converts the ASCII IP address (using dot-notation) into the equivalent binary. It also converts into the network ordering (you don't need to call htonl() on the result). Here are a few others:

Call	Description
inet_aton()	Converts dot-notation (###.###.###.###) into network-ordered binary. It returns zero if it fails and nonzero if the address is valid.
inet_addr()	Obsolete (same as inet_aton). It does not handle errors correctly. If an error occurs, it returns -1 (255.255.255.255—the general broadcast address).
inet_ntoa()	Converts a binary, network-ordered IP into ASCII dot-notation.
gethostbyname()	Asks the name server to convert the name (such as www.linux.org) into one or more IP address.
getservbyname()	Gets the port and associated protocol for a service in the /etc/services file.

The libraries offer you many more function tools than these. This book covers only a few that are consistently useful. For more information on these function calls, see Appendix B.

> ## Aiming for Portability
>
> For those of you who think that you may not have to worry about these conversion tools, consider this: The whole idea of writing Linux software is to make it compatible with all systems, right? It does not hurt anything to use these calls despite the platform. Generally it's good programming practice to program as if it were to be ported to another processor.

If you are trying to convert one format to another, you may find the appropriate converter in some library. That's the beauty of using established technology like POSIX compatibility. Of course, that means that there are many tools to look through. It helps to have the tools grouped by function. (That is why this book includes several relevant manual pages in the appendices.)

Applying the Tools and Extending the Client

The next step is to extend the time reader's functionality with the capability to send a message and get the reply. Again, the socket descriptor is interchangeable with the file descriptor. Just as you can use read(), you can use write():

```
#include <unistd.h>
ssize_t write(int fd, const void *buf, size_t count);
```

Here are some common errors you may encounter:

- EBADF fd is not a valid file descriptor or is not open for writing. For example, the program already closed the socket descriptor, or the socket was never properly opened (check the return value of the socket() call).

- EINVAL fd is attached to an object that is unsuitable for writing. This might happen if the program had previously shut down the writing channel.

- EFAULT An invalid user space address was specified for a parameter. The buf pointer is not pointing to legal space. When the call tried to access the memory region, it got a segmentation violation.

- EPIPE fd is connected to a pipe or socket whose reading end is closed. When this happens the writing process receives a SIGPIPE signal; if it catches, blocks, or ignores this, the error EPIPE is returned. This error occurs only upon the second write() call. A scenario might be

  1. A client connects to the server and sends some data.
  2. The server reads part of the message, then closes the connection (or crashes).
  3. Not knowing any problem, the client sends the next block of data.

Likewise in the write() call, you can substitute the file descriptor (fd) with the socket descriptor (sd). As an example, here is a snippet showing a typical socket output with write():

```
int sd, bytes_written = 0, retval;
sd = socket(AF_INET, SOCK_STREAM, 0);
... /*** Connect to host ***/
while ( bytes_written < len )   /* repeat sending until all */
{                               /*...bytes of message are sent */
    retval = write(sd, buffer+bytes_written, len);
    if ( retval >= 0 )
        bytes_written += retval;
    else
        /*---report connection error---*/
}
```

On the other hand, here is a snippet showing a typical socket output with fprintf() by converting the socket descriptor into a FILE*:

```
FILE *sp;
int sd;
sd = socket(AF_INET, SOCK_STREAM, 0);
... /*** Connect to host ***/
sp = fdopen(sd, "w");           /* create FILE* from socket */
if ( sp == NULL )
    perror("FILE* conversion failed");
fprintf(sp, "%s, %s, %s\n",Name, Address, Phone);
```

Note that in the first example, the program has to loop on the write() to get all the bytes out. Even though this is a socket stream, you cannot guarantee that the program sends all the bytes at once. The second instance does not have that limitation, because FILE* has its own data-buffering subsystem. When you write to a FILE* buffer, the subsystem forces you to wait until it sends all the bytes.

There is, of course, a dedicated socket write call: send(). Like the recv() call, send() gives the programmer more control over the execution of the transmission. The prototype declaration is

```
#include <sys/socket.h>
#include <resolv.h>
int send(int sd, const void *msg, int len, unsigned int flags);
```

All the parameters are the same as write() except for the last—flags. The send() system call has several options that help revise the call's behavior:

- MSG_OOB   Send "Out Of Band" data. As used above, it allows you to send one byte to the peer, client, or server indicating an urgent condition. The receiver has only one byte dedicated for OOB data; subsequent OOB messages overwrite the last message. When an OOB message arrives, the operating system issues a SIGURG (urgent signal) to the responsible program.

- MSG_DONTROUTE   Don't allow routing the packet. This causes the packet to bypass the routing tables, forcing the network to try to contact the receiver directly. If the destination is inaccessible directly, the call yields an ENETUNREACH (network unreachable) error. Only diagnostic or routing programs use this option.

- MSG_DONTWAIT   Don't wait for send() to finish. This option allows the program to proceed as if the send() were done (or delegated). If used, the operating system issues a SIGIO signal, indicating a completed write() operation. If the operation blocks because the send() queue is full, the call returns an error and sets errno to EAGAIN.

- MSG_NOSIGNAL   Don't issue a SIGPIPE signal. If the other end closes early, and if your program sends another message, your may get a SIGPIPE signal. If you are not prepared for this signal, your program aborts.

Using the send() system call is similar to using recv(). If you want to aggregate the flags, you use the arithmetic OR operator:

```
/***********************************************************/
/*** Do a normal write to socket pipe                   ***/
/***********************************************************/
```

```
int bytes_sent;
bytes_sent = send(sd, buffer, MAXBUF, 0);
...

/*--------Send any out of band data from socket pipe--------*/
int bytes_sent;
bytes_sent = send(sd, buffer, MAXBUF, MSG_OOB | MSG_NOSIGNAL);
...
```

The second example selects MSG_OOB and MSG_NOSIGNAL. Remember that these examples differ from the write() system call by adding a new parameter for controlling the socket. Also, the socket must be connected to the server or host in order to use write(). Here are some errors you may encounter:

- EBADF   An invalid descriptor was specified. The likely cause is the program did not check the return value of the socket() call.
- ENOTSOCK   The argument is not a socket. Perhaps it mixes file and socket descriptors.
- EMSGSIZE   The socket requested the kernel to send the message atomically, and the size of the message to be sent made this impossible. Broadcast messages cannot be fragmented, or the program set the socket option for "don't fragment."
- EAGAIN   The socket is marked nonblocking and the requested operation would block. This is not an error, merely a "not ready yet." Try sending again later.
- EPIPE   The local end has been shut down on a connection-oriented socket. In this case the process also receives a SIGPIPE unless MSG_NOSIGNAL is set. (Same as EPIPE in the write() system call.)

You use the send() system call to prompt a server. For example, if you want to use the network finger on a server, you open a channel to the server's port (79), send the username, and read the response. This algorithm is typically what the client does.

You don't need any special options to do this task. However, you may want to read as much information as the server sends you. Sometimes the reply may be larger than your buffer size. The following program listing excerpt shows you the implementation of the algorithm. You can get the complete program listing on the CD-ROM that accompanies this book.

```
/***********************************************************/
/*** Expanding the port tester - add the capability to   ***/
/*** access any port and to send a message.              ***/
/***********************************************************/
int main(int count, char *strings[])
{   int sockfd;
```

```
        struct sockaddr_in dest;
        char buffer[MAXBUF];

        /*--- Create socket and assign a port number ---*/
        sockfd = socket(AF_INET, SOCK_STREAM, 0);
        bzero(&dest, sizeof(dest));
        dest.sin_family = AF_INET;
        dest.sin_port = htons(atoi(strings[2]));
        inet_addr(strings[1], &dest.sin_addr.s_addr);

        /*--- Connect to server & send request ---*/
        if ( connect(sockfd, &dest, sizeof(dest)) != 0 )
            PANIC("connect() failed");
        printf(buffer, "%s\n", strings[3]);
        send(sockfd, buffer, strlen(buffer), 0);
        /*--- Clear buffer and read SHORT reply ---*/
        bzero(buffer, MAXBUF);
        recv(sockfd, buffer, MAXBUF-1, 0);
        printf("%s", buffer);
        close(sockfd);
        return 0;
}
```

If you want to use this algorithm to get a long reply, you need to change the last section to the following:

```
/***********************************************************/
/*** Revising the code to get lengthy replies           ***/
/***********************************************************/
/*--- Clear buffer and read SHORT reply ---*/
do
{
    bzero(buffer, MAXBUF);
    bytes = recv(sockfd, buffer, MAXBUF, 0);
    printf("%s", buffer);
}
while ( bytes > 0 );
close(sockfd);
```

This addition works correctly if the server closes the connection after sending you the data. Otherwise, your program waits indefinitely for data.

Waiting for information is a particular problem with socket programming. Sometimes you can trust the server to close the connection when it is done sending. However, some servers expect to leave the channel open until the client closes it. Be aware that if your program waits for a long time, you may be facing that type of problem.

Different Kinds of sockaddr

The network supports several different types of protocols. Each protocol has specific functions and features. To the network, it is all just packets. Packet types include

Named Sockets	PF_LOCAL	Actually does not connect to the network. This is strictly for processing queues using the file system.
Internet Protocol	PF_INET	(Already demonstrated.)
Novell Protocol	PF_IPX	For communicating with Novell networks.
AppleTalk	PF_APPLETALK	To communicate with AppleTalk networks.

You can find more of the defined and supported protocols in Appendix A. Each type uses its own naming systems and conventions, and all of them use the Socket API. This should make programming them rather straightforward. Regrettably, there is too much to include here, so this text primarily focuses on the Internet Protocol.

UNIX Named Pipes

Just briefly, consider how syslog works. Here's the problem: how do you coordinate several applications that may issue errors or messages at different times? The syslog is a tool that accepts messages like these. The Socket API already has this coordination built in.

Named sockets allow several local programs to submit messages (or packets). They are *named*, because they actually create a file in the file system. The communication is local only; nothing passes through the network, and no network client can connect to it.

It works like a regular socket: You can create a stream connection or a datagram connection. The only difference is, as stated earlier, the sockaddr. Here is how you set up the named pipe:

```
/**********************************************************/
/*** Unix named socket example                        ***/
/**********************************************************/
#include <sys/un.h>
int sockfd;
struct sockaddr_un addr;
sockfd = socket(PF_LOCAL, SOCK_STREAM, 0);
bzero(&addr, sizeof(addr));
addr.sun_family = AF_LOCAL;
strcpy(addr.sun_path, "/tmp/mysocket");        /* Assign name */
if ( bind(sockfd, &addr, sizeof(addr)) != 0 )
    perror("bind() failed");
```

Everything should look relatively familiar. The sun_path field allows a path of up to 104 bytes (including the NULL termination). From here, you can use all the regular API calls. This is the same for all supported protocols.

After you run this fragment, you can look in /tmp to see the new file. Be sure to delete this file before running the program again.

Summary: Applying IP Numbering and Tools

The Socket API is a very flexible interfacing tool for network programming. It supports several different protocols, allowing you to connect to and interconnect with other networking protocols.

The Internet Protocol uses addressing that builds in routing messages and clustering groups of computers. This makes each message autonomous from the originator: A message dropped on the network can get to the destination through routing and ARP tables. However, because of the addressing flexibility and sparse allocation, the addressing allocation is losing blocks of legal addresses.

Part of the TCP/IP stack abstracts the network with ports. The majority of connections use ports to communicate with specific programs on other network computers as if they own the network connection. This feature eases programming and reduces the flood of messages that your program could actually receive.

The network uses specific types and byte-orders (endianness) to hand messages back and forth. sockaddr defines the protocol, address, and port of the connection. Because of all these different data formats, the Socket API offers you many conversion tools for addressing (for example, inet_addr(), inet_aton(), inet_ntoa()) and endianness (htons(), ntohs(), htonl()).

TCP and UDP offer different interfacing levels to your program. The next chapter defines the different types and capabilities of each protocol within the IP.

Different Types of Internet Packets

IN THIS CHAPTER

The physical network supports different types of logical networks like Novell (IPX), Microsoft (NetBEUI), AppleTalk, and of course, TCP/IP. Each logical network uses discrete data messages called packets, as defined in the last chapter. The packets can be actual messages on the transmission line (which has a lot more information included) or simply the message you're sending.

The logical network packet at the generic level consists of information about the source, destination, and data payload. Each logical network offers varying degrees of features and interfaces (protocols). All packet types and protocols are available with network programming. Each type has significant strengths and weaknesses. Like shopping for tools, your choice of packet type depends on how you use it.

You can choose from four basic Internet packet protocols: raw IP, ICMP, UDP (unreliable messaging), and TCP (streaming) all layered on top of the physical network (see Figure 3.1). This chapter describes each type and presents their advantages, disadvantages, and typical uses.

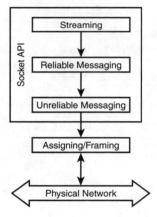

FIGURE 3.1
The Sockets API provides different levels of reliable messages.

The Fundamental Network Packet

If you could actually see the bits that travel from one computer to the other, what would you see? Each protocol is very different, but they all share one common necessary feature: They all carry the program's message. Some protocols include a source address, while some require a destination. You may think that not requiring a destination is a little unusual, but some protocols (like UUCP) use the connection as the address to the destination.

The Internet Protocol (IP) [RFC791] requires a packet to have three basic elements: source, destination, and data. (The data payload includes its length.) These elements provide the packet a level of autonomy. No matter where a packet is, you can identify where it came from, where it's going, and how big it is.

The packet's autonomy is an important feature of the Internet. As long as the packet is *alive* (the data is timely and relevant), routers can move data to its destination when the packet is launched onto the network.

> ### Packet Aliasing
>
> Packet autonomy also has a downside. While a packet provides a way of getting to anywhere from anywhere, a malicious programmer can easily trick the network. The network does not require that the source host's address be validated. *Aliasing* or *spoofing* (masking the true identity and assuming a different one) the hardware address is difficult, but programs can alias other IDs. Please note that later Linux kernels do not allow spoofing.

As discussed in Chapter 2, "TCP/IP Network Language Fluency," the network packet is in network byte (or big endian) order. With that in mind, take a look at a structure definition of how the network packet appears in Listing 3.1, and Figure 3.2 displays the physical layout.

LISTING 3.1 IP Structure Definition

```
/**************************************************************/
/*** IP Packet definition                                ***/
/**************************************************************/
#typedef unsigned int uint;
#typedef unsigned char uchar;

struct ip_packet {
    uint version:4;       /* 4-bit version [note] */
    uint header_len:4;    /* header length in words [note] */
    uint serve_type:8;    /* how to service packet [note] */
    uint packet_len:16;   /* total size of packet in bytes */
    uint ID:16;           /* packet ID [note] */
    uint __reserved:1;    /* always zero */
    uint dont_frag:1;     /* flag to permit fragmentation */
    uint more_frags:1;    /* flag for "more frags to follow"*/
    uint frag_offset:13;  /* to help reassembly */
    uint time_to_live:8;  /* permitted router hop cnt [note] */
    uint protocol:8;      /* ICMP, UDP, TCP [note] */
```

LISTING 3.1 Continued

```
    uint hdr_chksum:16;   /* ones-comp. checksum of header */
    uint IPv4_source:32;  /* IP address of originator */
    uint IPv4_dest:32;    /* IP address of destination */
    uchar options[];      /* up to 40 bytes [note] */
    uchar data[];         /* message data up to 64KB [note] */
};
```

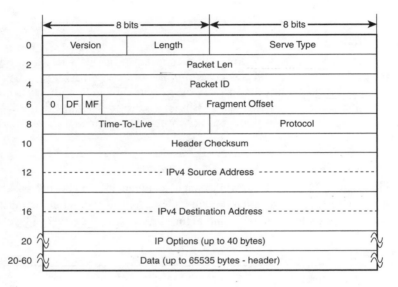

FIGURE 3.2

IP header layout.

Notice that the packet structure includes many more fields than the basic four fields discussed earlier in this chapter. The IP subsystem uses these additional fields for controlling the packet. For example, the dont_frag field tells the network that, instead of cutting up the message into smaller chunks, it should either accept the message completely or drop it.

Most of the fields are simple enough that the comments next to them provide sufficient description. The remaining fields require a longer description. The following sections define the IP fields that you can modify or use. This text is not exhaustive; if you want to learn more about each field, please refer to a good text on TCP/IP protocols.

version Field

The first IP field is the version number for the IP protocol version. Most of the values are either reserved or unassigned; for example, IPv4 places a 4 in this field. The few defined values are listed in Table 3.1.

TABLE 3.1 version Field Values

Value	Description/Use
4	IPv4
5	Stream IP Datagram mode (experimental IP)
6	IPv6
7	TP/IX (the "next" Internet Protocol)
8	The "P" Internet Protocol
9	TUBA

The only chance you have to fill this field is when you create a raw socket *and* you elect to fill the header yourself (using socket option IP_HDRINCL). Even then, you may set the field to 0. The zero flags the kernel to fill in the appropriate value for you.

header_len Field

This field tells the receiver the header length in 32-bit words. Since the value 0 is reserved (and meaningless), the greatest length is 15 words or 60 bytes. Again, the only circumstance in which you fill this field is with a raw socket packet and IP_HDRINCL. Since all IP headers are at least 20 bytes, the minimum value for this field is 5 (20/4) bytes.

serve_type Field

The serve_type field indicates how to manage the packet. It has two subfields: a precedence subfield (ignored on most systems) and a type of service (TOS) subfield. You normally set TOS with the setsockopt() system call. TOS has four options: Minimum Delay, Maximum Throughput, Maximum Reliability, and Minimum Cost (monetary). No special service selected means normal management. (See Chapter 9, "Breaking Performance Barriers," for details on setsockopt() and its values.)

ID Field

The IP subsystem gives each packet a unique ID. With only a 16-bit field, you can imagine that the numbers get used up quickly. Nevertheless, by the time the IP subsystem reuses an ID, the previous packet of the same value will probably have expired.

The ID helps reassemble fragmented packets. If you elect to manage the header (IP_HDRINCL), you must manage the IDs yourself.

3

DIFFERENT TYPES OF INTERNET PACKETS

> ### Custom IDs
>
> Keep in mind that your program is not the only one that may send messages if you choose to manipulate the header yourself. The IP subsystem keeps track of the IDs. You must use caution (and extra programming) to reduce the likelihood of selecting an ID that the subsystem recently used or may use.

`dont_frag`, `more_frags`, `frag_offset` Flags and Field

These flags manage how (or if) your packet fragments. If while traversing the network a lengthy packet has to go through a constricted network segment (one that cannot support the frame size), the router may try to break up the packet into smaller pieces (*fragmentation*). A fragmented packet remains fragmented until it arrives at the destination. Because each fragment adds its own IP header, the overhead diminishes performance.

> ### Kernel Fragment Reassembler
>
> You can choose to reassemble fragmented packets with the Linux kernel when the host is a router. This option is part of the firewall/router section in the kernel configuration. Please note that it takes time to reassemble packets, especially if they are scattered and arrive at different times. However, since the destination has to reassemble the packet anyway, selecting this option reduces traffic on the network inside the firewall.

The `dont_frag` bit tells the router or host not to break up the packet. If you set this bit and the packet is too large for a constricted network segment, the router drops the packet and returns an error (ICMP) packet.

The `more_frags` bit tells the destination to expect more pieces of the fragmented packet. The last fragment sets this bit to 0. (A nonfragmented packet sets this bit to 0.) If you are configuring the header manually, always set this bit to 0.

The `frag_offset` field indicates where in the packet the fragment belongs. Because packet fragments may travel through different routes in the network, they may arrive at different times. The destination has to reassemble the packet, and it uses the offset to place the fragment in its proper location.

The `frag_offset` field is only 13 bits long—far too short for a packet that can be up to 64KB. The offset is multiplied by 8 to place the actual byte position in the packet. This means that each fragment (except the last) must be a multiple of 8. The IP subsystem completely manages the fragmentation and reassembly of your packet; you don't need to worry about it.

With these fields and the packet ID, the IP subsystem can fragment and reassemble your packet. If the subsystem cannot get all the pieces within a specified time, it drops the packet and sends an error back to the originator.

time_to_live (TTL) Field

This field originally counted the number of seconds a packet could survive on the network during transit. Later, the meaning changed to the number of router hops. A *hop* is the transition through a host or router (*node*) where the node actively moves a packet from one network to another.

This 8-bit field permits up to 255 router hops before being discarded. When a router or forwarding host gets the packet, it decrements this field by one. If the field equals zero before arriving at the destination, the node drops the packet and sends an error to the source. The TTL field keeps the network from bouncing a packet around indefinitely.

Use the IP_TTL socket option to set this value (see Chapter 9). Alternatively, you can set it directly if you elect direct IP header manipulation (IP_HDRINCL).

protocol Field

Every packet on the Internet has an assigned protocol value, and ICMP (IPPROTO_ICMP or 1), UDP (IPPROTO_UDP or 17), and TCP (IPPROTO_TCP or 6) each own a code. The protocol tells the system how to treat the incoming packet. You can set this value with the SOCK_RAW option in the socket() system call. The protocol value is the last parameter of the call. The kernel's netinet/in.h header file lists many more. (Remember that even though the kernel includes a protocol definition, it might not support it.)

options Field

The IP subsystem can pass several options with each packet. These options include routing information, timestamps, security measures, routing record, and route alerts. This field can be up to 40 bytes long. Because some of the options are system dependent, you are unlikely to ever touch these options directly.

data Field

Your message goes here and can include up to 65,535 bytes (minus 60 bytes, the maximum size of the header). The data section includes any header information that the higher protocols need. For example, ICMP requires 4 bytes, UDP requires 8 bytes, and TCP requires 20–60 bytes.

The Internet packet system bases all its IPv4 packets on this structure. Each layer on top of this adds features and reliability.

Dissecting the Various Packets

The Internet Protocol offers several packet protocols that range from very fast to very reliable. All of them rest on the lowest layer—the basic IP packet. However, each layer has evolved to solve specific problems. To select the correct packet type, you must know about what you're transmitting.

The packet types most likely to be of interest are TCP, UDP, ICMP, and raw. Knowing the advantages and disadvantages of each type can help you choose the most appropriate for your application. Each packet type has different benefits, as summarized in Table 3.2.

TABLE 3.2   Packet Type Benefits

	Raw	ICMP	UDP	TCP
Overhead (bytes)	20–60	20–60+[4]	20–60+[8]	20–60 +[20–60]
Message Size (bytes)	65,535	65,535	65,535	(unlimited)
Reliability	Low	Low	Low	High
Message Type	Datagram	Datagram	Datagram	Stream
Throughput	High	High	Medium	Low
Data Integrity	Low	Low	Medium	High
Fragmentation	Yes	Yes	Yes	Low

In this table, notice that each packet type contains comparisons. A reliability of Low value only means that you cannot rely on the protocol to help reliability. While the differences may seem extreme, remember that they are merely comparisons.

Considering the Packet's Issues

Each protocol addresses issues in the transmission. The following sections define each issue and associated category from Table 3.2. This information can help you see why certain protocols implement some features and skip others.

Protocol Overhead

Protocol overhead includes both the header size in bytes and the amount of interaction the protocol requires. High packet overhead can reduce throughput, because the network has to spend more time moving headers and less time reading data.

Strong protocol synchronization and handshaking increase interaction overhead. This is more expensive on WANs because of the propagation delays. Table 3.2 does not include this measurement.

Protocol Message Size

To calculate network throughput, you need to know the packet size and the protocol's overhead. The transmission size gives you the maximum size of a sent message. Since all but TCP use a single-shot message, this limitation is typically due to the limits of IP packet (65,535 bytes). The amount of data your program transmits per packet is the transmission size less the headers.

Protocol Reliability

Part of the problem with networks is the possibility of lost messages. A message could be corrupted or dropped as it moves from one host or router to another, or the host or router could crash or fail. In each case, a message may simply be lost, and your program may need to follow up.

Also, you may need to make sure that the destination processes the packets in the correct order. For example, you may compose a message that does not fit in one packet. If the second packet arrives before the first, the receiver must know how to recognize and correct the problem. However, the order is not important when each message is independent and self-contained.

The packet's reliability indicates the certainty of safe arrival of messages and their order. Low reliability means that the protocol can't guarantee that the packet gets to the destination or that the packets are in order.

Protocol Message Type

Some messages are self-contained and independent from other messages. Pictures, documents, email messages, and so on are a few examples that may fit the size of the packet. Others are more in the form of a flowing stream, such as Telnet sessions, HTTP's open channel [RFC2616], large documents, pictures, or files. The message type defines which style best fits each protocol.

HTTP's Protocol

HTTP 1.0 could effectively use UDP for transferring messages instead of TCP. The client simply sends the request for a specific document, and the server replies with the file. Effectively, no conversation occurs between client and server.

Protocol Throughput

The most noticeable aspect of data transmission is network throughput. Getting the most out of your network is the best way to make your users happy. To get the best performance, you need to know the throughput. Often, the bits-per-second is a small part of the whole equation; it only indicates how the network could perform under ideal circumstances.

The protocol throughput measures how much real data the originator can send to the destination within a period of time. If the headers are large and the data small, the result is low throughput. Requiring acknowledgment for each message dramatically reduces throughput. By default, high reliability and integrity result in low throughput and vice versa.

Protocol Data Integrity

The networking technology currently has a lot of safeguards for data integrity. Some network interfaces include a checksum or cyclical redundancy check (CRC) for each low-level message. They also include special hardware technology that can filter out noise and get to the real message. Additionally, each protocol includes measures to detect errors in the data. These errors may or may not be important to you.

The importance of data integrity depends on the data; that is, some data requires very careful oversight, while less important data is less critical. Here are some types of data:

- Fault-Intolerant—Life-critical data. Anything that can affect public or private health/life. For example, life signs and vital signs from medical equipment and missile launch commands.
- Critical—Important and reliable data. Data that if out of sequence or faulty can cause harm to property or security. For example, financial transactions, credit cards, PIN numbers, digital signatures, electronic money, trade secrets, virus scanner updates, and product updates.
- Important—Data that requires proper functionality. Any loss can cause malfunction. For example, X11 connections, FTP downloads, Web pages, server/router addresses, and Telnet connections.
- Informational—Data that can be less than 100% reliable for proper functionality. For example, email, news feeds, advertisements, and Web pages.
- Temporal—Data that is date/time bound. Unless the program uses the information within a specific time, its importance lessens. For example, weather data, surveillance data, and time.
- Lossy—Data that can degrade without loss of usefulness. These are typically audio or visual. For example, movies, audio files, photos, and spam (of course).

Prior to choosing the packet type or protocol, try to categorize data according to this list. Also include the additional (or external) constraints of the program. These may be regulatory constraints as well.

Protocol Fragmentation

Large messages on slow networks can frustrate other users. All networks place a maximum frame size so those large messages don't dominate the network. Keep in mind that the routing host may still carve up, or fragment, large messages that go through a constricted network.

Each protocol has a different likelihood of fragmentation. Since reassembling fragmented messages is part of IP, the reassembly may be transparent to the higher protocols. Certain circumstances, however, may require the packet's wholeness. This is particularly important for network performance. When routers carve up the packet into smaller chunks, the router has to take the time to chop up the message, and the resulting packet overhead increases. By blocking fragmentation, the network drops the packet and returns a message-too-big error to your program.

Packet Types

The following sections describe each packet, showing its statistics and header definition (if there is one). Each section uses a quick-reference style to help you quickly see the features of each protocol. Use this style to help you choose the right packet for your applications.

The Raw Packet

A raw packet has direct access to an IP packet and header. It is useful in writing special or custom protocols. Its attributes are listed in Table 3.3.

TABLE 3.3   Raw Packet Attributes

Message Size (bytes)	65,535 (65,515 max data payload)
Overhead (bytes)	20–60
Reliability	Low (network may drop or rearrange packets)
Message Type	Datagram
Throughput	High (low system overhead)
Data Integrity	Low (system does not validate message)
Fragmentation	Yes

Linux provides the option to work with different layers in the Internet Protocol stack (refer to Chapter 5, "Understanding the Network Layering Model," for a complete definition of the layers and IP stack). The most basic TCP/IP message is the raw IP message. It has no information other than the most basic.

You can use the IP packet itself to create the most basic layer to create your own custom protocols. Access the IP packet by selecting SOCK_RAW in the socket() system. For security, you must have root privileges to run a raw socket program.

The raw socket lets you play with the guts of the IP packet. You can configure the socket to work on two levels of detail: data only or data and header manipulation. Data manipulation is like UPD data transfers but does not support ports. In contrast, header manipulation lets you set the header fields directly.

Using this message has both advantages and disadvantages. As a datagram message, it offers no guarantees of arrival or data integrity. However, you can send and receive messages nearly at network speed. For more information on raw packet manipulation, see Chapter 18, "The Power of Raw Sockets."

IP Control and Error Messaging (ICMP)

The Internet Control Message Protocol (ICMP) is one of the layers built on top of the basic IP packet. All Internet-connected computers (hosts, clients, servers, and routers) use ICMP for control or error messages. It is used for sending error or control messages. Some user programs also employ this protocol, such as traceroute and ping. ICMP's attributes are listed in Table 3.4.

TABLE 3.4   ICMP's Attributes

Message Size (bytes)	65,535 (65,511 max data payload)
Overhead (bytes)	24–64
Reliability	Low (same as raw IP)
Message Type	Datagram
Throughput	High (same as raw IP)
Data Integrity	Low (same as raw IP)
Fragmentation	Yes (but unlikely)

You can reuse your socket to send messages to different hosts without reopening the socket if you employ the ICMP in your own program. Send messages using the sendmsg() or sendto() system call (described in the next chapter). These calls require an address of the destination. With a single socket, you can send messages to as many peers as you want.

The advantages and disadvantages of an ICMP packet are essentially the same as raw IP (and other datagrams). However, the packet includes a checksum for data validation. Also, the likelihood that the network may fragment an ICMP packet is very small. The reason is because of the nature of ICMP messages: They are for statuses, errors, or control. The message is not going to be very large, so it may never require reassembly.

While you can use the ICMP for your own messages, it is usually for error messages and control. All networking errors travel the network through an ICMP packet. The packet has a header that holds the error codes, and the data part may contain a more specific message describing the error.

Part of the IP protocol, ICMP gets an IP header and adds its own header. Listing 3.2 shows a definition of the structure.

LISTING 3.2   ICMP Structure Definition

```
/*************************************************************/
/*** ICMP structure definition                          ***/
/*** Formal definition in netinet/ip_icmp.h             ***/
/*************************************************************/
typedef unsigned char ui8;
typedef unsigned short int ui16;

struct ICMP_header {
    ui8 type;          /* Error type */
    ui8 code;          /* Error code */
    ui16 checksum;     /* Message checksum */
    uchar msg[];       /* Additional data description */
};
```

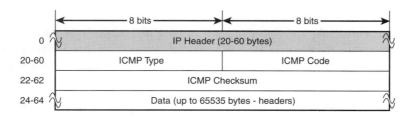

FIGURE 3.3
ICMP layout.

Type and code define what error occurred. msg can be any additional information to help detail what went wrong. For a complete list of types and codes, see Appendix A.

User Datagram Protocol (UDP)

The User Datagram Protocol (UDP) is used mostly for connectionless (independent messages) communications. It can send messages to different destinations without re-creating new sockets and is currently the most common connectionless protocol. UDP's attributes are listed in Table 3.5.

TABLE 3.5   UDP Attributes

Message Size (bytes)	65,535 (65,507 max data payload)
Overhead (bytes)	28–68
Reliability	Low
Message Type	One-shot
Throughput	Medium
Data Integrity	Medium
Fragmentation	Yes

Each layer up the IP stack provides more focus on data and less on the network. UDP hides some of the details about error messages and how the kernel transmits messages. Also, it reassembles a fragmented message.

A message you send via UDP is like an email message: The destination, origin, and data are all the information it needs. The kernel takes the message and drops it on the network but does not verify its arrival. As with the ICMP packet, you can send to multiple destinations from a single socket, using different send system calls. However, without the verification, you can experience near-maximum throughput.

Without arrival verification, the network can lose data reliability. The network can lose packets or fragments and corrupt the message. Programs that use UDP either track the message themselves or don't care if something gets lost or corrupted. (Please note that, while datagrams are unreliable, it does not mean that something will go wrong. It just means that the protocol makes no guarantees.)

Of the different data types (previously defined), Informational, Temporal, and Lossy best fit the UDP services. The primary reason is their tolerance for loss. If your Web camera fails to update every client, the end user is unlikely to either notice or care. Another possible use is a correct time service. Because correct time is Temporal, a host may drop a couple of clock ticks without losing integrity.

UDP offers the advantage of high speed. Moreover, you can increase its reliability yourself in the following ways:

- Break up large packets. Take each message and divide it into portions and assign a number (such as 2 of 5). The peer on the other end reassembles the message. Bear in mind that more overhead and less sent data decrease throughput.

- Track each packet. Assign a unique number to each packet. Force the peer to acknowledge each packet because, without an acknowledgment, your program resends the last message. If the peer does not get an expected packet, it requests a resend with the last message number or sends a restart message.

- Add a checksum or CRC. Verify the data of each packet with a data summation. A CRC is more reliable than a checksum, but the checksum is easier to calculate. If the peer discovers that data is corrupted, it asks your program to resend the message.

- Use timeouts. You can assume that an expired timeout means failure. Your originator could retransmit the message, and your receiver could send a reminder to the sender.

The Critical and Important data types require the reliability found in TCP or better. Fault-Intolerant requires much more than any of these protocols offer. These outlined steps mimic the reliability of TCP.

UDP relies on IP's features and services. Each UDP datagram packet receives an IP and a UDP header. Listing 3.3 defines how the UDP structure appears.

LISTING 3.3   UDP Structure Definition

```
/**************************************************************/
/*** UDP (datagram) structure definition                  ***/
/*** (Formal definition in netinet/udp.h)                  ***/
/**************************************************************/
typedef unsigned char ui8;
typedef unsigned short int ui16;

struct UDP_header {
    ui16 src_port;      /* Originator's port number */
    ui16 dst_port;      /* Destination's port number */
    ui16 length;        /* Message length */
    ui16 checksum;      /* Message checksum */
    uchar data[];       /* Data message */
};
```

3

DIFFERENT TYPES
OF INTERNET
PACKETS

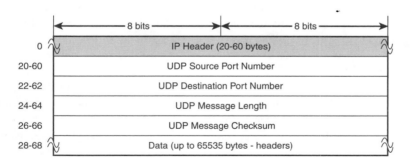

FIGURE 3.4
UDP layout.

UDP creates a virtual network receptacle for each message in the form of ports. With the port, IP can rapidly shuffle the messages to the correct owner. Even if you don't define a port with `bind()`, the IP subsystem creates a temporary one for you from the ephemeral port list (see Chapter 2).

Transmission Control Protocol (TCP)

Transmission Control Protocol (TCP) is the most common socket protocol used on the Internet. It can use `read()` and `write()` and requires re-creating a socket for each connection. TCP's attributes are listed in Table 3.6.

TABLE 3.6 TCP Attributes

Message Size (bytes)	(unlimited)
Overhead (bytes)	40–120
Reliability	High (data receipt checked)
Message Type	Stream
Throughput	Low (compared to other protocols)
Data Integrity	High (includes checksums)
Fragmentation	Unlikely

Taking reliability one step further requires ensuring that the destination gets the exact message the originator sent. UDP has the speed but does not have the reliability that many programs require. TCP solves the reliability problem.

The network, however, has several fundamental problems that make it unreliable. These problems are not limitations. Instead, they are inherent in the design of the network. To get reliable, streamable messages through the tangled Web, TCP/IP has to incorporate many of the ideas to improve reliability suggested in the section on UDP. The Internet has three hurdles: dynamic connections, data loss, and constricted paths, as discussed in the following sections.

Dynamic Connections

One host sends a message to another host. That message travels the networks, going through various routers and gateways. Each message sent may use a different path. Networking segments (connections between computers) often appear and disappear as servers come up and go down. The power of the Internet is its capability to adapt to these changes and route the information accordingly.

Adaptability is one of the driving forces behind the Internet. Your computer can make a request, and the network tries possible avenues to fill the order. Unfortunately, this advantage means that the path between your computer and the server or peer can change, lengthening and shortening the distance.

As the path lengthens, propagation times increase. This means that your program could send successive messages and many would arrive at different times, often out of order.

TCP ensures that the destination has correctly received the last message before it sends the next message. Compare this to a series of numbered messages (this is really how TCP works). Your program may send 10 messages in succession. TCP takes each message, attaches a unique number, and sends it off. The destination accepts the message and replies with an acknowledgment. Upon receiving the acknowledgment, TCP lets your program send the next message.

Sliding Window Protocol

TCP uses a better technique than the send/wait (or ACK/NACK) protocol, which is too slow for anyone's patience. Instead, it uses a sliding window: It gauges when and how often to reply with an ACK. Slower or dirtier connections may increase the acknowledge messages. Connections that are faster and lose less allow more messages to ship before expecting acknowledgments. This is part of the Nagle Algorithm. You can disable this using socket options (see Chapter 9).

Data Loss

When the destination gets your message, it determines the integrity of the data. The data may travel along less-than-optimal communication paths that may drop or corrupt message bits. Remember that the network sends every message one bit at a time. TCP sends with the message a checksum to verify the data. TCP is the last layer that can detect and remedy corrupted data.

If the destination detects any errors, it sends back an error, requesting a retransmittal from your program. Likewise, if your computer does not get an acknowledgment within a specific amount of time, the TCP subsystem automatically resends the message without your program's intervention.

Constricted Paths

Going back to the single message sent to a particular host, suppose that the message is too long for the intervening segments. The problem that the packet encounters as it passes through the network is the different technologies and transmission carriers. Some networked computers permit lengthy packets; others place limits on the size.

UDP tries to send the largest message that it can. This can be a problem with the constricted data paths. The IP algorithms anticipate that the routers may fragment data. Likewise, IP expects that it has to reassemble the incoming message.

TCP, on the other hand, limits every packet to small chucks. TCP breaks up longer messages, before the network has the chance to touch them. The size TCP chooses is one that a majority of networks can accept intact. By default, TCP uses 536 bytes and typically negotiates up to 1,500. To increase that size manually, set the MSS (maximum segment size) TCP socket option (see Chapter 9).

The receiver may find that the message's packets are out of order. TCP reorders them before handing the message to your program.

Solving all these network problems adds protocol and header overhead to TCP's algorithm. Of course, the added overhead of all TCP's techniques slows performance noticeably.

The TCP Header Definition

TCP had to add a lot of information to its header to support all the features that it offers you. The size, in bytes, of the TCP header is about three times that of the UDP header. See Listing 3.4 for a definition of the structure.

LISTING 3.4   TCP Structure Definition

```
/***************************************************************/
/*** TCP (streaming socket) structure definition        ***/
/*** (Formal definition in netinet/tcp.h)               ***/
/***************************************************************/
typedef unsigned char ui8;
typedef unsigned short int ui16;
typedef unsigned int ui32;
typedef unsigned int uint;

struct TCP_header {
    ui16 src_port;     /* Originator's port number */
    ui16 dst_port;     /* Destination's port number */
    ui32 seq_num;      /* Sequence number */
    ui32 ack_num;      /* Acknowledgment number */
    uint data_off:4;   /* Data offset */
    uint __res:6;      /* (reserved) */
    uint urg_flag:1;   /* Urgent, out-of-band message */
    uint ack_flag:1;   /* Acknowledgment field valid */
    uint psh_flag:1;   /* Immediately push message to process */
    uint rst_flag:1;   /* Reset connection due to errors */
    uint syn_flag:1;   /* Open virtual connection (pipe) */
    uint fin_flag:1;   /* Close connection */
    ui16 window;       /* How many bytes receiver allows */
    ui16 checksum;     /* Message checksum */
    ui16 urg_pos;      /* Last byte of an urgent message */
```

LISTING 3.4   Continued

```
    ui8 options[];    /* TCP options */
    ui8 __padding[];  /* (Needed for aligning data[]) */
    uchar data[];     /* Data message */
};
```

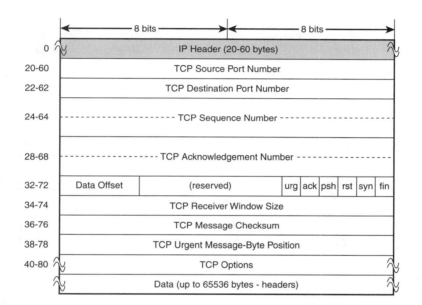

FIGURE 3.5
TCP layout.

The header may have a variable size, so the `data_off` field points to the beginning of the data. To save header space, this field acts like the IP's `header_len` field: It gives the count of 32-bit words that physically precede your data.

TCP uses some of the fields exclusively for opening a connection, flow control, and connection closure. During a communication session, some of the header is empty. The following paragraphs describe a few interesting fields.

The TCP header uses the same port number found in UDP. But `seq_num` and `ack_num` provide traceability to the stream. When you send a message, the IP subsystem attaches a sequence number (`seq_num`). The receiver replies that it got the message with an acknowledgment number (`ack_num`) that is 1 greater than the sequence number. This feature lets acknowledgment packets carry data as well.

Looking at the TCP Interactions

When you open a streaming connection, your program and server exchange the messages listed in Table 3.6.

TABLE 3.6   The Three-Way Handshake

Client Sends	Server Sends	Description
SYN=1 (syn_flag)		Request a virtual connection (pipe).
ACK=0 (ack_flag)		Set sequence number.
	SYN=1 (syn_flag)	Permit and acknowledge a virtual connection.
ACK=1 (ack_flag)		
SYN=0 (syn_flag)		
ACK=1 (ack_flag)		Establish a virtual connection.

This is called the *three-way handshake*. During the transfers, the client and server specify the buffer size of their receiving buffers (windows).

On the other hand, closing a connection is not as simple as it may appear, because there may be data in transit. When your client closes a connection, the interaction shown in Table 3.7 may occur.

TABLE 3.7   TCP Connection Closure

Client	Server	Description
FIN=1 (fin_flag)	Transmits data	Client requests close.
	Receives data	
ACK=1	Transmits more	Server channels flushed.
	Receives more	
ACK=1	FIN=1	Close accepted. Server closes and awaits client ACK.
ACK=1		Client closes its side.

Closing the TCP connection makes it impossible to reuse the socket for other connections. For example, if you connect to a server, the only way to sever the connection is to close the channel, which closes the socket as well. If you then want to connect to another server, you must create a new socket. The other protocols do not have that limitation.

How the IP Protocols Fit Together

While interfacing with the network, you may wonder how all these protocols fit together. In some cases, it may seem that they don't fit together at all. They do use some of each other's features, but they really don't work so closely together that they are inseparable.

The raw IP, ICMP, UDP, and TCP protocols fulfill specific roles. You can use these roles to fit your needs when you design your network application. Of course, while TCP has more reliability and features than the other protocols, you cannot replace ICMP with TCP. Because the Linux subsystems require different features from TCP/IP, each packet type is important for your system to work correctly.

The ICMP, UDP, and TCP packets physically rely on the raw IP packet. Their headers and data reside in the IP's data section, following the IP header.

Snooping the Network with Tcpdump

Observing packets on a live network effectively shows you what the kernel does with messages and how the network subsystem resolves address requests. From the raw IP packet to TCP, tcpdump is a tool that displays data on the network. For security, you need root access to run tcpdump.

By default, tcpdump uses promiscuous mode so that you can see everything on the network. Promiscuous mode manipulates the hardware interface directly to accept any and all messages.

The Balance of Network Ethics

Knowing how to do many things is very powerful and holds a lot of responsibility. With root privilege, you can do a lot good and a lot of harm to the network. When you install Linux on your computers, the distribution assumes that you act with the same good intentions as those who afforded you the ability to snoop others' packets. One effective way to destroy the Free Software movement is to abuse the power and trust that other good and well-intentioned people gave you.

Normally, the hardware interface adapter picks up only those messages that it recognizes from the ethernet address. Recall from Chapter 2 that every ethernet hardware adapter has a unique 6-byte ID. The adapter uses this ID to ignore all packets except for the ones that match the ID.

Programmable Ethernet IDs

Some OEMs (original equipment manufacturers) offer their network interface cards (either PCI or PCMCIA) that support a programmable MAC address (or ethernet ID). This makes mass production possible for a few card manufacturers while serving several hundred name-brand companies. Unfortunately, you may get a card that has a bogus ID, because the name-brand company did not program it correctly. This error can make your card non-unique on the network.

If you do not want promiscuous mode, you can turn it off with one of the options. Tcpdump has many options to help you filter out unwanted messages and select displayed data and data redirection. Here are a few interesting command-line options:

- `-a`   Try to assign names to network and broadcast addresses. This requires access to a nameserver.
- `-c <count>`   Stop after getting the specified count of messages.
- `-n`   Don't convert the node addresses to their names (this is useful when you don't have a name server).
- `-p`   Don't put the interface into promiscuous mode. If you have a small network or cluster, seeing all the packets may be interesting. Otherwise, with promiscuous mode enabled, the network could easily overwhelm your computer.
- `-v`   Print a slightly more verbose dump. This includes the time-to-live (TTL) field.
- `-vv`   Print a lot more information in the dump.
- `-w <file>`   Write the raw packet to a file.

Tcpdump can run without any options, and it displays most information you need. You can also see interesting interactions, such as the ARP (address resolution protocol) asking for and acquiring the ethernet ID from the IP address. Here's an example capturing 100 verbose packets without a time stamp:

```
tcpdump -v -t -c 100
```

The `-t` option suppresses the time stamp. Because the messages often scroll off the screen very quickly, you may want to redirect the results to a file.

Tcpdump does have a few anomalies; for example, it does not pick up messages to itself. It does not see the packets from `ping 127.0.0.1`, because the network subsystem does not send those messages down to the lower protocol layers where tcpdump hooks in.

Writing a Custom Network Snooper

How does tcpdump work? You can read the lengthy Open Source program, or you write your own network snooper (a tcpdump, of sorts). The only thing you need to know is how to capture any and all messages for a host. The tool that this section describes helps you write a network snooper that disassembles packets intended for the host. It does not support promiscuous mode, however.

For security (like tcpdump), you need to be root to run a network snooper. The snooper captures all messages destined for your computer. To get all messages, you use the following calls:

```
sd = socket(PF_INET, SOCK_PACKET, filter);
bytes_read = recvfrom(sd, buffer, sizeof(buffer), 0, 0, 0);
```

Notice the new socket type: SOCK_PACKET. This is a read-only hardware-level socket.

You can use several filters for SOCK_PACKET. The filters tell the IP layer what kinds of packet you want to capture. A few of these filters are

- ETH_P_802_3   802.3 frames
- ETH_P_AX25   AX.25 frames
- ETH_P_ALL   All frames (be careful!)
- ETH_P_802_2   802.2 frames

The filter to use is ETH_P_ALL. As the note indicates, be careful with this filter, because when you select it, it gives you everything. The resulting call is

```
sd = socket(PF_INET, SOCK_PACKET, ETH_P_ALL);
```

After successfully completing the call, each recvfrom() system call you make returns a network frame (a physical network message). The network frame includes the hardware addresses (for example, the ethernet addresses) and header.

The SOCK_PACKET provides access to the hardware-level frames and all associated data from each transmission. With it you can see how the network subsystem constructs the frames.

You can use the IP structure defined at the beginning of this chapter. However, recall that the storage is hardware-dependent, so the bitfields may be in the wrong order. The structure assumes that bit #0 is the first bit in the frame stream.

The program example on the Web site, snooper.c, rearranges the fields to match the actual hardware frame for a little endian processor (Intel-compatible) and GNU compiler. If you have a different processor (even a different compiler), you may have to tweak the structure.

Summary: Choosing the Best Packets for Sending Messages

You can use tcpdump and the snooper to print the different kinds of packets that your computer sends and receives. These packets, in the case of IP, may be raw IP packets, error messenger ICMP packets, UDP datagrams, or TCP stream messages. Each packet type fills a specific role while leaving plenty of room for expansion.

Each packet has its own header. ICMP, UDP, and TCP attach their headers to the IP header. The total dedicated to these headers ranges in size from 20 bytes to 120 bytes. The balance between the headers and the real data affects the network throughput.

TCP has the least throughput because of the header-to-data ratio. Because it provides the most reliable communication between two computers, it is the most-used protocol on the Internet. TCP offers streaming interface that allows you to use the higher library I/O functions, such as fprintf() and fgets().

You can use UDP to send single messages to different hosts without reconnecting. It virtualizes the network using ports, making it seem that your connection has exclusive access to the network. UDP provides good throughput but unreliable transmission.

The most commonly used protocol is TCP, because of its reliability. UDP follows distantly behind it. The network today has stepped away from trying to use the very-low-level packets and interfaces and toward sending messages. The performance is not as important as the reliability, but users continue to notice the performance issue.

Sending Messages Between Peers

IN THIS CHAPTER

You can think of message passing from two different angles: continuous and without interruption (TCP) or discrete packets of information (UDP). While continuous data flow is like a telephone transmission, the discrete packet is like a letter in an addressed envelope.

The continuous flow requires you to have an established connection with the destination. This makes sure that no information is lost during the interchange and is in order when it arrives. The discrete messages permit you to make a connection merely to ease programming. Without the connection, your program has to place an address on each message.

This chapter discusses connection-based and connectionless interfaces. The comparisons and examples may help you choose the most appropriate type for your applications.

What Are Connection-Based Sockets?

Linux (and all UNIX-type operating systems) offers essentially three different levels of communication for your programs. All the levels require using the `socket()` system call. These levels expose you to the dynamics of network programming and can make programming challenging.

The three basic protocols (raw IP, UDP, and TCP, as defined in Chapter 3, "Different Types of Internet Packets") abstract the network and add reliability while necessarily whittling away performance. The highest level, TCP, has the greatest reliability of all protocol levels. It guarantees that the data reaches the destination correctly and in order. It is so reliable that you could consider it like a file or an interprocess pipe. That is why TCP sockets are *connection-based* sockets.

Open Channels Between Programs

TCP sockets provide an open bi-directional channel between two programs. Like a microphone headset, the channel sends and receives streaming information without break. The programs may send information to each other simultaneously without having to reassemble the dialog from individual messages.

TCP also remembers who you are talking to. Each message in lower levels of the IP protocol has to provide the destination address with each message. That is like dialing your friend's number each time you want to take your turn to speak.

When you connect to the other program (using the `connect()` system call), your socket then remembers the destination address and port. Also, you can use the higher-level library calls designed for streamed I/O, like `fprintf()` and `fgets()`. This simplifies programming tremendously.

As you design your program, the TCP protocol helps you avoid the data loss problems that may occur with other protocols. This simplicity lets you focus on your program.

Reliable Communications

TCP's streamed I/O, high reliability, and access to the higher level I/O imply that the data path is clear and unencumbered. TCP guarantees reliable communications: The peer receives everything the program sends. The network subsystem that includes the devices and protocol stacks (either on the server or client) accepts a message, checks it, and passes it on to the program.

If the check fails and the subsystem detects an error, the subsystem takes care of it by asking for a retransmission. Both ends of the communication path perform this validation check. As described in the last chapter, some messages have a unique and sequential packet ID. The ID is important for ensuring reliability and order. You get this feature when you select the TCP protocol.

The two biggest problems with network communication are packet loss and packet reorder. Suppose your program sends a message. Programs cannot detect absolutely that the destination gets the message unless it gets a response from the destination. For example, your program sends the message, and the destination waits for the packet to arrive. If the destination does not receive anything for a while, it sends a message to your program indicating the last sequence number it reliably received. This collaboration tightly couples your program with the destination.

On the other hand, the destination may get some parts of the message out of order with the rest of the message. When this happens, the destination holds on to the message fragment until it gets your intervening pieces. The destination then reassembles the message using the sequence number as the ordering key.

As noted before, the higher-level library calls expect an open channel and also require the reliable communication path. The TCP protocol focuses on your message channel so that the information appears to flow in a nonpacketized stream. Alternatively, lower-level protocols focus on the packet, so they could not support high-level I/O library calls like printf().

The less-reliable protocols provide you with a very fast channel for your program to send messages. UDP, in particular, tries to get the message out on your network quickly without regard to order. Similarly, the destination accepts each independent message, not expecting any order.

Order is an important concern for your design. You may not expect that your data is order dependent when, in reality, it may be. Here are a few questions that can help you decide whether or not your messages require streams (with quick, parenthetical summaries).

- **Does your data form an independent request?** Your program can accept the reply in any order when the message is an independent request. For example, the order of execution is unimportant in the case of unrelated requests: A program can request a file and then go on to request the peer's status. However, if you were sending coordinate points for a player on a network game—that is, an interdependent request—the order of the positions is very important. (Yes=UDP; No=TCP)

- **If you randomly reorder the messages, does your program eventually respond with the same results?** This is the real litmus test of message-based channels. Streams cannot tolerate reordering of the packets. TCP carefully reorders the messages into a continuous message. (Yes=UDP; No=TCP)

- **Do you picture your dialog as a pipe connecting the two programs or as a FedEx courier?** On one hand, the flow of information between your program and the peer can compare to water in a pipe. This information has an order. On the other hand, a single packet of information can compare to a parcel. The information is unordered and packetized. For example, you can receive several parcels in any order and may only reply to a couple. The flow-pipe cannot support this without information loss. (FedEx=UDP; Pipe=TCP)

- **If you disconnect and reconnect between each message, does the server or peer have to keep track of where you were or the state of the transaction?** Some transactions may simply be "Give me this," and the reply is "Here." The server remembers nothing from transaction to transaction. Other transactions force you to pass through different states. A Telnet session has two states: logged-in and not logged-in. (No=UDP; Yes=TCP)

- **Must your program track who said what while serving several connections?** Sometimes you need to have dialogs (with/without data streams) in which the server must track the client. For example, personalization on the Internet lets the user customize his working environment. Some programs may do similarly. (Yes=UDP; No=TCP)

- **Could the network lose a message without affecting the destination's computations?** The originator may have to deal with the lost data, but as long as the destination does not depend on each message arriving safely, you could use the nonstreamed protocol of UDP. For example, it may be inconsequential to lose an unordered request, while in fact quite another matter to lose ordered requests. For example, stock prices require a careful flow of information, but weather statistics can hit a few blips without hurting the forecast. (Yes=UDP; No=TCP)

After answering these questions, if you find that just one answer is TCP, you may have to either use TCP or beef up the UDP protocol. These rules are not hard and fast; you may choose to accept the issues with the less-reliable UDP so that you can get the performance you need.

Lower Protocol Connections

It's possible to use the `connect()` system call on a UDP socket. This may be appealing when you do not need higher-level I/O, because UDP offers a performance boost with self-contained messages. However, the UDP connection functions a little differently from the way TCP handles connections.

Chapter 3 described the process as a three-way handshake. This handshake establishes the communication level for streaming your data between programs. Since UDP does not support streams, the connect() system call only simplifies the message passing.

The connect() system call on a UDP connection merely records the destination of any messages you send. You can use read() and write() like a TCP connection, but you do not have the reliability and ordering guarantees. The algorithm presented in Listing 4.1 is very similar to that of TCP programming.

LISTING 4.1   A Simple Connected Datagram

```
/*************************************************************/
/*** Sample datagram example with connection          ***/
/*** Excerpt from connected-peer.c                     ***/
/*************************************************************/
int sd;
struct sockaddr_in addr;
sd = socket(PF_INET, SOCK_DGRAM, 0);       /* datagram socket */
bzero(&addr, sizeof(addr));
addr.sin_family = AF_INET;
addr.sin_port = htons(DEST_PORT);
inet_aton(DEST_IPADDR, &addr.sin_addr);
if ( connect(sd, &addr, sizeof(addr)) != 0 )    /* connect! */
    perror("connect");
/*---Note: this is not a streamed send---*/
send(sd, buffer, msg_len);                 /* send like TCP */
```

Normally, when using UDP, you use the sendto() or recvfrom() system call (described later in this chapter). The send() system call assumes that the program has already registered the destination with a connect().

The peer (or server) that waits for the connection may use the same connection interface, or it could use sendto() and recvfrom(). However, for the program to connect to the peer, it is necessary for the peer to publish its port number with the bind() system call. For a complete description of the bind() system call, please refer to the "Sending a Direct Message" section, later in this chapter.

The example code fragment in Listing 4.1 refers to DEST_PORT. This number is an agreed-upon port interface between the two programs. The listening peer sets up the port by calling bind() to request DEST_PORT. When your message arrives, the destination may issue a connect() system call itself.

Unlike TCP's connect() system call, your program can reconnect as many times as you wish to other peers or servers without closing the socket. With TCP, you cannot connect to other peers or servers unless you close and then reopen the socket. One of the most important features UDP offers is the capability to send messages to different destinations without closing the socket. Using the `connect()` system call with UDP protocol still affords you this flexibility.

Again, if you use UDP in any form, you elect the unreliability that goes with it. You could lose packets, or the packets may arrive out of order. The `connect()` system call for UDP only records the destination and does not increase the reliability of the channel between your programs.

Reliably Delivered Messages (RDM)

The Reliably Delivered Messages (RDM) protocol [RFC908,RFC1151] provides the guaranteed delivery that TCP offers but also lets you have the message-based (non-streamed) speed of UDP. RDM may still get the messages out of order, but it provides a good compromise between UDP and TCP. Unfortunately, even though this protocol has been on the books for a number of years, Linux (and other UNIX operating systems) does not yet support it.

Example: Connecting to the HTTP Daemon

The most common protocol users connect with is HTTP. It describes a very simple interface that includes a query. The server, in turn, interprets the query and replies with a message that the client can understand. That message may be any document inside a simple email header format.

The simplicity of the interface demonstrates for you many of the transactions on the network. Most client-server interactions are single-transaction based. All of the overhead of TCP interfacing and reliability checking can be wasteful on a single transaction. Still, that is the accepted standard.

Simplified HTTP Protocol

To send a request to an HTTP server, you only need to know a single command. This is an oversimplified representation of the HTTP protocol. Chapter 6, "A Server Primer," covers the protocol in greater depth:

```
GET <query> HTTP/1.0<cr><cr>
```

The query typically looks like a directory path, but it can take parameters and variables. When you enter the URL http://www.kernel.org/mirrors/ in your browser, your browser opens a socket to www.kernel.org and sends the following message:

```
GET /mirrors/ HTTP/1.0<cr><cr>
```

It may also send a lot of other information about what kind of data it can receive. This helps data translation. The last two <cr>s are newlines that indicate the end of the message. The client can send any number of parameters and settings, but it must end the message with two newlines.

The connection is streamed, so you don't know if you have hit the end of the message. This could lead to waiting indefinitely for something that never arrives. The two newlines tell the server that the client is done talking.

Getting an HTTP Page

Composing the query is the easiest part of the connection. The query also gives you a lot of flexibility in adding what you need. The only requirement is to make sure that the server can understand your message. Listing 4.2 presents one way of getting a Web page. This program opens a connection specified on the command line and sends an HTTP request. The program prints the results on stdout.

LISTING 4.2   Getting a Web Page from an HTTP Server

```
/*******************************************************/
/*** Excerpt from the http-client.c (on Web site) file.   ***/
/*******************************************************/
int sd;
struct servent *serv;
if ( (serv = getservbyname("http", "tcp")) == NULL )
  PANIC("HTTP servent");
if ( (sd = socket(AF_INET, SOCK_STREAM, 0)) < 0 )
  PANIC("Socket");

/*---Initialize server address/port struct---*/
bzero(&dest, sizeof(dest));
dest.sin_family = AF_INET;
dest.sin_port = serv->s_port;              /* HTTP Server */
if ( inet_addr(Strings[1], &dest.sin_addr.s_addr) == 0 )
    PANIC(Strings[1]);

/*---Connect to server---*/
if ( connect(sd, &dest, sizeof(dest)) != 0 )
    PANIC("Connect");

/*---Compose the query and send it---*/
sprintf(buffer, "GET %s HTTP/1.0\n\n", Strings[2]);
send(sd, buffer, strlen(buffer), 0);

/*---While there's data, read and print it---*/
do
```

LISTING 4.2   Continued

```
{
    bytes_read = recv(sd, buffer, sizeof(buffer)-1, 0);
    buffer[bytes] = 0;
    if ( bytes_read > 0 )
        printf("%s", buffer);
}
while ( bytes_read > 0 );
```

The program in Listing 4.2 opens the connection, sends the command-line request, and displays everything it gets until the server closes the connection. Later versions of the HTTP protocol (1.1 and the proposed HTTP-NG) include the capability to leave the channel open, taking advantage of the TCP connection. Again, this feature emphasizes the need to tell the receiver when the sender is done talking. You can read much more about the new versions of HTTP in the RFCs found at www.w3c.org.

What Are Connectionless Sockets?

Not every communication requires having a full bi-directional channel open between peers. If the telephone is an example of a streaming connection, the postal system best represents a message-based (or *connectionless*) system. Like the postal system, UDP composes messages, assigns a destination, and ships it off without any tracking of the message as it travels to the destination. (Just to reiterate: A datagram's unreliability means that it offers no guarantee of delivery. That does not mean that it does not work.)

Setting the Socket's Address

The full installation of a Linux distribution usually includes tools that allow you to send and receive notes from other workstations on the network. The tools require only a machine address and maybe a username. You could implement this kind of tool on your own using a UDP socket. To do this, you need to see if the current user is the recipient of the message.

These messenger-style tools use the two pieces of data (hostname and username) to identify the recipient uniquely. The tool has no streamed data, so your implementation could use a connectionless interface.

The connectionless interface does not make the connect() system call, but you can't call send() or recv() without a connection. Instead, the operating system offers two lower-level system calls that include the destination address: recvfrom() and sendto(). These calls act similarly to recv() and send(), but you provide the destination as part of the call:

```
#include <sys/socket.h>
#include <resolv.h>
```

```
int sendto(int sd, char* buffer, int msg_len, int options,
      struct sockaddr *addr, int addr_len);
int recvfrom(int sd, char* buffer, int maxsize, int options,
      struct sockaddr *addr, int *addr_len);
```

The first four parameters are the same as `recv()` and `send()`. Even the options and possible error conditions are the same. The `sendto()` system call adds the socket address of the destination. When you send a message to your destination, you fill the `addr` structure and call `sendto()`. Listing 4.3 illustrates an example.

LISTING 4.3   `sendto()` Example

```
/*************************************************************/
/*** Sendto() example.                                   ***/
/*************************************************************/
int sd;
struct sockaddr_in addr;
sd = socket(PF_INET, SOCK_DGRAM, 0);
bzero(&addr, sizeof(addr));
addr.sin_family = AF_INET;
addr.sin_port = htons(DEST_PORT);
inet_aton(DEST_ADDR, &addr.sin_addr);
sendto(sd, "This is a test", 15, 0, &addr, sizeof(addr));
```

This example sends a message directly to `DEST_ADDR:DEST_PORT`. Of course, you could use either raw data or ASCII in the message body. It does not matter.

The `recvfrom()` system call is a little different. Like the `sendto()` call, the first five parameters are effectively the same. The behavior of `recvfrom()` is similar to `recv()`, and when executed it waits for a message to arrive from some sender.

The last parameter has a different type. It is a pointer to an integer. The last two parameters of `sendto()` are the destination. The last two parameters of `recvfrom()` are the address of the originator. Because the struct `sockaddr` family can be different sizes, you could possibly get a message from a source that is different from the socket type (the default being `AF_INET`).

Passing the Address's Length

The `recvfrom()` call (like `recv()`) passes the pointer to the structure's length. This is an artifact from a different protocol family, `PF_LOCAL`. When the call finishes, you need to know how much of the `addr` data region the call used. You also need to tell the call how much is available to use. Thus, the parameter is pass by reference so that the system call can return the number of bytes it actually used.

Because recvfrom() may change the addr_len parameter, you need to set the value each time you make the system call. Otherwise, the value in addr_len could potentially grow smaller with each system call. Here is an example of using recvfrom():

```
/***********************************************************/
/*** Recvfrom() example.                                ***/
/***********************************************************/
int sd;
struct sockaddr_in addr;
sd = socket(PF_INET, SOCK_DGRAM, 0);
/*---bind to a particular port---*/
while (1)
{   int bytes, addr_len=sizeof(addr);

    bytes = recvfrom(sd, buffer, sizeof(buffer), 0, &addr,
        &addr_len);
    fprintf(log, "Got message from %s:%d (%d bytes)\n",
        inet_ntoa(addr.sin_addr), ntohs(addr.sin_port),bytes);
    /****process request****/
    sendto(sd, reply, len, 0, addr, addr_len);
}
```

In this example, you create the socket and bind the port. The while loop waits for the incoming message, logs the connection, processes the request, and replies with the result. The loop resets the value of addr_len so that the size of addr does not appear to shrink with each system call. You can use the information in addr as the return address for your reply.

If you use the recvfrom() system call, you must supply a valid addr and addr_len; you cannot set them to NULL (0). Because UDP is connectionless, you need to know the source of the request. The easiest way to do that is to keep addr intact while processing the request.

Some Programs Just Need the Message

The connectionless protocol simplifies the handshaking. TCP requires a three-way handshake: The client sends a connection request, the server accepts the request and sends its own connection request, and the client accepts the server's connection request.

Connectionless UDP effectively has no handshaking; the message itself is the only collaboration shared remotely. This means that the protocol does no checking for a connection. Eventually, if the peer cannot be found or some transmission error occurs, you may get a network error message. However, that message may arrive a long time after the network detects the error (one to five minutes).

UDP's handshakeless protocol reduces the significant overhead of TCP handshaking. To support this, you may see one or two total setup packets. Not bad for high speed communications.

Transaction TCP (T/TCP): A Connectionless TCP

The TCP three-way handshaking, as compared to the UDP protocol, requires up to 10 setup packets. This slow startup is very costly when the requestor needs only a single transaction. During the startup process, the two ends of the connection verify each other's services and channel reliability. Similarly, the shutdown process requires an additional handshake (refer to Chapter 3).

TCPv3 [RFC1644] adds a new feature that provides some of the connection speed of UDP while retaining the reliability of TCP. Transaction TCP (T/TCP) does the connection, transmission, and shutdown all in one single sendto() system call. How does it do this?

TCP establishes your connections using the three-way handshake, and it closes or shuts down the connection using a particular handshake. These steps are necessary to ensure that the client and server get all sent data in the proper order. To meet that goal, the TCP packet has to use flags to indicate when to establish connection (SYN), acknowledge data (ACK), and close the channel (FIN).

Chapter 3 describes the format of the TCP packet. The packet header includes several fields that may appear to be mutually exclusive. For example, it has separate flags for SYN, ACK, and FIN. Why do you want to waste the precious space of the packet when only one bit of each field is likely to be active at the same time?

T/TCP uses these fields simultaneously. When the T/TCP client connects, it sends the message to the server while requesting the connection (SYN). It also sets the FIN flag to close the connection as soon as the server completes the transaction. See Figure 4.1.

The server replies with its own connection request, a close request, and an acknowledgment of the client's close. (The connection request acknowledgment is implied.) This packet includes the data that the server generated. Lastly, the client acknowledges the server's close.

T/TCP can be very fast. There is one problem: All the information must be transmitted within TCP's MSS (Maximum Segment Size), which is only 540 bytes. However, you can change that setting up to 64KB. Also, the program is not limited to sending one message; it can send several messages.

The server program does not have to do any more work to support T/TCP. The algorithm for a normal TCP connection serves T/TCP as well, because all the server-side support is programmed in the network subsystem. All the work is on the client side. You may use the following algorithm in the client:

```
/***********************************************************/
/*** T/TCP basic algorithm.                          ***/
/***********************************************************/
int flag=1;
```

```
int sd;
sd = socket(PF_INET, SOCK_STREAM, 0);
if ( setsockopt(sd, IPPROTO_TCP, TCP_NOPUSH, &flag,
        sizeof(flag)) != 0 )
    PANIC("TCP_NOPUSH not supported");
/****set up addr to destination****/
if ( sendto(sd, buffer, bytes, MSG_FIN, &addr, sizeof(addr))
        < 0 )
    PANIC("sendto");
...
```

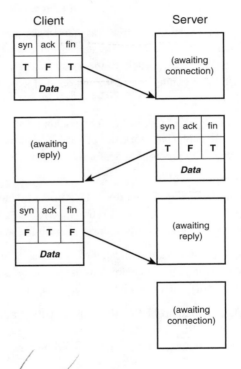

FIGURE 4.1

The T/TCP handshake opens, sends, and closes a dialog in three packets.

With T/TCP you have to disable TCP from flushing its buffers too quickly. That is what the setsockopt() system call is doing in the example. Also, you can send as many messages as you want, but the last message must have MSG_FIN (see above) in the sendto() system call.

T/TCP and Linux

Linux, unfortunately, does not currently support T/TCP. In the future it will, but for now, you may use these techniques on other UNIX operating systems. You can see some flags that indicate a work in progress in the Linux kernel (for example, `MSG_EOF` and `MSG_FIN` are defined in `linux/socket.h`). Still, you can try out the T/TCP programs found on the Web site.

TCP, as mentioned before, requires you to re-create a TCP socket for every new connection, because you can close a connection only by closing the socket itself. T/TCP may have a side benefit of not requiring you to re-create a socket like TCP, because its connection and shutdown are implicit.

T/TCP gives you the benefit of short bursts of interaction with any supporting server, while minimizing startup and shutdown times. The benefits of T/TCP help your program respond faster to servers.

Sending a Direct Message

Up to this point you have worked with a connected channel to send and receive messages that is best compared to using a telephone. A directed message is unconnected, meaning that it does no handshaking. Creating a directed message (not a pipe) to a peer requires a sender and a receiver. The sender transmits the message, and the receiver accepts the message. It's that simple.

Each message needs a destination (the kernel places the return address in the packet for you). The `send()` and `recv()` assume that they have a connected channel, which automatically defines the destination. Instead, you must use the `recvfrom()` and `sendto()` system calls, because both provide the addressing each message requires.

Prior to sending the message, you build the destination address, which includes the host address and the port number. As described in previous chapters, if your program skips selecting a port, the operating system assigns one to the socket randomly. This is not a good idea for peer programs. The calling peer must know the destination port to address the message properly.

Checking Linux `sockaddr` Support

The Linux kernel supports several different types of addressing protocols, but not all protocols are directly included in the distribution kernels. For example, the distribution kernels often omit the amateur radio protocols. If you are uncertain which binding protocols your compiled kernel supports, simply run your program. The `bind()`, `sendto()`, `connect()`, and `recvfrom()` system calls complain if they receive a `sockaddr` they don't understand. You can find a list of the supported `sockaddr` in Appendix A, "Data Tables."

The UDP/TCP senders must know what port the receiver is listening on so that the operating system routes the packet to the correct program. This port is usually an agreed-upon port number between sender and receiver. For example, the `/etc/services` file lists the published port numbers that provide standard services.

Binding the Port to Your Socket

You can request a specific port number from the operating system using the `bind()` system call. You may have seen this call before, and regrettably most UNIX manual pages define it as a way to "name the socket." This definition refers to PF_LOCAL or PF_UNIX sockets that use the file system. A better description is "to bind a port number or other publishable interface to the socket."

Name and Port Binding

The port assignment and socket naming vary dramatically between each `sockaddr` family member. Some, such as AF_LOCAL and AF_AX25, are alphanumeric names; others, like AF_INET and AF_IPX, use ports. The port numbers must be unique, so in general no two TCP or UDP sockets can have the same port numbers (at least with AF_INET). However, you can have a UDP socket and a TCP socket share the same port number. That is how some services (in `/etc/services`) offer you both connections.

The prototype definition of the `bind()` system call is

```
#include <sys/socket.h>
#include <resolv.h>
int bind(int sd, struct sockaddr *addr, int addr_size);
```

This section only introduces `bind()`; for an in-depth description, see Chapter 6. The use is similar to the `connect()` system call where you need to initialize the `addr` parameter first:

```
/*************************************************************/
/*** Bind() example.                                     ***/
/*************************************************************/
struct sockaddr addr;
int sd;
sd = socket(PF_INET, SOCK_STREAM, 0);
bzero(&addr, sizeof(addr));
addr.sin_family = AF_INET;
addr.sin_port = htons(MY_PORT);       /* request specific port */
addr.sin_addr_s_addr = INADDR_ANY;        /* any IP interface */
if ( bind(sd, &addr, sizeof(addr)) != 0 )
    perror("bind");
...
```

If you compare this `bind()` system call example with that of the `connect()` system call, you may note two main differences: Here, the code snippet is requesting `MY_PORT`, and the address is `INADDR_ANY`. Your program needs a specific port number for your peers to connect to.

The `INADDR_ANY` is a special flag (essentially `0.0.0.0`) that indicates that any peer can connect from any interface. Some computers have more than one network interface (for example, two LAN cards, a modem with a LAN card, aliased IP addresses). Each hardware or logical interface has its own IP address. Using the `bind()` system call, you can specify whether to serve any one or all of these interfaces. You can use this feature for cross-firewall translations or filters, and it applies to both TCP and UDP protocols. To indicate a specific interface, you can use the following:

```
if ( inet_aton("128.48.5.161", &addr.sin_addr) == 0 )
    perror("address error");
...
```

This makes the request that the port listen on `128.48.5.161`. You could use the network byte-ordering conversions like `htonl()`:

```
addr.sin_addr.s_addr = htonl(0x803005A1);  /* 128.48.5.161 */
```

Either way, it functions the same. You may note that `INADDR_ANY` does not use the `htonl()` conversion call. It doesn't need it, since it is all zeros, and it is guaranteed to be in network byte order.

Tossing the Message Around

Sending and receiving UDP messages looks a little like playing catch in the fog. The players take turns tossing and catching, even though they can't see each other. The sender is the first to toss the ball. The receiver must have a known location and port number, established with the bind() system call. The sender does not need to establish its port number, because each message includes the return address. The potential exists for a player to toss the ball to an empty space.

The sender does very little initialization and often does no more than one message request. You could place this in a loop, if you want to toss messages back and forth. The code for the sender is seen in Listing 4.4 and on the Web site in connectionless-sender.c.

LISTING 4.4   Datagram Sender Example

```
/**********************************************************/
/*** Sender example.                                    ***/
/*** (Excerpt from connectionless-sender.c)             ***/
/**********************************************************/
struct sockaddr addr;
int sd, bytes, reply_len, addr_len=sizeof(addr);
char *request= "select * from TableA where field1 = 'test';";
char buffer[1024];

/*---set up socket---*/
sd = socket(PF_INET, SOCK_DGRAM, 0);
bzero(&addr, sizeof(addr));
addr.sin_family = AF_INET;
addr.sin_port = htons(9999);        /* request specific port */
if ( inet_aton(DEST_ADDR, &addr.sin_addr) == 0 ) /* Dest IP */
    perror("Network IP bad");

/*---send message---*/
if ( sendto(sd, request, strlen(request), 0, &addr, addr_len) < 0 )
    perror("Tried to reply with sendto");

/*---get reply---*/
bytes = recvfrom(sd, buffer, sizeof(buffer), 0, &addr, &addr_len);
if ( bytes > 0 )
    perror("Reply problem");
else
    printf("%s", buffer);
...
```

Assuming that the receiver's port is 9999, the sender in this example transmits a SQL request.

The sender does not need to request a specific port, because the receiver picks that information from the data recvfrom() places in addr. (Again, remember that all sockets require a port. If you don't request one, the kernel chooses one for your program.)

Catching the Message

Unlike the sender, the receiver program needs to set the port number (using `bind()`). After creating the socket, it must publish the agreed-upon port number, so that the peer can communicate with it. The code in Listing 4.5 shows an example of a receiver. You can find the whole program in the file `connectionless-receiver.c` on the Web site.

LISTING 4.5   Datagram Receiver Example

```
/******************************************************/
/*** Receiver example.                            ***/
/*** (Excerpt from connectionless-receiver.c)     ***/
/******************************************************/
struct sockaddr addr;
int sd;

/*---Set up socket and request port allocation---*/
sd = socket(PF_INET, SOCK_DGRAM, 0);
bzero(&addr, sizeof(addr));
addr.sin_family = AF_INET;
addr.sin_port = htons(9999);        /* request specific port */
addr.sin_addr_s_addr = INADDR_ANY; /* any IP interface */
if ( bind(sd, &addr, sizeof(addr)) != 0 )
    perror("bind");

/*---Get & process all requests---*/
do
{   int bytes, reply_len, addr_len=sizeof(addr);
    char buffer[1024];

    /*---Await message, if OK process request and reply---*/
    bytes = recvfrom(sd, buffer, sizeof(buffer), 0, &addr,
        &addr_len);
    if ( bytes > 0 )                        /* if valid return */
    {                           /* ...declare connect and reply */
        printf("Caught message from %s:%d (%d bytes)\n",
            inet_ntoa(addr.sin_addr), ntohs(addr.sin_port),
            bytes);
        /****Process message****/
        if ( sendto(sd, buffer, reply_len, 0, &addr,
                addr_len) < 0 )
            perror("Tried to reply with sendto");
    }
    else
        perror("Awaiting message with RecvFrom");
}
while ( !quit );
...
```

In this excerpt, the receiver requests a port and then waits for an incoming message. If it gets a message, it processes the request and replies with the result.

The sender just transmits one message. The receiver, on the other hand, acts more like a server, receiving, processing, and replying to every message that arrives. This presents a fundamental problem between these two algorithms: allocating enough space for the entire message.

If your program requires a variable-length message, you may have to create a larger buffer. The largest UDP message is about 64KB; that is ultimately your largest size.

> **Large UDP Messages**
>
> If the message is larger than the buffer, the message queue drops any remaining bytes of the incoming message. This applies to many of the protocol families that support datagrams.

Ensuring UDP Message Arrival

Dropping a message that is only half read may not seem like a good idea. When using the UDP protocol, there are several issues that you need to be aware of. As mentioned above, you need to know how big the message is. UDP is also unreliable, meaning that you cannot guarantee that the destination got your message.

You might think that in all cases you need reliability, but not all systems really need it. For instance, some messages are very time critical. As soon as the time expires, the significance of the message reduces to nothing.

If you want to beef up UDP (without going 100% to TCP), you could take several steps. In fact, you could exceed the reliability of TCP rather easily.

Strengthening UDP's Reliability

The whole idea behind TCP is to provide a streamable interface between the client and the server. TCP introduces overhead that reduces performance perceptibly throughout the communication. Still, unlike UDP, it can guarantee the arrival of each message. If you want that guarantee in UDP, you have to add your own code.

For the sake of discussion, each message has several UDP packets. Ensuring that the destination gets the message introduces two interesting problems:

- How does the receiver know that a packet is supposed to arrive?
- How does the sender know whether the receiver got the packet?

Solving the first problem helps prepare the receiver to track each packet of a message. If there appears to be a sequencing problem, the receiver could request a specific packet. Also, the sender could expect an acknowledgment of each packet.

One method you could use is to assign a unique sequence number to each packet (like TCP's acknowledgment mechanism). As each packet arrives, your beefed-up UDP code checks it off. If a packet is lost, your program may request a retransmission with the specific packet number. The main problem with this method is that the sender must retain a record of all the packets it sent. It could drop off very old packets, but that packet history could become very long.

A way to solve lengthy packet histories is to acknowledge each packet. This method solves the second problem and requires the receiver to reply to each packet with its own message indicating what it successfully received by sequence number. This technique is in essence what TCP does. However, using this technique, your program experiences some of the performance hit that TCP has.

The problem is that most physical networks are not truly bi-directional. Each transmission takes up some of the network bandwidth, keeping others from transmitting. Also, each packet has the IP header and the UDP header (28-byte minimum). If the receiver replies to each packet individually, most of the acknowledgment is header overhead (4 or 5 bytes for your sequence ID acknowledgment and 28 bytes for the UDP/IP header). Therefore, keeping the receiver silent as long as possible helps reduce network congestion.

A solution could be to group the acknowledgments into a few packets. For example, if each packet is 1,024 bytes and the sender has to transmit a 1MB message, the receiver could get about 1,000 packets. Within that 1,024-byte limit, the receiver could easily acknowledge 10 packets at a time. This limits the history to 10×1,024 bytes. You need to know the network performance and the host memory limitations in order to implement this properly.

This introduces another problem: How does the receiver know when the sender is done? For instance, if the receiver acknowledges every tenth packet and the sender only has five packets, you may run into two problems:

- The receiver may never send an acknowledgment.
- The sender may assume that the receiver never got the packets, so it retransmits.

To solve this, you could tell the receiver the total number of packets to expect. When the receiver gets the last packet, it transmits the shortened acknowledgment message.

Sequencing Packets

Each packet of a message under the UDP protocol could arrive at the destination out of order with respect to other packets. This occurs because the Internet is very dynamic (see Chapter 3). Stalls, congestion, and dropped links may force routers to delay or reroute your message.

One of the solutions for ensuring packet arrival is to include a unique number. This solution can help packet sequencing. For this to work, the number must be sequential and unique between messages.

If the packet gets out of order, your protocol may hold back higher-numbered packets until the lower-number messages arrive. For example, if packets 1, 2, 4, and 5 arrive, packets 4 and 5 wait until 3 arrives.

Potentially, the network could drop packet 3 during transmission, in which case the receiver could either request packet 3 specifically or acknowledge the packets that arrived. Either way, the sender retransmits the missing message.

Packet Redundancy

The network may cause mirroring of packets, resulting in duplicates arriving at the destination. The most common cause is when a very late packet arrives after the destination requests a retransmittal. Sequencing eliminates redundant packets. The receiver simply drops the packet with the duplicate sequence ID.

Verifying Data Integrity

Packets move from source to destination through networks and routers. At any time, the network could corrupt the message (and often does on a congested network). One collision forces the originating hosts to retransmit. In the example above, where packet 3 is lost, the host most likely sent the packet. However, the network could easily have blasted it.

Both UDP and TCP use one's-complement checksums on their data. The IP layer checksums only its own header and ignores the data message. Checksums are useful for detecting minor errors, but it is possible for the errors to cancel each other out. Some networking interfaces include a hardware cyclical redundancy check (CRC) or error correction codes (ECCs) for finding and repairing corrupted data.

Again, packet 3 could actually arrive, but the contents might be corrupted while still passing the IP and UDP checksums.

You could incorporate your own checksum, CRC, hash, or ECC in your packets and messages. Algorithms for these are available on the Internet from the Open Source community. When you choose the validation algorithm, balance it against these items:

- The amount of data you're transmitting. Increasing your header size can significantly reduce the network throughput.

- The reparability of your data. Some data may be easily reparable because of redundancy or low criticality.

- Data value versus data position. Checksums are good at quick data value computation, but they lose byte-order significance. A CRC requires more computation but can easily identify bit errors up to the CRC size. For example, a 32-bit CRC can reliably detect bit errors up to 32 bits in length. Beyond 32 bits, it loses reliability.

Data reliability is important for most applications. Checking, validation, and sequencing help ensure safe and orderly arrival of a message. Making sure that the sender and receiver communicate helps smooth the data flow.

Data Flow Glitches

Communication between peers is not always clear. Each may assume that the other is supposed to talk first (network deadlock). Another problem is like being placed on hold forever: You are never sure that the person hasn't put you on hold and taken a coffee break for the rest of the day.

Starvation occurs when a requestor waits indefinitely for a response. The cause may include a bad network, slow peer, rebooted peer, and so on. In most cases, you can solve a starved receiver by programming a tickler, which is simply a message to remind the sender that your receiver program is still waiting.

The tickler should wait a period of time before getting impatient. You could include the last sequence ID sent and even a time stamp in the message. After hearing nothing from the sender, the receiver may reset the connection. This process does require the sender to understand the tickler and connection reset messages.

A network deadlock can happen when one of the messages is lost during a packet interchange. The sender waits for the reply, while the receiver still waits for the lost message. Your tickler could help break the deadlock as well. For example, in the packet interchange example, the receiver tickles your sender with the last sequence ID it got. Your program, in turn, retransmits the lost message.

Juggling Tasks: A Multitasking Introduction

Going back to the sender and receiver programs, why use two programs? Why not use just one? Using one program is possible, but when you want to send and receive at the same time, you essentially need two programs.

Suppose that you had a distributed program (a program that uses the network as a multiprocessor) that processes image data very quickly. Your network uses several stages to process the image: image capturer, deflecker, smoother, quantizer, and serializer. Each of these is on a different computer, and the information flows from one stage to the next. The smoother receives data from the deflecker, processes the information, and passes it on to the quantizer. Each middle stage must receive and send nearly at the same time, like a bucket with a hole in the bottom.

In this example, you cannot easily combine two stages. Each stage has to be separate, so that the information going in does not get muddied with the results going out. Of course you could toss in the issue of image error: How do you get an error message *up* the cascade?

Dividing the task into well-defined responsibilities is part of the concept of *multitasking*. You can run several programs at the same time in their own contexts to ensure that the inputs and outputs never mingle. This avoids corrupted results. The examples you see in this chapter use a form of multitasking because they run as separate programs.

The programs are actually similar enough that you could merge them into one so that they talk to themselves. In that case and to simplify the interactions, you must create a separately running task for each, indicating which one sends the first message.

Multitasking is integrally embedded in network programming. Chapter 8, "Choosing when to Wait for I/O," discusses multitasking in greater detail.

Summary: Connected Versus Connectionless Models

Passing messages between peers or clients and servers involves either connection-based or connectionless communication. With connection-based messages, you can simply open a channel, connect to a peer, and proceed to send and receive information. The connection keeps track of your destination for you, so you don't have to restate it. Both TCP and UDP support a connection; however, only TCP encompasses connection with reliability and ordering. UDP's connection offers a mere shorthand, so you can use higher I/O services than `sendto()` and `recvfrom()`.

Connectionless message passing is similar to mailing a letter: You need to address each message before sending. To do this, you must use calls other than send() and recv() that the connection-based communication uses. These are sendto() and recvfrom(). These system calls mirror the other calls but add destination and source addresses.

Transaction TCP (T/TCP) is essentially a connectionless TCP. If supported (Linux does not yet support T/TCP), T/TCP helps you to avoid the lengthy setup and shutdown times. This speeds transmission of your messages. Also, the abbreviated protocol focuses on the packet instead of the stream and reduces interaction to three message packets.

By default UDP is connectionless, but you may connect the UDP socket to ease programming. Unlike TCP, you can reconnect the same socket to different peers.

TCP provides you reliability but also carries a load of overhead. You can add reliability to UDP one piece at a time by ensuring data arrival, sequencing packets, eliminating redundancy, verifying data integrity, and removing data flow problems. TCP and UDP provide different levels of reliability and interaction. TCP lets you view the information like a stream; UDP gives your program access to the individual messages. Each of these builds on IP's architecture, functionality, and model.

Understanding the Network Layering Model

IN THIS CHAPTER

One of the most delicious European desserts is the torte, a kind of very rich cake. The torte typically has several (five to eight) layers. Each layer rests its weight on the lower layers and has a different flavor and color. The torte has a firm frosting that covers the crest to the platter.

If you look at how the conceptual network subsystem (or *protocol stacks*) is designed, you find a similar layering. On the surface it shows a common interface with the layers underneath. Each layer of the network rests on top of another to support its features. This dependence is very important: If any part of the lower layers fails, the whole subsystem either crashes or functions less optimally.

Partitioning the network responsibilities provides the support for the weighty features of higher-level functions. The network subsystem is a large and complicated mix of hardware, memory, security, data, kernel, and application. Coordinating all these technologies is the network challenge. All too frequently, unless you really understand the synergy of the technologies, coordinating their fusion burdens the network challenge.

Network modeling addresses the network challenge without losing portability. This chapter introduces the network challenge and presents two models that attempt to solve it.

Solving the Network Challenge

Network programming involves so many parts of computer science and software engineering that working at a low level is very complicated. Similar to building a house, if you focus on cutting the timber, you may never complete the house. But, by combining the proper tools and materials, you can think more about your finished product and the potential features.

The challenges network programming introduces are what makes this particular technology so interesting. However, to program the network from the ground up, you must be a guru (or master of all computer trades). The challenges of network programming include hardware, transmission, operating system interfacing, and program interfacing.

Networking Hardware Issues

Technology provides many options for implementing a network. The options include conducted versus nonconducted media (some physical conduit to carry the signal), electrical versus nonelectrical transmission, directed versus undirected paths, and short versus long distance. Table 5.1 lists a few forms of network connections.

TABLE 5.1   Network Media Have Different Characteristics and Limitations

Media	Conducted	Electrical	Directed	Distance	Top Throughput
Coaxial cable	yes	yes	connected	<2Km	10Mb/s
Twisted pair	yes	yes	connected	<150m	100Mb/s
Fiber optic	yes	no	connected	(unlimited)	100Gb/s
Wireless: HF	no	yes	broadcast	>1000Km	<10Kb/s
Wireless: VHF/UHF	no	yes	broadcast, line of sight	<30Km	<40Kb/s
Wireless: microwave	no	yes	yes, line of sight	<30Km	<1Mb/s
Satellite	no	yes	yes	(unlimited)	<10Mb/s
Infrared	no	no	yes, broadcast	<10m	<1Mb/s
Laser	no	no	yes	very long	<100Gb/s

Fortunately, the kernel hides all these technologies from your direct interaction. Imagine how difficult it would be to know what kind of medium and transmission the computers use. Yet all of these technologies have to deal with several common problems.

One problem with many technologies is *signal attenuation*, or line loss, from media resistance. Electrical types of transmission are particularly susceptible to this problem. The message may degrade from the medium itself. Line signal loss is a real problem for certain technologies (for example, twisted pair and coaxial cabling). The physics of electric and radio transmission attenuate your message as it passes through the medium.

Another problem is *collisions*. Several computers sharing the same medium (conducted or non-conducted) may cause collisions where they transmit messages at the same time. If your computer sends a packet while another is being transmitted, the resulting collision garbles both packets. The two computers must detect collisions, back off, recover, and retransmit.

Interruptions in the conductor cause signal loss and packet degradation. Because of the physics involved, if you disconnect a coax cable from an active network, any active electrical signal reflects off the open connection as if it were a mirror. Any transmission ends up being completely garbled.

Directed transmissions like laser, microwave, or infrared also can suffer interruptions. An obstacle placed between the transmitter and receiver can completely block the signal. Other issues like smoke, smog, and birds cause problems as well.

Hosts connect to a common network medium, sharing time and resources, so hardware identification suddenly can be an issue. Each packet needs a destination on a shared network. If the network connection is just two computers (a point-to-point network), the packet does not need a destination. The destination would be implied. However, the shared network needs a hardware address so that the network interface can select its messages from the myriad that zip by.

Ethernet LAN cards provide their own ID: the MAC, a six-byte ethernet address. When your computer sends a message, the networking subsystem divides the message into several frames, the smallest transmitted container. On an ethernet, each frame includes the source and destination MAC. Eventually the network associates the logical IP address with an actual physical (MAC) address. With the physical address, the LAN card listens for its address. When a matching address arrives, it opens its buffers and lets the message flow in.

Networking Transmission Issues

The hardware issues focus on the technology of the physical communication channel. The next networking issue is moving the packet around the network. The packet faces many hazards that can corrupt or lose it entirely. Often the sender and receiver get little-to-no notification of a packet failure. Sometimes the receiver times out because it has not received a message from the sender when, in reality, the route between them may be severed.

Troubles regarding packets at the networking level typically involve problems with routing. Because the network changes while messages move from one place to another, knowing ahead of time what the symptoms are can help you identify the problem and effect a solution.

Changes in network topology (or *propagation dynamics*) is a concern with even the most controlled network configurations. While its causes vary, it results in lost transmissions. One type of propagation dynamic is the network itself losing messages in transit. You may have experienced or heard about those networks in cubicles where someone moves his feet and shuts down someone else's cluster. Networks between computers change; connections between computers appear and disappear.

Another cause of propagation dynamics is excessive packet aging. As the packet propagates through a path, each node that forwards the packet tracks how old it is using a time-to-live (TTL) field. A packet expires when it exceeds the number of router hops it's allotted. Each packet can get up to 255 hops; by default the value is 64 hops. Usually that is enough for your message to get where it's destined to go.

The limit on the number of hops is important to keep the network from becoming overcrowded with long-dead packets. It's easy for a packet that shows no tracking to cycle around endlessly. For example, suppose router A gets a message. A's routing tables indicate that the best path is through B, so it sends the packet to B. Router B, however, lost its link, so it may send the packet back to A. Router A has no record of receiving the packet, so the packet bounces back and forth (until the TTL field expires or routers A and B synchronize their tables). The TTL field limits how long a packet goes around in a cycle.

Routing lists and host tables can become very large. Careful table management can help you avoid lengthy delays in calculating the best path to the destination.

While the complexity of the network is challenging, it is likewise complex to detect path loss, recovery, and cycles. Often, when a network segment disappears, cycles (or network loops) form that cause packets to age and die quickly. The network rarely notifies your sending and receiving hosts of the problem; the packets simply expire.

Sometimes pathway ambiguity can cause a packet in a message to be copied during transit (*packet-mirroring* or *ghosting*). This strange occurrence is undetectable unless each packet holds an ID or sequence number. Not only can the network duplicate information needlessly, but the network can also lose data through disappearing routers during a transmission or even packet corruption so that an error message never arrives back to the sender.

Packet loss happens all the time. Without accounting and acknowledgements, the originator may never determine whether the destination got the message.

Lastly, the segments may have router-data incompatibilities. Some routers or networks cannot support full 8-bit bytes or large packet sizes. The routers must convert the packets or return an error.

Fortunately, the networking issues arise only when you use lower-level protocols. If you don't have the time or want to face these challenges and are satisfied with the slower throughputs, use the tested and proven high-level protocols. Most network applications use them. Once you have tested your algorithm with a high-level protocol, consider tuning your program for more performance with lower-level protocols. Then, when the dust of the project-building frenzy clears, hone and tune your algorithm to squeeze out more performance.

Network to Operating System Interfacing

The network must be able to interface with the operating system for several reasons. To get its job done, the operating system handles the resources that the network subsystem needs, such as interrupts, ports, and memory. Also, while the networking subsystem manages the details of the network, it has to reside in the kernel for best performance.

The network-kernel interface is complex—especially if the kernel is not reentrant. Fortunately, the Linux kernel is now over the reentrancy hurdle and can handle the associated issues.

When a message arrives, the hardware sends an interrupt to the CPU to pick off the message. If the kernel (where the interrupt handler resides) is slightly late, another message may overrun the first message. This is especially true when the network card is put into *promiscuous mode* (accepting any and every message it hears). Chapter 3, "Different Types of Internet Packets," first introduced the promiscuous mode.

Except for simulated networks like PPP, CPUs rarely work with the hardware networking interfaces directly. The CPU uses a coprocessor on the network interface card. The CPU loads the data into the network interface and instructs it to transmit. When done, the card raises an interrupt to the CPU. This instructs the kernel that the network card is again ready to accept another message. PPP on the other hand requires a lot more CPU interaction, but because the interface is much slower, it's not as much of a burden as it could be.

A message queue holds the outgoing and incoming messages. When the kernel gets a notification that the card is ready for another frame, it takes the message directly from the message queue. If your program sends a message when the interface is not ready, the kernel places the request or message on the queue for later processing. The network is a limited resource; no two programs can access it at the same time. As a result, the operating system has to queue and process the requests one at a time.

Also, the kernel has to prepare each message for transmission, or it has to disassemble the incoming message for the receiver. The buffering subsystem tracks the constructed frames and readies them for the network or the client process (such as disk I/O).

Part of the process of packaging the message is assigning identification. Hardware identification (like the MAC) is clumsy and difficult to manage on a large network. So the network subsystem provides a logical identification (for example, the IP number).

Each packet needs the identification so that the operating system can quickly determine where to send it. IP numbering provides the network operating system a way of grouping computers together into subnetworks.

Network to Program Interfacing

A main area of concern is how to interface the network to your program. Because network programming has so many angles and caveats, consider the specifics of each situation separately and then determine how they interrelate. This section discusses some of those issues.

The first issue is receiving and dealing with errors and exceptions. The operating system and your program must be able to receive and handle network errors or exceptions. Some errors and exceptions are asynchronous to the running program. C and Java can intercept them, but some languages cannot (for example, Pascal). So, as you consider how to write your application, keep in mind that not all languages lend themselves well to the demands of network programming.

The second issue is data and packet reliability. Some programs expect high data reliability; others don't. Analyze what kind of data you have and how reliable it needs to be. In Chapter 2, "TCP/IP Network Language Fluency," you can find a list of data types and their criticality. Use this list to help you choose the right protocol.

The third issue is synchronization and concurrency. Your network program interfaces with another concurrently running program. You must coordinate the programs to avoid deadlock and starvation problems (discussed in detail in the section "Client-Server Concurrency Issues" in Chapter 10, "Designing Robust Linux Sockets").

Lastly, consider examining real versus virtual connections. The network offers your program a simpler form of interfacing by making it look like your program owns the network connection. These virtual connections (ports) deliver only those messages that the connection is supposed to see.

While the program-interfacing issues are complex, they make programming the network challenging and fun. This list is not comprehensive. However, the Socket API hides a lot of network programming challenges from your program.

Several years ago, groups of programmers tackled the networking challenge and invented several modeling standards. The standards typically build on top of each other in the form of layers. New layers can depend on the solutions of lower layers. Like peeling an onion, the heart of networking is the physical transmission medium (electricity, radio, or light).

Two models covered in this section, OSI and IP, are similar to many other network models. With this information, you may see why they choose their course of action.

Open Systems Interconnection (OSI) Network Model

The most prominently recognized network model—OSI—uses the layering approach and has seven layers. Each layer of the model abstracts the interface between the hardware and the program. This model even extends the interface into the user space.

The programs and applications on your workstation provide you with tools necessary to get your job done. The user space defines your customer's working area. Focus your attention on this area, because good design makes user interactions with your program seamless and intuitive.

The OSI network model provides a common interface so that once a user understands the procedures, he can use the same methods on other OSI implementations. The OSI model intentionally hides and abstracts away the implementation details of specific hardware. This gives the user the same feel regardless of the platform.

The OSI model's interface tries to answer each of the other specific challenges of network programming. At the same time, however, it provides interfaces (or *hooks*) into the lower levels so that power programmers can still play. The model has seven layers, beginning with the hardware layer, as shown in Figure 5.1. Each layer from bottom to top abstracts the network implementation from the user and your program.

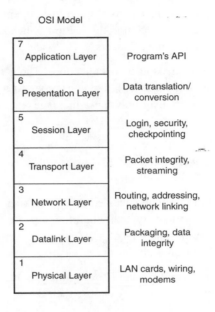

OSI Model

7 Application Layer	Program's API
6 Presentation Layer	Data translation/ conversion
5 Session Layer	Login, security, checkpointing
4 Transport Layer	Packet integrity, streaming
3 Network Layer	Routing, addressing, network linking
2 Datalink Layer	Packaging, data integrity
1 Physical Layer	LAN cards, wiring, modems

FIGURE 5.1

Most people associate network layering with the OSI model. Each layer adds functionality and reliability while abstracting the network and reducing performance.

Layer 1: Physical

The Physical layer encompasses all the hardware-related interfaces: the medium and signal. The medium (for example: twisted pair, coax, fiber) carries the signal to its destination.

Part of the Physical layer is the network adapter. The network adapter acts as the go-between for the kernel and the physical medium. On one end, it accepts transmit requests from the kernel drivers and transmits message packets (*frames*). When finished, it notifies the kernel with an interrupt.

The adapter's microcontroller listens for a quiescent network before it tries to send a frame. It detects and handles collisions and retransmissions. If necessary, it notifies the kernel of transmission problems. The kernel's drivers then manage their own retries or pass the errors up the protocol stack.

On the other end, the adapter listens to the network for messages that match its hardware (ethernet) address. When matched, the adapter fills an internal buffer and issues an interrupt to the kernel. To do this, the hardware layer provides its own hardware identification.

Data frame repeaters accept all network messages and pass them on to a new segment of the network. Data repeaters are dumb in that they do not select from packet to packet and ignore the hardware identifications. A data repeater has less programming intelligence than a typical repeater, which selectively permits packets between segments and resides in the Physical layer. Use a data repeater to extend the network length and amplify the attenuated signal.

Lastly, some ethernet adapters now include a checksum or CRC of their own to perform data validation checks. If CRC finds an error, the card flags the data as suspect for the Datalink layer to fix. This may give you a little more confidence in the datagram protocols.

Other physical networks may have other mechanisms. For example, the PPP connection may include a parity (most don't). FDDI has checksumming or CRCs. Some obscure radio protocols simply send each character twice.

Layer 2: Datalink

The Datalink layer rests on the Physical layer. The primary role of the Datalink layer is to provide data transfer from host to host. It packages messages into frames for the hardware. It checks for and tries to correct transmission errors. If the hardware does not support checksums or CRCs, the Datalink layer does the calculations itself.

The Datalink layer interfaces the kernel to the network hardware. Typically, the Datalink layer is a network driver that resides in the kernel. The driver uses a uniform interface so that the kernel can work blindly with vastly different technologies.

This layer prepares the data frames for transmission and disassembles received messages. The driver waits for interrupts that indicate a message was sent or a message was received. When it gets a message-sent notification, the Datalink driver loads the next frame to send.

The Datalink works closely with the buffering subsystem of the kernel. Most of the time, it only needs 10–60KB of system RAM. Linux's kernel configuration lets you define the size of the buffering and frame beyond 1MB for very fast transfers (100MB/s or higher), if you have enough memory. This is useful for very high-speed connections that may receive large frames or high throughput. To use this feature, you may have to recompile the kernel, because many Linux distributions do not enable it.

Network bridges reside in the Datalink layer. The Linux kernel's bridge option is still experimental at the time of this writing. If you want to experiment with it, you may have to reconfigure and compile the kernel to include the drivers.

The Network layer rests on top of the Datalink layer and provides address resolution and routing.

Layer 3: Network

The Network layer rests on top of the Datalink layer. Its primary function is to work with the routing tables, routers, and gateways to find the destination host. In a non-routed network, this layer is essentially inactive.

The Network layer provides a uniform addressing mechanism for heterogeneous networks. If, for example, you have two physical networks such as AppleTalk and Ethernet, this layer bridges them using a frame translation.

Network routers reside in this layer, providing a connection between homogeneous and heterogeneous physical networks.

Layer 4: Transport

The Transport layer rests on top of the Network layer, relying on the data integrity and routing of the Datalink and Network layers. Its primary responsibility is to deliver a message intact, in order, and without duplication. This layer adds many functions to provide streaming and communication integrity.

The Transport layer is the last place that the model can address any data or communication errors. (*Data errors* here refers only to the integrity of the data, not the meaning. For example, this layer does not catch a malformed HTTP request, but it does catch checksum errors.) If the layer detects packet loss or corruption, it requests a retransmission from the sender. To do this checking, it adds more checksums to the packet.

This layer introduces the concept of a *virtual network* or *multiplexing*. With this feature, each connection has the perception of having an exclusive connection to the network (like the TCP/IP port concept). Your program gets all the messages other programs sent to it, despite the fact that your host may have several network programs running.

Because of the reliability, the Transport layer is the layer most commonly used by applications that communicate with one another over the Internet. It provides all the features needed to hold networking sessions.

Layer 5: Session

The Session layer heavily depends on the Transport layer to provide the streaming and reliability it needs. Its primary responsibility is to provide controls over the connection and data flow.

The connection may be unstable, so this layer provides *checkpointing*. For example, suppose the connection is transferring a file and the connection drops. All the time spent getting the first part of the file is lost if at reconnect the file has to start over. Checkpointing locks down parts of the transfer so that the new connection has to receive only the missing parts.

As implied earlier, the Session layer automatically reestablishes dropped connections. It also provides security and login procedures.

It also provides data flow management. One of the problems with client/server connections is controlling who talks first and how to hold a dialog. One method this layer uses is passing a token: The host that has the token can do critical operations. This flow control lessens the likelihood of deadlock, starvation, or data corruption (discussed in detail in the section, "Client-Server Concurrency Issues" in Chapter 10).

Layer 6: Presentation

The Presentation layer manages the data and does needed conversion (for example: decompression, formatting, layout, image display, character set conversions). Remote Procedure Calls (see Chapter 15, "Network Encapsulation with Remote Procedure Calls (RPCs)") are a practical example of this layer.

Layer 7: Application

The last layer, the Application layer, provides network services such as file transfer, terminal emulation, messaging, and network management. Essentially, most applications use this layer, since it provides the Application Programming Interface (API). However, it is not the actual user application; it is the set of library calls and services to help the applications work with the network. Network File System (NFS) is an example of this layer that hooks into the operating system's virtual file system architecture. It builds on top of the RPC tools to provide the function interfaces.

Internet Protocol Suite

Linux (like most other UNIX operating systems) does not use the OSI network model directly. However, the model is a starting point to understanding the IP Stack. Linux uses the Internet Protocol suite to manage its native network interface.

> **NOTE**
>
> The IP protocol sprang from the ARPAnet (Advanced Research Projects Agency Network) funded by DARPA (Defense Advanced Research Projects Agency) in 1972. BBN Corporation implemented the first vestiges of the network. Later, UNIX, a free operating system offered by Bell Labs, adopted the model as well. The universities involved used UNIX to test out a concept of linking several computers together throughout the United States. The Sockets API originated with BSD 4.2 in 1983.

The Internet Protocol suite has four layers that map closely to the OSI model. The highest layer is called the Application layer. The IP suite's Application layer encompasses OSI's layers 5–7 (see Figure 5.2). Refer to Figure 5.1 for a comparison.

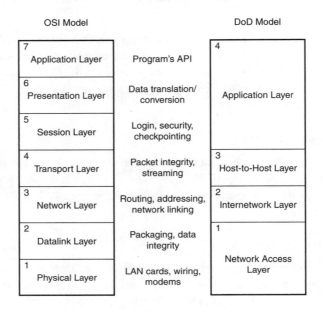

FIGURE 5.2

The DoD or Internet Protocol Stack compares closely to the OSI model. The Socket API stops at OSI's Transport (4) layer. The protocol leaves the remaining layers to high-level programs like Telnet, FTP, and Lynx.

Layer 1: Network Access Layer

IP's first network layer most closely matches OSI's Physical and Datalink layers. Because the hardware and drivers are so closely tied together and the hardware support varies so widely, you cannot isolate one from the other.

The characteristics are similar: The driver works closely with the hardware interfaces to provide a common set of functionality to the kernel. The kernel, in exchange, gives the driver direct access to the ports and interrupts. If an interface is lacking in any features that the kernel needs, the drivers take up the slack.

Linux adds another feature that complicates this layer: hot swapping network adapters. This is found in PCMCIA support. When you insert a PC card, the PC card manager recognizes it, allocates the appropriate ports and interrupts, inserts the defined kernel modules, and configures your network. Likewise, when you remove the card, the manager disables the network and removes the kernel module.

Layer 2: Internetwork Layer (IP)

The IP layers (both IPv4 and IPv6) depend on the device drivers to provide a common interface and functionality. Both versions are different in this layer. They compose different protocol stacks that translate to and from IPv4 and IPv6, as needed, to ensure compatibility.

The IP layer best aligns with the OSI Network layer. It provides the logical addressing and routing functions of that layer. The one part that the IP layer lacks is the error messaging of the Network layer.

Layer 2: Control/Error Messaging Extensions (ICMP)

ICMP (Internet Control Message Protocol) adds the missing error messaging of the OSI Network layer. ICMP provides the message protocols for errors and exceptions in the routing and forwarding of messages. Typical exceptions include `network not reachable` and `host not found`.

This protocol works with other systems to perform various functions. For example, it works with the routing tables (ARP) when hosts become unreachable. Additionally, it works with TCP to speed up or slow down the communication and change the sliding window. IPv6 has even added control for multicast group management.

What's interesting about ICMP is that it stands alone. Neither UDP nor TCP uses its layer. They do accept its messages for their own processing.

Layer 3: Host to Host (UDP)

Contrary to popular opinion, UDP (User Datagram Protocol) does *not* match perfectly with the OSI Transport layer (see Figure 5.3). The Transport layer guarantees delivery, in-order packets, error-free packets, and stream-like functions. UDP does not; see Table 5.2.

TABLE 5.2   Transport Layer Versus UDP

Transport Layer	UDP
Reliable data	Reliable data (checksums)
Reliable delivery	No guaranteed delivery
Negotiated window size	Fixed window (determined by program)
Record oriented	Packet oriented
Built on Networking layer	Built on IP

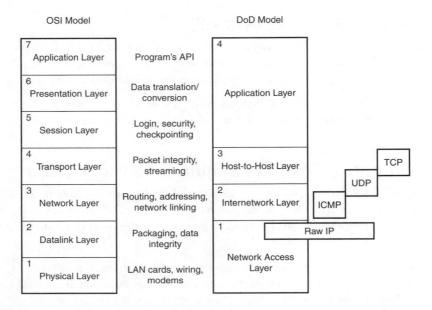

FIGURE 5.3

The IP Stack focuses more on functionality than encapsulation. Revising the diagram to better reflect the coverage from one layer to another shows that UDP dips little into the OSI Network (3) layer.

UDP adds one primary feature of the Transport layer: virtual networks with ports. As described in Chapter 4, "Sending Messages Between Peers," this particular feature abstracts the network and lets your network program act like it solely owns the connection. All other features are like the IP layer. If properly positioned, UDP straddles the Network and Transport layers, leaning more on the Network side.

Layer 3: Host Streams (TCP)

The TCP layer matches the OSI Transport layer very well. Both provide the reliability, streaming, ordering, and error management needed for building sessions. It is important to emphasize that TCP does not rest on UDP. It has its own header and own path in the network subsystem. For a side-by-side comparison, see Table 5.3.

TABLE 5.3 Transport Layer Versus TCP

Transport Layer	UDP
Reliable data	Reliable data (checksums)
Reliable delivery	Guaranteed delivery

TABLE 5.3   Continued

Transport Layer	UDP
Negotiated window size	Sliding window
Record oriented	Stream oriented
Built on Network layer	Built on IP

Layer 4: Application Layer

This is where the TCP/IP model stops. According to the model, the Application layer comprises OSI's Session (5), Presentation (6), and Application (7) layers. The TCP/IP model has a few applications that fill these roles. Some examples of this layer are Web browsers, gateways, Telnet, and FTP (File Transfer Protocol). Remote Procedure Calls (RPCs) best align with the Presentation layer. Network File System (NFS) depends on RPCs and appears to fit the Application layer. Still, these applications blur the boundaries so that assigning them to any particular layer is difficult.

The Application layer rests on top of the Host Streams layer (UDP and TCP). However, it may accept messages directly from ICMP.

Fundamental Differences Between OSI and IP

Both the OSI and IP models use layering to define the roles of each protocol stack. They also move from the hardware-dependent code to the abstract application. But you may have noticed some differences.

OSI layers the data as well as the protocol. Referring back to Figure 5.1, each layer of the stack has its own header information. As the data moves down the stack toward the Physical layer, each layer encapsulates the message inside its own packet.

For example, if you send a Session layer message, the Physical layer sees a list of headers in reverse order: datalink, network, transport, and session. The message itself follows all these headers at the end of the data. Each layer uses this process, including the Physical layer. Eventually, you may have up to seven headers on a single packet.

The receiver reverses the process. It uses the encapsulated data to determine whether to pass your message up to the next layer. In the previous example, your message arrives at the Physical layer. Each layer peels off its header. If it sees another header, it passes the message up to the next layer. Eventually, the message stops at the Session layer.

The IP model operates differently. Attaching a header for every layer can make your message header heavy, reducing throughput. Instead, the IP model places the protocol type in the IP header. When IP gets the message, it checks that field and routes the message directly to the protocol you chose, after removing its own header.

Also, as indicated at the end of Chapter 3, each of IP's protocols fills a specific role. Unlike the OSI model, where each layer rests squarely on the back of the lower layers, all protocols rest on IP raw protocol.

Again, the IP model uses a protocol to address a particular need. ICMP is for error messaging, UDP is for directed messages and connectionless communications, and TCP is for streaming. The raw IP is for developing new protocols.

What Services What?

The next step is how to use the DoD Network model. If you want to access the all the different layers of the IP Stack, use the socket() system call.

TABLE 5.4 DoD Layer Summary

DoD Layer	Programmer/User Access
4—Application	FTP, Gopher, Lynx, Netscape, IRC
3—Host to Host (TCP)	socket(PF_INET, SOCK_STREAM, 0);
3—Host to Host (UDP)	socket(PF_INET, SOCK_DGRAM, 0);
2—Internetwork (ICMP)	socket(PF_INET, SOCK_RAW, IPPROTO_ICMP);
2—Internetwork (IP)	socket(PF_INET, SOCK_RAW, protocol);
1—Network Access	socket(PF_INET, SOCK_PACKET, filter);

This interface may differ from your expectations. Linux allows read access to the low-level driver messages using SOCK_PACKET. This Linux-specific feature gives you access to any and all messages on the network. You used this feature to build your own network snooper in Chapter 3.

Summary: From Theory to Application

This chapter examines the interface between the different network elements that need to work in harmony. The network challenge includes computer hardware interfacing, network connection issues, operating system linking, and application interfacing. Each has specific problems that get in the way of giving your program access to other computers. Networking addresses these problems using carefully designed models to help you program in a consistent way.

Two networking models, OSI and IP (or DoD), separate the solutions into layers. The layers rest on top of each other like layers of a cake. The support that the lower layers provide increases the data reliability and interfacing of higher layers. The layers also offer you a wide selection of speed versus reliability.

The first layer addresses the physical interfacing between computers. In succession, each layer strengthens message reliability, arrival, and flow. When you use interfaces from the middle layers of the protocol stack, you can expect that the data will arrive correctly.

Higher levels work as if the network is the computer, whereas the lower levels function as if you are sending messages in a bottle. Each has a use for your program data.

The Server Perspective and Load Control

IN THIS PART

A Server Primer

IN THIS CHAPTER

Network programs always have a sender and a receiver. Generally, the sender is a client that connects to a service offered by a networked computer. Part I of this book, "Network Programming from the Client Perspective," covers in detail the client's standpoint—how to connect to a server, how to create connectionless communications, and how to use the IP-supporting tools. This chapter introduces the other half: the receiver or the server's perspective of the process.

The server's perspective completes the client/server interaction. To illustrate the relationship between the client and server, you might compare the network to a telephone system and the server to the central phone number of a large company that routes calls to its employees. The client connects to one of the employees through the central number and an extension. From this example, you can see how a server on the network accepts connections from a client. The main number is the host's address and the extension is the service port.

Servers request a specific port number—the port that the client knows. Similar to publishing a telephone number, if the server does not get the number it wants, the client cannot call it.

This chapter turns the perspective around from asking for services, as discussed in Part I, to offering them. It takes you step by step through the process of writing and building a server. At the conclusion, a small HTTP directory server shows you how to connect to a Web client and how to package HTML messages.

Mapping the Socket: The Server's General Program Flow

The process for creating a server always begins with creating the socket. Just as the client requires specific calls at certain times, the server uses a similar path but adds a few extra system calls. The server calls `socket()`, but it must do the extra work that was optional for a client, as seen in Figure 6.1.

The client program you wrote in the first chapters followed the client diagram. In order, the client called: `socket()`, `connect()`, `read()`, `write()`, and `close()`. The `bind()` system call was unnecessary because the operating system performed that function for you. The port number was not needed because the program calls the server. The client always makes an *active connection* because it actively pursues a connection.

Server programs, on the other hand, need to provide a consistent and specific port number for client programs if your server is to serve them. The server diagram shows a few differences from the client. The server program you write must call `socket()`, `bind()`, `listen()`, `accept()`, and `close()`. And while the client program is an active connection, the server is a passive connection. The `listen()` and `accept()` system calls make a connection only when the client requests a connection (like answering a ringing telephone).

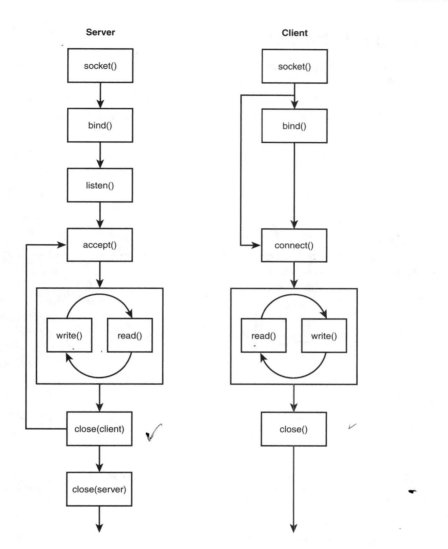

FIGURE 6.1

The program flows for the client and server are similar but have distinct differences in the way they connect to the network. This is a map of system calls for the client and server programs.

Chapter 4, "Sending Messages Between Peers," introduced the bind() system call. This chapter defines it a little more formally. Likewise, this chapter describes two new calls— listen() and accept().

A Simple Echo Server

Before talking about the different system calls you use to create a server, you may want to see the general program flow of the server example. The example is the standard Echo Server. Like the Hello, World example for C programming, Echo Server is the example for socket servers. You can find the full source of this program on the Web site, and it is named `simple-server.c`.

The simplest test for most communications is an echo. Just as a telephone salesman repeats your order back to you to ensure correctness, you can use an echo to start your own server. Basically, writing the program this way helps you build and test your critical application.

> ## Build and Test Paradigm
>
> You may have noticed that this book cites many computer science–based disciplines. Network programming requires a greater focus on testing, checking, and construction. It is fraught with so many different fundamental issues that you must use the simplest programming approaches to minimize program errors. The build and test paradigm (a small facet of rapid-prototyping) lets you focus on a specific problem. After you solve the problem, the result becomes a building block for the rest of your development.

The generic server requires that you call a series of system calls in a particular order. The Echo Server is a good demonstration of this order without muddying the example with server-specific processing. The following is the general program flow for the Echo Server:

1. Create a socket with `socket()`.
2. Bind the port with `bind()`.
3. Convert the socket into a listening socket with `listen()`.
4. Wait for a connection with `accept()`.
5. Read the message with `recv()` or `read()`.
6. Echo the message back with `send()` or `write()`.
7. If the message is not bye, go back to step 5.
8. Close the connection with `close()` or `shutdown()`.
9. Go back to step 4.

The program flow demonstrates the difference from a connectionless interface by not closing the connection until the client tells it to do so (with a bye command). Chapter 4 presented a comparison between connection-based and connectionless sockets. The server completes that comparison. You can think of a connectionless, waiting peer as a quasi-server.

This program flow is important to see what's ahead when you create servers. The first obvious step (creating a socket) was discussed in Chapter 1, "Introducing the Cookbook Network Client." And, as noted there, all network communications begin with that step. The next step, binding the port, is critical to your server.

Binding Ports to the Socket

The connection-based socket begins, as always, with a call to socket(). The server typically uses the reliable TCP protocol layer, so you can use the SOCK_STREAM flag. But, you must take it one step further—the clients need to know to which port to connect.

The bind() system call asks the system if your program can own a particular port number. Just like a sales company requests and publishes a central phone number for its clients, bind() selects a port number. If your server doesn't specify a port number, the operating system assigns the next available one from its pool of numbers. This port can be different each time you run the program if the OS assigns one for you.

You can also tell if the server is already executing if you request—but don't get—a specific port number. The operating system assigns the port to only one process.

The bind() system call looks like the following:

```
#include <sys/socket.h>
#include <resolv.h>
int bind(int sd, struct sockaddr *addr, int addrsize);
```

The sd variable is the socket descriptor you first created. First defined in Chapter 1, the variable addr points to a socket name (the port number) from the family of sockaddr records (defined in Chapter 2, "TCP/IP Network Language Fluency"). The last parameter you provide, addrsize, is the length of the sockaddr record.

The program needs to provide the size of the record to the operating system because of the whole concept of the Sockets API: one interface but many architectures. The operating system supports many protocols, each using its own naming structure, and each structure having a different size.

To use bind(), you need to create and fill addr (see Listing 6.1).

LISTING 6.1   Using `bind()` in a TCP Server

```
/*******************************************************/
/*** INET socket example: Fill the sockaddr_in struct   ***/
/*** variable addr.                                      ***/
/*******************************************************/
struct sockaddr_in addr;  /* create an internet socket name */
bzero(&addr, sizeof(addr));       /* start with a clean slate */
addr.sin_family = AF_INET;              /* select IP stack */
addr.sin_port = htons(MY_PORT);    /* designate port number */
addr.sin_addr.s_addr = INADDR_ANY; /* allow any host IP addr*/
if ( bind(sd, &addr, sizeof(addr)) != 0 )   /* request port */
    perror("Bind AF_INET");
```

Use the code segment in Listing 6.2 to bind to a named socket (`AF_UNIX` or `AF_LOCAL`).

LISTING 6.2   Using `bind()` in a LOCAL Server

```
/*******************************************************/
/*** LOCAL Socket Example: Fill the sockaddr_ux struct   ***/
/*** variable addr                                       ***/
/*******************************************************/
#include <linux/un.h>
struct sockaddr_ux addr;     /* create a local named socket */
bzero(&addr, sizeof(addr));      /* start with a clean slate */
addr.sun_family = AF_LOCAL;        /* select a named socket */
strcpy(addr.sun_path, "/tmp/mysocket");    /* select name */
if ( bind(sd, &addr, sizeof(addr)) != 0 )      /* bind name */
    perror("Bind AF_LOCAL");
```

With this particular code segment, you can look in the /tmp directory and see the socket file. The system message logger, syslogd, uses LOCAL sockets to get its information: system processes open a connection to the logger's socket and send messages to it.

The following are the typical errors you can get from the call:

- EBADF   The socket descriptor is not valid. This can occur if the socket() system call failed and you didn't check the return value.

- EACCES   The requested port number is restricted to root access only. Remember that if you use ports between 0–1023, you must be root when you run the program. For more information, see the section on host port numbers in Chapter 2.

- EINVAL   The port is already being used. You may have another program that owns this port. Also, if you try to rerun a server shortly after it dies, you may get this error. The operating system takes its time freeing up an allocated port (up to 5 minutes!).

In all cases, the bind() system call attempts to allocate a specific name or port to your server's socket (use the /etc/services file as a guide for available or standard ports). The clients use this port to establish the connection and begin sending and receiving data.

Creating a Socket Listening Queue

The socket interface gives your program a way to connect with other programs on the network. The connection is exclusive: once a program connects, no other programs can connect. One way around this is to create a waiting queue.

You enable the socket waiting queue with the listen() system call. Referring back to the earlier example in this chapter, if the company only has one telephone, it could not handle more than one call at a time; so it is not unlikely to receive a busy signal. The solution is to add call waiting.

The listen() system call is similar to a call waiting queue. When the server calls listen(), it designates the number of queue slots. The call also converts the socket into a listening-only socket. This conversion is important so that you can later use the accept() system call.

```
#include <sys/socket.h>
#include <resolve.h>
int listen(int sd, int numslots);
```

Again, the sd parameter indicates the created socket descriptor from the socket() call. The numslots parameter allocates the number of pending connection slots. The code segment in Listing 6.3 shows a typical use.

LISTING 6.3   Listen() Example

```
/*************************************************************/
/*** Listen-Conversion Example: Convert the socket to a   ***/
/*** listening socket for client connections.             ***/
/*************************************************************/
int sd;
sd = socket(PF_INET, SOCK_STREAM, 0);
/*** Bind port ***/
if ( listen(sd, 20) != 0 )   /* convert to listening socket */
    perror("Listen");        /* ...with 20 pending slots */
```

Typically, servers set the queue depth between 5 and 20 pending connections. A queue depth more than 20 is often wasteful in normal production (multitasking) environments. Without multitasking, you may have to increase that to a number close to the timeout you set (such as 60 for 60 seconds).

The following are the errors usually returned from a listen() system call:

- EBADF   The socket descriptor is not valid (see the description for bind()'s system call).
- EOPNOTSUPP   The socket protocol cannot support a listen call. For example, TCP (SOCK_STREAM) supports the listening queue, but UDP (SOCK_DGRAM) does not.

The next step after converting the socket into a listening socket is to wait for and accept connections, as discussed in the next section.

Accepting Client Connections

Up to this point, the program has created the socket, bound a port number, and set up a connection queue. Now, it can accept connections. The accept() system call makes the socket descriptor a dispatcher for all connections. This is where things get a little strange, and the initial rules are broken. When you convert the socket into a listening socket, it is no longer a bidirectional channel for data. Your program really can't even read data; the listening socket allows you only to accept connections. The accept() system call waits (or *blocks*) until a connection arrives.

When the client makes a connection, the listening socket creates a new bidirectional channel for that client using the same port. The accept() system call implicitly creates a new socket descriptor for the program. In effect, every new connection creates a new dedicated line between the client and server. From this point, you interact with the client through the new channel.

Additionally, you can determine who is connecting to your server because a couple of the call's parameters get the client's connection information. Chapter 4 presented a similar system call, recvfrom(), that got data and the return address. This address information is useful for tracking the computers that connected to your server.

```
#include <sys/socket.h>
#include <resolve.h>
int accept(int sd, sockaddr *addr, int *addr_size);
```

As always, the sd parameter is the socket descriptor. As with the recvfrom() system call, the last two parameters provide the call a place to write the client's address and port number. Unlike the recvfrom() system call, the last two parameters of accept() are optional. If you do not want to pick up the caller's address and port number, simply set these parameters to zero.

Be sure to make the addr parameter size large enough to accept the address it's expecting. Don't worry about corruption due to buffer overflow; the call does not exceed addr_size bytes. In most cases, the client connections are the same size as the protocol (for example, AF_INET for sockaddr_in or AF_IPX for sockaddr_ipx). The call passes addr_size by reference so your program can determine the actual number of bytes used (see Listing 6.4).

LISTING 6.4 Accept() Example

```
/**************************************************************/
/*** Accept Example: Wait for and accept a client      ***/
/*** connection.                                       ***/
/**************************************************************/
int sd;
struct sockaddr_in addr;
/*** Create socket, bind it & convert it to a listener ***/
for (;;)                         /* repeat this indefinitely */
{   int clientsd;               /* the new socket descriptor */
    int size = sizeof(addr);   /* reassign the size of addr */

    clientsd = accept(sd, &addr, &size); /*await connection */
    if ( clientsd > 0 )                  /* no error occurred */
    {
        /**** Interact with client ****/
        close(clientsd);        /* clean up and disconnect */
    }
    else                                    /* accept error */
        perror("Accept");
}
...
```

Communicating with the Client

Notice that the listing closes `clientsd`. The `clientsd` socket descriptor differs from `sd`, the main socket descriptor. It's important to close `clientsd` because each connection generates a new descriptor. Failing to close each connection can cause you to eventually run out of file descriptor slots.

> ### Reusing the `addr` Variable
> You can reuse the `addr` local variable from the `bind()` system call. After you have completed the `bind()` for the server port, the server no longer needs that information. It's then safe to use that variable for other purposes.

Remember that most of the parameters are in network byte order. You can get the address and port number from `addr` using the conversion tools described in Chapter 2 (see Listing 6.5).

LISTING 6.5   Accept() with Connection Logging

```
/***************************************************************/
/*** Accept Example (revised): Add client-connection      ***/
/*** logging. Compare with Listing 6.4                    ***/
/***************************************************************/
/**** (Inside the loop) ****/
...
client = accept(sd, &addr, &size);
if ( client > 0 )
{
    if ( addr.sin_family == AF_INET )
        printf("Connection[%s]: %s:%d\n", /* log connection */
            ctime(time(0)),            /* time-stamp connection */
            ntoa(addr.sin_addr), ntohs(addr.sin_port));
    /*---interact with client---*/
...
```

If the accept() system call yields an error, it returns a negative value to your server. Otherwise, it returns a new socket descriptor. The following are some common errors:

- EBADF   The socket descriptor is not valid (see the description for bind() in Chapter 4).

- EOPNOTSUPP   The socket must be a SOCK_STREAM for this call.

- EAGAIN   The socket is set for non-blocking and the listening queue has no pending connections. A call to accept() with no one on the queue blocks the task unless the socket is made non-blocking.

The Echo Server simply sends back what it receives until it gets a bye message (see Listing 6.6).

LISTING 6.6   Echo Server Example

```
/***************************************************************/
/*** Echo Service Example: Send back whatever we get      ***/
/*** until "bye<ret>". (Compare with Listing 6.5)         ***/
/***************************************************************/
/**** (Inside the loop & after accept()) ****/
...
if ( client > 0 )
{   char buffer[1024];
    int nbytes;

    do
    {
```

LISTING 6.6   Continued

```
        nbytes = recv(client, buffer, sizeof(buffer), 0);
        if ( nbytes > 0 )          /* if real data, echo back */
            send(client, buffer, nbytes, 0);
    }
    while ( nbytes > 0  &&  strncmp("bye\r", buffer,4) != 0 );
    close(client);
}
...
```

Notice that the end condition is looking for a `"bye\r"`, not `"bye\n"`. Depending on how the input processing works (Telnet does none), the server may get one or the other. For robustness, consider testing both. Try out this program with Telnet as your client. The complete program, named `simple-server.c`, is on the Web site.

General Rules About Defining Protocols

When communicating with other computers, your programs need to agree on a procedure of interaction. Two very important actions are "Who talks first?" and "When are we done?" This agreement defines a transaction-protocol.

The client and server use these procedures to ensure that they don't transmit at the same time or blindly wait for each other to transmit first. As you build servers, consider the questions in the following subsections.

Which Program Talks First?

Most servers talk first. But, high security systems sometimes wait for the client to send the first message. The process you use can have the client identify itself (more than the standard host ID and port). At the same time, you may want a more user-friendly system that provides some identification and protocol listing upon connection.

Another consideration is unneeded interaction. If the server talks first, it usually says the same thing each time it gets a connection. Does the client need to know that? Does the added interaction slow the communication channels a little?

Which Program Drives the Conversation?

Often, clients drive the interaction with the server. The client connects to the server and sends requests. The server, in turn, processes the requests and issues a reply.

But, you may have to switch roles sometimes. For example, a client requests some database information from your server. After transmitting the data, a different client updates a few fields that the first client requested. If the first client works exclusively from the first data set, it could make the wrong decisions.

In that type of situation, the server should send the unsolicited updates to the client, and the client needs to accept them. Consider how the client interacts with the server and peers interact with each other and notice exceptions and define ways to address them.

What Level of Certification Do You Need?

To write a highly secure system, it's essential to know to whom the server is talking. In turn, the server must know or certify the user, or minimally the machine.

The certification process can include usernames and passwords. It can also use a trusted certificate issuer for the users' machines. Chapter 16, "Adding Security to Network Programs and SSL," discusses the Secure Socket Layer (SSL) and presents a couple possible solutions to this problem.

On the other hand, you may not need certification, but want some kind of logging instead. How often does a demographic hit your server? Do you need to beef up certain server pieces to meet user needs? How can you unobtrusively get to know your customer?

Each of these questions are important to consider as you program your server. The Web has several examples of how to get demographics and user needs/trends. This information can also offer information about software defects and even system crackers. A simple way is to ask. Some browsers and Web servers use much more elaborate methods.

What Type of Data Do You Use?

Most servers you interact with use ASCII for correspondence, while most Web pages are text/HTML. It's a good idea to consider the questions "Is that the most efficient data form to use?" and "Does the client support compressed data?" As you look at your server and your customer's clients, consider how to decrease the delays on the server, network, and client.

Compressing data can have some real benefits. Compressed ASCII can yield between 50% and 80% reduction in data size. Even compressed data can be ASCII without too much inflation, so the network won't lose any binary high bits. The following subsections provide more detail on how to handle data.

How Do You Handle Binary Data?

Binary data—especially compressed—is more efficient than ASCII. Problem: some networks only support 7-bit bytes. This is a real problem for 8-bit binary data. These networks are typically dinosaurs that cost too much to replace. Fortunately, the routers connected to these networks often recognize the incompatibility and convert the data down or up as needed. This conversion requires computation time and thus slows propagation. The data reformatting affects the receiver-host, because the host has to reassemble the fractured data.

Also, do you start with non-binary and then switch to binary? If so, either your client or server needs to tell the other when to switch. Similarly, you may want to switch back at some point.

How Do You Know when There Is a Deadlock?

You may run into instances when the server and client are waiting for each other (deadlock). As they wait, they are tying up valuable resources and may be taxing your users' patience.

Try to identify the situations that cause deadlock before determining if your particular problem is deadlock. If you have deadlock, the only solution is to sever the connection and try again. When you have to reconnect, you lose the context of the connection (where you are at in the interaction), and you may lose data.

The client or server may encounter *starvation* (indefinite waiting for resources). Starvation typically occurs when a client or server is doing things other than managing the connection. Like deadlock, the standard solution is to timeout and reconnect.

Do You Need Clock Synchronization?

Although it is challenging, clock synchronization (coordinating the real-time clocks between hosts) is essential when you have time-critical issues, such as financial transactions. This is a nasty problem. First, determine how accurate the synchronization needs to be.

The server has to establish its clock relative to the client. However, most clients do not synchronize with network time. Because the client is rarely accurate, both use an arbitrator (a time server). However, this presents its own problems (the delay in getting the correct time off the network).

One solution for a synchronization problem is to set all transactions at the server (moving more of the responsibility away from the client). After the server completes the transaction, it replies to the client with the time and date of posting.

How and When Do You Restart the Connection?

At some points during an interaction, the server and client may have to start over without losing connection. Losing connection can mean significant loss of information, so reestablishing a connection is out of the question.

The TCP/IP protocol offers a priority message that you can use as a reset message. For more information on priority messages and out-of-band data, refer to Chapter 9, "Breaking Performance Barriers." This message is only a beginning; both your server and the client have to return to some starting point. That is a challenge in structured programming.

Reconnecting is a direct way of starting over. The urgent message can tell either the client or the server to close the connection. Then, the client can reconnect to re-establish communication. Reconnection, however, may lose more information than you desire. So, a reset can force both the client and server back to some known point. Your data's criticality plays a very important role in connection recovery.

When Are You Finished?

The server and client have connected and passed packets back and forth. Now it's time to say goodbye. Knowing when the interaction is complete may not be as easy as it seems. For example, when you write an HTTP server, you complete the interaction by sending two newlines. However, you may wait indefinitely for the client's request when you have insufficient buffer space for a single read and you read with either read() or recv(). In this case, the server may timeout and declare the connection ended.

Similarly, it can be difficult to decide which program should close the connection first. A client gets a pipe broken error (EPIPE) when the server closes the connection before the client completes the transmission.

It all comes down to what the protocols require. HTTP interactions require a pair of newlines to indicate an end-of-transmission. You may have to define your own, because a streaming socket gives you a lot of latitude.

An Extended Example: An HTTP Directory Server

Echo Server is a great starting point for several different servers. One common server that's on the minds of many folks is an HTTP server. Now, a full-blown HTTP server is a little outside the scope of this text, but you can create a much smaller one that responds to requests from any browser.

This section describes a small server that creates HTML dynamically instead of getting a file from the file system. In a way, this makes the program easier and more enjoyable to work with. You can find the complete program listing on the Web site, and it is called html-ls-server.c.

As described in the last section, HTTP 1.0 has a specific protocol that defines how the client and server interact. Listing 6.7 shows the difference from the Echo Server example in Listing 6.6.

LISTING 6.7   Simple HTTP Responder Example

```
/*************************************************************/
/*** Simple HTTP responder.                              ***/
/*************************************************************/
...
while (1)
{   int client;
    int size = sizeof(addr);

    client = accept(sd, &addr, &size);
    if ( client > 0 )
    {   char buffer[1024];
        /*--- Message for client ---*/
        char *reply = "<html><body>Hello!</body></html>/n";

        bzero(buffer, sizeof(buffer));          /* clear buffer */
        recv(client, buffer, sizeof(buffer), 0); /* get msg */
        send(client, reply, strlen(reply), 0);/* send reply */

        /*--- display client's 'hello' message on server ---*/
        fprintf(stderr, "%s", buffer);''
        close(client);
    }
    else
        perror("Accept");
}
...
```

Each time the client connects, it sends a message that looks similar to the following:

```
GET /dir/document HTTP/1.0
(some protocol definitions)
```

The first line is the request. All the following messages tell the server what the HTTP client can accept and interpret, and it can include configuration information to help the server determine how to interact with the client. The most relevant line to examine is the GET command. GET has two parameters—the request and the understood protocol. Your server can parse the request to get the path and document requested. (Of course, the request can be more complicated than a fully qualified filename.)

The HTTP 1.0 protocol allows spaces in the path, so scanning the line requires getting everything from the initial / to the HTTP/. The path can include letters in hexadecimal notation, but the example server's basic program flow ignores those.

Additionally, the protocol uses some of the MIME header protocols when the server replies. The client expects the document to have certain fields and a status:

```
HTTP/1.1 200 OK
Content-Type: text/html
...
(empty line)
(empty line)
<html>
<head>
...
```

The first line is the status. If you have ever wondered where the infamous 404 (request not found) error comes from, the first line of the reply tells your client how successful the query was. Refer to Appendix A, "Data Tables," for a complete list of HTTP 1.1 status codes.

However, you can skip returning the status and MIME information because the client assumes the default is HTML. The program can simply send the generated HTML source.

As you write a simple HTTP server, you may run into a few snags. For one, the server does not know ahead of time how large the resulting document may be, so the server needs to convert the socket channel into a FILE* structure (see Listing 6.8).

LISTING 6.8   Expanded HTTP Responder Algorithm

```
/**************************************************************/
/*** HTTP 1.0 Example: Accept connection, get request,    ***/
/*** open directory, and create HTML directory listing.   ***/
/**************************************************************/
...
/**** Create socket, bind it, convert it to listener ****/
for (;;)
{   int client;
    int size = sizeof(addr);

    client = accept(sd, &addr, &size);  /* await connection */
    if ( client > 0 )                   /* if successful... */
    {   char buf[1024];
        FILE *clientfp;

        bzero(buf, sizeof(buf));             /* clear buffer */
        recv(client, buf, sizeof(buf),0);     /* get packet */
        clientfp = fdopen(client, "w"); /* convert to FILE* */
        if ( clientfp != NULL ) /* if conv. successful,... */
        {
```

LISTING 6.8   Continued

```
              /**** Get path from message (buf) ****/
              /**** Open directory ****/
              /**** For all files,... ****/
              /****    Read each file name ****/
              /****    Generate HTML table ****/
              fclose(clientfp);              /* close FILE ptr */
       }
       else
          perror("Client FILE"); /* can't convert to FILE */
       close(client);               /* close client's socket */
    }
    else
       perror("Accept");  /* an error occurred in accept() */
}
...
```

You can improve on the program listing by sorting the filenames, recognizing the file types, including the HTTP 1.1 error codes, and so on. The existing program flow only works with directories. The server places an FTP link for any regular file. Again, you can get the complete program on the Web site.

Summary: The Server's Basic Elements

This chapter shows you how to view matters from the server's perspective. This helps you see how much of the network fits together and enhances your network programming skills. With this in mind, you can offer clients many services while controlling and centralizing critical data and operations. You have a wide variety of capabilities in distributing load, reaching more clients, and increasing data manageability.

Network server applications use three new calls—bind(), listen(), and accept()—above those that the typical client uses. You use these to select the port number (bind()), define the connection queue (listen()), and accept new connections (accept()). The accept() call creates a new socket connection for each new connection, opening your program to allowing multiple simultaneous connections through a single port.

The server definition requires you to consider transaction-protocols. These protocols describe how the client and server interact and how they should behave. Step by step, analyze the client/server interaction and the best way to meet each request correctly and efficiently.

Dividing the Load: Multitasking

IN THIS CHAPTER

Imagine all the tasks you could do if you could work on many disparate activities at the same time. This *parallel tasking* allows you to focus efficiently on different tasks without distraction. In fact, the mind is able to do just that. For example, you can clean out the basement while contemplating a particularly hard algorithm; or you can stew on a mathematical problem while reading some science fiction. Each is an example of parallel- or multitasking.

Up to this point, you have created a few clients that connect with network servers, programmed peers to share information, and written a couple servers. But in all these cases, each program does only one task at a time. The server allows only one client; and an incoming client-connection has to wait while the server services current client. Wouldn't it be great to accept more than one connection at a time? How about connecting your client to several servers at once?

Multitasking is very powerful and can ease programming if you think of parallel or multiple tasks with designated responsibilities. Above all, write your code to be comprehensible by your peers. Revising your good source code to implement multitasking without proper planning can easily yield unwelcoming and unmanageable code.

This chapter encompasses the often confusing topic of multitasking, covering both processes and threads. Along with how and when to use them, this chapter describes their uses, differences, strengths, and weaknesses. Additionally, this chapter introduces signals, locking, and deadlock.

As you might guess, the topics presented in this chapter are rather extensive. You can find entire college texts devoted to these issues. However, this chapter presents only the multitasking essentials for network programming. So, the discussion focuses on the information that you need to get your job done quickly and easily.

For clarity, this chapter uses the term *task* to mean a executable system entity. Under this definition, *processes* and *threads* are tasks to simplify the discussion and help you understand multitasking within this context.

Defining Multitasking: Processes Versus Threads

With multitasking, you can access the sheer power of Linux and other UNIX clones because you can use it to allocate the CPU time into independent slices of time (*timeslicing*) and space (system resources). Programs can accomplish more and work more efficiently if properly designed for multitasking.

Tasks are separate executable units on your system. Every active thing you work with is a task. Computer multitasking is divided into two camps—processes and threads (or *lightweight processes*). These two terms are actually two extremes along a wide spectrum of data sharing. To understand how multitasking works, you need to know how the operating system separates individual tasks from one another.

Each task groups information into different partitions of memory (*pages*). The operating system assigns each task a *page table*—a set of pages with each page performing a different function. The task uses these pages through the virtual memory (VM) subsystem of the microprocessor. The VM is a table that translates the program's effective addresses to physical locations. When the operating system begins a task switch, it saves information about the task—the *context*—and loads the next task's page table into the VM.

> ### Purpose of the Virtual Memory
>
> The virtual memory page table includes more information than just memory translation. It includes references to access rights (read/write/execute). The operating system also flags those pages that are swapped out to secondary storage. That way, when the program accesses the page, the microprocessor issues a page fault (page is missing). The page-fault handler then loads the missing page from secondary storage.

The tasks can share different pages, depending on how they were created. For processes, Linux uses a *copy on write* algorithm. Processes do not share any data, but rather than copying everything all at once, the VM copies only those pages that the parent or child revises. Copy on write reduces the overhead of process creation, increasing your workstation's performance. Part of the great performance you see in Linux is due, in part, to this delayed memory copy.

Processes and threads each have their respective roles and rarely cross lines. These roles can help you to decide which to use. For example, you use a process to call an external program and get information from it. On the other hand, you can use the thread to process an image for display while loading it. This simple rule can help you decide between processes or threads: If you need to share data, use a thread.

Figure 7.1 shows what parts of a task you can share. In all cases, the tasks cannot share the stack and the context. The current thread's library implementation defines a thread to share everything except the process ID (PID).

During a task switch, the operating system replaces the current page table entries with those of the incoming task. This overhead can take several CPU cycles. You may see task switching overhead between 1μs and 0.1ms, depending on the microprocessor and its clock rate. That can be a long time—especially when Linux task switching is 100 times per second (every 10ms). Each task gets a portion of the CPU's time, and part of this allocation is the task switch itself.

On some UNIX versions, threads run faster because the task switcher has to flush fewer page table entries. The 2.0 and 2.2 Linux kernel versions showed a nearly identical switching time. This similarity is due to the finely tuned switching algorithms.

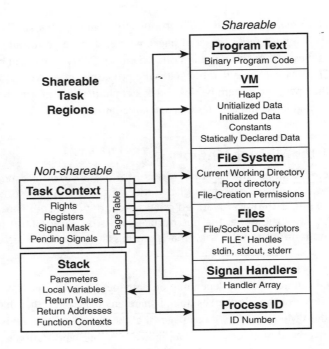

FIGURE 7.1

Linux tasks own several regions of memory.

Linux and other operating systems also support symmetric multiprocessing. If you write your programs to support multitasking, you get an automatic turbo charge when they run on symmetric multiprocessors. Basically, the rules are the same in Linux, only there are two or more processors to run the tasks. (At the time of this writing, Linux supports a maximum of 16 symmetric CPUs.)

When to Use Multitasking

When should you use multitasking? Generally, a user should always have control over a program. Sometimes the program has to wait for other operations to complete, so it must use multitasking to interact with the user while waiting for the other operations. In the same way that Netscape allows you to access its menus while downloading a Web page, the parent program you design should delegate all network I/O operations to child-tasks. In fact, because different servers have varying response times, splitting off a few threads to load information from them may use your network channel more efficiently.

Dividing the Load: Multitasking

CHAPTER 7

137

7

DIVIDING THE
LOAD:
MULTITASKING

Here is a good rule of thumb for when to use multitasking: While waiting for I/O, the program could simultaneously

- Do other work—Process information or delegate tasks
- Respond to the user—User input or status reporting
- Serve other computers/people—One task waits and accepts a connection while another serves an established connection

Mixing threads and processes in the same program may seem to be unusual. However, this is actually common in large, interactive applications. Internet browsers usually mix them in that each browser window is a standalone process, while each request, such as page loading, results from the browser firing off several threads. You can mix and match threads and processes as you need them.

Multitasking Characteristics

Notice some common features in every task in a process listing (using either the top or ps aux command). These features help you work with them in a consistent way.

First, every task has a parent. Well, this is almost true. The process table listing shows a program called init; this is the mother of all tasks on the system. Its primary responsibility is to manage the tasks running on the system. The parent task creates and manages the tasks it uses to delegate responsibilities. When the child completes, the parent should clean up after its termination. If the parent does not clean up, eventually init has to.

Every task uses memory, I/O, and priorities. The most interesting programs that you write work with more information than the context can hold—16–32 registers are not much. The memory is always measured in terms of the RAM and swap that you set up on your computer. Programs use this memory to store their current state (this is different from the task's context).

Your programs need to interact with something, such as you or some file. This implies I/O. Every task gets three standard I/O channels:

- stdin   Standard input (input only), typically keyboard
- stdout   Standard output (output only), typically display
- stderr   Standard error (output only), typically display or log

You can change (or redirect) all of these channels from within your program or when you execute it. Your choice of redirection destinations can include other devices, files, or a different task. When creating (or *spawning*) a task, the child task inherits all the parent's open files. How closely coupled this inheritance is depends on the type of task.

Every task has an independent hardware stack. This is very important—especially if you use the low-level task-creation system call (clone(), see later in this chapter). Programs use the hardware stack to track function return values, local variables, parameters, and return call addresses. If tasks did share their hardware stack, they can immediately corrupt each other's work.

Lastly, every task has a unique priority. You can change the amount of CPU time your program uses by raising or lowering the priority.

> **Linux's Task Scheduling**
>
> Multitasking operating systems use many different methods for scheduling tasks. Linux uses a prioritized round robin scheduling scheme. In a round robin, each task gets a portion of the CPU time in turn. To implement priorities, this scheduling scheme moves higher priority tasks up the task list more quickly than lower ones.

Task Differences

The differences between processes and threads are subtle. When working with them, keep the following styles and features in mind.

Processes	Threads
From the point of a successful call, there are two processes running inline.	The caller supplies the name of the function to run as the child.
The child must be explicitly terminated with an exit() system call.	The child can explicitly or implicitly terminate with a pthread_exit(void* arg) or a return statement.
	No shared data. The only information passed to the child is the snapshot of the parent's data before the system call. The child shares the parent's data, accepts a parameter, and/or returns a value.
The child is always associated with the parent. When it ends, the parent must clean up the child.	The child can be detached from the parent. Thus, the child can terminate without parental intervention. (Unless the child is detached, the parent has to clean up the thread as well.)
Because each process's data is independent from the others, there is no contention for resources.	All contended data must be identified and locked so no corruption can occur.

Processes	Threads
Independent file system.	Linked file systems. The child sees any changes the parent makes to the current working directory (chdir), the root file system (chroot), or the default permissions on file creation (umask).
Shared file tables. If the child closes a file, the parent loses access to the file.	Open file tables are not shared. The operating system copies the tables so that the two processes have the same file open, but closing one channel does not affect the other process.
No shared signals.	Signals are shared. One thread can block a signal using sigprocmask() without affecting the other threads.

Use whichever fits the circumstances better and with which you are most comfortable. There are clear advantages to getting the free shared-data that threads offer, but the simplicity and independence of processes make them appealing as well.

How Do I Create a Process?

Multitasking is most often achieved with processes. It shares nothing, creates a new instance of your program, and inherits copies of the parent's open I/O channels. To spawn a process, use the fork() system call:

```
#include <unistd.h>
pid_t fork(void);
```

The fork() system call has a very simple and unassuming interface: you call it, and suddenly you have two identical processes running at the same time. The fork() system call has three ranges of values:

- Zero—The program in question is the child. If the call returns a zero, the fork() was successful and the currently running task is the child. To obtain the child's process ID (PID), use the getpid() system call.
- Positive—The program in question is the parent. If the call returns a positive value, the fork(), again, was successful and the currently running task is the parent. The return value itself is the PID of the new child.
- Negative—An error occurred; the call was unsuccessful. Check errno or use perror() to determine the nature of the error.

Most programs place the fork() system call in a conditional statement (such as if). The conditional statement helps separate the parent from the child. Listings 7.1 and 7.2 show two typical examples that use the call.

LISTING 7.1   Task Splitting Example

```
/********************************************/
/* Parent and Child following unique paths */
/* Task-splitting style of multitasking     */
/********************************************/
int pchild;

if ( (pchild = fork()) == 0 )
{   /* You're in the child */
    /*---Do some child-ish things---*/          ——— child
    exit(status); /* This is important! */
}
else if ( pchild > 0 )
{   /* You're in the parent */
    int retval;
    /*---Do some parent-ish things---*/         ——— parent
    wait(&retval); /* await child's end */
}
else
{   /* Some kind of error */
    perror("Tried to fork() a process");
}
```

LISTING 7.2   Job Delegation Example

```
/********************************************/
/* Parent (server) and Child (job proc)     */
/* Job-delegation style of multitasking      */
/********************************************/
int pchild;
for (;;) /* Loop Forever */
{
    /*---Wait for job request---*/
    if ( (pchild = fork()) == 0 )
    {   /* Child */
        /*---Process the request---*/
        exit(status);
    }
    else if ( pchild > 0 )
    {
        /* parent clean up */
        /* notice NO WAIT() -- you must */
        /* use signals (see later) */
    }
```

LISTING 7.2   Continued

```
    else if ( pchild < 0 )
    {   /* Some kind of error */
        perror("Can't process job request");
    }
}
```

Listing 7.1 creates a child in a safe environment. The parent does some work and then waits for the child to terminate. Alternatively, you can use an algorithm, such as that seen in Listing 7.2, that makes the parent into a job delegator. When some outside entity requests an operation, the parent creates a child to do it. Most servers use that seen in Listing 7.2.

You may want to use multitasking to get different jobs done at the same time. The jobs can be the same algorithmically, but they use different data. Without this concept, programs can waste computation time in duplicated effort. *Differentiation* separates the tasks so that they do not duplicate effort. While there is nothing syntactically wrong with the source code in Listing 7.3, it defeats the purpose of multitasking because it does not differentiate.

LISTING 7.3   Forking Without Differentiation Example

```
/**************************************************************/
/*** This is an example of "running together".  If fork() ***/
/*** is called without some differentiation, the two      ***/
/*** tasks duplicate each other's work, thus wasting CPU   ***/
/*** time.                                                 ***/
/**************************************************************/
/*---do something---*/
fork();
/*---continue---*/
```

This book refers to multitasking without differentiation as *running together* or *confluence*. As a general rule, avoid this condition. Running together can also occur if the process does not properly terminate with an explicit call to the exit() system call.

Implementing Fault-Tolerance with Confluence

You can use this powerful running together technique as part of a fault-tolerant system. A fault-tolerant system can duplicate computations to check for accuracy. When a processor begins to degrade, the computational results can vary. You can implement this technique by running together two or more tasks and locking them to a particular CPU (not currently supported on Linux). Each task runs the same computations on its designated processors. And, at a certain interval, the tasks send their current results to an arbitrator validation. The system shuts down the odd-processor-out.

7

DIVIDING THE
LOAD:
MULTITASKING

If you get any error from a `fork()` system call, you may have problems with your process table or memory resources. One symptom of an overburdened operating system is being denied resources. Memory and process table entries are foundational to a properly functioning OS. Because these resources are so important, Linux limits the total amount of resources a process can have. When you can't get a reasonably sized chunk of memory or you can't create a new task, you may have problems with your program or you don't have enough memory.

How Do I Create a Thread?

Threads offer you the power of closely shared resources between parent, children, and siblings. Use threading to delegate data tasks for a common goal. For example, one thread retrieves a picture, while another converts it for display. In contrast, processes help you when you don't need such closely connected interactions.

One specific implementation of threading you may have heard about is Pthreads. Pthreads is a set of library calls that offer threading in a POSIX 1c–compliant way. The programs you write using Pthreads are likely to be compatible with other POSIX-compliant operating systems. The library call for creating new Pthreads is `pthread_create()`:

```
#include <pthread.h>
int pthread_create(pthread_t* child, pthread_attr_t* attr, void*
(*fn)(void*), void* arg);
```

The Difference Between Library and System Calls

The difference between a library call and a system call is the amount of work done in libraries versus the kernel. A `fork()` system call really is an interface into the kernel system services. The `pthread_create()` is in a different library that translates the call into the `clone()` system call. In this case, to compile C programs with threads, be sure to include `-lpthread` as the last argument on the `cc` command line. For example, to compile `mythreads.c` and link it with the Pthreads library, use the following:

```
cc mythreads.c -o mythreads -lpthreads
```

As with the `fork()` system call, at the point you successfully execute `pthread_create()`, you have another task running. However, creating threads is more complicated than the `fork()` system call. Depending on how many features you want to use, you may have to do more preparatory work. Each parameter provides the materials needed to start the new thread (see Table 7.1).

TABLE 7.1   The Function of Each Parameter for the `pthread_create()` Library Call

Parameter	Description
child	The handle to the new thread. You use this variable after the call to control the thread.
attr	A set of attributes or behaviors for the new thread. You can define how the thread is to work and interact with the parent at the time of instantiation. A few of these behaviors include priority, attachment, and scheduling. This parameter can be NULL.
fn	A pointer to a function that is to house the thread. Every thread runs in a specified program subroutine (unlike `fork()`). When the thread returns or exits the subroutine, the system terminates the thread. This helps avoid the task confluence problem (see above).
arg	A parameter to be passed to the function. You can use this to configure the thread's initial settings. Be sure to make the data block that this parameter points to available to the thread. In other words, don't refer to a stack variable. The parameter can be NULL as well.

As previously noted, you have two threads running after successfully completing the call—the parent and the child. Both share everything except the stack. The parent keeps a handle (`child`) of the child thread, and the child executes in own routine (`fn`) with configuration (`arg`) and behavior (`attr`). If you set the attributes to NULL, you can still change the thread's behavior later. Keep in mind that until you change the attributes, the thread behaves in the default manner.

Essentially, the call reduces to two specific parameters. You can compare the basic algorithms for processes and threads in the following code. The algorithms almost mirror each other to reflect the primary differences. Compare Listings 7.4 and 7.5 to see the differences in creating processes and threads.

LISTING 7.4   Process Creation Examples

```
/*********************************/
/* This example creates a process */
/*********************************/

void Child_Fn(void)
{
```

LISTING 7.4   Continued

```
    /* do whatever a child does */
}

int main(void)
{   int pchild;

    /*---Initialization---*/
    /* Create new process */
    if ( (pchild = fork()) < 0 )
        perror("Fork error");
    else if ( pchild == 0 )
    {/* here is the child */
        /* close unneeded I/O */
        Child_Fn();
        exit(0);
    }
    else if ( pchild > 0 )
    {/* Here is the parent */
        /*---close unneeded I/O---*/
        /*---do other work---*/
        /* wait for child to end */
        wait();
    }
    return 0;
}
```

LISTING 7.5   Thread Creation Examples

```
/*********************************/
/* This example creates a thread */
/*********************************/

void *Child_Fn(void *arg)
{   struct argstruct *myarg = arg;
    /* do whatever a child does */
    return NULL; /* any value */
}

int main(void)
{   struct argstruct arg = {};
    thread_t tchild;

    /*---do some other initialization---*/
    /* Create new thread; report error in failed */
```

LISTING 7.5 Continued

```
if ( pthread_create(&tchild, NULL, &Child_Fn, &arg) != 0 )
    perror("PThreads error"); /* error */

/***Note that threads don't have a child section***/
/* We are implicitly still in the parent */

/* do some other work */
/* wait for child to end */
pthread_join(tchild, NULL);

return 0;
}
```

When you spawn a process, you use the fork() system call. The only difference is the conditional program statement to separate the execution paths. With a Pthreads spawn, you provide attributes (how the thread is to behave), a child routine (where the child is to run), and a parameter (what specific data with which to call the child).

Processes require a specific call to exit() to avoid running together, which you place at the end of the child's path. With Pthreads, you don't have to worry about that. A return statement (or even falling through without a return statement) implicitly terminates the child thread.

The __clone() System Call: The Call for the Brave

Linux offers you a low-level system call that gives you a lot more control over the creation of processes and threads. It is a Linux-specific call that allows you to select from six different memory types to share. Use this single call to access the full spectrum of task-data sharing. Referring back to the previous VM pages diagram, use this call to enable/disable sharing of any combination of the shareable pages of a task.

> **Be Careful with __clone()**
>
> The __clone() system call is not for the faint of heart. With all this power, you can easily blow up your program (and make your debugging task nearly impossible!).

If you still want to play, __clone() looks like the following:

```
#include <sched.h>

int __clone(int (*fn)(void*), void* stacktop,
    int flags, void* arg);
```

This call requires a little explanation. Similar to the `fork()` system call, the `__clone()` system call returns either the child's PID or a `-1` if an error occurred. Table 7.2 describes the meaning and use of each parameter.

TABLE 7.2 The Parameters of the `__clone()` System Call

Parameter	Description
fn	Similar to the `pthread_create()`, this is a pointer to a function that the child executes. When the function returns (with a `return` statement or an explicit call to the `exit()` system call), the task terminates.
stacktop	This points to the top of the child's stack. Most processors (except for the HP PA RISC) grow their stack from top to bottom. Therefore, you need to pass the first legal byte of the stack. (For portability, you have to use conditional compiling.)
flags	This parameter indicates what is to be shared and what signal to raise when the child terminates. Table 7.3 lists the possible sharing options. While you can specify any signal upon child termination, you might want to stick with `SIGCHLD` (the standard).
arg	Similar to the `pthread_create()` library call, use this parameter to pass information to the child's `fn` parameter.

Clone's Stack-Spaces

Because threads share everything and sharing the stack is a bad idea, the parent has to set aside some space for the child's stack. This space is still part of everyone's shareable data region. If you have a misbehaving task or insufficient stack space for your child, your debugging is going to be challenging.

Again, referring to the processor's VM diagram (Figure 7.1), you can use the flags in Table 7.3 to enable different forms of data sharing. If omitted, the operating system assumes you mean to copy that data region between tasks.

TABLE 7.3 Different Types of Shareable Task Data with `__clone()`

Flag	Description
CLONE_VM	Share the data space between tasks. Use this flag to share all static data, preinitialized data, and the allocation heap. Otherwise, copy data space.
CLONE_FS	Share file system information—current working directory, root file system, and default file creation permissions. Otherwise, copy settings.

TABLE 7.3   Continued

Flag	Description
CLONE_FILES	Share open files. When one task changes the file pointer, the other tasks see the change. Likewise, if the task closes the file, the other tasks are no longer able to access the file. Otherwise, create new references to open inodes.
CLONE_SIGHAND	Share signal tables. Individual tasks can choose to ignore open signals (using sigprocmask()) without affecting peers. Otherwise, copy tables.
CLONE_PID	Share process ID. Use this flag carefully; not all the existing tools support this feature. The Pthreads library does not use this option. Otherwise, allocate a new PID.

The __clone() system call is an all-encompassing task creator. With everything shared, the child is a thread; with nothing shared, the child is a process. Consider that the __clone() system call effectively replaces the fork() system call and pthread_create() library call if properly configured.

Listings 7.6 and 7.7 show code sections implementing with fork() and pthread_create() compared with an equivalent __clone() system call.

LISTING 7.6   Code Illustrating fork() and pthread_create()

```
/************************/
/* The fork() system call */
/************************/
void Child(void)
{
    /*---child's responsibility---*/
    exit(0);
}

int main(void)
{   int pchild;

    if ( (pchild = fork()) == 0 )
        Child();
    else if ( pchild > 0 )
        wait();
    else
        perror("Can't fork process");
}
```

LISTING 7.6   Continued

```
/***********************************/
/* The pthread_create() library call */
/***********************************/
void* Child(void* arg)
{
    /*---child's responsibility---*/
    return &Result;
}


int main(void)
{   pthread_t tchild;

    if ( pthread_create(&tchild, 0, &Child, 0) != 0 )
        perror("Can't create thread");
    pthread_join(tchild, 0);
}
```

join to get return from child.

LISTING 7.7   Code for an Equivalent __clone() System Call

```
/**************************************************/
/* The equivalent __clone() system call to fork()*/
/**************************************************/
void Child(void* arg)
{
    /*---child's responsibility---*/
    exit(0);
}
#define STACK    1024
int main(void)
{   int cchild;
    char *stack = malloc(STACK);
    if ( (cchild = __clone(&Child, stack+STACK-1, SIGCHLD, 0)
            == 0 )
        {/** In child -- section unreachable **/}
    else if ( cchild > 0 )
        wait();
    else
        perror("Can't clone task");
}
/*****************************************************/
/* The equivalent __clone() system call to pthread_create()*/
/*****************************************************/
void Child(void* arg)
{
    /*---child's responsibility---*/
```

LISTING 7.7   Continued

```
    exit(0);
}
#define STACK    1024
int main(void)
{   int cchild;
    char *stack=malloc(STACK);
    if ( (cchild = __clone(&Child, stack+STACK-1, CLONE_VM |
          CLONE_FS | CLONE_FILES | CLONE_SIGHAND | SIGCHLD,
          0)) < 0 )
        perror("Can't clone");
    wait();
}
```

You can use the `__clone()` system call basically anywhere you can use the other two calls. However, note that it is not 100 percent compatible with the implementation of Pthreads. For one, a cloned task only returns an integer (like a process). Pthreads, on the other hand, allows a thread to return any value. Also, task termination differs. Unless you expect to use your code exclusively on a Linux-compatible computer, you may want to focus on the standard task-spawning calls.

Task Communication

You create unique tasks by differentiating them so that they don't duplicate work. The two types of differentiation—specified paths and communication—help you design and delegate the responsibilities in logical ways. For example, consider playing a hand of poker. The game uses several phases and modes of operation to ensure players play correctly. Because each gets a different hand to play, divergent playing styles, and varying funds to bid with, the game becomes interesting. Similarly, you achieve optimal results when you take into account the differing functions of tasks and responsibilities.

Initialization: Setting the Child's State

In poker, every player buys a set of chips, and the dealer deals out the hand. The players may have different techniques to place a value on their hand; and the dealer has an added responsibility of managing the deck. In programming, one form of communication is simply the state with which the task starts. Both processes and threads typically follow a different execution path than the parent after the parent sets up the shared data.

Use the parent to set up the environment with which the children work. After the children have what they need, they can begin processing. The parent can have a little control over the child, but—like the dealer and the players—these are usually directive ("You can't do that!"), not procedural ("Go on! Bid your house!").

When you create threads, you follow a procedure like creating processes. First, you set up the shared environment for processes and threads, and then create the task. Additionally, threads can accept a void* parameter (like a procedure call) for initialization. The void* data type is C's way of doing abstract data types. With it, you can pass any value around and it's up to the receiver to interpret the real meaning. This parameter is like accepting the hand to play.

> ## Using the void* Data Type
>
> Passing a void* type may seem very powerful, but be careful how you create the type. The data has to be either an allocated block (using the malloc() library call), global data, or static data. In other words, it should not be stack (or *auto*) data. The reason is simple: As the program makes the procedure calls/returns, the stack is going to change. The data may not exist for the child to see.

Shared/Common Memory

When you play poker, you eyeball two particular resources—the pot and the deck. These are limited and shared resources. How you play and when you fold depends on those factors. During play, the dealer takes from the deck and distributes among players. Players evaluate the hand they receive and toss money bids into the pot. Likewise, it's necessary to keep in mind the memory resources available to your program.

You can program processes and threads to passively pass information to everyone else holding common or shared memory. Threading offers you common memory inherently: the parent and child (and even siblings) share the same data regions by default. The stack is the only unique region between threading tasks. Just make sure that no two people have their hands in the pot at the same time.

You can create shared memory in your processes by using the shmget() system call. Shared memory in this fashion sets aside a block of memory for communicating with other processes. However, this slows computation time because the process has to use the system to manage the memory access.

Interprocess Communication (IPC)

During the poker game, the players send messages to each other and to the dealer. Some of these messages are instructional, some emotional (as you might guess). Still, the players direct the message to a particular player or to the entire group.

The tasks you design and program can use interprocess communication (IPC). IPC usually comes in the form of pipes; your task can direct messages to other tasks using these pipes. Pipes are unidirectional, like using stdin and stdout I/O channels. The system call `pipe()` creates the following pipe:

```
#include <unistd.h>
int pipe(int fd[2]);
```

The parameter fd is an array of two integers. You provide this array to accept the two new file descriptor references. Two common errors are

- EMFILE   Too many files are already open.

- EFAULT   fd is not pointing to an array of two integers.

The following is an example of using pipe:

```
/***************************************************************/
/*** Example of using the pipe() system call               */
/***************************************************************/
int fd[2];       /* create the array to hold the descriptors */
if ( pipe(fd) != 0 )                      /* create the pipe */
    perror("Pipe creation error");
...
read(fd[0], buffer, sizeof(buffer)); /* read from input end */
...
```

Indexing File Descriptors

Every I/O channel is assigned a file descriptor number. This is an index into a file descriptor table. By default, every process gets three channels: stdin (0), stdout (1), and stderr (2). When you create a pipe, it takes the next two available slots (one for input and one for output). For example, if a task has no other files open, calling `pipe()` sets aside pipe-input (3) and pipe-output (4).

Setting up a pipe with multitasking is more complicated and can be a little mind-bending, but once you've done it a couple of times, it won't induce migraines any more.

Listing 7.8 and 7.9 contrast the different ways of creating pipes in threads and processes for parent tasks. Since the programmer has to pay special attention to cloned tasks, the examples do not include them.

LISTING 7.8   Creating Pipes in a Parent Process

```
/************************************************************/
/***                   Parent Process                   ***/
int FDs[2];       /* create the place holder for the new pipe */
pipe(FDs);   /* create the pipe: FDs[0]=input, FDs[1]=output */
char buffer[1024];

/*---Create the process using fork() ---*/
close(FDs[0]);                              /* Make write-only */
...
write(FDs[1], buffer, buffer_len); /* send message to child */
...
/*---do processing---*/
wait();
close(FDs[1]);
```

LISTING 7.9   Creating Pipes in a Parent Thread

```
/************************************************************/
/***                   Parent Thread                    ***/
int FDs[2];       /* create the place holder for the new pipe */
pipe(FDs);   /* create the pipe: FDs[0]=input, FDs[1]=output */
char buffer[1024];
...
/*---Create the thread using pthread_create() ---*/
write(FDs[1], buffer, buffer_len); /* Send message to child */
...
/*--- (Leave pipe closure to child) ---*/
pthread_join(pchild, arg);
```

The child process or thread fulfills different roles. While similar to each other and due to the constraints on threads, they work slightly differently with pipes. Compare Listing 7.10 with Listing 7.11.

LISTING 7.10   Creating Pipes in a Child Process

```
/************************************************************/
/***                   Child Process                    ***/
int FDs[2];       /* create the place holder for the new pipe */
pipe(FDs);   /* create the pipe: FDs[0]=input, FDs[1]=output */
char buffer[1024];

/*---Create the child process---*/

dup2(FDs[0], 0); /* replace stdin */
```

LISTING 7.10   Continued

```
close(FDs[0]); /* not needed now */
close(FDs[1]); /* no writing to parent */


read(0, buffer, sizeof(buffer)); /* get message from parent */
...
/*---do processing---*/
printf("My report...");
exit(0);
close(FDs[1]);
```

LISTING 7.11   Creating Pipes in a Child Thread

```
/******************************************************/
/***                    Child Thread              ***/
int FDs[2];      /* create the place holder for the new pipe */
pipe(FDs);  /* create the pipe: FDs[0]=input, FDs[1]=output */
char buffer[1024];

/*---Create the child process---*/

read(FDs[0], buffer, sizeof(buffer));/* get msg from parent */
...
/*---do processing---*/
printf("My report...");
...
close(FDs[0]); /* close input pipe */
close(FDs[1]); /* close output pipe */

pthread_exit(arg);
```

You can create a pipe between two tasks using Figure 7.2 as a guide; use the following steps to further understand what is happening.

1. The parent declares a file descriptor array. When you call the pipe() system call, the call places the descriptors in this array.

2. The parent creates the pipe. The kernel creates a queue and places the reading descriptor in fd[0] and the writing descriptor in fd[1].

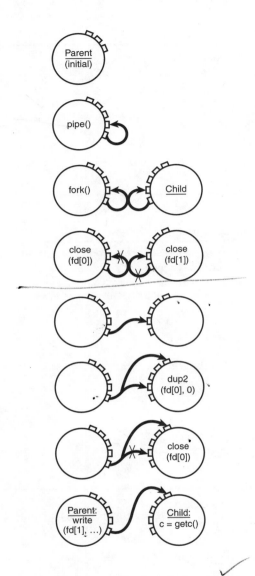

FIGURE 7.2
When you create a pipe between tasks, you have to follow a particular sequence of redirecting and closing channels.

Using Pipes Requires Closing One End

When the system creates a pipe, it connects the input channel to the output channel: The pipe effectively loops in on itself—whatever the program writes can be read by the same task (as if it were talking to itself). The same message still goes to the child, but the parent sees its own message in the input. Most communication paths are in one direction: the parent telling the child what it should process, so your process closes the unneeded channels. However, if you want true bi-directional communication, you need to call `pipe()` twice—one pipe for each direction (see Figure 7.3).

3. The parent spawns the new task. The process gets an exact copy of everything (including the pipe). The pipe between the parent and child is intertwined.

4. The parent communicates with the child using the file descriptor array.

5. The child process redirects its own standard input (this is optional) and communicates with the parent using the open pipe. It also closes the output channel.

6. The parent needs only the output channel of the pipe to communicate with the child, so it closes the input channel.

You cannot redirect the I/O channels in threads because they share the file descriptor tables. This means that if you close the file in one thread, you essentially close it in all other threads of your program. Processes, on the other hand, make a copy of the file descriptor tables, so closing one channel does not affect the other processes in the program.

Figure 7.2 showed you how to create a unidirectional connection between a parent and the child. To create a bi-directional connection, you need to follow Figure 7.3.

Refer to this diagram to help you create pipes and redirection for your programming.

Signaling a Course Change: Folding

The poker game has few direct, asynchronous controls. A player can fold (step out of the current game) at any time. If the game were held in the Old West, a cheater might meet a sudden, asynchronous termination. In any case, the dealer picks up the dropped cards. Likewise, after you have started a process, you can change its course or your parent task can get notified of termination with signals.

Every task you program should handle all useful signals. There are approximately 30 different kinds of signals (two signals are user-defined). Most signals you can ignore or not capture because the likelihood that they occur is slim or to capture them is not meaningful. Many uncaught signals usually terminate your program, and some of these are important to multi-tasking programs. For example, the system notifies the parent when a child terminates with a `SIGCHLD` signal.

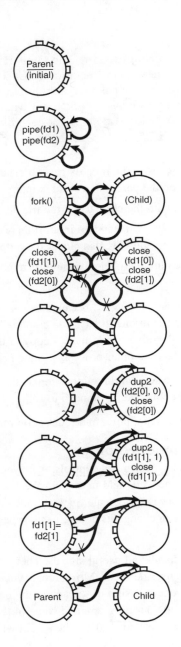

FIGURE 7.3

Your program can create an additional connection back if you want bi-directional communication between the parent and the child.

A signal is similar to an interrupt; the only information is that the signal occurred. When the signal arrives, the task stops what it is doing and jumps to a specified routine (called a *signal handler*). For SIGCHLD, you can call wait() to clean up the child's termination. You also can support other signals, such as math errors or Ctrl+C breaks.

Linux supports two styles of signals: System V (a one shot signal that reverts back to the default handler when the system calls your custom handler) and BSD (that keeps its handler until told otherwise). If you use the signal() system call, the single-shot is the default. You may not be interested in this feature—you should expect to capture the signal repeatedly.

Resetting the Signal Handler

To reset the handler, some programs used to fix the one-shot System-V behavior by placing a call to the signal system call directly in the signal handler. Unfortunately, this can create a race condition; a signal could come in before the call to reset it. As a result, the signal may be lost.

Instead of using signal(), the preferred system call is sigaction(). The sigaction() system call provides you more control over the behavior of the signal subsystem. The following is its prototype:

```
#include <signal.h>
int sigaction(int sig_num, const struct sigaction *action,
        const struct sigaction *old);
```

You use the first parameter to define which signal to capture. The second parameter defines how you want to handle the signal. If you set the last parameter to a non-NULL value, the call stores the last action definition. The structure definition for the second and third parameters is as follows:

```
struct sigaction
{
  /* Function pointer to handler */
    void (*sa_handler)(int signum);
  /* Specialized sigaction callback */
    void (*sa_sigaction)(int, siginfo_t *, void *);
  /* Bit array of signals to block while in handler */
    sigset_t sa_mask;
  /* behavior to perform */
    int sa_flags;
  /* (deprecated--set to zero) */
    void (*sa_restorer)(void);
};
```

To use this structure, you set the first field (sa_handler) to different values than a function pointer. If you place SIG_IGN in this field, the program ignores the specific incoming signal. Also, the program returns the behavior to the default if you use SIG_DFL.

To permit or deny cascading signals (one signal interrupting another), use the second field, sa_mask. Each bit (there are 1,024 possible bits) represents a signal to permit (1) or block (0). By default, a specific signal blocks like signals while servicing the first. For example, if you are servicing a SIGCHLD signal and another process terminates, your handler ignores that signal by default. You can change that behavior with SA_NOMASK.

The sa_flags determine the behavior of the handler. Most of the time, you can set it to zero:

- SA_ONESHOT   Use the System V behavior of resetting the handler once a signal is caught.
- SA_RESETHAND   Same as SA_ONESHOT.
- SA_RESTART   Restart some system calls if a signal interrupts it. Use this flag to restart system calls such as accept().
- SA_NOMASK   Allow the same signal to interrupt while handling an earlier signal.
- SA_NODEFER   Same as SA_NOMASK.
- SA_NOCLDSTOP   Does not notify parent if a child process just stops (SIGSTOP, SIGTSTP, SIGTTIN, or SIGTTOU). This flag is important for this chapter.

Listing 7.12 shows you an example of how to capture the SIGFPE (float-point exception) and ignore the SIGINT (keyboard interrupt).

LISTING 7.12   SIGFPE and SIGINT Handler Example

```
/***********************************************************/
/*** Capturing SIGFPE and ignoring SIGINT example      ***/
/***********************************************************/
#include <signal.h>

/* Define the signal catcher */
void sig_catcher(int sig)
{
    printf("I caught signal #%d\n", sig);
}

int main(void)
{   struct sigaction act;

    bzero(&act, sizeof(act));
    act.sa_handler = sig_catcher;
    sigaction(SIGFPE, &act, 0);     /* Capture a float error */
```

LISTING 7.12   Continued

```
    act.sa_handler = SIG_IGN;             /* Ignore signal */
    signal(SIGINT, &act, 0);    /* Ignore the ^C (interrupt) */
    /*---do processing---*/
}
```

Losing Signals in Signal Handlers

If you take too long in a signal handler, your program can lose pending signals. The signal queue is only a single flag—if two signals arrive, only one gets recorded. So, try to minimize the amount of CPU time spent in the signal handler. Also, making the handler short and succinct ensures that your program gets more CPU time.

Servers and clients can receive several different signals. To make code more robust, capture all reasonable and applicable signals. (Some signals, such as SIGFAULT, are best uncaught. If you get this one, there is something wrong in your code or data, and you won't recover.)

Reducing Code with Shared Signal Handlers

You can merge your signal handlers into one handler. The system passes the handler the signal number. Once inside the handler, simply check that value to do the appropriate actions.

You can send any signal to a task you can control. In other words, signals follow the same security rules as everything else. To issue a signal from the command line, you can use the kill command. Likewise, you can call the kill() system call in a program. The kill() system call's prototype is as follows:

```
#include <sys/types.h>
#include <signal.h>
int kill(pid_t PID, int sig_num);
```

You can get the lengthy (and convoluted) options for this call by reading the manual pages. Essentially, your program calls kill() with the process ID and the signal that you want to send to the process.

Child's Results

Returning to the poker example, when the hand ends or when a player folds, the dealer has to clean up and shuffle the deck. In fact, some players may demand to see the results of the winning hand before the winning player collects the pot. In similar manner, the parent cleans up and checks the results of each child.

The last method of communication is the termination results. The parent uses this information to decide the success of the child. When a process ends, it always returns a signed integer. The thread, on the other hand, can return an abstract object using a void*, an abstract object like that of the thread's parameter.

Be certain to use caution when supplying the result this way—it must persist between the transition. For example, don't return an object built from a stack variable. Instead, use the heap or a global variable. In fact, as long as the parent expects the parameter to change and it's not shared between threads, you can use the same parameter variable to pass data back.

Beating the Clock: Race Conditions and Mutexs

The power that threads offer you is very enticing. If threads are correctly managed, your programs run more quickly and experience fewer stalls. However, this feature has one catch—resource contention. If two threads revise the same data at the same time, they may corrupt the results. And trying to debug a contended resource can require long hours from you. The following subsection discusses the issues of race conditions.

Race Conditions

You may be familiar with *race conditions*, primarily two threads in a race to get their data stored. Earlier, this chapter presented an example of a race condition in resetting signal handlers. A *critical section* is the section of source code where the resource contention occurs. Consider the examples in Listings 7.13 and 7.14, assuming that Thread 1 and Thread 2 execute at the same time.

LISTING 7.13   Race Condition for Thread 1

```
/*************************************************************/
/*** Example of a race condition where two threads are    ***/
/*** contending for a queue data object.                  ***/
/*************************************************************/
int queue[10];
int in, out, empty;
/************** Thread 1 ************/
/* Read queue */
if ( !empty ) /* avoid queue underflow */
{   int val = queue[out];
    out++;
    if ( out >= sizeof(queue) )
```

LISTING 7.13   Continued

```
      out = 0;  /* wrap around */
   empty = ( out == in );
}
```

LISTING 7.14   Race Condition for Thread 2

```
/*******************************************************/
/*** Example of a race condition where two threads are  ***/
/*** contending for a queue data object.                ***/
/*******************************************************/
int queue[10];
int in, out, empty;
/************* Thread 2 ************/
/* write queue */
if ( !empty  &&  out != in ) /* avoid overflow */
{  queue[in] = 50;
   in++;
   if ( in >= sizeof(queue) )
      in = 0;  /* wrap around */
   empty = ( out == in );
}
```

For clarity, be sure to notice that the program increments the pointer variables after referencing the queue. These look okay as long as they run parallel and line by line. Unfortunately, that rarely happens. Suppose Thread 1 lags Thread 2 by a few lines. It's possible that Thread 2 could execute the empty test just before Thread 1 resets variable out. This instance would create the problem of an invalid test because out would never equal in.

This problem has a different twist if the two threads are switching back and forth (multitasking instead of parallel tasking). A task switch could occur just after the out++ statement in Thread 1. Thread 2 then resumes with potentially bad data in variables out and empty because they don't complete their tests.

Effectively, the two routines are contending for four data resources: queue, in, out, and empty.

Mutual Exclusion (Mutex)

You can handle critical sections by locking out (*mutual exclusion* or simply *mutex*) other processes from using the resource. This *serialization* (allowing only one task at a time) ensures that the threads don't corrupt data in the critical sections. A mutex *semaphore* is a flag that serializes access and acts like a traffic light. As long as the flag is clear (green), the thread can enter the critical section. If the flag is set (red), the thread blocks until clear (green) again.

To manage resources, programs use either of two methods: coarse- or fine-grained locking. Coarse-grained locking basically locks everyone out of doing anything while the program is in a critical section. One coarse-grained method turns off timeslicing. You face two big problems with this approach: it blocks unrelated tasks, and it does not work in multiprocessing environments.

Fine-grained locking offers you control over the contended resource instead of the tasks. A thread requests access to a shared resource. If it is unused, the thread owns it until released. If your thread finds the resource is already reserved, your thread blocks and waits until the resource is released by the task currently using it.

The Pthreads library offers you a wide selection of tools for managing your threaded applications. Included is the Mutex API. The method of using mutexes is straightforward (see Listing 7.15).

LISTING 7.15   Creating a Semaphore Example

```
/**************************************************************/
/*** Define the global mutex semaphore.  The value       ***/
/*** indicates the checking algorithm to use.            ***/
/**************************************************************/
pthread_mutex_t mutex = PTHREAD_MUTEX_INITIALIZER;
...
/* Begin critical section */
pthread_mutex_lock(&mutex);
...
/*---Work on critical data--*/
...
pthread_mutex_unlock(&mutex);
/* End critical section */
...
```

The parameter mutex is the semaphore you use to lock the section. A full-code example (called thread-mutex.c) is included on the Web site. Initialize it with one of three behavior values:

- Fast (default)—(PTHREAD_MUTEX_INITIALIZER) Just check the lock. If the same thread tries to lock a mutex twice, it deadlocks.
- Recursive—(PTHREAD_RECURSIVE_MUTEX_INITIALIZER_NP) Verify that the owner is locking the mutex again. If so, it keeps count (*counting semaphore*) of the number of locks. The mutex has to be unlocked as many times as it was locked.
- Error-Checking—(PTHREAD_ERRORCHECK_MUTEX_INITIALIZER_NP) Verify that the thread unlocking a mutex is the same one that locked it. If it is not the same, it returns an error while leaving the lock intact.

The library offers an additional call to lock without blocking. The `pthread_mutex_trylock()` library call attempts to lock the semaphore. If it can't, it returns an EBUSY error.

Playing Fair by Avoiding Critical Section Lockouts

Try to limit computation in a critical section to just the contended items. For example, don't call I/O or manipulate unrelated data unless you absolutely can't avoid it. If necessary, you can copy the data into local variables for computation outside the section. Keep in mind that I/O mixed with critical sections leads to deadlock-potential.

Pthread Mutex Problems

You do have a few limitations with Pthreads. First, Pthreads' mutex has no reference to the critical section of memory. It's just a flag. Using the traffic light analogy again, the contended resource is the intersection—not the traffic light. The light would function with or without the intersection. The primary function of mutex is for you to use it exclusively for the contended data. For instance, if not careful, you could program two threads to use a single semaphore for unrelated data. This is not dangerous—you won't crash, deadlock, or corrupt data. You may, however, block a thread unnecessarily.

Second, you could have several threads working on a large block of data, such as a table. Each of the cells is unrelated, and the threads are working in different sections. You don't want to lock the whole table, only sections of it (called *zone locking*). Pthreads mutexes give you the ability to block concurrent accesses, but it can't dynamically determine where your thread is working.

Finally, you may also want to prioritize access. There is no harm in reading some data, and you can have several readers at the same time (known as *shared locking*). But, no other thread can write to it. Similarly, you want only one writer; this only works if the contended data is atomically updated. Pthreads are limited to exclusive access—either you have it or you don't.

If the current version of Pthreads mutexes does not meet all your needs, you could build your own extensions on top of them.

Deadlock Prevention

Imagine two toddlers playing with some toys. One child sees what the other child is playing with and vice versa. They want each other's toys, but they are not willing to give up what they have. Essentially, they are deadlocked.

When using threads, be sure to consider the possibility of resource contention and critical sections. After isolating and grouping the critical data, you need to identify who needs what and when. Sometimes you may find that two resources need to be locked (called *interlocked*) before work can proceed. If you are not careful, you can cause a deadlock to occur.

Consider the following deadlock example:

Thread #1	Thread #2
1. Lock Savings Fund.	1. Lock IRA Fund.
2. Lock IRA Fund.	2. Lock Savings Fund.
3. Using IRA Fund, change Savings Fund.	3. Using Savings Fund, change IRA Fund.
4. Unlock IRA Fund.	4. Unlock IRA Fund.
5. Unlock Savings Fund.	5. Unlock Savings Fund.

Thread #2 deadlocks at step 2. Using a standardized naming policy, the deadlock is more apparent:

Thread #1	Thread #2
1. Lock Funds_Mutex_ 1.	1. Lock Funds_Mutex_ 2.
2. Lock Funds_Mutex_ 2.	2. Lock Funds_Mutex_ 1.
3. Using Funds_Mutex_ 2, change Funds_Mutex_ 1.	3. Using Funds_Mutex_ 1, change Funds_Mutex_ 2.
4. Unlock Funds_Mutex_ 2.	4. Unlock Funds_Mutex_ 2.
5. Unlock Funds_Mutex_ 1.	5. Unlock Funds_Mutex_ 1.

The deadlock occurs because the two threads want each other's resources. The following are a few rules that can reduce deadlock potential:

- Group Naming—Identify interdependent groups of resources and give their mutexes a similar name (for example: Funds_Mutex_1 and Funds_Mutex_2).
- In-Order Locking—Lock the resources numerically from least to greatest.
- In-Order Unlocking—Unlock the resources numerically from greatest to least.

By following these deadlock policies, you can avoid the nasty debugging required in unraveling a deadlock.

Controlling Children and Killing Zombies

You have created a couple of threads or processes. After you have created children, you do have some control over them. The question is, how do you control their behavior? As mentioned before, you can communicate with them using signals, messages, and data.

Give the Child More Attention: Priority and Scheduling

You can lower the child's priority so other tasks get more CPU time. (As you may know, only a `root`-privileged task can increase a task's priority.) The system calls to use to change priority are `getpriority()` and `setpriority()`.

Unlike processes that offer little control over the children, threading allows you to change its scheduling algorithm or disown it. Linux uses a prioritized round robin scheduling algorithm (as introduced earlier in this chapter). Pthreads offer you three different scheduling algorithms:

- Normal—This is like the Linux scheduling algorithms. (default)
- Round Robin—The scheduler ignores priority and each thread gets a slice of time until terminated. You might use this in real-time environments.
- FIFO—The scheduler queues up and runs each thread to completion. Again, use this scheduling form primarily for real-time environments.

Burying the Zombies: Cleaning Up after Termination

Perhaps it escaped your notice that some of the process table examples you've worked on may have some zombies floating around. Sorry, this is not a Halloween thriller, but the problem can cause horror to any system administrator. After you get them in your process table, they sometimes won't go away without rebooting.

If you like taking risks and don't know what a zombie is, you might consider creating one on your system. *Don't do this if you can't reboot your computer.* They won't harm your computer, but they can take up valuable resources (memory and process table entries). Run the Multitasking Echo-Server code (found on the Web site). Connect to it, and then, type **"bye"**. It closes the connection. Now type **ps aux|grep *<username>*** (substituting your username as appropriate). You may see an entry with a status of *z*. This does not mean it's sleeping. You usually can kill it by killing the parent (Echo-Server).

When the child ends, it exits with a numeric return value. The value indicates either a success or some error code. Normally, you have to program the parent to wait for the child task to complete using the `wait()` system call. `wait()` retrieves the child's return value for the parent to examine. If you do not wait for the child, the child waits indefinitely for you.

Getting Process Zombies

The parent should care for all its children. Sometimes it doesn't. When the parent ends without reckoning with all its completed children, the init program inherits them. The init program's primary responsibility is to schedule, run, and clean up processes. Occasionally it can't. This is when zombies begin to proliferate in your process table. You won't be able to use the `kill()` command to remove them. The only solution is to reboot your system. (You can try `init s` or `init 1` to flush the process table, but there's no guarantee that it will work.)

Unlike processes using the `fork()` or `__clone()` system call, Pthreads allow you to disown (or *detach*) a thread. Detaching a thread lets you proceed without having to wait for it to terminate. The library call is simply

```
#include <pthread.h>
int pthread_detach(pthread_t tchild);
```

The parameter `tchild` is the reference you got from calling `pthread_create()`. The call returns the following errors:

- `ESRCH`   No thread could be found corresponding to that specified by `tchild`.
- `EINVAL`   The thread `tchild` is already in the detached state.

You can use `pthread_create()` in the following way:

```
/*************************************************************/
/*** Example of detaching a thread from a parent.  This   ***/
/*** allows the parent to proceed without checking for    ***/
/*** the child's termination.                             ***/
/*************************************************************/
/* Create the variable to reference thread */
pthread_t tchild;
...
/* Create thread */
if ( pthread_create(&tchild, 0, Child_Fn, Child_Arg) != 0 )
    perror("Could not create thread");
else
    /* Detach it */
    pthread_detach(tchild);
...
```

After calling `pthread_detach()`, your parent task can continue with its own computation. Processes, on the other hand, do not have that flexibility. But, at the same time, it's unnecessary to wait for every child; that defeats the purpose of delegating responsibilities.

Dividing the Load: Multitasking

CHAPTER 7

167

7

DIVIDING THE
LOAD:
MULTITASKING

You can capture the notification of a child's termination asynchronously with signals. When a
child ends, the operating system sends the parent a SIGCHLD signal. All you have to do is capture it and call wait() in the handler.

```
/**************************************************************/
/*** Example of signal handler for capturing child        ***/
/*** termination notifications.                            ***/
/**************************************************************/
#include <signal.h>

void sig_child(int sig)
{   int status;

    wait(&status);                      /* Get the final result */
    fprintf(stderr, "Another one bytes the dust\n");
}
```

To get any notifications, you need to connect the signal handler with the signal, as follows:

```
{   struct sigaction act;

    bzero(&act, sizeof(act));
    act.sa_handler = sig_child;
    act.sa_flags = SA_NOCLDSTOP | SA_RESTART;
    sigaction(SIGCHLD, &act, 0);        /* Capture child TERM */
}
```

Avoiding exec() Zombies

To fire off an external program, you must capture the child's termination notification,
even when using the exec() system call (discussed in the section "Calling External
Programs with the exec Server," later in this chapter). It may seem to you that the
external program is no longer related to the parent, but the parent actually still owns
the task space.

If you want to see if anything went wrong with the child, check the return value—passed
through the status variable. The parent, of course, has to interpret the meaning of the result.
So, for example, the child can return 0 (zero) for successful termination or a negative value for
an error.

> **Process Return Value Limits**
>
> Only the lowest 8 bits are retained, and the value is shifted by 8 bits. So if you return a value 500 (0×01F4), the wait() system call gets 0×F400. The upper 0×0100 is lost.

The status value returned from wait() is not directly interpretable. It has encoded states along with the process's exit code. The libraries offer a simple way of isolating the exit code, two of which are WIFEXITED() and WEXITSTATUS(). Take a look at the man pages for waitpid() for information on these macros.

Extending Current Clients and Servers

You can apply the concepts from this chapter to examples from previous chapters and extend them with processes and threads. You can add multitasking to the Echo Server by adding the calls to fork() or pthread_create(). Because you are now creating new tasks, the fork() system call requires you to capture and dispatch child-termination signals. To get the complete source listing, please see echo-server.c on the Web site.

Now after compiling and running this program, you can connect to this server with the telnet command. In fact, you can have several connections running at the same time. This is precisely what a user expects—an apparent exclusive connection to the server. Creating tasks and delegating responsibilities helps you provide that service.

Calling External Programs with the exec Server

No one likes to reinvent something that works well. You probably prefer to use the ps command over building that information yourself in a program. Also, using Perl to do some operations is a lot easier than writing a parser in C. So, how do you use these established commands?

The exec() system call API extends the fork() system call by allowing you to call external programs and interact with them. This is essentially what CGI (Common Gateway Interface) calls are on the Web, as shown in the following:

- A host on the network offers a CGI server that takes a command. The command has command-line parameters typically in the following form:

  "http://www.server.com/cgi/<command>?param1+param2+..."

- The client sends a message, for example

  "http://www.server.com/cgi/ls?tmp+proc"

- The server creates a child process and redirects the stdin, stdout, and stderr to the client's channel.

- Next the server calls the program using the exec() system call.

Notice the power of multitasking by the simple fact that running external programs cannot be done effectively without multitasking. The exec() system call comes in five flavors:

- execl()   Variable parameter list, first is the command with fully qualified path. All of the following parameters are the command-line arguments, beginning with the zeroth argument (arg[0]). The list ends with a zero or NULL.

```
/* For example: */
if ( execl("/bin/ls", "/bin/ls", "-aF", "/etc", NULL) != 0 )
    perror("execl failed");
exit(-1);
/* actually the "if" is redundant -- exec does not return unless it failed */
```

execl()'s First Two Parameters

The execl() system call may appear redundant; Why are the first and second parameters the same command? The first parameter is the actual command name (to be executed), and the second is the zeroth command-line parameter (like arg[0] in main() of a C program). Don't forget to include the name—some external commands check the name to figure out what behavior to use. Also, don't forget the last NULL or zero; it indicates the end of the parameter list.

- execp()   Similar to execl(), but the command searches the execution path.

```
/* For example: Find the program 'ls' in execution path */
if ( execl("ls", "ls", "-aF", "/etc", NULL) != 0 )
    perror("execp failed");
exit(-1);
```

- execle()   Similar to execl(), but the last parameter is an array of strings representing the environment. Remember to end the list of parameters with a NULL or zero.

```
/* For example: */
char *env[]={"PATH=/bin:/usr/bin", "USER=gonzo", "SHELL=/bin/ash", NULL};
if ( execle("/bin/ls", "/bin/ls", "-aF", "/etc", NULL, env) != 0 )
    perror("execle failed");
exit(-1);
```

- execv()   Has two parameters. The first is the fully qualified path of the command. The second is an array of command-line arguments. The last entry in the array is a zero or NULL.

```
/* For example: */
char *args[]={"/bin/ls", "-aF", "/etc", NULL};
if ( execle(args[0], args) != 0 )
    perror("execle failed");
exit(-1);
```

- execvp()   Like execv(), but the command searches the execution path.

```
/* For example: */
char *args[]={"ls", "-aF", "/etc", NULL};
if ( execle(args[0], args) != 0 )
    perror("execle failed");
exit(-1);
```

If successful, the exec() system call does not return to your program. The operating system replaces the task context with the external program, so you don't even need the if statement; any executed statement after an exec() means it failed.

To use this system call in a socket server, replace the main client-waiting loop with the following:

```
/*--------------------------------------------------------*/
/* Code fragment for accepting client connections and     */
/* calling an external program ("ls -al /etc").           */
/*--------------------------------------------------------*/
...
while (1)
{   int client, addr_size = sizeof(addr);

    client = accept(sd, &addr, &addr_size);
    printf("Connected: %s:%d\n", inet_ntoa(addr.sin_addr),
                                 ntohs(addr.sin_port));
    if ( fork() )
        close(client);
    else
    {
        close(sd); /* Client doesn't need access to the socket */
        dup2(client, 0); /* Replace stdin */
        dup2(client, 1); /* Replace stdout */
        dup2(client, 2); /* Replace stderr */
        execl("/bin/ls", "/bin/ls", "-al", "/etc", 0);
```

```
        perror("Exec failed!"); /* something went awry */
    }
}
...
```

Refer to `ls-server.c` on the Web site for the full listing.

Difference Between `fork()` and `vfork()`

On other UNIX versions, you may want to use the `vfork()` system call. Because processes do not share their data, the child must get a snapshot of the parent's data space. If you just want to call `exec()` after the `fork()`, that copy is a waste of time and space. To solve this problem, some UNIX versions introduced the `vfork()` system call to suppress the copy. However, Linux uses a copy-on-write procedure (copying the parent's pages only if the child or parent revises them). The exec-child does not revise the data pages, so the system does not copy any data pages. Therefore, Linux does not need the `vfork()` system call. It mapped the `vfork()` system call to `fork()`.

The two primary differences between a normal parent-child creation are the I/O redirection and the `exec*()` call. You need to redirect all standard channels, including `stderr`, to supply the external program all the I/O it needs to work correctly.

You can use the `exec()` system call in both threads and processes. With many tools available, this becomes very useful. Threads have a caveat; because they cannot redirect the standard I/O without affecting any peer thread's I/O, threads that call `exec()` share the same I/O with the peer threads.

Using an `exec()` Call in a Thread

Here's an interesting problem: What happens if a thread calls `exec()`? The external program could not replace the caller without affecting the peers. The Linux kernel uses the policy that the call won't share the data, but the existing file channels remain shared. So, when the external program terminates, it closes the `stdin` and `stdout` file handles. This affects the peer threads. Recommendation: Use `fork()` instead if you want to `exec()` an external program.

Summary: Distributing the Process Load

Multitasking gives your programs the extra kick they need to increase accessibility and flexibility. You can use threads and processes to speed up your clients and boost your servers. With task management and communications, you can ease programming and increase reliability.

This chapter introduced you to the topic of multitasking and the different types of tasks—processes and threads. You also learned how to create them with high-level tools like Pthreads or `fork()` or the low-level tool `__clone()`.

After you have created the task, you can control thread interactions with synchronization. Synchronization further helps you serialize (or coordinate) access to the contended data. Serialization ensures data integrity.

Every task can accept messages through pipes or other I/O and signals to handle asynchronous events. The pipes allow you to direct information to children, offloading the parent. They also allow you to redirect standard I/O for simpler interaction. Signals capture events that can help your programs be more robust.

The next chapter extends the concepts of I/O and provides alternatives to multitasking.

Choosing when to Wait for I/O

IN THIS CHAPTER

With today's time demands, it's a good idea to investigate time-saving methods for your network. So it's good to keep in mind that your computer has a fundamentally critical, limited resource: the CPU. Every task on the system demands time from it, and every task has to share that time in small portions. At the most basic level, every task shares CPU time with time-slicing. Linux uses a more dynamic scheduling algorithm that adapts to CPU use and I/O blocking.

When a program runs, it is either executing or waiting for something (*blocking*). The program encounters two kinds of blocking: I/O-bound (spends more time waiting for I/O) and CPU-bound (spends more time in computation). During the I/O down time, other tasks can run and complete their assignments. This is how most tasks cooperate and share the CPU's limited time. When a task has to wait for I/O, it yields (*blocks*) so that another task can run.

You may not want to wait for a particular I/O to complete before continuing other tasks. For instance, consider how annoying it would be to have a browser that allows you to quit only *after* it has completely loaded a page. On the other hand, think of a client that simultaneously connects and loads resources from several servers. When you manage your pipeline well, it is always full, and you get the most out of your network connection.

When you retain control of the CPU while waiting for I/O to finish, you can increase the program's usability and reduce user frustration. One way to retain this control is through non-blocking I/O and timeouts. Nonblocking I/O lets you check the I/O subsystem or gets the kernel to tell your program when it's ready for more data. This frees up your program to focus on the user or some CPU-intensive algorithm.

Effective management of I/O blocking may work with or be an alternative to multitasking and multithreading. It's another programming tool to help you get your job done.

Choosing when to block and when not to block is very tricky. This chapter presents some ideas and rules of thumb to help you select the best situations.

I/O Blocking: Why?

The multitasking environment empowers you to do many things at the same time. In fact, when designed right, the result is 100% scalable to symmetric multiprocessing. This power has some limitations and rules. If you don't abide by those rules, the system suffers.

One rule to consider is that every task has to yield time to other tasks. The system builds this rule into everything that it does. For instance, each task gets a slice of time from the CPU. If there is nothing to do, the task yields up its slice. But how does the task know whether there is anything to do? Isn't it always doing something?

Well, yes and no. The primary cause of having nothing to do is waiting for some I/O to complete. Just for scale, consider the speed of the processor against the speed of the disk or the network.

Even with very fast disk arrays, you may have a transfer rate of 160MB/s and a seek/latency time of 5ms. If a task is running on a 500MHz Pentium III, each instruction is effectively taking one clock tick. You can expect an average of 2–4ns per instruction. In the amount of time that a seek takes to finish, your program could have executed about 1,250,000 assembler instructions (*opcodes*).

EnergyStar Delays

Most new computer systems today conform to *Green* or *EnergyStar* standards. One requirement is that the drive powers down when not used for a period of time. The drive takes about 1 or 2 seconds to spin up from idle.

Likewise, a 10Mb network transfers an average of 300KB/s from computer to computer (this is a measured optimum for a network running TCP/IP). A 100Mb/s network may increase this average only by a factor of 10 (3.0MB/s). Not counting the transmission, routing, and request-processing time, your client may have to wait an equivalent of 1000 instructions (on a similarly configured system). With these other factors, you can easily multiply that estimate by 1000 to 5000.

An average number of opcodes per line of compiled C source is 10:1. In other words, a network delay of 20ms could mean that your task could have executed about 5,000,000 opcodes, or 500,000 lines of C code.

So, how does the operating system deal with these time lags? It basically puts your task to sleep (*blocking*). When the system request finishes, your task wakes up and continues running.

Blocking I/O-bound tasks is usually the rule rather than the exception. To see how many tasks are actually running on your computer, run ps aux. All the tasks labeled R are running; those labeled S are stopped. You can have only one task running: the ps command itself.

When Do I Block?

You may let a program block (stop processing and wait) when an I/O resource takes its time to finish. Any time your program makes a system call, the operating system may force your task to wait for the transaction to finish. In most cases, the task waits for the I/O to send or receive information. Blocks occur under the following circumstances:

- Reading—A read-block occurs when no data has arrived yet. Internally, even one byte can cause the read() to return after a designated period of time.
- Writing—A write-block occurs when the internal buffers are full and waiting for transmission and your program requests more data to be sent. Linux sets aside memory for buffers for all I/O subsystems. These buffers store the data temporarily until the I/O subsystem transmits it. If the buffers fill up, subsequent calls block until some buffers free up.
- Connecting—A connection-block occurs when the accept() and connect() system calls find no pending connections in the listening queue. Blocking while waiting for a connection may actually be a good idea; otherwise, you may want to delegate the I/O request to a separate thread or task.

The following sections discuss further considerations regarding blocking.

Alternatives to I/O Blocking

What are some alternatives to blocking that you can use? You may want your program to do other things while waiting for a system request to finish. The program could

- Test the integrity of its data.
- Start and track other requests.
- Wait for several socket connections.
- Process some CPU-intensive calculations.

It can be pretty enticing to avoid I/O blocking, considering how much you can accomplish while waiting for a request. But, it's difficult to create the environment for nonblocking unless you design it in from the start. (Retrofitting nonblocking support is very challenging and can involve a lot more work.) Choose from these three methods to help avoid blocking: polling, timeouts, and asynchronous I/O.

Asynchronous I/O Versus Signal-Driven I/O

The algorithms for asynchronous I/O presented in this chapter are essentially signal-driven I/O, letting signals determine when I/O buffers are ready to read-from or write-to. True asynchronous I/O, as defined in POSIX.1, never blocks. In fact, starting a read would immediately return. The receiving buffers are considered unsafe until the read finishes and the program receives a signal. Linux does not (like many other operating systems) comply with POSIX.1 asynchronous I/O on sockets. To be consistent with the majority of the industry, this chapter uses the term "signal-driven I/O."

Comparing the Different I/O Programming Interactions

To increase throughput and responsiveness, perhaps your most important tool is the creative use of the I/O subsystem. Your programs are subject to getting information from outside sources. Controlling when and how you block makes your program more responsive to the user. Linux offers essentially four different styles of I/O interaction. It's helpful for you to take into account that each of the four different styles of I/O interaction has strengths and weaknesses. Figure 8.1 shows a task reading a packet with the different interaction styles. The process begins with no data waiting in the kernel buffers.

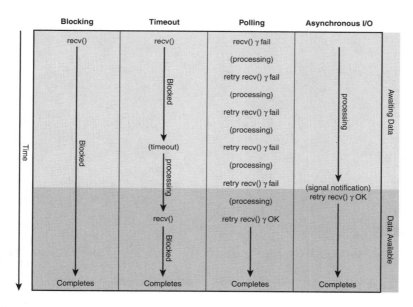

FIGURE 8.1

Each style of I/O control varies the amount of time available to the task during a read.

With the blocking style, the program waits until data arrives. The polling style repeatedly calls the recv() system call until the data arrives. The timeout style, on the other hand, may not get the data if the data does not arrive in time. Still, with the timeout style, you do not lose the message; the kernel holds it for you until you call for it again. Lastly, with the asynchronous style, the kernel notifies the task when it gets data.

Notice that it's a different story with how each style handles the interface when you send a message. The kernel's buffers take up the slack to speed up the processing in a nonblocking call. In all cases, a blocking call stops until the kernel completely sends the message. (This is not completely true, since the kernel really waits until it can send the message before waking the task, but to simplify programming you can assume that the message is gone when the task resumes.) Polling and asynchronous calls store the message in the buffers and return immediately. Figure 8.2 assumes that the data is too large to store entirely in the buffers.

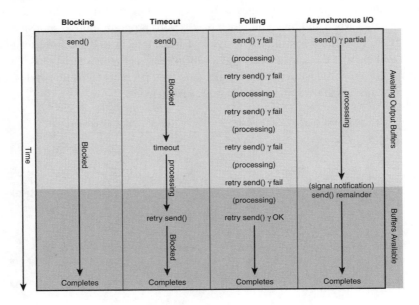

FIGURE 8.2

The write operation offers more time to the task by using buffers.

The following sections show you how to use polling, timeout, and asynchronous I/O.

Polling I/O

The program may have several things to do besides waiting for a packet. Once you call `send()` to send a message, it's not a concern how or when the message leaves the computer. As far as you are concerned, the I/O subsystem sends the message complete and intact. Often this is not the case; most messages are chopped up to fit the limitations of the network. Similarly, you may not want to get pieces of a message. Instead, you want to fill your buffer. In both cases, your program stops and waits for the task to finish.

Polling helps you avoid being blocked in I/O communication by checking to see if the channel is ready. To use polling, configure the channel for nonblocking. Then, check the return value of a system call. If the call returns `EWOULDBLK` (or `EAGAIN`), try again a little later. Programs often place this in a loop that has some localized processing, such as is found in the following polling algorithm:

```
/***********************************************************/
/*** General Polling Algorithm                        ***/
/***********************************************************/
...
while ( /*** Transferring Data ***/ )
{
    if (/*** check a channel for readiness ***/)
        /*** process the channel ***/
    /*** Do some computation ***/
}
...
```

What is important in this code segment is the computation section. Linux uses a prioritized round-robin style of scheduling. As a task does more CPU-bound processing (less I/O-bound), its effective priority increases. If you omit the computation section, your task runs in a *tight loop,* increasing scheduling favor while essentially doing nothing. Tight loops are very nasty to task scheduling. Your task can eventually dominate the scheduling time while accomplishing very little.

Also, if you can't think of anything to do while waiting for a channel to free up, don't use a delay loop or sleep(). Unless you need a real-time response, a delay loop or sleep() defeats the purpose of polling. Either use a timeout or let the program block instead.

A Polling Reader

Polling lets you get pieces of information that the task can process while waiting for more. With a polling reader, the program gets and processes data. Usually, the processing and the data read are related, and you must enable nonblocking I/O to do polling at the read/write level. Use the fcntl() system call to enable nonblocking I/O as shown here:

```
#include <fcntl.h>
int fcntl(int fd, int command, int option);
```

Similar to the read() system call, this command accepts either a file descriptor (fd) or a socket descriptor (sd). The command is F_SETFL, and the option is O_NONBLOCK. This system call has many more options. Refer to Appendix C for a more expansive listing.

```
if ( fcntl(sd, F_SETFL, O_NONBLOCK) != 0 )
    perror("Fcntl--could not set nonblocking");
```

For example, suppose you are writing an audio player plug-in. Instead of waiting for the entire clip to arrive off the Internet, you may want to play while receiving the data. Of course, since the data is probably compressed, the program has to convert the data into a machine-readable form. The program snippet might look like the code found in Listing 8.1.

LISTING 8.1   Polling Read Example

```
/*************************************************************/
/*** Polling Read Example: reading an audio stream,     ***/
/*** processing the data, and playing it.               ***/
/*************************************************************/
...
if ( fcntl(sd, F_SETFL, O_NONBLOCK) != 0 )
    perror("Fcntl--could not set nonblocking");
...
done = 0;
while ( !done )
{   int bytes;
    Queue ProcessingQueue;
    Queue OutputQueue;

    /*--- Get any pending data ---*/
    if ( (bytes = recv(sd, buffer, sizeof(buffer), 0)) > 0 )
        QueueData(ProcessingQueue, buffer);

    /*--- Convert a certain number of bytes from the ---*/
    /*--- processing queue--typically faster than recv() ---*/
    ConvertAudio(ProcessingQueue, OutputQueue);

    if ( /*** output queue is far enough ahead ***/ )
        PlayAudio(OutputQueue);

    /*--- If data stream is done & output queue empty... ---*/
    if ( bytes == 0  &&  /*---output queue empty---*/ )
        done = 1;
}
...
```

This example accepts data, enqueues it, and processes it. However, it does have a problem: If there is no data in either queue, the `while` statement becomes a tight loop. To solve this problem, you could insert a delay, since audio is a real-time issue.

Polling Writer

The program runs several times faster than any I/O function. (In fact, to improve the performance of your computer, get more memory and replace old, slow I/O. Just getting a faster CPU is not as effective.) So, when your program transmits a message or makes any request, the operating system puts your program on hold for quite a while.

The polling writer has a similar algorithm to the polling reader. It's a good idea to couple data generation and processing with the transmitter. The preparation is the same. Use the fcntl() system call with the same parameters.

The problem you may have to deal with in a polling writer is the exact opposite from the reader. The reader may have no data to work with, thus placing the reader into a tight loop. The writer can generate data more quickly than send() can transmit it (*writer pileup*).

For instance, consider the algorithm in Listing 8.2 to send photos from a digital camera to a few clients.

LISTING 8.2   Polling Writer Example

```
/*********************************************************/
/*** Polling Writer Example: sending an image to several  ***/
/*** clients.                                             ***/
/*********************************************************/
...
int pos[MAXCLIENTS];
bzero(pos, sizeof(pos));
for ( i = 0; i < ClientCount; i++ )
    if ( fcntl(client[i], F_SETFL, O_NONBLOCK) != 0 )
        perror("Fcntl--could not set nonblocking");
...
done = 0;
/*--- repeat until all the clients get the whole message ---*/
while ( !done )
{   int bytes;

    done = 1;
    /*--- For all clients... ---*/
    for ( i = 0; i < ClientCount; i++ )
        /*--- If still more to send to client... ---*/
        if ( pos[i] < size )
        {
            /*--- send msg, tracking how many bytes sent ---*/
            bytes = send(client[i], buffer+pos[i],
                size-pos[i], 0);
```

LISTING 8.2   Continued

```
            if ( bytes > 0 )
            {
                pos[i] += bytes;
                /*--- if all the clients are done, exit ---*/
                if ( pos[i] < size )
                    done = 0;
            }
        }
    }
}
...
```

In this code, the clients have to be tracked individually, because they may be accepting data at different rates. The pos integer array tracks byte position in a buffer where each client is processing. You could expand this algorithm to encompass timeouts.

Another problem may be that your server may get another image while the first is still being sent out, causing writer pileup. To solve this problem, choose one of these options:

- Append the new message onto the old.
- Cancel the last message and begin to send the new one.
- Change the camera's frame rate.

In all cases, base your choice of options on how critical the data is, how much could be lost, and how variable the connections are. See Chapter 4, "Sending Messages Between Peers," for a list of guidelines.

Polling Connections

A more rare polling algorithm involves connecting clients from different ports. The server waits for a client to connect, and typically, the server program offers only one port. While this is customary, you can have as many ports open as you want within a program. However, designers think of a program as having a specific purpose and a port as providing a specific service.

Some port services are so fundamental and trivial that writing programs for each is a waste of time, effort, and memory. But a socket may connect to only one port. Instead, consider writing a polling socket program, as shown here:

```
/**********************************************************/
/*** Polling Connection Example: check various ports for ***/
/*** connections creating a new task to answer each      ***/
```

```
/*** request.                                                 ***/
/*************************************************************/
...
/*--- Set nonblocking for each socket ---*/
for ( i = 0; i < numports; i++ )
    if ( fcntl(sd[i], F_SETFL, O_NONBLOCK) != 0 )
        perror("Fcntl--can't set nonblocking on port#%d", i);
...
for (;;)                                    /* Do this forever */
{   int client;

    for ( i = 0; i < numports; i++ )
        if ( (client = accept(sd[i], &addr, &size)) > 0 )
            SpawnServer(sd[i], i);
    /**** Do housekeeping ****/
}
...
```

This may seem like a great idea, but creating a separate task for each accept() may be more manageable. In fact, the best solution is to use the select() system call, which waits for a number of I/O channels to unblock (refer to Chapter 7, "Dividing the Load: Multitasking," for more information on select()).

Asynchronous I/O

Getting the operating system to tell you when a channel is ready for more I/O requests turns around the problem of file I/O in your favor. This affords more time for the program to spend on computation and less time stalled in various system calls.

An asynchronous read is similar to the blinking light on an office phone indicating voicemail. In the same vein, the telephone callback feature is like the asynchronous write. Picture asynchronous I/O as a notification of channel availability.

The system implements this asynchronous I/O with the SIGIO signal (sometimes called *signal-driven I/O*). Programs get a SIGIO when data is ready for reading or when a write channel is ready for more data. As with all signals, you know nothing more than a signal occurred. So, in the case of a program getting an SIGIO when two channels are open, it is not readily apparent which channel to check.

Exceptions present another problem. The kernel does not issue a signal if an error occurs on the channel. It's not readily apparent when a program loses connection with the client, unless you actually test the channel in the program.

The program begins the signal-driven I/O by instructing the kernel to accept a SIGIO signal. When the signal arrives, the signal handler sets a flag that the main program watches. The main program loop in turn begins processing, occasionally checking the flag that indicates the signal arrived. The handler may do the I/O processing itself and then flag the main loop, or it could just leave the I/O for the main loop.

How does this differ from polling? Both algorithms need to check periodically if the I/O channel is ready. Polling calls don't block the system calls but do require periodic checking. Similarly, the main loop has to poll on the flag being set by the signal-driven I/O.

The primary difference is how much time the program spends in the system calls. The signal-driven I/O spends very little time in the send() and recv() system calls: the kernel tells your program when it is ready. On the other hand, polling has to repeatedly make system calls.

The algorithm in Listing 8.3 provides a general idea how the process works.

LISTING 8.3   Signal-Driven I/O Algorithm

```
/*************************************************************/
/*** General Asynchronous or Signal-Driven I/O Algorithm   ***/
/*************************************************************/
int ready=0;
...
void sig_io(int sig)
{
    /**** IF RECV(): Get all pending data ****/
    /**** IF SEND(): Send all processed data ****/
    ready = 1;    /* tell main loop: "transaction complete" */
}
...
for (;;)
{
    if ( ready > 0 )
    {
        /**** Block SIGIO temporarily ****/
        ready = 0;
        /**** IF RECV(): copy data into processing area ****/
        /**** IF SEND(): fill output buffer from ****/
        /****     ...processed data queue ****/
        /**** Unblock SIGIO ****/
    }
    /**** Process incoming data ****/
    /**** -OR- ****/
    /**** Generate more data to send ****/
}
...
```

Blocking a SIGIO signal may appear to be a little unusual. Because the signal handler and the main loop share the same variables, you have a critical section (see the section "Mutual Exclusion (Mutex)" in Chapter 7). Turning off the signal handler is an important mutual exclusion device (mutex).

Queued Messages

To get all the pending messages, you may have to call the send() and recv() calls several times in the handler. The kernel may issue several signals at once to your program, but your program gets only one signal type at a time. If two identical signals arrive very closely together, your program gets only one.

You start the SIGIO messages using the fcntl() system call. This system call not only tells the kernel to make the socket descriptor asynchronous (remember that this applies to all file descriptors) but also tells the kernel to direct the signals to a specific process. For example, the following code segment turns on the SIGIO signals and directs them to the current task:

```
/*********************************************************/
/*** Code fragment to start the flow of SIGIO signals    ***/
/*********************************************************/
...
if ( fcntl(sd, F_SETFL, O_ASYNC | O_NONBLOCK) < 0 )
    PANIC("Can't make socket asynch & nonblocking");
if ( fcntl(sd, F_SETOWN, getpid()) < 0 )
    PANIC("Can't own SIGIO");
...
```

When your program claims ownership of the I/O signals, it claims all of them, not just SIGIO. Another signal you may get is SIGURG, used in getting out-of-band data. For more information see the section "Sending High-Priority Messages" in Chapter 9, "Breaking Performance Barriers."

On-Demand Reading

Programs can process data as it arrives using an asynchronous read, or *on-demand reading*. As the data arrives, the kernel signals the program. The program picks it up and then processes it. As in a factory or assembly line, the needed materials arrive and move along.

The best use of this feature is one that does a lot of CPU computation while waiting for a single source of data. (Please keep in mind that although several channels may be open for I/O, you need to check it manually to see which channel issued the signal.) Consider using a Virtual Reality Modeling Language (VRML) document for this task, as shown in Listing 8.4.

LISTING 8.4 Asynchronous Processing Algorithm

```
/*************************************************************/
/*** VRML Async Reading Example: process data while      ***/
/*** waiting for more to arrive.                         ***/
/*************************************************************/
int ready=0, bytes;
...
void sig_io(int sig)
{
    /*--- get pending message ---*/
    bytes = recv(server, buffer, sizeof(buffer), 0);
    if ( bytes < 0 )
        perror("SIGIO");
    ready = 1;     /* tell main loop: "transaction complete" */
}
...
/*--- Enable Asynchronous, Nonblocking I/O ---*/
if ( fcntl(sd, F_SETFL, O_ASYNC | O_NONBLOCK) < 0 )
    PANIC("Can't make socket asynch & nonblocking");
/*--- Claim ownership of SIGIO and SIGURG ---*/
if ( fcntl(sd, F_SETOWN, getpid()) < 0 )
    PANIC("Can't own SIGIO");
while ( !done )
{
    if ( ready > 0 )
    {
        /**** Block SIGIO temporarily ****/
        ready = 0;
        FillQueue(Queue, buffer, bytes);
        /**** Unblock SIGIO ****/
    }
    /**** Process incoming data for a short time in the  ****/
    /**** VRML rasterizer, or until the variable "ready" ****/
    /**** changes.                                       ****/
}
...
```

Again, avoid doing much in the signal handler. Your handler, in this circumstance, could simply notify the main loop to load the data itself. But, because the queue manager may use memory management, filling the image processing queue should be done outside of the handler.

> ## Trigger-Happy Read Events
>
> The receive buffer notifies the task when it passes the low-water mark (the minimum number of bytes required before the kernel issues a SIGIO). The low-water mark is set to 1 by default, so your program could get signaled every time the buffers get 1 byte. On some systems, it's possible to change this to a greater value with setsockopt() (see Chapter 9). However, Linux does not appear to support writing to this parameter.

Asynchronous Writes

You program the asynchronous write a bit differently because of the kernel's buffers. When your program first calls send(), it's likely that the kernel's buffers can store the entire data block. But it's also possible that it can't, and the kernel caches only a part.

So, check the return value of every write() to make sure that all the data gets sent. It may even be essential for you to keep all outgoing data for a channel in a single queue. This reduces the code complexity involved with multiple buffers. Still, making the buffering flexible is important as well, so that the queue may grow and shrink as needed.

A database query example serves well in this situation. It generates lots of data that can be processed or gathered while sending the reply, as shown in Listing 8.5.

LISTING 8.5   *Asynchronous Writer Algorithm*

```
/*****************************************************************/
/*** Database Query Async Writer Example: process query    ***/
/*** while generating results.                             ***/
/*****************************************************************/
int ready=0, bytes, size=0, pos=0;
...
int sig_io(int sig)
{
    if ( size > 0 )
    {
        bytes = send(client, buffer, size+pos, 0);
        if ( bytes > 0 )
        {
            pos += bytes;
            ready = 1;
        }
    }
}
...
```

LISTING 8.5 Continued

```
/**** Enable nonblocking, signal-driven I/O; claim SIGIO ****/
while ( !done )
{
    if ( /*** channel available ***/ )
        /*** Send message, no blocking ***/
else
    /*** queue message ***/
}
...
```

Every time the channel clears and is ready for more data, the kernel sends the process a
SIGIO signal. Use that signal as shown in the previous example to funnel data out in an
on-demand way.

On-Demand Connections

You can create an on-demand connection server (theoretically). Essentially it looks like an on-
demand reader, but instead of reading a file, the program calls accept(). The handler needs
three global variables to communicate with the main loop: the socket acceptor (sd), an array of
descriptors, and the current number of connections. Any local variable your signal handler creates is lost at the end of the handler.

The handler might look like this:

```
/*************************************************************/
/*** On-Demand Connection Example:  Make connection in    ***/
/*** signal handler.  Main loop cycles though each open   ***/
/*** socket for messages. (Excerpt from demand-accept.c   ***/
/*** on CD.)                                              ***/
/*************************************************************/
...
int Connections[MAXCONNECTIONS];
int sd, NumConnections=0;
void sig_io(int sig)
{   int client;

    /*--- Accept connection. If too many, error & close ---*/
    if ( (client = accept(sd, 0, 0) > 0 )
        if ( NumConnections < MAXCONNECTIONS )
            Connections[NumConnections++] = client;
        else
        {
            send(client, "Too many connections!\n", 22, 0);
```

```
                close(client);
          }
     else
          perror("Accept");
}
...
```

While an on-demand server is useful, the clear advantage of multitasking is that it allows you to retain the local variables, and it sets aside a specific task for each connection.

Unless your server is prone to task-overload (the program creates so many processes that the performance drops), using on-demand connections may encumber your programming. For all the effort in designing and implementing an on-demand connection server, you probably won't get the same bang for the buck. It's simply easier to use either the multitasking or polling technique.

Solving Unwanted I/O Blocking with `poll()` and `select()`

Linux offers two tools to help you work with multiple open channels at the same time. These tools are more efficient (and may be easier to implement) than manual polling. The whole idea behind each tool is that the system call blocks until any channel changes state.

A state change includes conditions such as data being available to read, a channel is clear for writing, or an error occurred. Upon return, one or many of the channels may have changed state. The return value from the call represents the number of channels that changed.

However, the `select()` system call is a little more complex and involves several macros to help manage the descriptor lists:

```
#include <sys/time.h>
#include <sys/types.h>
#include <unistd.h>
int select(int maxfd, fd_set *to_read, fd_set *to_write,
    fd_set *except, struct timeval *timeout);
FD_CLR(int fd, fd_set *set);          /* remove fd from set */
FD_ISSET(int fd, fd_set *set);     /* check if fd is in set */
FD_SET(int fd, fd_set *set);            /* add fd to set */
FD_ZERO(fd_set *set);             /* initialize set for use */
```

The main routine is the `select()` system call. It has several helper macros (`FD_CLR()`, `FD_ISSET()`, `FD_SET()`, `FD_ZERO()`) to manage the descriptor lists. The parameters are defined in Table 8.3.

TABLE 8.3   Parameters for the `select()` System Call

Parameter	Description
maxfd	One more than the highest-numbered file descriptor in the set. (See below for more.)
to_read	The set of descriptors that await reading. This is the set that you want to test for reading.
to_write	The set of descriptors that await writing.
except	The set of descriptors that await priority messages.
timeout	The time in microseconds to wait before giving up. (See below for more details.)
fd	The file descriptor to add, delete, or test for.
set	The set of descriptors to manipulate.

The `maxfd` parameter is the highest-numbered descriptor slot in any of the three sets plus 1. Each task gets a number of I/O descriptor slots (typically 1024). Each I/O channel occupies a slot (`stdin` is 0, `stdout` is 1, and `stderr` is 2). If the sets had descriptors [3,6] in `to_read`, [4,5,6] in `to_write`, and [3,4] in `except`, `maxfd` becomes 6 (the highest descriptor number) plus 1, or 7.

The `timeout` parameter gives you the flexibility of setting a limit to how long the system call waits:

- If `NULL`, wait indefinitely.
- If positive, wait the specified microseconds.
- If zero, return immediately after checking all descriptors once.

For example, if you had three channels open to clients numbered [3,4,6], you could wait for them to send the program data like this:

```
/***********************************************************/
/*** Select() Example.                                 ***/
/***********************************************************/
int count;
fd_set set
struct timeval timeout;
...
FD_ZERO(&set);                             /* Clear set */
FD_SET(3, &set);           /* Add client channel #3 */
FD_SET(4, &set);           /* Add client channel #4 */
FD_SET(6, &set);           /* Add client channel #6 */
```

```
timeout.tv_sec = 5;              /* Timeout after 5.25 seconds */
timeout.tv_usec = 250000;

/*--- Wait for select() ---*/
if ( (count = select(6+1, &set, 0, 0, &timeout)) > 0 )
    /**** Find the descriptors that changed ****/
else if ( count == 0 )
    fprintf(stderr, "Timed out!");
else
    perror("Select");
...
```

In this example, when the `select()` system call returns with a positive value, one of the three channels has data to read. To find out which channel is ready, add the code needed and read in the data. However, if the return value is zero, the call exceeded the 5.25-second time limit.

The `poll()` system call is similar to `select()` and may be a little easier to manage. It uses an array of structures to define the behavior:

```
struct pollfd
{
    int fd;         /* the descriptor to test */
    short events;   /* requested events to watch */
    short revents;  /* events that fired */
};
```

The first field, `fd`, is the file or socket descriptor. The second and third fields, `events` and `revents`, are bit masks for specific events:

- `POLLERR`   Any error condition. Return if any error occurs on channel.
- `POLLHUP`   Hang-up on other end. Return if peer hangs up.
- `POLLIN`   Incoming data. Return if data ready for reading.
- `POLLINVAL`   fd not open. Return if the channel is not an open file or socket.
- `POLLPRI`   Priority messages. Return if a priority message arrives.
- `POLLOUT`   Channel availability. Return if a `write()` won't block.

The system call to `poll()` looks like this:

```
#include <sys/poll.h>
int poll(struct pollfd *list, unsigned int cnt, int timeout);
```

The program fills an array of `pollfd` structures before it uses this system call. The cnt parameter is the number of legal socket descriptors in the array. (Remember to keep these descriptors contiguous; if one closes, compress the array. Not all implementations deal well with an empty slot.) The `timeout` parameter acts like the `select()` timeout but in milliseconds.

Either the select() or the poll() system calls provide the power to monitor several channels at the same time. With good planning, you can avoid some of the overhead problems multitasking encounters.

Implementing Timeouts

A simple alternative to polling I/O channels is to tell the operating system that you do not want to wait longer than a specified time. The Linux system calls do not provide a direct way of doing this. Consider using these ways to implement timeouts:

- With the timeout in the select() or poll() system call
- With a signal (SIGALRM) to wake up the task

Linux Socket Timeout Support

The socket options include timeouts for sending (SO_SNDTIMEO) and receiving (SO_RCVTIMEO). Unfortunately, these parameters are read-only for now; on Linux, they default to OFF. If you try to port some code that uses these parameters, you may have to use the other two methods.

The select() and poll() system calls (described previously) supply a timeout parameter in microseconds. Using these system calls is perhaps the easiest way to implement timeouts, but the timeouts apply to all channels in the call.

This situation can be a problem: Suppose you have three channels, and one of them is not very responsive. Using just these system calls, you cannot detect that the failing channel should have timed out and closed. You can manually keep individual times for each channel, resetting the time with each response. Still, that may be a lot of unnecessary checking and logging.

You can use an alternative instead: an alarm signal. An *alarm* is a clock that runs in the kernel. When the alarm goes off, the kernel sends a wakeup call to the task in the form of a signal. If the task is waiting in a system call, the signal interrupts the call, the task enters the signal handler, and then the system call returns with an EINTR error.

Every task can send itself a signal, but the task needs to know what to do with the signal. On some systems, the sleep library call uses the alarm() system call, first setting up the task to capture the SIGALRM signal. Please look at the following example:

```
/**************************************************************/
/*** Example: Timeout example using the alarm() system     ***/
/*** call. (Excerpt from echo-timeout.c on CD.)            ***/
/**************************************************************/
...
```

```
int sig_alarm(int sig)
{/*** do nothing ***/}
...
void reader()
{    struct sigaction act;

    /*--- Initialize signal structure; reset to default ---*/
    bzero(&act, sizeof(act));
    act.sa_handler = sig_alarm;
    act.sa_flags = SA_ONESHOT;

    /*--- Set the signal handler ---*/
    if ( sigaction(SIGALRM, &act, 0) != 0 )
        perror("Could not set up timeout");
    else
        /*--- If signal handler installed, set timer ---*/
        alarm(TIMEOUT_SEC);

    /*--- Call the I/O that might timeout ---*/
    if ( recv(sd, buffer, sizeof(buffer), 0) < 0 )
    {
        if ( errno == EINTR )
            perror("Timed-out!");
    }
}
...
```

The example shown sets up the signal handler, sets the timer, and calls the I/O. If recv() gets no data by the time the timer expires, the task gets a signal. The signal interrupts the recv() system call, and the system call returns with an error (EINTR).

To get this behavior, leave off the SA_RESTART option from the sa_flags field. Chapter 7 advises you to include this option with signals. In that case, omit this option for the timeout timer to work.

One final note: Avoid using the alarm() system call with sleep(), because it can cause problems in your program. Instead, use the Linux SIGALRM signal or use sleep()—don't mix them.

Summary: Choosing the I/O Techniques

The network program interacts with other programs through the network. Since the performance and response times vary from machine to machine and network to network, it's important to know when and how to use nonblocking I/O to improve the I/O management in your clients and servers.

Used carefully and properly balanced, blocking and nonblocking I/O increases your client's and server's responsiveness to the user.

This chapter covered several topics on blocking (what it is, when it's useful, why it's used) and nonblocking (what are the different types, when to use them, how to use them). It discussed the main tool to select nonblocking I/O: the `fcntl()` system call.

The two primary nonblocking tools are polling and asynchronous I/O. Polling repeatedly tries to use an I/O system call. Asynchronous (or signal-driven) I/O places the burden on the kernel to determine when a channel is free. Polling focuses on the I/O, while signal-driven I/O focuses on local processing.

Another tool to manage blocking is a timeout. You can deploy timeouts in the `select()` or `poll()` system call or use a timer signal that wakes up the process when a call takes too long.

Breaking Performance Barriers

IN THIS CHAPTER

How do you get everything out of your server or client? Linux has several tools in the Sockets API that make this process relatively straightforward. However, you have to look at the programming problem from several angles at the same time, because each aspect touches on and affects another.

Your network program has three distinct aspects: the task, the connection, and the messages. You work with each one of these in the course of the program. The task involves working with all related processes, or threads. The connection is the socket itself and its behavior, and the messages interact with the I/O processing that receives and sends messages. To get the most out of your network program, you have to balance the tasks with the messaging. The socket enables you to specialize the connection to meet your needs.

This chapter takes you through several ideas and best practices that address the task, connection and messaging. You need to know the concepts presented in previous chapters to fully use these algorithms.

Creating the Servlets Before the Client Arrives

To this point you have seen how to create a server, implement multitasking, and control I/O blocking. Each of these building blocks helps you interact with your clients and control the throughput. Chapter 7, "Dividing the Load: Multitasking," showed you how to delegate the task of accepting and serving incoming connections, creating child processes as you need them.

On some systems, however, creating a new task each time consumes time and resources. Also, you may not want to dedicate the entire computer resources to just serving network clients. (On the other hand, you *may* want to do just that, but there are logical and effective limits you must place on server access to ensure performance.) You may have other programs that need to execute on a regular basis, or even local/remote logins. In any form, you need to control the growth of your server program. And, controlling the number of connections requires extra programming.

Placing a Cap on the Number of Client Connections

If you recall from the previous chapters, the server creates a new child process as soon as the client connects. Your program has to change here to incorporate the control over too many processes (once called *rabbit processes* because they multiply too quickly to control). The standard algorithm that follows does just that.

```
/******************************************************************/
/*** Standard create-processes-as-you-go algorithm          ***/
/*** ("test-server.c" on the Web site)                      ***/
/******************************************************************/
int sd;
```

```
struct sockaddr_in addr;
if ( (sd   = socket(PF_INET, SOCK_STREAM, 0)) < 0 )
    PANIC("socket() failed");
bzero(&addr, sizeof(addr));
addr.sin_family = AF_INET;
addr.sin_port = htons(MY_PORT);
addr.sin_addr = INADDR_ANY;
if ( bind(sd, &addr, sizeof(addr)) != 0 )
    PANIC("bind() failed");
if ( listen(sd, 20) != 0 )
    PANIC("listen() failed");
for (;;)
{   int client, len=sizeof(addr);
    client = accept(sd, &addr, &len);
    if ( client > 0 )
    {   int pid
        if ( (pid = fork()) == 0 )
        {
            close(sd);
            Child(client); /*---Serve the new client---*/
        }
        else if ( pid > 0 )
            close(client);
        else
            perror("fork() failed");
    }
}
```

You saw this algorithm in Chapter 7, and it serves a long-term connection very well. Long-term connections include logins, database interfacing, and any other interaction where the client and server correspond for several iterations.

This algorithm has a major flaw: What happens if you run out of PIDs? What happens if you start thrashing your swap because you don't have enough RAM to support the number of processes? This is exactly the problem with rabbit process generators.

Difference Between RAM and Memory

You may think that the virtual memory system with all your swap space can save your system. Actually, that's quite misleading. When you want performance, you need to keep all the active processes with their data available in RAM. If they become swapped out, the time that the kernel requires to load it back in wipes out any perception of speed. Knowing your system, the memory, processors, and I/O is the first hurdle to squeezing out performance.

One method you could try is keeping count of processes:

```
/****************************************************************/
/*** Algorithm revised to limit the number of children    ***/
/*** ("capped-servlets.c" on Web site)                    ***/
/****************************************************************/
int ChildCount=0;

void sig_child(int sig)
{
    wait(0);
    ChildCount--;
}
...
for (;;)
{   int client, len=sizeof(addr);
    while ( ChildCount >= MAXCLIENTS )
        sleep(1);   /*---You could "sched_yield()" instead---*/
    client = accept(sd, &addr, &len);
    if ( client > 0 )
    {   int pid
        if ( (pid = fork()) == 0 )
        {/*---CHILD---*/
            close(sd);
            Child(client); /*---Serve the new client---*/
        }
        else if ( pid > 0 )
        {/*---PARENT---*/
            ChildCount++;
            close(client);
        }
        else
            perror("fork() failed");
    }
}
```

In this example, the parent keeps track of the number of children. If there are too many children, the server simply yields the CPU until one of the connections closes and the child terminates. You can use this method rather easily and, because the only writer to the ChildCount variable is the server and its signal handler, you don't have to worry about race conditions.

Again, this algorithm works well for your long-term connections. However, if you have a lot of short-term, single-transaction connections, the cost of creating and terminating child processes can eat away at your server's performance. The idea is to have a set of processes running, all waiting for a connection to arrive.

Preforking Your Servers

Your server could have 5–20 processes waiting for a connection to arrive. This is what the distribution-loaded HTTP server does. (If you have HTTPD installed and running, look at your process table and you may see several instances of it running.) How does the child get the data if the processes don't share data? The answer is in the following code fragment.

```
/***********************************************************/
/*** Code fragment of the child process             ***/
/***********************************************************/
if ( (pid = fork()) == 0 )
{
    close(sd);
    Child(client); /*---Serve the new client---*/
}
```

This excerpt shows the child closing the socket descriptor (sd). The client socket descriptor provides the connection to your client. Why does the child close sd?

When you create a child process, the child shares the open file of the parent. If the child doesn't need that file, it should close it. However, the child could leave the file open and read or write just like the parent. This leads to how you may create several processes serving the same socket:

```
/***********************************************************/
/*** Creating a set of child-servers to await connection  ***/
/*** ("preforking-servlets.c" on Web site)            ***/
/***********************************************************/
int ChildCount=0;

void sig_child(int sig)
{
    wait(0);
    ChildCount--;
}
...
main()
{
    /**** Attach signal; create & bind socket ****/
    for (;;)
    {
        if ( ChildCount < MAXPROCESSES )
        {
            if ( (pid = fork()) == 0 )        /*---CHILD---*/
                for (;;)
                {
```

```
        int client = accept(sd, 0, 0);
            Child(client);   /*---Serve new client---*/
        }
    else if ( pid > 0 )                 /*---PARENT---*/
        ChildCount++;
    else                                /*---ERROR---*/
        perror("fork() failed");
    }
    else
        sched_yield();                  /*--- OR, sleep(1)---*/
    }
}
```

This reverses the order of the `accept()` and `fork()`: Instead of creating the process after a connection, this algorithm waits for the connection after creating the child processes.

This code fragment may create 10 processes, for example. All the child processes enter the forever loop waiting for and processing connections. Assuming no connections are waiting, all 10 processes I/O block (sleep). When a connection arrives, all of the process wake up, but only one gets the connection. The remaining nine go back to sleep. This cycle continues indefinitely.

What happens if one of the child processes crashes or terminates? This is why the parent never makes the `accept()` system call. The parent's primary role is to make sure that the correct number of children are always available.

At first, the parent creates the quota of child processes. When a child terminates, the signal handler picks up the notification and decrements the quota by one. When the parent resumes, it creates a new child. If the parent does not need to create more, it yields the timeslice to another task.

Adapting to Different Load Levels

The parent's primary responsibility is to make sure that enough child processes are available to serve the incoming connections. This responsibility must be balanced against your computer's resource load. If you are not careful, the clients may begin to drop off due to timeouts because your server does not have enough listeners serving connections.

Using a dedicated number of listeners (*servlets*) forces a limit on the number of active connections. This is the primary restriction on having preforked servlets. Nevertheless, the idea of limiting the number of processes that your program creates and destroys is a good one. It lessens the turmoil on your process table and system resources. What might be a good way to minimize creation and destruction while meeting the needs of connecting clients?

You could make the servlet algorithm adaptable to the demands of the system. Your server has to respond to two different challenges: knowing when to create more servlets and knowing when to terminate extra ones. The second challenge is simple: The servlet terminates itself if it is idle for a while.

The first challenge, knowing when to create more servlets, is not so direct. You may recall that every TCP server has a listening queue (that is what the `listen()` system call does). The network subsystem enqueues every connection request, and the `accept()` system call acknowledges and creates a dedicated channel to the client. If a client sits in a queue too long, it may only wait for a couple of minutes before giving up.

Being able to see how many pending connections the queue has and what is the longest waiting request might help server tuning. You could use this information to monitor the system's responsiveness to the requests. As the queue fills, the server can create more servlets. If the connection delay gets too long, you may simply adjust the servlet's self-termination delay. Unfortunately, this is not something that the API calls offer. If you want servlet adaptability, you must use another approach.

One method of creating new servlets to respond to a volume of requests is like chumming fish. Where legal, fishermen cast out samples (chum) of different kinds of bait. The bait the fish eats is the bait the fisherman uses. The fish's response also indicates how large the school is.

Like chumming, the server throws out an extra servlet every once in a while. As long as the same number of extras terminate as were created (because there's nothing to do), the server continues this process. When the servlets stop terminating, your server increases the number of extra servlets it creates until the number stabilizes again.

The purpose of preforking is to minimize the time of creating and cleaning up after servlets. Creating and terminating servlets haphazardly brings you back to forking for every new connection. You have to plan carefully to avoid this result. Also, your algorithm must have a minimum number of servlets running for this to work.

This is where statistics help a little. The adapting algorithm has to face three possibilities: The number of connections is stable, it is increasing, or it is decreasing. If the number of connections is stable, the server sees the same number of servlets terminating as are created during a given period of time. For example, if your server creates a servlet every 60 seconds (with a 30-second idle timeout), you may see the first pattern in the diagram in Figure 9.1.

If the number of connections is increasing, there are fewer being terminated than there are being created. If your server does not see a termination within the prescribed time, you can assume that it is serving a connection. At that point, your server doubles the rate of servlet creation (see the second pattern in Figure 9.1). This process continues until the number of servlets hits a ceiling or your server reaches the maximum creation frequency (every 5 seconds, perhaps).

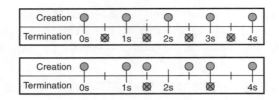

FIGURE 9.1

Extra servlets are thrown out to see if connections are pending.

Again, suppose your server creates a new servlet every 60 seconds (with a 30-second idle time-out). If the extra servlet does not terminate within the prescribed time, you can cut in half the time delay between creations, thus doubling the frequency. You can repeat this process until the connection rate begins to stabilize.

Finally, when the connections begin to dwindle, the pending connections (if any exist) have more than enough servlets for the queue, and the server begins to see servlet termination. When the extra servlets begin to terminate, you can reset the server's frequency to normal.

```
/*************************************************************/
/***   Chumming connections example                     ***/
/***   ("servlet-chummer.c" on Web site)                ***/
/*************************************************************/
int delay=MAXDELAY;                 /* for example, 5 seconds */
time_t lasttime;
void sig_child(int signum)
{
    wait(0);                        /* Acknowledge termination */
    time(&lasttime);                    /* get the time stamp */
    delay = MAXDELAY;                   /* reset chummer back */
}


void Chummer(void (*servlet)(void))
{
    time(&lasttime);                    /* Initialize timestamp */
    for (;;)
    {
        if ( !fork() )                  /* first, set the chum */
            servlet();  /* call the task (must have exit()) */
        sleep(delay);                   /* dream for a while */
        /* If no child terminated, double frequency        */
        if ( time(0) - times[1] >= delay-1 )
            if ( delay > MINDELAY )  /* don't go below min */
                delay /= 2;         /* double chum frequency */
    }
}
```

This code fragment shows how to track the formation of servlets and test for a load increase by noting the time that the last child terminated. The termination also resets the timer so that the current connection can stabilize and the process can restart.

Extending Control with a Smart Select

Using processes to manage the flow of connections is an intuitive way to distribute the tasks. Furthermore, placing limits on the number of processes running and preforking the processes ensure that the connections get the attention they require. There is a fundamental problem, however, with all these approaches: the scheduler storm.

The Scheduler Storm

The scheduler storm presents two problems that expose you to the limits of multitasking and the reasons why single-CPU systems can become overwhelmed. The first problem shows the effect a large process table has on servlets. The second problem affects the preforking concept.

The process table can easily handle a few hundred processes. Depending on memory and swap, theoretically you could have many more. Still, consider the limits: Linux switches between processes every 10ms. This does not include the time delay of unloading old process contexts and loading a new one.

For example, if you had 200 servlets running, each process could wait 2 seconds for a small slice of CPU time on a system that switches tasks every .01 second. If each timeslice could send out 1KB within that small slice, you may see about 200KBps throughput on the 10Mbps LAN connection (about par for TCP/IP). However, each connection gets only 512 bytes per second. This is the primary risk of letting the process table grow without barrier.

The second problem is at the heart of preforking: Several processes all wait for one connection. Your server may have 20 servlets I/O blocked when a connection request arrives. Since all are waiting for a connection, the kernel awakes all 20. The first one gets the connection, while all the rest return to an I/O blocked state. Some programmers call this a *scheduling storm* or a *thundering herd*. In either case, this problem emphasizes the need to minimize the number of waiting servlets and adapting based on the connection load.

> ### Solving the Thundering Herd in the Kernel
> One of the problems with writing a book on an ever-evolving technology like Linux is that the information becomes obsolete very quickly. Linux 2.4 solved the thundering herd problem in the kernel by waking up only one I/O-blocked process.

Overburdened `select()`

One solution to these problems is to avoid multitasking altogether. In a previous chapter you read about the I/O multiplexer system calls: `select()` and `poll()`. These system calls could act in a similar manner as several processes.

Instead of 20 servlet processes all waiting for a connection, you could offer one process that waits for a connection. When the connection request arrives, the server places the connection (the client channel) in an I/O list. These system calls wait for any one to send a request or command. The system call returns to your server with the channels that are ready, and your server retrieves and processes the command.

The temptation to skip multitasking altogether and use these multiplexers may lead to some loss in performance. When using a single task to process information, your program or server has to wait for I/O at various times during the life of the process. If you don't take advantage of this downtime, your servers may lose significant opportunities to do other things. For example, if you have ever compiled the kernel, you may find that it compiles in less time if you force multiple jobs with the `-j` make option. (If you have the memory, two or three jobs per processor cuts the compilation time noticeably.)

Compromising with a Smart Select

As you create your high-powered, high-demand server, you can use various ways to distribute the load. Two are multitasking and I/O multiplexing. However, if used exclusively, multitasking may lose control of the scheduler and erode precious time to context switching, while I/O multiplexing loses unused CPU bandwidth. An alternative to using either exclusively is a combination of both. Combining the two into a *Smart Select* could help you diminish the disadvantages of each, while giving you their capabilities.

A Smart Select dispatches a few processes. Each process owns a connection channel and a set of open client channels. An I/O multiplexer manages all of the channels. Here is an algorithm for the process:

```
/*************************************************************/
/*** Smart Select example: each child tries to accept a    ***/
/*** connection.  If successful, it adds the connection    ***/
/*** to the select() list.                                 ***/
/*** ("smart-select.c" on Web site)                        ***/
/*************************************************************/
int sd, maxfd=0;
fd_set set;
FD_ZERO(&set);

/*** Create socket and fork() processes ***/
```

```
/*---In Child---*/
maxfd = sd;
FD_SET(sd, &set);
for (;;)
{   struct timeval timeout={2,0};              /* 2 seconds */
    /*---Wait for some action---*/
    if ( select(maxfd+1, &set, 0, 0, &timeout) > 0 )     —— Smart
    {
        /*---If new connection, connect and add to list---*/
        if ( FD_ISSET(sd, &set) )
        {   int client = accept(sd, 0, 0);
            if ( maxfd < client )
                maxfd = client;
            FD_SET(client, &set);
        }
        /*---If command/request from client, process---*/
        else
            /*** Process client's request ***/
            /*** If client just closed, remove from list ***/
    }
}
```

You can use this algorithm to create a few processes—much less than the number you can create in a purely multitasking server—for example, 5–10 servlets. Each servlet, in turn, could support 5–10 connections.

Select Collision ✓

You may have heard of a BSD problem called *select collision*. The previous algorithm assumes that the select() can wait on several descriptors and wake up only when the descriptors change state. The BSD 4.4 implementation has a limitation that causes all processes blocked in a select() to wake up. It appears that Linux does not have this limitation.

This approach could easily support hundreds of connections without interfering with each other. The balance between the number of tasks and the number of connection helps minimize the impact on the process table. However, having so many connections can lead to problems if you need to track your protocol's state.

You can use this algorithm easily with stateless servers. A stateless connection remembers nothing about previous transactions. This requires all transactions sent to your server to have no relationship with other transactions or each connection to have a single transaction. Also, if your server requires short- to medium-term connections, you can use this approach. Some examples are an HTTP server, a DB query server, and a Web redirector.

Implementation Problems

As you might have noticed, this approach does have a couple of limitations. First, the primary server cannot balance the number of connections between each servlet. You can add code to place a ceiling on the number of connections:

```
/*********************************************************/
/*** Limiting the number of connections to a servlet     ***/
/*********************************************************/
if ( FD_ISSET(sd, &set) )
    if ( ceiling < MAXCONNECTIONS )
    {   int client = accept(sd, 0, 0);
        if ( maxfd < client )
            maxfd = client;
        FD_SET(client, &set);
        ceiling++;
    }
```

This approach effectively yields the connection to another servlet. However, the distribution of connections between your servlets may be random.

The other problem is with regard to the context of your connection. When a client connects to your server, unless it is a single-transaction connection, your server passes through different states. For example, state one is login and state two is a session.

The previous code fragment always returns to the point of waiting for and getting some message. If you want to incorporate states, you must track where each connection is. With this information, you can program the servlet to compare the connection with the message it receives. It's not difficult, but you have to plan your program a little more.

The last limitation of this algorithm is its support of long-term (deep transaction) connections. This algorithm remains stable, if you have a client and server doing single transactions or short interactions. However, deep transaction connections usually require multiple states. This complicates your server tremendously. Also, because the connection is active longer, the possibility of getting your load out of balance increases.

Redistributing the Load

You can solve the load distribution limitation if you switch to threads instead of using processes. As described above, the server cannot easily distribute the number of connections per task. (You can do this with IPC, but it's more trouble than it's worth.) Threading lets you share everything between tasks, including the file descriptor table.

In a similar vein, your server may have several threads running, making it difficult to assign connections. You have a descriptor array and can use the poll() system call. (You can use the select() call, but the algorithm is not as straightforward.) Each thread owns one portion of the array. This works only if the parent accepts all connections. When your server sees a connection request, the parent accepts it and places it in the array of descriptors.

Depending on the implementation of poll(), your threads may have to time out frequently so that they can pick up any changes to the descriptor array. A few implementations simply cycle through testing each descriptor; others (more likely used in Linux) actually register the descriptors into a system call. The system call waits and reports on descriptor activity. Therefore, if the parent adds a new descriptor, the thread must call poll() again to begin processing it.

```
/****************************************************************/
/*** Fair load distribution example: parent accepts       ***/
/*** and assigns connections to various threads.           ***/
/*** ("fair-load.c" on Web site)                           ***/
/****************************************************************/
int fd_count=0;
struct pollfd fds[MAXFDs]; /* cleared with bzero() */

/*---parent---*/
int sd = socket(PF_INET, SOCK_STREAM, 0);
/***Bind() and listen() socket***/
for (;;)
{   int i;
    /*--- Find an available slot before accepting conn. ---*/
    for ( i = 0; i < fd_count; i++ )
        if ( fds[i].events == 0 )
            break;
    if ( i == fd_count  &&  fd_count < MAXFDs )
        fd_count++;
    /*---If you have an available slot, accept connection---*/
    if ( i < fd_count )
    {
        fds[i].fd = accept(sd, 0, 0);
        fds[i].events = POLLIN | POLLHUP;
    }
    else                /* otherwise, yield for a little while */
        sleep(1);                  /* or, some yielding delay */
}

/*---child---*/
void *Servlet(void *init)
{   int start = *(int*)init;       /* get the fd-range start */
    for (;;)
    {   int result;
```

```
                              /* wait for only 0.5 second */
        if ( (result = poll(fds+start, RANGE, 500)) > 0 )
        {   int i;
            for ( i = 0; i < RANGE; i++ )
            {
                if ( fds[I].revents & POLLIN )
                    /*** Process incoming message ***/
                else if ( fds[I].revents & POLLHUP )
                    /*** close connection ***/
            }
        }
        else if ( result < 0 )
            perror("poll() error");
    }
}
```

This shows the responsibilities of the parent and the children. The parent accepts connections and places them in the fds[] array. The children wait on each range of connections. (If the events field in the pollfd structure is zero, your call to poll() skips that entry. If the array has no active descriptors, poll() just waits for the timeout period before returning zero.)

Your client program can use the advantages of a threaded connection as well. As you read in Chapter 7, threads do very well in sending out multiple independent requests, gathering the information, and summarizing it. Your client can do all this in tandem, because most of the time spent in network communication is waiting for the servers. Since threads inherently share their data, you can fire off several requests and interpret some results while waiting for the rest.

Delving Deeper into Socket Control

Controlling your algorithms around the sockets and connections is one part of increasing server and client performance. You also need to control the socket itself. Previous chapters mention a few options you can use to configure the socket to your needs. This section defines many more.

You can control all socket configuration options using the getsockopt() and setsockopt() system calls. These system calls configure general and protocol-specific options of your socket. Appendix A, "Data Tables," has a summary of all available options. The prototypes for these calls are as follows:

```
int getsockopt(int sd, int level, int optname, void *optval,
    socklen_t *optlen);
int setsockopt(int sd, int level, int optname,
    const void *optval, socklen_t optlen);
```

Every option has a level. Currently, Linux defines four socket levels: SOL_SOCKET, SOL_IP, SOL_IPV6, and SOL_TCP. Each option has a type: Boolean, integer, or structure. When you set or get an option, you place the option in optval and declare the size of the value in optlen. When you get an option, the call returns the number of bytes it used through optlen.

For example, if you want to disable SO_KEEPALIVE, use the following:

```
/*********************************************************/
/*** setsockopt() example: disable keepalive          ***/
/*********************************************************/
int value=0; /* FALSE */
if ( setsockopt(sd, SOL_SOCKET, SO_KEEPALIVE, &value,
        sizeof(value)) != 0 )
    perror("setsockopt() failed");
```

Likewise, if you want to know the socket type (SO_TYPE), you can use this example:

```
/*********************************************************/
/*** getsockopt() example: socket type                ***/
/*********************************************************/
int value;
int val_size = sizeof(value);
if ( getsockopt(sd, SOL_SOCKET, SO_TYPE, &value,
        &val_size) != 0 )
    perror("getsockopt() failed");
```

The following sections define each of the options you can use.

General Options

The general options apply to all sockets. The level for these options is SOL_SOCKET.

- SO_BROADCAST   This option permits your socket to send and receive broadcast messages. The broadcast address sets the active subnet bits (see Chapter 2, "TCP/IP Network Language Fluency") to all ones. Not all networks support broadcasting (ethernet and token ring do). Those networks that do support it allow only datagram messages. (Boolean, disabled by default.)

- SO_DEBUG   This option enables logging of information about all messages sent or received. TCP is the only protocol that supports this feature. To learn how to read this queue, refer to the TCPv2 RFC. (Boolean, disabled by default.)

- SO_DONTROUTE   In rare circumstances, you may not want your packets routed to get to the destination. An example of this is router configuration packets. This option enables/disables routing. (Boolean, disabled by default.)

- SO_ERROR   Get and clear any pending socket error. If you do not pick up this error before the next I/O operation, errno gets the error. (Integer, 0 by default, get only.)

- `SO_KEEPALIVE`   If your TCP socket does not hear from the external host for 2 hours, it sends a series of messages trying to reestablish connection or determine a problem. If it finds a problem, the socket posts an error and closes itself. (Boolean, enabled by default.)

- `SO_LINGER`   The socket does not close immediately if it still has data in its buffers. The `close()` system call flags your socket for closure (without closing it) and returns immediately. This option tells the socket to force your program to wait until the close completes. It uses the `linger` structure, which has two fields: `l_onoff` (enable/disable lingering) and `l_linger` (maximum wait in seconds). If enabled and `l_linger` is zero, a socket close aborts the connection and drops all buffered data. On the other hand, if `l_linger` is nonzero, a socket-close waits for the data to transmit or times out. (`struct linger`, disabled by default.)

- `SO_OOBINLINE`   You can send very short messages that the receiver does not place in the data queue. Instead, it accepts the message separately (out of band), so you can use it for transmitting urgent messages. This flag forces the out-of-band data into the data queue where your socket could read it normally.

- `SO_PASSCRED`   Enable/disable passing of user identification (see `SO_PEERCRED`). (Boolean, disabled by default.)

- `SO_PEERCRED`   Set peer credentials (user ID, group ID, and process ID). (`struct ucred`, zero by default.)

- `SO_RCVBUF`   You can use this option to resize the input buffers. For TCP you should set this to 3 or 4 times the size of MSS (Maximum Segment Size, see `TCP_MAXSEG` below). UDP does not have flow control, however, and you lose any messages that exceed the receive-buffer's size. (Integer, 65,535 bytes by default.)

- `SO_RCVLOWAT`   Like `SO_SNDLOWAT`, this works with I/O multiplexing system calls and signal-based I/O. As soon as the socket receives the indicated number of bytes, the socket notifies your program. On Linux this option is read-only. (Integer, 1 byte by default.)

- `SO_RCVTIMEO`   Like `SO_SNDTIMEO`, this places a limit on the amount of time waiting for input. If the reading call (`read()`, `readv()`, `recv()`, `recvfrom()`, or `recvmsg()`) exceeds the time without getting any data, the read returns with an error. (`struct timeval`, 1 byte by default, get only.)

- `SO_REUSEADDR`   Using this option, you can create two sockets that share the address:port connection. You can share a port with different sockets in the same process, different processes, or different programs. Most of the time this is useful when your server crashes and you need to restart it quickly. The kernel typically reserves a port for several seconds after the termination of the owner. If you get a `Port Already Used` error in the `bind()`, use this option to get around it. (Boolean, disabled by default.)

- `SO_SNDBUF`   This option lets you define the size of the output socket data buffer. (Integer.)

- `SO_SNDLOWAT`   This is the low water mark for transmitting information. The I/O multiplexing system calls report that a socket is writable when you can write that many bytes to the socket. If you are using signal-based I/O, you get a signal upon reaching the low water mark. On Linux this option is read-only. (Integer, 1 byte by default.)

- `SO_SNDTIMEO`   This option allows you to set a timeout on all your write calls (`write()`, `writev()`, `send()`, `sendto()`, and `sendmsg()`). If one of these calls in your program takes too long, it aborts with an error. (`struct timeval`, 1 byte by default, get only.)

- `SO_TYPE`   This option returns the socket type. This number matches the second parameter in the `socket()` system call. (Integer, no default, get only.)

IP-Specific Socket Options

The IP-specific socket options apply mostly to datagrams and managing lower-level details. To use these options, you must set the `level` parameter in `getsockopt()` and `setsockopt()` to `SOL_IP`.

- `IP_ADD_MEMBERSHIP`   Join a multicast membership. (`struct ip_mreq`, no default, write-only.)

- `IP_DROP_MEMBERSHIP`   Drop multicast membership. (`struct ip_req`, no default, write-only.)

- `IP_HDRINCL`   This option allows you to build the raw IP packet header information. The only field you don't fill is the checksum. This option is for raw packets only. (Boolean, disabled by default.)

- `IP_MTU_DISCOVER`   Lets you open the MTU (maximum transmission unit) discovery process. The MTU is the agreement between the sender and receiver on how large the packet should be. This has three values:

  `IP_PMTUDISC_DONT (0)`   Never send DF (don't fragment) frames.

  `IP_PMTUDISC_WANT (1)`   Use per-route hints.

  `IP_PMTUDISC_DO (2)`   Always use DF frames. (Integer, disabled by default.)

- `IP_MULTICAST_IF`   Sets the outgoing multicast interface. This is the IPv4 address assigned to a hardware interface. Most machines have only one interface and one address, while some may have more. This setting lets you indicate which address interface to use. (`struct in_addr`, `INADDR_ANY` by default.)

- `IP_MULTICAST_LOOP`   Enables multicast loopback. Your receive buffer gets a copy of whatever you transmit. (Boolean, disabled by default.)

- IP_MULTICAST_TTL   Sets the maximum number of hops (Time To Live) the multicast message is allowed. For any effective Internet multicasting, you must set this value, because it allows only one routing by default. (Integer-byte, 1 by default.)

- IP_OPTIONS   Lets you select specific IP options. The options are notes in the IP header that tell the receiver specific notes (for example, timestamping, security levels, and alerts). Look at the TCPv1 and TCPv2 RFCs for more information. (Byte array, none by default.)

- IP_TOS   This option lets you determine the type of service (TOS) that the outgoing packets require. You can select from four types: IPTOS_LOWDELAY (minimize delay), IPTOS_THROUGHPUT (maximize throughput), IPTOS_RELIABILITY (maximize reliability), and IPTOS_LOWCOST (minimize cost). (Integer, no extra services by default.)

- IP_TTL   Set the time to live (TTL) of each packet. This indicates the maximum number of router hops before the packet expires. (Integer-byte, 64 by default.)

IPv6-Specific Socket Options

The IPv6-specific socket options apply to extended features of IPv6 or IPng. To use these options, you must set the level parameter in getsockopt() and setsockopt() to SOL_IPV6.

- IPV6_ADD_MEMBERSHIP   Like the IPv4 version, this option lets you join an IPv6 multicast group. (struct ipv6_mreq, none by default, write-only.)

- IPV6_ADDRFORM   This option allows you to convert the socket between IPv4 and IPv6. (Boolean, disabled by default.)

- IPV6_CHECKSUM   When working with raw IPv6 sockets, this option lets you tell the socket the byte offset to the checksum in the packet. If the value is -1, the kernel does not calculate the checksum for you, and the receiver skips it as well. (Integer, -1 by default.)

- IPV6_DROP_MEMBERSHIP   Like the IPv4 version, this option lets you unsubscribe from a IPv6 group. (struct ipv6_mreq, none by default, write-only.)

- IPV6_DSTOPTS   This setting allows you to retrieve all options from a received packet. This information appears in the recvmsg() system call. (Boolean, disabled by default.)

- IPV6_HOPLIMIT   If you use the recvmsg() system call and have enabled this option, you can get the number of hops remaining in a received packet in the ancillary data field. (Boolean, disabled by default.)

- IPV6_HOPOPTS   If you use the recvmsg() system call and have enabled this option, you can get the hop-by-hop options in the ancillary data field. (Boolean, disabled by default.)

- IPV6_MULTICAST_HOPS   Similar to the IPv4 version (TTL), this option lets you define the maximum number of router hops before expiring. (Integer-byte, 1 by default.)

- IPV6_MULTICAST_IF   Similar to the IPv4 version, this option lets you define which interface (by IP address) to use for multicasting messages. (`struct in6_addr`, zero by default.)

- IPV6_MULTICAST_LOOP   Like the IPv4 version, this option echoes every message you send on multicast. (Boolean, disabled by default.)

- IPV6_NEXTHOP   This option lets you specify the next hop for a datagram when you use `sendmsg()`. You need to have `root` access to perform this operation. (Boolean, disabled by default.)

- IPV6_PKTINFO   Normally you can't get very much information about the received packet. This option lets you get the arriving interface index and destination IPv6 address. (Boolean, disabled by default.)

- IPV6_PKTOPTIONS   Similar to the IPv4's IP_OPTIONS, you can directly specify the options using a byte array. In most cases you send IPv6 options via the ancillary data of the `sendmsg()` system call. (Byte array, none by default.)

- IPV6_UNICAST_HOPS   Similar to the IPv4's IP_TTL, this option lets you specify the maximum number of router hops before expiring the packet. (Integer-byte, 64 by default.)

TCP-Specific Socket Options

The TCP-specific socket options apply to the streaming capabilities of the TCP layer. To use these options, you must set the `level` parameter in `getsockopt()` and `setsockopt()` to SOL_TCP.

- TCP_KEEPALIVE   The SO_KEEPALIVE waits for 2 hours before checking for a connection. This option lets you change that delay. The value's units are in seconds. On Linux the `sysctl()` call replaced this option. (Integer, 7200 by default.)

- TCP_MAXRT   This option lets you specify the retransmit time in seconds. A `0` selects the kernel default, and a `-1` forces the network subsystem to retransmit forever. (Integer, `0` by default.)

- TCP_MAXSEG   The TCP stream is packetized into chunks of data. The Maximum Segment Size (MSS) specifies the amount of data in each chunk. The network subsystem coordinates this value with the peer's MSS. You cannot increase this value over the peer's MSS, but you can decrease it. (Integer, 540 bytes by default.)

- `TCP_NODELAY` TCP uses the Nagle Algorithm, which forbids sending any message that is smaller than the MSS until the receiver acknowledges (ACK) all outstanding messages. If you enable this option, you turn off the Nagle Algorithm, making it possible to send several short messages before getting the ACKs. (Boolean, disabled by default.)

- `TCP_STDURG` This option specifies where in the stream to find the OOB data byte. By default it is the byte following the OOB flag. Since all implementations recognize this default, you may never need to use this option. Linux replaced this option with the `sysctl()` system call. (Integer, 1 by default.)

Recovering the Socket Descriptor

You may write many servers as you learn how to do network programming. You may run into a problem that the `bind()` fails because of an `address in use` error. This is the most common error programmers get (even experienced ones) and one of the most common questions asked on the Usenet. The problem comes from the way the kernel allocates the ports.

Most kernels wait for a few seconds before reallocating a port (some specifications claim up to a minute). This policy is important for security. The delay makes sure that floating packets are dead before permitting a new connection.

You can get around this problem if you use the `SO_REUSEADDR` option. In fact, some say that you should enable this option on all your servers. As stated in the previous section, this option lets you reconnect quickly even though the kernel may still have it allocated. To enable the option, you can use the following excerpt:

```
/*************************************************************/
/*** Reusing a port example (for servers that die and    ***/
/*** need to restart).                                   ***/
/*************************************************************/
int value = 1; /* TRUE */
int sd = socket(PF_INET, SOCK_ADDR, 0);
if ( setsockopt(sd, SOL_SOCKET, SO_REUSEADDR, &value, sizeof(value)) != 0 )
    perror("setsockopt() failed");
/**** Bind(), listen(), and accept() ****/
```

Another procedure you could follow is to retry the `bind()` system call if it returns the `EAGAIN` error. One caveat for using this option is that no other programs should be using your port. The `SO_REUSEADDR` option lets your programs share ports. That may cause problems. You don't want two HTTP servers running at the same time, both using port 80. Also, trying to start a server that's already started is a common sysadmin goof.

Some programmers leave this feature disabled and retry a few times to detect if the program is already running. If you want to use this option (which actually is a good idea), be sure to use a different locking mechanism, like the PID in `/var`.

Sending Before Received: Message Interleave

One aspect of server responsiveness is its quick recovery. Another aspect is how quickly the client can get the request out to the server. You can also use TCP_NODELAY to assist your server's performance by getting out the client's query as quickly as possible.

As previously mentioned, TCP uses the Nagle Algorithm to limit the number of small messages on a WAN. It forbids sending any message that is smaller than the MSS until the receiver acknowledges (ACK) all outstanding messages. Of course, if the send buffer has more than MSS bytes of data, it sends it as quickly as possible. What this means to you is that if you have several short requests, you may wait longer for their replies. This is because they are not sent as soon as you write() them, but they are serialized into send-ACK-send interactions.

The only loss possible when using this approach is loss of network throughput, but you can control that. Remember that if the number of bytes in the header begins to outweigh the data itself, the throughput suffers. If you can limit the messages so that they are not too small (try building them manually first into a buffer), then you can send them in a burst. The result is getting the throughput of instant transmission while minimizing the throughput drain.

Noting File I/O Problems

As you look at the options for building the messages, you may be tempted to use the standard file I/O system calls or the higher-level FILE* library calls. Up to this point, this text tells you that this interchangeability is great.

Using the standard calls is very useful for quick prototypes and fast development. They are familiar and have several features that can make your programming very easy. In fact, as you do rapid prototyping, use those calls that most closely match the ones in the Sockets API. Try to limit those, like printf(), which may be harder to convert.

The problem with using the file I/O calls stems from the way the libraries and system manage them. When you make one of the file I/O calls with a socket descriptor or you use fdopen(), the system may copy your data a few times from the file buffers to the socket buffers. This dings your client's or server's stellar performance. Even the low-level file I/O, read() and write(), looks at your descriptor, determines that it needs socket I/O, and makes the appropriate call.

Eventually, you might want to use the Sockets API exclusively. This can also help readability and maintainability of your code; it makes it very easy to see that your program is working on a file versus a socket.

Using Demand-Based I/O to Recover CPU Time

Your servers, clients, and peers all share two common features: your algorithms and the I/O subsystem. You can control your programs by good design and profiling. The I/O subsystem is not as flexible. (One of the most appealing aspects of Linux is that you can get into it and change it.) The I/O system calls in the Sockets API offer you a lot of control over how you send and receive your data. Mixed with the control from fcntl(), this provides some very powerful tools.

In most cases, the kernel simply buffers the messages you send. This means you can focus on getting information and processing it. Chapter 8, "Choosing when to Wait for I/O," explains how to use asynchronous I/O (or demand-based I/O) for letting the kernel do some of the work for you.

Asynchronous I/O (not the real-time definition) works with your program by placing the burden of notification on the I/O subsystem. During the life of your program, you may do several reads and writes.

Speeding Up a send()

When you send a message, the kernel copies the message into its buffers and starts the process of constructing the packets. Upon completion, the kernel returns to your program with a status. The only reason for the delay is to generate the results of the send(). If you have any problems with your message, the kernel can reply with an error message.

However, most errors after you have connected come from transmission, not from the send() command. Unless you have something such as an illegal memory reference (which the call detects quickly), you may not get an error until after the send() finishes. You can get these errors from the SO_ERROR socket option before the library's errno gets it.

You can speed up the send() operation with the MSG_DONTWAIT system call option. With this option, the call copies your data and immediately returns. From that point you can proceed with other operations. However, it is your responsibility to check the error codes carefully.

The only time that a write operation blocks is when the transmit buffers are full. This does not happen very often when you have a lot of unused memory. If it does, you can use asynchronous I/O with signals to let you know when the buffers are available.

Offloading the recv()

Unlike the send() system call, most recv() system calls I/O block, because your program usually runs faster than the arriving data. If the receive buffers have data, the read operation copies the information and returns. Even if one byte is ready in the buffers, the read operation returns with that one byte. (You can change this behavior with the MSG_WAITALL option in the recv() system call.)

Generally, you don't want to wait for data to arrive when your program could be doing other things. You have two options: Spawn threads that manage that particular I/O or use signals. If you use threads, you may have another process that is I/O blocked on the recv(). This may not be an issue, but keep in mind the system's resources. If you have several processes or threads already in your program (or other programs), you may not want to load up the process table.

The alternative, asynchronous I/O or signal-driven I/O, lets your program run. When a message arrives, the kernel sends a signal (SIGIO) to your process. Your signal handler accepts the signal and issues the read call. When done, the handler sets a flag indicating that data is ready.

Remember that the signal only tells your program that data arrived, not how much data. Also, the danger of doing I/O in signal handlers is the chance that you lose other signals. You can solve these problems by not forcing the call to give more data than is available and setting the flag and leaving the reading to the main program.

Either algorithm—threading or signal-driven I/O—essentially does the same things. Both get the data as soon as it arrives, and both have to set a global flag when the data is ready.

Sending High-Priority Messages

During the interchange of messages, your program may need to wake up the other end or stop some operation. The TCP protocol supports urgent messages that essentially jump the input queue. These urgent messages are the out-of-band (OOB) data you may have read up to this point. (Other protocols support urgent messages, but they differ in implementation.) This option is not as glamorous as it sounds. According to the specifications, urgent messages are never allowed more than a one-byte message.

In fact, if your program gets two urgent messages in succession, the second may overwrite the first. This is due to the way the networking subsystem stores urgent messages. It has only a one-byte buffer for each socket.

Originally, this feature served transaction-based connections like Telnet, which needed a way to force an interrupt (like ^C) across the network. You can use them to tell the client or server a very specific operation, such as reset-connection or restart-transaction. Really, you can't do much more than that. (You can get very inventive with the 256 possibilities, though.)

If you do not select the SO_OOBINLINE socket option, the kernel notifies your program of OOB data with a signal (SIGURG). (Your program ignores this signal by default unless you capture it.) Within the signal handler, you can read that message with the MSG_OOB option in the recv() system call.

If you want to send an urgent message, you need to use the MSG_OOB option in the send() system call. Additionally, like asynchronous I/O, you need to enable capturing this event with a
system call to fcntl():

```
/***********************************************************/
/*** Claim ownership of SIGIO and SIGURG signals      ***/
/***********************************************************/
if ( fcntl(sockfd, F_SETOWN, getpid()) != 0 )
    perror("Can't claim SIGURG and SIGIO");
```

This call tells the kernel that you want to get asynchronous notification of SIGURG and SIGIO.
Remember that the call uses only one byte of that message as the OOB data.

You can use the urgent (OOB) messages to make sure that the listener is alive, because unlike
regular data, flow control does not block them. You might use this for a heartbeat:

```
/***********************************************************/
/*** Heartbeat between programs: Server replying to beats ***/
/*** ("heartbeat-server.c" on Web site)               ***/
/***********************************************************/
int clientfd;
void sig_handler(int signum)
{
    if ( signum == SIGURG )
    {   char c;
        recv(clientfd, &c, sizeof(c));
        if ( c == '?' )                      /* Are you alive? */
            send(clientfd, "Y", 1, MSG_OOB);     /* YES! */
    }
}

int main()
{   int sockfd;
    struct sigaction act;
    bzero(&act, sizeof(act));
    act.sa_handler = sig_handler;
    sigaction(SIGURG, &act, 0);     /* connect SIGURG signal */

    /*** set up server & connection client to clientfd ***/
    /*---claim SIGIO/SIGURG signals---*/
    if ( fcntl(clientfd, F_SETOWN, getpid()) != 0 )
        perror("Can't claim SIGURG and SIGIO");
    /*** do your work ***/
}
```

In this example, the server replies to the messages that the client sends (you can reverse it as well). Most of the items listed set up and respond to the message. The client is a bit different:

```c
/*************************************************************/
/*** Heartbeat between programs: Client sends beats.     ***/
/*** ("heartbeat-client.c" on Web site)                  ***/
/*************************************************************/
int serverfd, got_reply=1;
void sig_handler(int signum)
{
    if ( signum == SIGURG )
    {   char c;
        recv(serverfd, &c, sizeof(c));
        got_reply = ( c == 'Y' );                    /* Got reply */
    }
    else if ( signum == SIGALRM )
        if ( got_reply )
        {
            send(serverfd, "?", 1, MSG_OOB);     /* Alive?? */
            alarm(DELAY);                         /* Wait a while */
            got_reply = 0;
        }
        else
            fprintf(stderr, "Lost connection to server!");
}

int main()
{   struct sigaction act;

    bzero(&act, sizeof(act));
    act.sa_handler = sig_handler;
    sigaction(SIGURG, &act, 0);
    sigaction(SIGALRM, &act, 0);
    /*** set up connection to server to serverfd ***/
    /*---claim SIGIO/SIGURG signals---*/
    if ( fcntl(serverfd, F_SETOWN, getpid()) != 0 )
        perror("Can't claim SIGURG and SIGIO");
    alarm(DELAY);
    /*** do your work ***/
}
```

These examples show you a heartbeat that the client drives. You can expand this to a bi-directional heartbeat simply by adding a test in the server. If the server does not hear from the client within a period of time, you know you have an error at the client end.

Urgent messages give you more control over the connection, as long as both ends expect that level of interfacing. This is part of establishing protocols that Chapter 6, "A Server Primer," discusses.

Summary: Pulling Together Performance Features

Each chapter up to this one has given you a piece of a large puzzle that can help you build a high-performance client and server. The network program (the client, server, or peer) has to manage the information that it sends and receives. Sometimes, using multitasking can limit the performance if you are not careful.

When balanced with I/O control and multiplexing I/O, you can take advantage of the power of each and lose little. This adds complexity to your programs, but with good design and forethought, you can overcome the problems it creates.

The socket options also give you fine control over how the socket manages the packets. One of the features includes sending a message even though the buffer is not full. As you send and receive messages, calling the Sockets API can speed execution.

The tools that the Sockets API offers increase control of your program. You might use many of them in a single program so that you can predict the reliability of your program. Reliability in a network program is very elusive and requires several tricks, tips, and hints. The next chapter takes you to another level of reliability.

Designing Robust Linux Sockets

IN THIS CHAPTER

So, you want to write commercial-grade clients and servers. That's a good goal—even if you might donate the work to Open Source. No one likes to be criticized for his code. So how do you make good code great? Good question.

You could consider what you're trying to accomplish. If you are writing for a specific type of user, do you have one in mind? Can you work with him and get ideas about the possibilities? How reliable do the clients and servers need it to be?

Writing robust network programs is similar to regular programming, but you have to look at the big picture first; your program always runs at the same time as any connected program. That opens the picture quite wider. You have to consider more than just making the source readable.

This chapter provides several gems of advice on how to deal with these issues. It cannot be comprehensive; entire books are available just on writing solid code. But it can help you avoid the more typical network programming obstacles.

Using Conversion Tools

The first step in creating good, robust socket programs is to use the Socket API's conversion tools. You have a wealth of tools that convert the addresses, names, and binary numbers back and forth. This is important if you want to ensure portability, testability, and longevity of your code.

As described in Chapter 2, "TCP/IP Network Language Fluency," the network uses the big endian binary storage format. You may have an alpha or 68040, which are themselves big endian as well. But, you probably want everyone in the Linux community to use your creative work. These tools automatically make the binary of the structures right. If you are on a big endian computer, you lose nothing—the libraries automatically map all conversion calls to do nothing, so your program does not spin its wheels in a useless call.

Thousands of programmers have tested all the libraries on your Linux machine. Some of these tests may admittedly be ad hoc. However, the GNU organization is very serious about the reliability of their packaged libraries. The thoroughness and almost nit-pickiness of these test procedures have made the libraries Linux uses solid. This foundation gives your program strength as well.

Some programmers like to reinvent the library with their own twists on interfaces or behavior. If you follow this approach without trying to use the standardized tools, you can spend more time inventing than developing. And, the result is larger, more complex, and harder to test. If, however, you find the libraries lack a needed function, try to follow the style and philosophy of the UNIX library calls. The following are some examples:

- Return 0 if the call completes without error.
- Return a negative value if the call is unsuccessful and submit error to `errno`.
- Use the standard error numbers.
- Pass structures as references.
- Try to define low-level calls and build high-level calls on top of them.
- Define all read-only pointer parameters as `const`.
- Struct definitions are preferred over typedefs.
- Lowercase variable and function names are preferred over uppercase. Constants are in all capitals.
- Use `syslog` to log events, errors, and any unusual activity.

These are just a few. The best solution is to find existing functions and mimic their interface style.

Writing your program in a familiar and readable way makes it easy for others to use it, revise it, and enhance it. Consider this: Linus Torvalds himself declared that he does not plan on owning the kernel forever. Using standard tools and practices lengthens its life span.

Eyeing Return Values

As you work with the Socket API calls, you need to look at their behavior and results. Network programming is unlike most other types of programming. Errors can happen at any time in your program, and sometimes the error arises irrespective of the current execution.

First you might want to check all return values. Some calls are very important, and some are crucial. Generally, conversion calls don't return an error or a very critical one. The following are some critical calls:

- `bind()` When you need a specific port, you must reserve it. If you cannot, you need to know as early as possible in the program. Errors you are likely to see are port conflicts (already in use) or something wrong with the socket.
- `connect()` You cannot proceed unless you have an established connection. You may see errors like host not found or host unreachable.
- `accept()` Your program can't begin communicating with the client unless the result of this call is greater than zero. (Yes, it's possible to have a zero for a legal socket descriptor, but that is an unusual program.) Often the error you may see is `EINTR` (call interrupted by signal). This is okay. Either program the `sigaction()` call to include `SA_RESTART` in the flags or ignore the error and manually restart the call.

- **All I/O (recv(), send(), and so on)**   These calls determine whether you successfully sent your message or the new message is real. You may return with a connection closed error or a call interrupted (as discussed earlier). If you use the higher level functions, such as fprintf(), you should use calls that return some kind of success or failure, and you should check that. You could lose the connection at any time, resulting in a SIGPIPE signal killing your program.

- **gethostbyname()**   If you get any error from this call, the value returned is zero (or NULL). So, if you de-reference the returned pointer when you get an error, your program aborts with a segmentation fault.

- **fork()**   The return value indicates whether you're in the child or in the parent. And, you might want to separate the child from the parent's execution path. Also, you can check for any errors. If the return value is negative, you have not created the child, and you may have more systemic problems.

- **pthread_create()**   Like the fork() call, you might want to verify that the call succeeded in creating the new child.

- **setsockopt()/getsockopt()**   The sockets have many options you can work with to tune the behavior. Generally, you may want to know if the call was successful so that you can proceed on that assumption.

All these calls share one common fate if they fail—your program may terminate or behave unpredictably. This is a good rule of thumb: If the call seriously impairs the reliability of your program, always check the return value. If any problem is evident, report it to the console. This alerts the user early of any problems.

The following are less important calls, a few that you could get away with ignoring the return value:

- **socket()**   The only time you fail this call is if you request a socket you can't have (permission or lack of kernel support), if you have a bad parameter, or you have a full descriptor table. In call cases, the bind(), connect(), or I/O call acts as backup to catch the fault with a "not a socket" error.

- **listen()**   You are unlikely to get an error from this call if bind() previously succeeded. It does have a limit to the depth of the listening queue. If you use 15–20 entries, your program can work well even with a large connection rate.

- **close() or shutdown()**   If the file descriptor is bad, the file is gone anyway. In either case (success or failure), the file is gone, and your program can move on. (You may want to check the location in your program that calls this if you suddenly start running out of file descriptors.)

API calls that are not as critical often have other important calls that can pick up the slack following right behind them. Also, if they fail, they may not cause any catastrophic failures. This is not a license to ignore the return values of these calls; in all circumstances, checking verifies success and thus increases your program's reliability.

You can use other measures to capture errors that occur while you may not be in a system or library call. These errors happen because of the dynamics of the network and the possibility that the server or client could go silent. The networking subsystem keeps track of some of these errors in the TCP protocols, because TCP constantly ensures that the channel is clear for bi-directional communications.

If your program does not send a message for a while, you need to check on the connection manually. If you do not, the error eventually appears as an I/O fault. To access this information, you can use the `getsockopt()` system call with SO_ERROR option:

```
int error;
socklen_t size=sizeof(error);
if ( getsockopt(sockfd, SOL_SOCKET, SO_ERROR, &error, &size) == 0 )
    if ( error != 0 )
        fprintf(stderr, "socket error: %s(%d)\n", strerror(error), error);
```

Using this approach can intercept errors before they get to the I/O subsystem. And because you captured the error early, you can fix it before the user discovers the problem.

Another way the system lets you know of an error is through signals. Most calls warn you once that an error occurred to the channel. Some errors, like a premature close or normal close, issue a signal to your program if you do not get the message the first time. Your program may ignore some of these signals by default, but capturing all relevant signals reduces the risk of long debugging nights.

Capturing Signals

The network program involves many technologies, and some of these technologies invoke signals. Your program must support collecting and processing these signals. The most commonly overlooked signal that can cause your program to abort is SIGPIPE.

Signal intercepting and processing has its unique problems, as noted in Chapter 7, "Dividing the Load: Multitasking." The first problem you must deal with is the fact that each process records only one signal per signal type. If you get more signals before completely processing the first, your program drops those events.

You have a few options to address this problem. First, you should do as little as possible in the signal handler. Any I/O can potentially lose further signals. The risk of I/O blocking in a signal handler can result in disastrous consequences (such as a program hang). Also, you should avoid loops; try to run straight through all your signal algorithms. This rule does have a few exceptions, but generally, it is a good idea to minimize processing.

Second, you can permit your handler to be interrupted. Be careful with this option; your signal handler may use a different hardware stack to accept each call. Because that special stack is not very deep by default, you can easily overflow that stack.

Third, your handler could accept the signal and place it in a queue for your main program to process. This, however, is not as useful as you might think. The signal only tells you that something happened. Besides the specific type of signal (Linux defines 32 types), you know nothing else. If you enqueue the messages, your queue-processing loop has to determine whether multiple signal events mean something or could actually collapse into one event.

Determining what to do with each signal event depends on the signal itself. Of the 32 defined signal types (listed in Appendix A of this book and in section 7 of the man pages), your program is likely to encounter or request six on a regular basis: SIGPIPE, SIGURG, SIGCHLD, SIGHUP, SIGIO, and SIGALRM. You could get other signals, but these are the more common and relevant ones.

SIGPIPE

One common signal is SIGPIPE. The UNIX manuals state that only naïve network programs ignore this signal. In normal, nonconcurrent programming, you may never encounter this event. On the other hand, if you do get this signal, it may not be very important to your program, and it's okay to terminate. However, when writing a server or client, you must watch the connection carefully so that your program can recover without terminating prematurely.

A pipe error happens when the destination host closes the connection before you are done sending (see sigpipe-client.c and sigpipe-server.c on the Web site). You get the same error when you pipe a long directory listing through a paging program like less. If you quit the paging program before reaching the bottom of the listing, you get a broken pipe message. You can avoid the signal by using the MSG_NOSIGNAL option in the send() system call. But that may not be the best approach.

What you do with the signal depends on what you need. First, you must close the file (or set a flag for the main loop) because the channel is now defunct. If you have several connections open and your program polls each connection, you need to find out which connection closed.

But you may have unfinished business with the other end. If the client or server knows your protocol, it is unlikely to close the connection in midstream. Two possible causes are that an error occurred on the client/server side and the path between fell apart. Either way, if you need the session to finish, you may want to re-establish the connection.

If the server or client disconnected or crashed, you can re-establish as soon as it is ready to connect again. You may want to give other programs a little time to come back up. Likewise, a faulty network needs a little time to quiet down after it readjusts the routing. If you can't reconnect after several attempts, you can notify the user and let him choose what to do (this is what some browsers do).

The network may continue to be unreliable even after waiting a while. After you reconnect, you can send shorter bursts that you can checkpoint along the way. This lets you pick up where you left off in the protocol.

SIGURG

The protocol between the client and server requires choosing all the features necessary to pass the information. You can include some key features, such as data-stream interrupts or a heart-beat (see Chapter 9, "Breaking Performance Barriers"), which require the out-of-band (OOB) data feature. But unless you plan it and design it into the protocol, you don't get the SIGURG signal. The behavior differs from the other signals. The default signal behavior is to ignore the signal, and your program must ask for the signal to get it.

The SIGURG signal is specifically for receiving OOB data. Your program has to follow several steps to intercept this message (see Chapter 9). Usually, if the client or server sent it to your program, it may be for a good reason. So, if you get this signal unexpectedly, you might want to capture it and log it for later review.

If your program gets more than one of this signal too quickly to accept and process, your program loses the last OOB data message. This is because the socket's incoming data queue reserves only one byte for an urgent message.

SIGCHLD

Unlike the SIGURG signal where you have to request the notification, you get the SIGCHLD signal if you use multitasking (specifically, processes) and the process terminates. When the child progress terminates, the kernel retains its context so that the parent can review the results. The kernel also notifies the parent with this signal. If your program ignores the signal, these contexts accumulate in the process table as zombies (see Chapter 7).

Typically, programs use this signal to call the wait() system call. However, it is possible to get the signal more quickly than a one-line system call like wait(). This is a nasty problem, but it is easy to solve. The SIGCHLD signal is the only signal that justifies using a loop to process all zombies.

Because wait() can block your program (blocking in a signal handler is not a good idea), use the waitpid() system call:

```
#include <sys/types.h>
#include <sys/wait.h>
int waitpid(int pid, int *status, int options);
```

The pid parameter can be several values; if you use -1, this call acts like the regular wait() system call. The status parameter is like that of wait(). To keep the call from blocking, set options to WNOHANG. If you have exhausted all the outstanding zombies, the call returns a zero. The following is an example of its use in a signal handler:

```
/*********************************************************/
/*** Improved zombie killer example                   ***/
/*********************************************************/
void sig_child(int signum)
{
    while ( waitpid(-1, 0, WNOHANG) > 0 );
}
```

Again, this instance is really the only time that you should use a loop in a signal handler. Spending too much time in a signal handler can lose pending signals. The reason why this example works with a loop is due to the way waitpid() works. You don't need a signal to pick up terminated child processes.

For example, you enter this routine because a child terminated. While your program processes the signal, another process terminates. Because you are in the signal handler for SIGCHLD, you lose that signal. However, the next iteration of waitpid() picks up the child's context. One call clears out all outstanding terminations—not just one.

SIGHUP

What happens to the child process when the parent terminates? The child gets a SIGHUP signal. Your program may get this signal if the user logs out. By default, the process that gets this message terminates. In most cases, you may want to leave this behavior alone, because you might not want the programs lingering after the controlling programs terminate.

Most servers run better in the background as daemons without a specific login. In fact, some daemons fire off a child process that assumes the whole responsibility of the program. When the child is ready, the parent terminates. This is similar to using the nohup command, and it has the added benefit of not appearing on the admin's job listing.

Also, one standard way of restarting a daemon is to send it a hang up signal. Usually this terminates the currently running process, and init starts a new instance. If you cannot depend on init to keep your server up and running, you can force a restart by exec()'ing a new instance (see `restart-example.c` on the Web site). Before doing this, you must manually terminate all current processes under the older parent. (You may have to use this restarting technique on all signals that can terminate your server.)

SIGIO

You can get a performance boost to your network program by offloading the I/O notification to the kernel. When implemented correctly, your program gets the `SIGIO` signal whenever the I/O buffers no longer block a read or write operation. For writing, this occurs when the I/O subsystem can accept at least one byte (see the write low water mark, `SO_SNDLOWAT`, socket option). For reading, this occurs when the I/O subsystem *has* received at least one byte (see the read low water mark, `SO_RCVLOWAT`, socket option). See Chapter 8, "Choosing when to Wait for I/O," for how to implement this signal, and see Chapter 9 for performance benefits.

SIGALRM

Like the `SIGIO` signal, you only get the `SIGARLM` signal if your program asked for it. This signal is typically the result of calling `alarm()` system call, a time-delayed wakeup call. Daemons often use this signal as a watchdog to ensure that the program is still alive or to check the solidarity of the connection. See Chapter 9 for using this as a connection heartbeat checker.

Resource Management

Signals are one small part of a program's resources. If you track and capture specific signals, you can reduce system corruption and may be able to increase performance. The *whole* program has much more than just signals. It includes files, heap, static/data memory, and CPU time. You have additional resources, such as child processes and shared memory. What makes a reliable server (or even client) is being careful with your resources.

File Management

Your program automatically gets three standard files when it starts up: `stdin`, `stdout`, and `stderr`. You should be familiar with these and the fact that the user can redirect any one of them. This is typically not a problem because the kernel flushes and closes these for you upon program termination.

New files and sockets are a different matter. You must remember to track and close each file. Even though the kernel closes all files for you upon program termination (such as the standard I/O files), all files require a portion of the kernel's and program's memories. All files that the program loses track of chew up more and more resources.

Even if you are working with one file, it is good programming practice to force a close somewhere in the program. Someday, in the course of revision, you may open more files.

Memory Heap

The memory heap (or dynamic memory allocation) is similar to opening and closing files where you must track each chunk of memory you carve out. But, the heap tends to be a really loose end for many programmers. Memory leaks are common and very hard to track. There are libraries to help you track these chunks (like ElectricFence), but some good practices can help you avoid the more common errors.

The first and perhaps the most common programming error is forgetting to check the return value of `malloc()` or `calloc()` (in C++ you need to capture any exceptions). If the size of memory you requested is not available, the call returns a `NULL` (zero) to your program. Depending on how much you need that space, you may design your program to terminate, clean up and retry, notify the user, and so on. Some programmers like to use `assert()` for every memory allocation. Unfortunately, that *always* aborts your program if it fails.

Be consistent with the allocation calls. If you use `calloc()`, use it for all memory allocations. Don't mix calls. In particular, the C++ `new` operator sometimes does not interface well with `malloc()` and `calloc()`. When you call `delete` on a `malloc()`'ed block of memory, you can see some unpredictable results.

Furthermore, when you release a block of memory, assign a `NULL` to the pointer variable. This is a quick way to find out if you have a *dirty reference* (using a pointer after its memory is freed).

When you allocate some memory, you can either get exactly what you need, or you can get what you expect you may need. These are two different approaches to the same problem. The first approach (*precise allocation*) carves out precisely the space that the variable needs when it needs it. The program that uses the other approach (*generous allocation*) typically requests a large chunk of memory and then uses the chunk for processing.

Table 10.1 summarizes the benefits of each programming style. Unlike mixing allocation calls, you can mix precise and generous allocation, but be sure to document your usage.

TABLE 10.1 Allocation Comparison

Precise Allocation	Generous Allocation
Gets exactly what you need.	Gets a large chunk that can be portioned out later.
Does not waste allocated memory.	Almost always wastes a portion of the memory allocated.
Requires several allocation and release calls.	Requires one allocation and one release.
More likely to fragment program memory.	Less likely to fragment memory.

TABLE 10.1   Continued

Precise Allocation	Generous Allocation
Effective in module- or program-wide memory usage.	Very useful in a single procedure-call where it uses a chunk of memory then releases it.
May waste allocation space because each allocated block requires an allocation descriptor. (This is how the allocation subsystem tracks memory use.)	Only generates one allocation header for the entire block.
Portable to other systems.	This is also portable, but it takes advantage of Linux's latent allocation. (Only the 1KB pages that are used are actually linked to real memory.)

`malloc()` Giving Segmentation Faults

If you get a segmentation fault in the `malloc()` system call, your program has corrupted the allocation block of some allocated memory. This fault typically occurs because of a misbehaving string operation or an out-of-bounds array. Test array index and limit string lengths to avoid this problem.

Your program can have several modules that use allocations in different ways. If you are interfacing with other programmers, be sure to establish who owns what. For example, if you pass a pointer to some memory to a routine, does the routine now own the pointer? Or, should it make a copy?

One typical approach is to leave the ownership to the routine/module that created it. This means that if you pass the reference to another module that needs its version, you must provide a way to clone the block. Some object-programmers call this a *deep copy* because all the references inside the block have to be copied as well.

Static Data Memory

Of the different types of resources, you may have the least problems with the static data memory. This memory includes both initialized and uninitialized data variables and stack variables. The following example shows the different types of data memory:

```
int Counter;                       /* Uninitialized data */
char *words[] = {"the","that","a",0}; /* initialized data */
void fn(int arg1, char *arg2)      /* parameters (stack) */
{   int i, index;                  /* "auto" variables (stack) */
```

The best way to avoid problems with this resource is to ensure that the program initializes everything before using it. You can use the `-Wall` C compiler option to show all warnings.

CPU, Shared Memory, and Processes

The last three resources, CPU, shared memory, and processes, require only a few notes. See Chapters 7, 8, and 9 for more information.

- Shared memory—Similar to file management. You open, lock, and close access to the shared regions of memory.
- CPU—Your programs can easily dominate the computer's scheduling time. Be sure to release some time by blocking at the right time.
- Processes—If you use multitasking, the system tells you the status of each child process. You need to accept and act on the notifications so that you don't fill the process table with zombies.

Critical Servers

Knowing the external and internal events (signals, for example) helps you know how to work from a system-level view. As you program your clients and servers, you need to determine *what* has to happen *when*. This determines the behavior your program must have in each circumstance. The primary difficulty in predicting behavior is that each computer can have a different configuration—even though the distribution installation may be the same. (It's an established fact that every system administrator has to tweak his workstation.)

The variability on a single computer is by itself daunting, but when you bring in network programming, you almost have to declare that all bets are off. However, you do have some control. If you have a complete understanding of what the program is supposed to do and what it interfaces with, you can rule out the other variables. You may want to define for the user that the external dependencies must behave correctly with their own dependencies.

For example, suppose you have a server that is to run as a daemon. If your server needs access to certain files on the destination system, you may want to stipulate that those files must reside in a particular directory and must retain a specified format. This helps the sysadmin to know that if anything goes wrong, he can look at the files to verify them.

Servers, in particular, are different in expectation and performance. Users expect your server to be available when they contact it. They also expect it to reply within a reasonable period of time. To keep users satisfied, you need to know the specifics of what "reasonable" means. Furthermore, you may want to determine how much uptime your server must have. If your server goes down, how quickly does the user expect the system to come back up? This all depends on how critical your server is.

What Qualifies as a Critical Server?

Unlike clients that can go up and down more often, users expect servers to be up and stay up. Clients can connect, establish protocols, transfer information, and shutdown comparably quickly. Of course, in a client, you *could* be more relaxed in memory and file management. Some Windows programs are. When the program exits, the memory manager releases all those resources (at least in Linux).

Servers, on the other hand, must remain up and running indefinitely. Like the genie in the lamp, you expect that your client can connect to the server at any time and fulfill any wish (within reason). The genie can't say, "Hold your horses while I reboot." The server must be available and ready.

The expected availability determines how critical your server is. Some servers are more critical than others. Like an HTTP server, some servers simply have to reply within a certain period of time. Others must track the transactions so that neither the client or the server loses any information, and all sessions appear seamless; a common example of this is a credit card purchase or money transfer.

Communication Events and Interruptions

During a purchase, your client's connection sudden drops. What can cause this? The TCP connection is supposed to be a reliable connection between client and server. What could possibly go wrong? Plenty.

Connection events and interrupts can result in loss of data, money, and possible life. Whenever you connect two computers together using any form of channel, you risk losing that connection. When looking at what *could* happen, you have to consider what kinds of information conduits exist and how TCP interacts with each.

Physical Interruptions

The network has so many different types of physical connections and different ways of *dropping carrier* (losing the electrical or optical signal that carries the packets) that listing them would be very laborious and not very useful. The simple point is that the connection between point A and point B can drop.

TCP works with these events very well. It does not matter if the physical media is wire, fiber, or radio waves. The original designers came from the days of nuclear paranoia, where the possibility of losing entire networks shaped the way the router sent messages. If the network has a different route to the same destination, the network detects it and reprograms the routers. The problem is simply that it takes time to discover the new path and cause the rerouting.

Your critical messages can encounter this problem and usually TCP recovers without your intervention. However, if the network can't establish a new path, your program may have to recover your session itself.

Routing Blips

Physical disruptions cause routing blips in the form of cycles. The message can bounce around between routers until discovered and fixed. This causes duplication and packet loss. Again, during a single TCP connection, your program does not encounter these problems because the protocol fixes them before getting to your program.

Server/Client Dropout

On the other hand, if you have to restart a session, you must take into account the possibility of duplications. You may have to restart a session if the client or server drops out. A server drops out or completely blacks out when it crashes. At the time of the crash, it loses all the transactions. When the client drops out, the information it sends at the time can be lost. The server's data loss is far more critical than the client's.

Session Recovery Issues

The client must reconnect to the server if either drops the connection. You face several issues to re-establish the connection. TCP usually solves these issues for you automatically. However, a session is connection-dependent—the user and server never seem to skip a heartbeat if the connection drops.

The first issue you have to address is transaction loss. During a transaction, the server could drop out either from a program failure or a system failure. If the client does not track each message but assumes that the server gets the transaction, the network could lose the message. Even when the server comes back up, the sent message may never arrive.

The second issue is the opposite of transaction loss—transaction duplication. This is different from packet duplication. During critical communications, both the server and the client track the messages they send. At certain times, both may have a copy of the same message until the receiver acknowledges the message.

For example, the client issues a request to transfer $100 from the savings account to the checking account. Until the client gets the confirmation from the server, it holds the message in a transaction queue. If the client drops out, the system saves the transaction queue. After coming back up, the client retries each outstanding transaction in the transaction queue. If the server executes the transaction again, the account manager transfers a total of $200 instead of $100.

The last typical problem you must address is the procedure of session re-establishment. Often, the sessions are not secure and do not require passing through different security walls. Insecure connections need no more than a reconnection. If, however, yours is a critical server, you have to authenticate. *Authentication* verifies the client has the right to connect. This can happen through a login prompt, a common form of security.

The other form establishes and verifies that the client is really who it claims to be (*certification*). The certification process requires a trusted third party-server (a *certifier*). When the server accepts a connection and begins the login process, the server asks the client for a certificate of authenticity. The server then forwards the certificate to the third party certifier. The certifier checks the certificate and responds with the authenticity.

You must consider these general issues and others you may have before implementation. If you consider security and session protocols after implementation, you create unpluggable holes in your design.

Session Recovery Techniques

Part of the security system includes session recovery. Because you may have critical data, you must consider ways of securing the data. The previous section introduces a couple of ideas to solve this problem.

Part of the process of auto recovery is minimizing user interaction. You also need to consider the issues discussed previously. The previous section provides some hints as to methods to help you recover a session.

The first problem is simply the connection. Even though your server notices the connection loss first, it cannot initiate the connection if the protocol foundation is TCP. Instead, the client must connect to the server. If you want to use the TCP protocol, your client must be intelligent enough to detect a connection dropout and re-establish it.

Back-Handshaking

Getting the client to realize that the connection has dropped out can be more difficult because it takes time for network errors to arise. You could *back-handshake*—connect in both directions. Normally, the client connects to the server. In back-handshaking, the server connects back to the client. You can use the backwards channel to send procedural messages back (such as reconnect). You can use a reliable UDP instead of TCP for this back channel.

The connection process can include forcing the recovering client to reauthenticate or recertify automatically or re-log in. This is a necessary step to recover a secure session. If your user is still using the application when it re-establishes the session, you could recall the previous authentication and log it in for him. However, the recertification needs to follow the same procedure as before. Fortunately, the user does not need to get involved or even need to know.

The user works with the session in the form of transactions. These transactions can get data or revise server data. To ensure that the data is always accurate, the client and server track each revision-transaction. As the program designer, you do not need to track data retrieval (unless that's part of your security).

You can avoid transaction loss by tagging, logging, and acknowledging all transactions. To acknowledge it, the transaction must have a unique ID tag. The unique tag is different from the TCP message ID because the tag is unique for all sessions. (The tag really does not have to be unique for all sessions. You could reuse the tags after a predefined time. This simplifies implementation a bit.)

For example, the client sends a request to withdraw funds from a credit card account. At the same time, it logs the transaction locally on permanent storage. The server follows two steps. First it acknowledges the message (the transaction is *posted*). After completing the transaction, the server sends another acknowledgment (the transaction is *committed*).

After the server acknowledges the transaction, the client discards the pending transaction. (Programs should never discard critical transactions. Instead, they should be moved into a secure archive.) The client can use the second acknowledgment as a flag to update current records.

Thin Clients

If you do not want to risk getting out sync with the server, you can make your client a *thin client* by keeping no information locally. The client that you program still tracks the transactions, but instead of keeping information locally (such as current balances), each information refresh becomes a request to the server.

If the session drops out, the client and server must recover the session. After recovering the session, the client and server have to work through the outstanding transactions. They compare transaction tags, discarding those that are finished.

This process also helps eliminate the duplicate transaction problem. The client and server only eliminate those transactions that they share. The remaining ones are outstanding and need reposting.

You may find other issues that require additional handling. The ones this section covers are standard for most critical servers. To discover others, create use cases with associated scenarios and try to discover your specific needs.

Client/Server Concurrency Issues

A session may not malfunction because of something as catastrophic as a crash or an abort. When you work with concurrently running programs, you encounter concurrency issues that can cause similar deadlocks and starvation that threads and processes (multiprogramming) do. However, these are harder to detect.

You need to understand that the concurrency problems found in network programming are not exactly like multiprogramming. The reason is simple; unlike the multithreaded program, client/servers and peers really don't share resources. They are isolated and separate. The only link is the physical media of the network. Furthermore, the multiprogramming-type of deadlock is very hard (if not impossible) to untangle. You can untangle a network deadlock, but they still can deadlock and starve each other.

Network Deadlock

Most network communications define a protocol of who talks first. For example, typically one sends requests while the other responds. That designation defines which end of the connection drives the protocol.

To illustrate the interaction, please consider HTTP and Telnet servers. An HTTP server accepts requests from the client, making the client the driver for the protocol. A Telnet session, on the other hand, prompts the user for a username and password. Once logged in, the only time that user knows that the server can respond is when he sees the command prompt. The Telnet session can accept an asynchronous command using a keyboard interrupt (Ctrl+C).

Network deadlock is simple: The client/server or peers forget which was to talk next, so they end up waiting for each other indefinitely. This form of deadlock is difficult to detect because it shows the same symptoms as a very congested network—both ends don't hear anything for a while.

You could place a timeout on the connections to solve this problem. This is a very good idea because no client or server (especially) should wait forever on the network. But timeouts do not tell you anything more than a message took too long to arrive.

Another way around deadlock is to switch roles every so often. If the server is driving the session, let the client drive the session after a specified time. If a deadlock occurs, eventually both switch roles and begin transmitting. Once they do that, they can quickly re-establish the protocol.

An effective way of preventing, detecting, and fixing deadlock is to use the heartbeat algorithm presented in the previous chapter. Instead of just sending an "Are you alive" query, both ends of the connection send each other a message indicating whether it is in listening mode or not (for example, driver-listening or responder-listening). You can even expand the messages to indicate the protocol's state.

Network Starvation

The other networking problem you can face is starvation. Network starvation, like network deadlock, is a flaw in the communication with the client. Suppose you have a server that has ten connections in a `select()`, and the server only has enough timeslice to answer five. It is possible that one connection never gets serviced.

You encounter this problem often when connecting very busy sites on the Internet. The only symptom you see is similar to that of a deadlock; you connect and then hear nothing for a long time. This is different from just connecting and waiting with no data transferred, which the TCP protocol causes when it establishes and enqueues the connection request. Instead, you see a few bytes sent to your client and then—silence.

The solution to this problem is not as direct as the deadlock solution. Like trying to tell a micromanager that he needs to delegate some tasks, a server that accepts more connections than it can really support appears productive. Instead, it just starves one connection after another.

The first step is to make sure that you have a good balance of processor/system performance to the number of active connections. When you set the listening queue depth, remember that pending connections are okay—as long as you serve them before they time out. You need to gauge how long each session is and adjust the queue depth accordingly.

You can take another approach to keep connections from starving. This is similar to the way processes get CPU time through scheduling. The concept you might try is *dynamic scheduling* or *priorities*. When you have, say, three processes that have equal CPU usage, only one can run at a time. So the scheduler increases the effective priority of the ones it passes over. This ensures fair distribution of CPU.

In like manner, you can use something like a priority scheme on each of your connections. This is advantageous because you can use the priorities in different ways. Those connections that have data ready get higher priority than others.

Denial of Service Attacks

Network perpetrators use a degenerate form of network deadlock or starvation. You need to know about this, even though it's one of the older network attacks. As described in previous sections, the network subsystem accepts a connection request from a client on a specific port. This port represents a server and the port has a listening queue.

The attacker connects to this port. The TCP three-way handshake completes, and the network subsystem redirects the connection to the listening queue. Your server gets to the connection and accepts the connection (remember that the connection is not fully complete until the `accept()` system call). Next your server hands off the connection to a servlet.

Here is the problem. If the attacker did nothing, sending no data, the TCP/IP stack eventually times out the connection and drops the attacker. That's good. However, the attacker is smarter than that; he sends a few bytes—insufficient to fill any buffer, but sufficient to force an I/O block (an *I/O stall*).

Your server gets the first bytes and then blocks on reading the rest. The attacker knows that your server has blocked on that connection. His program proceeds to make more connections. Eventually, your server could completely chew up system resources while accomplishing nothing. Even if you cap the number of connections, the attacker's program could eventually dominate the server's resources and queue. You're then blocked from serving anyone else.

You can take three steps to prevent this:

1. Always place a timeout on all your I/O calls. Timeouts are easy to do, and they keep you from losing control of your server.

2. Always leave one process free (typically the parent) to monitor the child processes. You can determine how many processes have stalled.

3. Limit the number of connections from a particular host ID or subnetwork. Every connection includes the source's host ID. This is a weak prevention because the attackers are very resourceful, and you can harm innocent access.

These steps can help your locate and disable a network attack. You can find other forms of attacks; you might want to watch your hit rates and connection logs.

Summary: Solid-as-a-Rock Servers

You can provide a reliable and stable server or client on which users can depend. You can recognize and avoid problems such as the network attacker, deadlock, and starvation. Likewise, by capturing signals, you strengthen your program to withstand some of the more common programming errors.

This chapter gives a few suggestions of robust programming. These are mostly common sense: Conversion tools help portability, and return values are always important to look at. But knowing which return values to watch lets you worry less about the errors and more about the program. Also, knowing that the conversion tools don't lose any performance on big endian computers reduces their risk.

Knowing about how your server works and how it interfaces with the client is the greatest way to tune your server and make it unbreakable.

10

DESIGNING
ROBUST LINUX
SOCKETS

Looking at Sockets Objectively

Saving Time with Objects

IN THIS CHAPTER

The battery in a clock supplies the clock the power it needs to run. If you need to replace the battery, you simply take one out and put in a new one. Imagine how easy it would be if we could do the same thing with programs—simply unplug the old and plug in the new.

Object technology attempts to reach that level of interfacing. It focuses on the responsibility of each component and provides a solid and unchangeable interface to which you can connect other components. To understand where the technology is going, you need to know where it has been.

This chapter covers the concepts behind object technology. It does not cover the wide expanse of all the theory, but it does introduce the main topics. It begins with the evolution of software engineering and concludes with ways to apply these concepts to non–object-oriented languages.

> **NOTE**
>
> This chapter precedes the chapters that discuss sockets in specific implementations. In order to cover properly the specific implementations in Java and C++, this chapter provides foundational information about objects. No book on objects should omit the foundational philosophies as a preamble. Generally, most programmers do not understand objects, so implementations skew slightly from the original intent of the technology.

The Software Engineering Evolution

The development of software and programming does not have the lengthy history of physics, mathematics, or other such sciences. One part of software engineering (the lifecycle of software development)—computer science—relies heavily, however, on the thought and process of mathematics, particularly Boolean algebra, group theory, and statistics. Still, the software engineering and computer science fields have made significant strides in technology. These strides have defined how you use your computer today.

After you understand how these pieces fit together, you can easily choose the right tools for the right job. This section describes each type of programming and modeling theory that the industry has developed over the last few decades. Essentially, the strides (or stages) in technology encompass each other as an expanding set of tools and methodology. The most significant stages are Functional, Modular, Abstract, and Object Programming. This section describes each stage.

Step-by-Step Functional Programming

The first method development came from the concept of flowcharting. The whole idea was that every program included a series of functions, decisions, data, and I/O. Flowcharts show the step-by-step stages of evaluation, transforming meaningful input into meaningful output.

Functional design evolved into Structured System Requirements (SSR), Structured System Analysis (SSA), and Structured System Design (SSD). Each phase defines the materials needed to solve a particular programming problem. The phases encompass each other like concentric circles, the center being actual implementation.

SSR looks at the needs of the system. Often called Level 0 (zero), SSR defines the boundaries between inside program scope and outside program scope. At this level, you, the designer, look at those systems or people that interact with the proposed design. The SSR defines what functions your design needs to offer the user.

The next stage, SSA, helps you ask the right questions to define some of the higher level functions and data that pass through the system. Levels 1 and 2 model and define the major system architecture and components. The data is not supposed to be concrete data but rather general information that each component operates on to complete a task. At this stage, the model uses circles for operations or functions and connecting arcs that show data paths (dataflow diagrams).

Level 3 is a transitional phase between SSA and SSD. You use it to define any system-dependent, legacy, or third-party interfaces. Some system interfaces include your user and network interfaces.

The last phase, SSD, takes the detail further by identifying how to divide the problem into functions or procedures. When using this approach, you may go so far as to write the general algorithms or use flowcharts.

SSR, SSA, and SSD can go as far as eight levels (Level 7 having the most detail), but only projects that are *very* large (millions of lines of code) ever go that far. The model is very flexible in this way; the designer only has to go as far as is needed.

Every programmer still uses something akin to a functional design—even if it is just writing code. A flowchart can always help you organize the steps to take in the detail of the program. Level 0 is also critical, as described later in this chapter.

Unfortunately, the mapping from design to actual source code is not very clear. You may note that—even at the SSD phase—no one has written any program source code. Even though the stages show a clear transition from abstract to detail, the programmer who gets the design often struggles with making the connection between paper and code.

Hiding Implementation with Modular Programming

The next stage puts more teeth in what some people call "good programming." Part of the problem with functional design is the tendency to violate scoping rules. The scope of defined variables, functions, procedures, and modules lays out "who has the right to see what." If he has no scoping rules (or the scope is not enforced), the programmer's temptation is to use all resources available to get the job done quickly. In a scopeless environment (which often happened with functional design), every function has access to all other functions and all variables. Creating global variables is one example of a scoping violation.

> ## Global Versus Scratchpad Variables
>
> Do not think that you cannot ever use global variables. In some instances (like embedded system programming), you must be very careful about wasted memory. Programs often use memory spaces for temporary calculations. If you are careful, you can share a few scratchpad variables without scoping violation. Just remember that doing this seriously affects concurrent (or threaded) programming.

Many programmers avoid global variables because of side effects. If several sections of the program depend on a specific variable and a code revision changes the variable, all the dependent sections must change as well. (This does not apply to global read-only data, because the program cannot revise it.)

Modular programming (a slight extension to structured programming) sets scoping rules that all programmers must follow. The programmer must surround all variables with a set of implementations or interfaces (described in the "Interfaces" section, later in this chapter). Another name for modular programming is *encapsulation*, described in the "Implementation Encapsulation" section, later in this chapter. Modular programming extends the concept further with support for concurrency—monitors. A monitor is a function or procedure that allows only one execution thread through at a time.

Modular programming offers you an understanding and interface with the outside world. If you organize your programs into modules with interfaces, you can change out a module and insert a new and improved one without very much reengineering.

Modular programming still had its drawbacks. But it did introduce a concept that has helped in defining many reusable libraries. Because it provided reliable interfaces that rarely changed, writing pluggable modules for other programmers became very inviting. Also, the programmer would not need to know the implementation details, so revisions to the code were more welcome.

Not Needing the Details: Abstract Programming

Some details are so remote from the implementation needs that programmers began to look at abstract computer science concepts. With modular programming, data could be simply blocks of data with little meaning to the module. A classic example is a queue or FIFO (first in, first out); the algorithm does not need to know what is going in—only that it must come out.

Some of the first abstractions include queue, stack, tree, dictionary, bag, set, array, and so on. Each of these has a particular set of methods that you can use every day. In fact, version 5 of UNIX, back before it split, had about 10 implementations of the queue. With data abstraction, the programmers could have avoided that duplication and focused on several more interesting problems.

When programming some problem, see if you can generalize some aspect of the program. With careful analysis and practice, you can see sections that can be useful elsewhere. Also, you can find many generalized algorithms already written for you.

Looking at the data abstractly was a really significant step in the computer science field. With abstraction, the programmer does not need to know everything about the data that his program passes around. He simply focuses on what it can do.

Getting Close to Nature Through Object Programming

The current programming trend is object programming, but perhaps a better perspective would be responsibility modeling. Object programming focuses on the things in the system you are trying to program. It extends the concept of modular programming with two questions: "What does it know?" and "What does it do?" This is why the term responsibility modeling might be closer to the intent.

Objects take one step further by trying to approximate nature. Everything in nature has features (attributes) and behaviors (functions or methods). They also have intrinsic capabilities. For example, the offspring can receive features and functions from the parent. The fact that a dog has certain behaviors may stem from parental genes or oversight.

Reaching Programming Nirvana

The end-all and be-all of programming is to avoid having to write the same code over and over. Wouldn't it be great to invent something equivalent to a hammer-program that you can use over and over, changing its behavior only slightly to meet the needs of the moment?

The programmer tries to reach that lofty height through two goals: reuse and pluggability. The following sections describe these goals in more detail.

Reusing Your Work

Correctly applied, object programming yields a design that others can leverage or reuse. The holy grail of all software engineering is to write-once and reuse-many times. Objects bring you closer to that idyllic state.

The problems you face from day to day as a programmer do not stray much from those faced by others who have programmed before you. In fact, most problems are just mutations of age-old designs. Some reusable designs include that of TCP messengers or servers, such as email or HTTP. Regrettably, much of their designs are locked behind the walls of proprietary software.

The power of reuse is the ability to take others' work and build on it. Consider how long it would take an architect to build your new home if he had to pour metal to make nails? Now, that industry can pump out very impressive, sturdy, and well-built homes in a factory and ship the pieces to the site in only three days! Why can't the computer industry do that? Well, it can, but it takes discipline.

NIH: Not Invented Here

When I worked at my first job, I was among the most intelligent and gifted engineers I had ever met. Trying to stand out of the crowd was a constant struggle. However, there was one trait many of them shared that limited their potential: NIH. *Not Invented Here* is a mindset that stipulates that "If we didn't do it, it was probably done wrong (or not perfectly)." I have learned that this erroneous (if not arrogant) viewpoint is prevalent throughout nearly all software firms.

You might want to consider two angles of reuse—accepting others' work and promoting your own. The first is really straightforward and requires a little trust between you and the provider. This is fine, as long as the provider is responsive to your needs.

The flipside makes you the provider for the user-programmer. To promote your work, the libraries must be robust and you need to respond quickly your users. A good and intuitive design keeps your customer coming back for later versions. Also, providing clear upgrade paths helps make a difficult transition easier.

Lastly, generalizing your design simplifies reuse. Look at the problem as a set of puzzle pieces. The closer you make the pieces to a generalized form, the more likely your users can reuse your work.

Strengthening Reuse with Pluggability

Another ultimate goal is the ability to replace a library with another, better library. For example, batteries have specific interfaces but many different styles of manufacture and features. Batteries can be simple dry cell or even the newer lithium-ion. Each still uses a pole-style of interface, one end positive and the other negative. The dry cell is cheaper, and the lithium-ion is more efficient, is rechargeable, and has a longer life.

Following this style, you want to select an interface and resist changing it. Therefore, no matter what happens, you can improve the implementation (boosting performance, increasing reliability, fixing defects). The ability to change libraries or modules in and out is *pluggability*.

You need to follow certain rules to produce pluggable code. First, define an interface and stick to it. A thoroughly thought out interface determines the longevity of the module. If the interface cannot keep pace with evolving needs, designers discard it for a newer (sometimes less proven) technology. A good (but often confusing) example of a flexible interface is the socket() system call itself. While initially less than intuitive, the interface is so flexible that it has survived several years of network development and many networking technologies.

The second rule for pluggable code is *minimalism*—making the interface as simple as possible increases the likelihood of adoption. *Coupling* is the number of distinct connections (or, in terms of modules, the number of distinct data elements passed in) a system has. Increasing the coupling increases dependence and reduces adaptability. Socket programming actually is a mixture of simplified interfaces with complex interfacing. To get a socket running, you have to make several system calls (up to seven). While this provides a lot of adaptability, it does nothing to help the programmer. The only reason sockets have survived for so long is their ability to change.

The third and final rule is layering. *Layering* does more than modularize a set of data; it places a single boundary around an entire technology. The TCP or OSI layering models do a good to great job of layering the technology. Each layer has rules to it, and each has interfaces. The rules always envision a product that can adapt to new technologies.

Laying the Object Foundation

As stated earlier, object-oriented programming stands on all good programming models invented to date. It extends a few ideas and places limits on a few others. The result is a set of concepts that you can use most of the time to solve programming problems. But before you get your expectations set too high, you may want to read the limitations in Chapter 14, "Limits to Objects."

This section identifies the foundations of objects. Some of these you may be familiar with; some may be very new. Object-oriented programming is founded on four intrinsic foundations:

A-PIE what know 4 do

Abstraction, Polymorphism, Inheritance, and Encapsulation. You can remember these concepts with the mnemonic A-PIE. (Some object purists say that objects have only three pillars, because abstraction is integral to polymorphism, inheritance, and encapsulation. Abstraction is still important to link back to the evolution of computer science.)

The section also shows you examples for each. What is most interesting about object programming is its ability to be applied anywhere—with or without an object-enabled language. Translation: You can use most of these concepts in nearly any programming language, including assembler. It all comes down to discipline.

Implementation Encapsulation

The first foundation of object technology is encapsulation. Enclosing the actual implementation details into a protected shell of interfaces is a critical requirement for reuse. In most respects, global data is a big no-no in object programming. Your program must inseparably and dedicatedly link the data with the implementation. If the program breaks this link, you lose reuse and pluggability.

> ### Global Objects
>
> No global data is a good rule to follow. It ensures that only the owner modifies the data. Question: Is a global object global data? For example, suppose you have an instance called MyAccount, and suppose it is in a global variable. The answer is that a global object is *not* global data. As a matter of fact, creating global objects is common and often required.

Encapsulation hides information that the outside does not need to know or guards access to certain data. You often have two different types of information that you may want to hide from the outside world—internal data and internal implementation. Internal data (all data should be internal) includes information about the structure and layout of the data.

For example, if you have two persistent variables inside an object that provide counting, you do not want the outside world to know how the program stores the numbers. That information would not contribute to the performance. Instead, if another part of the program accesses the variables directly, the coupling between the two sections of the program increases. And if you needed to change the way the counters work, you would have to change the external references as well.

Internal implementation refers to all local procedures or functions that support the object. In the process of writing a program, you may find the need to write a set of support routines that only simplify coding. These routines just divide the processing load into steps or functions and do not relate with the outside world.

All interfaces with the outside world should show relevance to what the object does or for what it is responsible. Typically, the industry calls these functions *services*. Everything else should be locked into the object.

Behavior Inheritance

Suppose you wanted to write a module that was the same as another but only changed a couple behaviors. For example, a toggle on a desktop application is just a mutation of a button that holds a depressed or released state. Object inheritance offers this foundation. There's an old adage that applies to this foundation: "Treat a child like the parent, and it behaves itself."

Objects let you define an object with a set of attributes and behaviors. Inheritance lets you reuse that work by adding specific derivations or mutations to the existing work. When the program creates a new object, inheriting it from another, the new object has all the capabilities of the parent (or *superclass*). Figure 11.1 shows the superclass Device as the parent to other concrete classes.

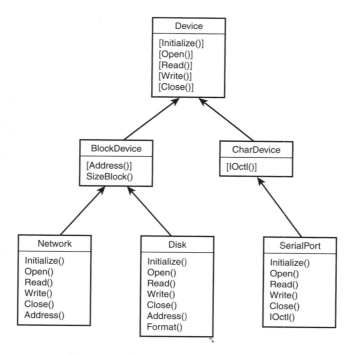

FIGURE 11.1

The inheritance hierarchy of Device *includes two abstract objects (*BlockDevice *and* CharDevice*) and three regular objects (*Network, Disk, *and* SerialPort*).*

A programming example might be "`SerialPort` is a `CharDevice`, and a `CharDevice` is a `Device`." `Device` would define the basic interfaces for `initialize()`, `open()`, `read()`, `write()`, and `close()`. `CharDevice` would extend `Device`'s interface with `ioctl()`. Lastly, `SerialPort` actually defines the implementation of each interface, applying the serial port's eccentricities.

Data Abstraction

The third foundation, data abstraction, is similar to the abstract programming model described earlier, but it extends the concept a little. Abstract programming allows the programmer to focus on the function and ignores the meaning of the data. This led to standard implementations of basic computer science structures, such as stacks and dictionaries.

Object programming extends this concept with a few of its own. By tacking on encapsulation, object programming allows you to work inside the sphere of the module you need to write and perfect. Abstraction works with the functions and operations from a generic viewpoint.

Abstraction gets a tremendous boost from inheritance. Inheritance coupled with abstraction allows you to create generalized objects that act as blueprints but really don't exist in nature. Taking an example from nature, a Chihuahua is a dog, and a dog is a mammal. Neither dog nor mammal exists in nature, but they do provide a blueprint for how to distinguish the dog from a cat or tree. An abstract object identifies the main responsibilities of the object and may leave some defined but not implemented.

Unlike an abstract object, all normal objects must define and implement all remaining behaviors. In the `Device` example shown previously, `CharDevice` and `Device` are not real objects but merely abstractions that provide blueprints for specific interfaces and behaviors. The behaviors are the basic interfaces mentioned earlier. You may note that you could program the default behaviors for a few interfaces; this would not reduce the power of abstraction. In fact, if done properly, the default behaviors would stand as a basis the inherited objects would enhance.

Abstraction's power lets you call a single interface (for example, `read()` from the earlier example) without knowing the specific implementation. The Device hierarchy definition (Figure 11.1) includes two other objects, `Disk` and `Network`. Abstraction lets you create any one of the non-abstract objects yet treat them like the abstract version. For example, you can do the following:

```
/**********************************************************/
/* Create a Disk object and place it in the Device        */
/* abstract reference                                     */
/**********************************************************/
Device *dev = new Disk();
dev->Initialize();
```

Even though `Device` does not define the `Initialize()` behavior but only provides the interface, the language is smart enough to call `Disk`'s implementation. Be aware that the interface `Address()` is invisible to `Device`, even though `Disk` defines it. To access that interface, you can revise the code:

```
BlockDevice *dev = new Disk();
dev->Address();
```

You set the access and interfaces by defining the interface as part of the variable declaration. Of course, you can cast the variable to the appropriate type, but not all languages keep *type-safeness* during the conversion.

Method Polymorphism

The fourth and last primary object foundation looks a little like abstraction—*polymorphism*. This foundation does not enhance the programming paradigm's power. It merely simplifies the defined interface—the method names are easier to remember.

Polymorphism uses both the name and the parameters of an interface to uniquely identify the behavior. For example, you could have two methods named `PlayVideo()` and `PlayMIDI()`. With polymorphism, you would have one name for two behaviors, `Play()`. The parameters would uniquely identify the behavior—`Play(Video)` and `Play(MIDI)`.

The linkers that compilers use are still not smart enough to handle matching both the name and parameter of a behavior, so the compiler has to provide the fix. How a language implements this foundation requires changing the name of the behavior to include the name and each parameter type. This is called *name-mangling*. The resulting name only partially resembles the original behavior name.

Object Features

To incorporate the foundations of object technology includes several features or definitions. These features may not be new, but they are important terms to use when talking the object technology language.

The seven features are access rights, class, object, attributes, properties, methods, and relationships. This section describes each feature.

The Class or Object

The first two features often confuse programmers. The class is the description of the object, and the object is the actual allocated thing. This is analogous to a blueprint (the class) and the house built from the blueprint (the object).

An experienced C programmer knows about the `struct` language element—it describes the contents of a compound data structure. The class similarly describes the elements that the object will have when it's created. Creating an object from a class is like creating the variable using the defined structure tag.

> ### Usage Note
> To this point, this chapter has used the term *object* to refer to both a class and an object. That was intentional to reduce confusion.

The inheritance hierarchy includes two special types of classes: the superclass and the subclass. The *superclass* is the class at the very top of the inheritance tree, and it usually is abstract. Each class that derives its behavior from some parent class is a *subclass*.

Attributes

The individual fields in a C structure are similar to the attributes in the class. Typically, attributes are all the class's fields both published and hidden. The elements of a class that are visible to the outside world are *published* as part of the interface. Most of the time, you want to hide (or encapsulate) all the attributes of a class.

Properties

Some attributes can be visible to the interface. These are the properties of the class. Do not use this feature unless you want to expose part of your class to the outside world. Usually, properties are either read-only definitions or are behind `Get()` and `Set()` guards. You never want to expose a pure variable to the outside.

> ### Programming CRUD
> The `Get()` and `Set()` methods are not really methods. They are part of a special set of functions that do nothing more than create, read, update, and delete (CRUD) information. Methods are responsibilities: They *do* something. CRUD provides no features and is always assumed. Therefore, it is never counted in the method set.

Subclasses inherit both properties and attributes from their parent classes.

Methods

Methods are the object responsibilities or behaviors. You can override inherited methods, add new methods, or enhance existing interfaces with polymorphism. When you override an inherited method, it is common to call the parent's original method. This helps the parent initialize its private attributes and behaviors.

Attributes, properties, and methods compose the class's *elements*.

Access Rights

Access rights ensure that part of the program accesses the right parts of the interface. Both Java and C++ offer three levels of access—private, protected, and public.

- private   Isolates the elements from everyone except the owner
- protected   Lets both the owner and its subclasses access the element
- public   Lets everyone access the element

You can loosen the strictness of the access rules by setting up friendships between classes.

Relationships

Objects interact with each other in three different ways. One way, inheritance, is described earlier in this chapter. You can remember these relationships with three keys: *is-a*, *has-a*, and *uses*. Professionals use these keys during object analysis and design, and they have their own graphical representation (which is beyond the scope of this text).

- *is-a*   Inheritance: One class derives its behavior from another.
- *has-a*   Contains: One class holds/owns another.   — → Containments
- *uses*   Works: One class works or uses another.

All object interactions involve these keys exclusively. Be careful when letting your objects interact: two objects should not have more than one interaction. For example, Object A should not contain and work Object B. If an analysis shows this kind of relationship, it's broken.

Relationship duality indicates a poorly done analysis. Objects must have one responsibility. An object that has more than one distinct responsibility can demonstrate this duality. The answer is simple—split the object in half or more.

Extending Objects

When you have a good thing (especially a really good thing like objects), the natural tendency is to extend the features or expand their meaning. These extensions are available in some object languages but not all. You should be aware that a design you produce may not be implemented in the language you intend.

Some extensions are natural consequences of objects, such as templates and streaming). Others, such as exceptions, are unrelated but are very important for good design. This section identifies a few common extensions.

Templates

Class abstraction and polymorphism take a set of functions and apply them as appropriate to the data. Imagine being able to extend that concept and create a class that can generate its own versions on new data. Templates (available in C++) let you define a generic responsibility without foreknowledge of the data.

A template establishes the behavior and responsibility. You create a new class based on this template by providing a specific type. A common use of templates is in creating generic containers of objects. For example, a queue or stack has behavior (putting in and taking out ordered data) that is independent of the data type.

Creating a template from scratch is arcane, and the syntax is strange. The easiest way is to create an instance of the class and generalize it. After you've tested it, go ahead and add the template notation.

Persistence

Most of the time, programmers think of objects *living* while the program is running. However, programs sometimes have parameters that help define their behaviors. Usually, these behaviors are tuned to the user's needs. When you need to save this kind of information while the program is not running, you typically save that information in some file.

Persistence lets you abstract that behavior. When the program comes up, it loads the parameters and continues where the user left off. Persistence is also helpful in system recovery. If carefully done, you can even seamlessly reestablish connections lost from a system failure.

Streaming

Another extension to objects is *streaming*. Imagine being able to tell the object to package itself up and save or send itself somewhere. When it arrives or a program loads it, it automatically opens itself up and tells you what it can do. This is very useful in persistence and distributed programming.

Streaming is part and parcel in Java. You can do some streaming techniques in C++, but object identification (called *introspection* in Java) is not possible.

Overloading

Many extensions just focus on one foundation. For example, operator overloading (supported in C++) is an extension of polymorphism. Some programmers mistakenly say that polymorphism includes operator overloading. It doesn't; it's simply an extension. Java does not support overloading, but it's considered to be an object language.

Operator overloading lets you add to (*not redefine*) the meaning of internal operators. You can use these operators in any way you want as if they were regular polymorphic method names. The extension, however, must place many restrictions on the new definition.

- *Extension not Redefinition*—You cannot change the meaning of an existing type. In other words, you cannot change the meaning of (int)+(int).
- *Not All Operators Available*—You can use most operators, but some cannot be redefined (for example, the arithmetic if ?:).
- *Must Retain Parameter Count*—The new operator meaning must use the same number of parameters as the original. All overloadable operators are either monadic (one-parameter) or didactic (two-parameter).

You may want to use caution when defining new meanings for operators. It can make your code less clear and result in unintentional results.

Interfaces

A really useful extension allows the object to keep its identity while being able to service others. One problem that C++ has is that for Class A to use Class B, Class A must either be aware of Class B when the programmer designs Class A, or Class B must inherit from a class that Class A knows about. When Class B has to support several interfaces, you get into some very nasty multiple inheritance problems.

The classes that have the greatest longevity have the most flexible interfaces. Java and other languages let you declare that the new class supports a particular interface. This declaration does not add very much overhead to the new class.

Events and Exceptions

The last common object extension lets the programmer worry more about the program than error recovery. If you have programmed much in C, you probably have run into the persistent problem of resolving errors. When an error occurs (either internal or external), the most appropriate place to handle the error is not likely to be at the location where you discovered it.

Exceptions let you define when and how you want to handle particular errors, and you don't have to be executing at the location of the error handler. Regrettably, all these languages do not support a resume feature, meaning that once the handler fixes the error, the program cannot continue where it left off.

Like exceptions, events are asynchronous internal or external situations that cause a redirection in the program. More common in GUI-style programs, event-based programming sets the stage to respond to the events and either waits for them or does processing between each event.

Again, like exceptions, few (if any) languages support all the capabilities of object-event programming. You can simulate much of it, but alternative implementations are likely easier.

Special Forms

Object technology has the same problems with data and design as other technologies. Not every data problem fits into the object mold. These degenerate forms are not necessarily bad design, but too many of them does indicate the lack of understanding of objects.

This section defines the types of degenerate classes, gives examples, and offers suggestions on how to avoid them if possible.

Record/Structure

An old rule states that a class without methods is just a record. Some records are necessary. If you cannot think of any responsibility, it may not have any. For example, databases just store data; they don't store methods. Nature, however, does not have any method-less objects. Everything can do something.

A record or structure is just a collection of data. It has no methods beyond CRUD. Very infrequently, you may run into one of these degenerate classes. If you do, try testing it with the following:

- *Are the elements (fields) strongly related?*—For example, if you change one, it should change the value or meaning of another. If not, you may have *collection* (a bag of unrelated items). Try to isolate all related groupings. Then, identify what they are responsible for.

- *Did you start with the class and then identify the supporting attributes?*—A common mistake is to find all the possible attributes and then try to group them into a class. That is backwards. A programming problem starts with a primary responsibility or task that you can divide into smaller and smaller subtasks.

- *Are you looking at a part of a very large system?*—Databases are great examples of collections. Each relationship has to be kept in a set of business rules so that you maintain data integrity. If you start out just looking at one part of the relational map, you may conclude that it has no function at all. The reality may be that you are losing the forest of data for the tree.

If you answered "Yes" to each of these, don't worry about it and create the record. Be sure to encapsulate it with CRUD.

Function Bag

The function bag is the opposite of the record or data bag. It does not have any data but plenty of functions. An excellent example of this is the math library. You might think that `float` is related to the functions in the math library. Actually, they are related but not *coupled*. To create a proper class, you must have good strong coupling between the data and the methods. If you don't, you don't have an object. The `exp()` function is related to but not coupled with the floating-point type (you can still have a `float` without the `exp()` function).

Unlike the data bag, function bags do exist in nature. You can find these in any physics or calculus textbook. They exist with the need of data.

If you find that you have deduced a function bag, test its validity with the following questions:

- *Have you carefully divided the responsibilities to a good level?*—You can easily go overboard with delegation and end up splitting the object atom—two or more objects that should have been one. Look for overly strong coupling between classes. You may actually have one or two objects after restructuring.

- *Do you have good, "healthy" coupling between classes?*—Just like tasks, if two or more classes depend on each other, you can get a form of deadlock or cyclical dependency. These dependencies indicate that the data or function is in the wrong class.

- *Do you have proper ownership of functions and data?*—If the data and functions are not strongly dependent or related, or you can easily partition them, you may not have the responsibilities in the right place.

- *Do the responsibilities interact with each other?*—One method should directly or indirectly change the behavior of other methods. If this does not happen, you don't have any coupling between them.

- *Do the methods use any internal (non-constant) data?*—A healthy class is going to have methods that change the state of the object. If nothing changes, you really have a *translation-function* instead of a method.

Function bags are much more common than data bags, but you still need to be suspicious of accidental function bags.

Language Support

Once you understand the capabilities of object technology, you would naturally want to try them. The features they offer are very attractive to most programmers and technologists. Even electrical (hardware) and embedded systems (firmware) engineers are jumping on the object bandwagon.

As you might expect, many languages now exist that support the demand for objects. You can even find versions of Object Cobol (for those who want a challenge). The classic object-oriented languages are SmallTalk and Eiffel. Lisp is a language that supported a form of object-orientation long before objects became popular. The next two chapters discuss sockets APIs in Java and C++.

Supporting Versus Enabled Versus Oriented

You may have noticed a few shades of terms—object-oriented and object-enabled. These are actual terms the object technology experts have defined for different languages. In reality, few object languages are truly object-oriented or *object-enforced*. SmallTalk is perhaps the only prevalent language that is object-enforced. Everything that you do in SmallTalk is with an object. Whether it is creating an instance, working with the source or compiler, or manipulating the framework, you simply cannot get around it.

Most languages are *object-enabled*: the language supports and encourages the foundations, features, and extensions to object technology. For example, C++ is an object-enabled language. You can circumvent many of the features and simply compile C code with it. You can even define quasi-objects with many of the features—except for encapsulation and privileges—of a class by using `struct` instead.

An object-enabled language lets you write code that does not force all the tenets of object technology. Even Java is object-enabled; you could write one huge `main()` in a single class definition with several supporting methods. True object-enforced languages are not limited to a single entry point; all the objects the program needs it instantiates (creates and runs) at startup.

The loosest form of object-orientation is *object-supporting*. Essentially, an object-supporting language has object-enhanced features, but they are optional and are appendages to the language structure. You can get similar or equal power out of the language with or without the object support elements. A good example of an object-supporting language would be Perl or Visual Basic. Of course, object-supporting languages have limitations. Typically, you lose inheritance.

To make up for the limitations, these languages often throw in a catch-all element. For example, Visual Basic offers the variant type to support abstraction and manual inheritance. Unfortunately, these catch-all elements break other foundations of object technology, such as encapsulation, reuse, maintainability, readability, and testability. Visual Basic's variant type leaves the type determination up to the receiver, forcing the receiver to know private information about the data that it gets.

How to Map Objects to Non-Object Languages

Object technology is great if you can program in an object-enabled programming language (such as C++ and Java). You gain a lot of benefits from the foundations and extensions and, if done right, your code becomes more reusable. However, not every shop supports or permits object languages. What can you do?

Believe it or not, much of the foundation and features of objects can be deployed in any programming language, including COBOL and assembler (except for inheritance). It just takes discipline and a particular programming style. Unfortunately, nearly all the extensions are lost.

Because much of object-orientation is based on previous technologies (abstraction, modular programming, and so on), the languages of that day have those features. The following are ways to get those benefits:

- *Encapsulation*—Make sure that all the interfaces with your modules are procedures or functions. Trust that the programmers don't crack open your code and use the variables and other private members. Also, name your methods with something such as `<ModuleName>_<ProcedureName>()`. However, some compilers may limit the name length, so you may want to check that.

- *Abstraction*—Languages that allow you to change the type of a variable with something like casting can do some form of abstraction. You can store the actual type as part of the record structure and get that to do the appropriate actions.

- *Polymorphism*—You can do your own name mangling (for example, `Play_MIDI()`).

- *Inheritance*—Some languages can simulate inheritance using function pointers, but this is difficult to debug and maintain.

- *Class and Object*—You have a good starting point if the language supports records.

- *Attributes*—These are simply the fields of the record.

- *Properties*—You create the CRUD interfaces for each published property.

- *Methods*—All languages support functions and procedures. If you do not have functions, you can simulate that with a parameter-value return.

- *Access Rights*—The access rights would be rules you set to use your module. If someone breaks those rules, all bets are off.

- *Relationships*—Contains and Works relationships are available. The Inheritance relationship depends on the language.

- *Templates*—Not available.   C++

- *Persistence*—You can keep track of the state and manually load each time the program starts.

- *Streaming*—The packaging and unpackaging of data requires knowledge about the data and the ability to cast data types. Identification of unknown structures is not possible because the methods would not be shipped along with the data.

- *Overloading*—Not available.

- *Interfaces*—You can use implicit interfaces, but that only assumes a dynamic-loading environment. This is not likely to be available.

- *Events and Exceptions*—You can simulate some event programming and exception catching, but you would need to use an inter-function jump (such as C's `setjump()`) to duplicate it. This is not a good idea.

You are not left out of the object programming loop. The good practices listed here can help you in whatever condition you work.

Summary: Object-Oriented Thinking

Object technology stands on top of a lot of good research and innovation in programming. The foundation of objects (abstraction, polymorphism, inheritance, and encapsulation) helps the programmer design and write good solid programs that others can leverage or reuse. The features define the parts of how object technology implements part of the foundation, and the extensions let the programmer grow into other capabilities.

When used carefully and with discipline, the result of object-oriented analysis and design is easier to reuse. It is also easier to maintain and extend than conventional programming. Lastly, it lets the programmer focus more on the problem than on the programming.

Using Java's Networking API

IN THIS CHAPTER

Up to this point, the book has covered sockets and network programming in C. The advantages of C-style programming is very clear to operating systems designers—the power without overhead is a real bonus. However, it does not always result in reusable or portable programs.

Alternatively, you could use an object-enabled language and create a set of reusable tools. Java is a great example of excellent reuse and even portability. The whole foundation of Java is to provide two levels of portability—source level and code level. Source-level portability means that all programs must be able to compile on any platform. (You may note that Sun Microsystems reserves the right to expire or *deprecate* certain interfaces, methods, or classes.) This is very powerful because you can reuse code on any platform that supports Java.

Code-level portability is not really new. The idea "Compile once, run everywhere" is easy to implement with the right tools. Java compiles to a byte code on which a virtual machine runs. The Java Virtual Machine (JVM) executes each command sequentially, acting somewhat like a microprocessor. Of course, interpreting the byte code cannot ever approximate the speed of native machine language (which C compiles into), but because of the speed of modern microprocessors, the performance degradation is less noticeable.

Java is a very powerful, simple, and fun language. If you know how to program in C/C++ and understand Object Technology, you've got a good start in programming in Java. The libraries in Java are expansive, covering many, many operations. You can easily get lost in all the available classes. Even if you learn Java and become thoroughly familiar with the class libraries, you may probably keep the Java Developers Kit (JDK) documents and a few printed references close at hand.

The last chapter introduced the purpose of Object Technology and how to design using it. This chapter covers one socket implementation in Java; the next chapter defines a custom C++ socket framework. Because a topic on Java is so vast, the topics in this chapter primarily assume that you already know Java and want to move into network programming. Likewise, some of the examples on the companion Web site contain Abstract Windowing Toolkit (AWT) program code—discussing GUIs and events is beyond the scope of this chapter.

The following sections discuss the classes that Java offers for sockets, relevant I/O, and threading. This chapter also discusses some of the newer methods that support socket configuration (as found in Chapter 9, "Breaking Performance Barriers").

Exploring Different Java Sockets

Like C, Java offers ways to access the Internet. In fact, some programmers say that the true benefits of Java arise from GUI independence and the inherent network programming. Java offers a few Internet protocols for your use, these primarily being TCP and UDP.

The Java-preferred networking channel is the TCP channel. It, as noted in the first part of the book, has the most reliability. Also, it's easier to use than the datagram-style of communication. Java still offers a UDP connection, but the I/O library does not offer any direct support for it.

Programming Clients and Servers

Streaming (or TCP) channels match Java's interface the best. Java tries to abstract the details and simplify interfaces. You can easily understand the decisions behind placing support for TCP in the I/O library. Java's approach to creating sockets really reduces the steps to a couple of objects and methods.

Java TCP Clients

For example, if you want a client socket, you just create it:

```
Socket s = new Socket(String Hostname, int PortNum);
Socket s = new Socket(InetAddress Addr, int PortNum);
```

A common implementation may look like the following:

```
Socket s = new Socket("localhost", 9999);
```

That's it. You don't have to do anything else to connect to a server. When the JVM creates the object, it assigns a local port number, does the network-byte order conversion, and connects to the server. You can even specify which local network interface and port to use with the following extensions:

```
Socket s = new Socket(String Hostname, int PortNum,
    InetAddress localAddr, int localPort);
Socket s = new Socket(InetAddress Addr, int PortNum,
    InetAddress localAddr, int localPort);
```

The InetAddress class converts the hostname or IP address into the binary address. Most of the time, you won't use the InetAddress object directly in the call unless you begin with it. Instead, the constructor that passes Hostname is a more common use. Most programs connect using the information a user provides to the program. This typically is by hostname or IP address.

Java's IPv4/IPv6 Support

Java currently and directly supports IPv4 and, according to project Merlin (see java.sun.com), IPv6 support should be available when the operating system supports it. Classes like InetAddress, which manages the names and conversion, should easily adapt to other protocols. Be aware, however, that the version you have may not support it yet. Some interfaces, such as InetAddress.getHostAddress(), need to change to support the extended address and new format.

Sending/Receiving Messages

After creating the socket, the program cannot directly send or receive data through this class, however. You must get the InputStream or OutputStream from the class instance:

```
InputStream i = s.getInputStream();
OutputStream o = s.getOutputStream();
```

Using these methods, you can read or write arrays of bytes:

```
byte[] buffer = new byte[1024];
int bytes_read = i.read(buffer); //--Read block from socket
o.write(buffer);    //--Transmit byte array through socket
```

You can even use InputStream to determine if data is waiting in the kernel's buffers with InputStream.available(). This method returns the number of bytes that the program can read without blocking.

```
if (i.available() > 100 )//--Don't read unless 100 bytes await
  bytes = i.read(buffer);
```

When you are done, you can close the socket (and all the I/O channels as well) with a single call to Socket.close():

```
//--Clean up
s.close();
```

Manual Versus Garbage Collection

Java uses new for all calls. The JVM passes everything (except scalars) as pointers, and the pointers are never exposed to your program. Everything must point to some data or null. The JVM calls a garbage collection process when resources begin to get scarce. All loose memory references during this process file back into the available pool. This means that you never have to release any of the memory you allocate. However, this does not apply to sockets. You must manually close all sockets. If the program does not close a defunct socket, the program may run out of available file descriptors eventually. The resulting program behavior may not be entirely unpredictable.

With these calls and objects, you can create an echo client as shown in Listing 12.1.

LISTING 12.1   An Example of a Simple Echo Client in Java

```
//***************************************************************
// SimpleEchoClient excerpt
//-------------------------------------------------------------
```

LISTING 12.1   Continued

```
Socket s = new Socket("127.0.0.1", 9999);    // Create socket
InputStream i = s.getInputStream();      // Get input stream
OutputStream o = s.getOutputStream();    // Get output stream
String str;
do
{
  byte[] line = new byte[100];
  System.in.read(line);                  // Read from console
  o.write(line);                         // Send the message
  i.read(line);                          // Read it back
  str = new String(line);                // Convert to string
  System.out.println(str.trim());        // Print message
}
while ( !str.trim().equals("bye") );
s.close();                     // Close connection
```

Listing 12.1 shows a simple reading and sending loop. It is far from complete, but it demonstrates the functionality. If you try to compile this snippet, the compiler complains about not catching certain exceptions. All network operations must capture exceptions. For the source, Listing 12.1, you surround the code with the following:

```
try
{
// <--Add all source here
}
catch (Exception err)
{
  System.err.println(err);
}
```

The try...catch block completes the example. You can drop this code directly in a main() block of a class.

Java TCP Servers

As you saw in the earlier sections, Java has simplified creating, reading, writing, and closing sockets. Writing the corresponding server is even easier. The call to create a server socket has three interfaces:

```
ServerSocket s = new ServerSocket(int PortNum);
ServerSocket s = new ServerSocket(int PortNum, int Backlog);
ServerSocket s = new ServerSocket(int PortNum, int Backlog,
    InetAddress BindAddr);
```

The Backlog and BindAddr offer the same features as the C-based system calls listen() (awaiting-connection queue) and bind() (to a specific network interface).

If you recall, a C-based server program takes about 7–10 lines to write. In Java, you can create an equivalent server in about two lines:

```
ServerSocket s = new ServerSocket(9999);
Socket c = s.accept();
```

And, like the C-style listening socket, you use the ServerSocket for only awaiting client connections. When a client requests a connection, the server gets a new Socket object that it can use to create the I/O streams.

Again, you can use these classes to create a SimpleEchoServer (see Listing 12.2)

LISTING 12.2   The Simple Echo Server in Java Uses Byte Arrays in the Input/Output Streams

```
//************************************************************
// SimpleEchoServer excerpt
//-----------------------------------------------------------
try
{
  ServerSocket s = new ServerSocket(9999);  // Create server
  while (true)
  {
   Socket c = s.accept();            // Await connection
   InputStream i = c.getInputStream(); // Get input stream
   OutputStream o = c.getOutputStream();//Get output stream
   do
   {
     byte[] line = new byte[100];    // Create scratchpad
     i.read(line);           // Read client's message
     o.write(line);             // Send it back
   }
   while ( !str.trim().equals("bye") );
   c.close();                 // Close connection
  }
}
catch (Exception err)
{
  System.err.println(err);
}
```

Listing 12.2 demonstrates how easy creating a server is in Java. These examples are sketchy and tend to be a little clunky, but the following sections fix the I/O limitations and can help you with more solid code.

Implementing Messengers

The last section covers streaming protocols (or TCP). For connection-based communications, streams should work fine for you. However, some messages may lend themselves to a message-based protocol, such as datagrams (UDP). The Java networking package has a couple classes that let you create sockets and send messages. These are `DatagramSocket` and `MulticastSocket`.

The `DatagramSocket` class lets you create a socket with a single call:

```
DatagramSocket s = new DatagramSocket();
```

Like the `Socket` class, you can manually set the local port and network interface:

```
DatagramSocket s = new DatagramSocket(int localPort);
DatagramSocket s = new DatagramSocket(int localPort,
    InetAddress localAddr);
```

After you create the datagram socket, you can send and receive messages. These messages do not interface directly with Java I/O package. Instead, you have to use arrays of bytes. The networking package includes the `DatagramPacket` class to manage the data and destination information of each message with:

```
DatagramPacket d = new DatagramPacket(byte[] buf, int len);
DatagramPacket d = new DatagramPacket(byte[] buf, int len,
    InetAddress Addr, int port);
```

You use the first constructor to create an object that you would read into. The second constructor is useful for creating messages you intend to send and adds a destination address/port. The buf refers to an allocated array of bytes; and len refers to the length of the array *or* the length of valid data.

To demonstrate the use of the `DatagramSocket` and `DatagramPacket`, consider a peer-source and peer-destination example. A peer-source program sends a message to the peer-destination. This is similar to the datagram programming demonstrated in Chapter 4, "Sending Messages Between Peers." Listing 12.3 shows an example of a peer-source using datagrams.

LISTING 12.3   Create a Datagram Socket and Send the Message

```
//************************************************************
// SimplePeerSource excerpt
//----------------------------------------------------------
DatagramSocket s = new DatagramSocket();   // Create socket
byte[] line = new byte[100];
System.out.print("Enter text to send: ");
int len = System.in.read(line);
```

LISTING 12.3 Continued

```
InetAddress dest =              // Convert hostname
    InetAddress.getByName("127.0.0.1");
DatagramPacket pkt =            // Create message packet
    new DatagramPacket(line, len, dest, 9998);
s.send(pkt);                    // Send message
s.close();                      // Close connection
```

This listing sends the message and immediately closes the socket. While seemingly an error, all sockets allow you to send anything and then close—even before the message leaves your local host. The socket's message queue stays around until all the messages are gone.

Peer-destination essentially does the same as the client, only it reads the message instead of sending it. Listing 12.4 shows simple peer destination.

LISTING 12.4 Receive the Datagram Message and Display It

```
//**************************************************************
// SimplePeerDestination excerpt
//-------------------------------------------------------------
DatagramSocket s = new DatagramSocket(9998); // Create socket
byte[] line = new byte[100];
DatagramPacket pkt =    // Create buffer for incoming message
    new DatagramPacket(line, line.length);
s.receive(pkt);                      // Get message
String msg = new String(pkt.getData());   // Convert data
System.out.print("Got message: "+msg);
s.close();              // Close connection
```

Java supports the datagram socket to the extent that you can create sockets and send messages, but that's about it. If you want more robust I/O capability, Java really does not offer it directly. Instead, you can use the memory I/O classes to build the messages in an array (described in the section "Classifying the I/O Classes," later in this chapter).

The advantages of sending directed messages instead of an open pipe are essentially the same advantages UDP offers. (For more details on these differences, please refer to Chapter 3, "Different Types of Internet Packets," and Chapter 4.) Java provides a simple wrapper over the datagram protocols.

Sending to Multiple Destinations

The datagram protocol lets you send a single message to an unconnected destination. An advantage to datagrams is being able to send to several destinations at once using broadcasting and multicasting. Chapter 15, "Network Encapsulation with Remote Procedure Calls (RPCs)," discusses in detail both of these methods of sending messages.

Current Java-Multicasting Support

At the time of this writing, the multicasting socket options are not working correctly. This support should be fixed soon. This was tested on the 1.3 beta version for WinNT and Linux.

Java offers multicasting in its networking wrapper, but it excludes broadcasting. Multicasting lets a program join a special IP address reserved for multicasting groups. Every program in this group gets messages sent to the address. To create a `MulticastSocket`, you can use one of two constructors:

```
MulticastSocket ms = new MulticastSocket();
MulticastSocket ms = new MulticastSocket(int localPort);
```

Even though you can create a multicast socket with no specified port, your program must select a port before you can expect any messages. The reason is that all multicast datagrams use the port to filter out unwanted messages.

After you have created the socket, it acts just like a `DatagramSocket`. You can send and receive directed messages. To get the extended multicast functionality, you need to join a group. IPv4 has set aside a range of legal multicasting addresses: `224.0.0.0–239.255.255.255`.

```
MulticastSocket ms = new MulticastSocket(16900);
ms.joinGroup(InetAddress.getByName("224.0.0.1"));
ms.joinGroup(InetAddress.getByName("228.58.120.11"));
```

From this point on, your socket gets messages sent to the `224.0.0.1:16900` and `228.58.120.11:16900` addresses. Like other datagrams, the program can take each message and respond directly to the sender, or the program can reply to the group.

You don't have to join a group to send messages. Because the multicast socket is still a UDP socket, you can send messages to the group without actually joining the group. To receive multicast messages, however, the socket must join the group.

> ## Objects and Planning for the Future
>
> IPv6 supports a UDP-based multicast and intends to support a TCP-based multicast. This extension removes the unreliability of the UDP protocol. But because the MulticastSocket derives from DatagramSocket, the current hierarchy cannot support the IPv6 plans for reliable datagrams. This design is a good example of not planning for the future. When you design and write any object framework, try to look ahead a little. Leaving a few places that need to be upgraded or extended is easier than fixing a hierarchy. MulticastSocket cannot support a IPv6 T/TCP socket simply because it inherits from a datagram.

Listing 12.5 gives you an example of how to create and configure a multicast socket.

LISTING 12.5   Create a Multicast Socket and Assign Port #16900 to It, Join Group, and Wait for Messages

```
//************************************************************
// SimpleMulticastDestination excerpt
//-----------------------------------------------------------
MulticastSocket ms = new MulticastSocket(16900); // New socket
ms.joinGroup(InetAddress.getByName("224.0.0.1"));// Join group
String msg;
do
{
  byte[] line = new byte[100];
  DatagramPacket pkt = new DatagramPacket(line, line.length);
  ms.receive(pkt);
  msg = new String(pkt.getData());
  System.out.println("From "+pkt.getAddress()+":"+msg.trim());
}
while ( !msg.trim().equals("close") );
ms.close();                     // Close connection
```

Listing 12.5 creates a socket for multicasting and requests a port through which it can get the packets. After joining the 224.0.0.1 (local host) group, it creates a packet for incoming packets.

Connecting Through I/O

Up to this point, the examples use very simple and often clumsy I/O interfaces. The power of Java's sockets is in its capability to connect through different I/O classes. Java has several classes that offer different forms of reading and writing data.

This section classifies and shows you how to use the I/O classes you may want to use with sockets. The coverage is not exhaustive because the I/O package has a lot of features. If you would like to know more, you may want to pick up other Macmillan books on Java (such as *Pure Java 2* by Kenneth Litwak or *Java Programming on Linux* by Nathan Meyers).

Classifying the I/O Classes

The Java I/O package includes several classes, each defined to perform a specific task. All of them send or receive information. Unfortunately, because it has so many classes, it is difficult to know which to use and when. Perhaps the easiest way to work with them is to group them according to their several responsibilities. Then you can easily see which class is best for socket use.

The I/O package essentially offers six primary types of I/O. Each type serves a specific purpose, and all derive from `Reader`, `Writer`, `InputStream`, or `OutputStream`:

- *Memory*—I/O based on memory buffers. The package accesses no hardware devices; instead, arrays in RAM serve as virtual I/O pools. This helps in parsing strings or even creating a buffer for datagrams. Examples include `ByteArrayInputStream`, `ByteArrayOutputStream`, `CharArrayReader`, `CharArrayWriter`, `StringReader`, and `StringWriter`.

- *File*—Reading, writing, and manipulating the file system. These classes provide you ways to create, read, write, delete, or manipulate files in a file system. Examples include `FileInputStream`, `FileOutputStream`, `FileReader`, and `FileWriter`.

- *Filters*—I/O that does some character-based translation or interpretation. For example, treating a newline like an end of record, recognizing fields by tabs or commas, or converting binary values into readable numbers. Examples include `FilterReader`, `FilterWriter`, `PrintWriter`, and `PrintStream` (deprecated).

- *Objects*—Sending and receiving of entire objects. This is most impressive; Java can send and receive instances without any coding on your part. In most cases, you only need to flag the class `Serializable`, and you can transmit and receive object instances. The classes are `ObjectInputStream` and `ObjectOutputStream`.

- *Pipes*—IPC (Inter-Process Communications) as you find in C. You create a pipe and link it with another pipe, and then two threads send each other messages. The classes are `PipedInputStream`, `PipedOutputStream`, `PipedReader`, and `PipedWriter`.

- *Stream*—Generalized buffered I/O communications. This is the form that sockets use. If you want to use the others, you need to convert the streaming class to another (see the next section). The abstract classes are `InputStream` and `OutputStream`. The basic conversion classes are `InputStreamReader` and `OutputStreamWriter`.

The package has several other classes that really don't fit in this classification. An example is SequenceInputStream, which allows you to merge two streams into one.

Of all these classes, you may want to familiarize yourself most with ObjectInputStream and ObjectOutputStream for sending and receiving custom classes or BufferedReader and PrintWriter for string I/O. Network programs often use these because they suit socket programming the best. Similarly, you can use the ByteArrayInputStream or ByteArrayOutputStream objects to provide interfaces for datagram messages.

Converting Between I/O Classes

Some features that one class owns may not be directly available in the I/O class that the socket hands you. The Socket class only offers two I/O classes—OutputStream and InputStream. These offer pretty much bare bones reading and writing of byte arrays. To get the different features, you need to convert these classes.

Suppose you want to read in strings, not byte arrays. The BufferedReader has a good String interface. You need to convert from the InputStream abstract class to the Reader abstract class. The InputStreamReader class acts as the go-between for this conversion:

```
Socket s = new Socket(host, port);
InputStream is = s.getInputStream();
InputStreamReader isr = new InputStreamReader(is);
BufferedReader br = new BufferedReader(isr);
String l = br.readLine();
```

You can also use the following customary shorthand:

```
BufferReader br = new BufferReader(new InputStreamReader(
  s.getInputStream()));
```

Sending a string (without actually converting the string) through a channel is a little easier:

```
String msg = new String(
  "<html><body>Welcome to my Java website</body></html>");
SocketServer ss = new SocketServer(9999);
Socket s = ss.accept();
PrintWriter pw = new PrintWriter(s.getOutputStream(), true);
pw.println(msg);
s.close();
```

The first parameter gives the new PrintWriter instance a reference to the socket's stream. The second parameter tells the object to *autoflush* whenever the program calls println(). Normally, the I/O in PrintWriter buffers up the data until it has enough to minimize bandwidth waste. Specifying autoflush says that you want to specify when a buffer is sent.

Using these I/O classes, you can create I/O messages that non–Java-based programs can interpret. However, you can still send/receive objects to/from another Java program using the ObjectOutputStream/ObjectInputStream classes. You can transmit any object that implements the Serializable interface.

```
String msg = new String("Test");
Socket s = new Socket(hostname, port);
ObjectOutputStream oos = new ObjectOutputStream(
  s.getOutputStream());
oos.writeObject(msg);
```

The receiving end can take the message as an object and convert it into a known type:

```
Socket s = ss.accept();
ObjectInputStream ois = new ObjectInputStream(
  s.getInputStream());
String newMsg = (String)ois.readObject();
```

If the message does not match the type being cast, the interpreter throws a ClassCastException. So if the program gets a class that you did not anticipate, you can use class reflection to get the correct type. If the program still does not know the type, you can dig deeper in the class and get the methods, inheritance, and implementations. While making the code more complicated, using this approach can result in a more extensible product.

Configuring the Java Socket

Chapter 9 lists several ways you can configure your socket to do different operations using socket options. Java versions up to 1.3 have exposed some of these capabilities in the API. Please note that if the operating system does not support certain socket options, Java cannot expose them. This section describes these exposed options.

Shared Java-Socket Configurations

All Java sockets share methods to configure the socket. The following determines how long a read waits for data. These methods expose the SO_TIMEOUT socket option, which determines how long a read waits. The SO_TIMEOUT option is archaic, and Linux uses fcntl(), poll(), or select() instead.

```
getSoTimeout()
setSoTimeout(int timeout)
```

The following code specifies the size of the internal send buffers in bytes. These methods expose the SO_SNDBUF socket option:

```
getSendBufferSize()
setSendBufferSize(int size)
```

The next code lines specify the size of the internal receive buffers in bytes. These methods expose the SO_RCVBUF socket option.

```
getReceiveBufferSize()
setReceiveBufferSize(int size)
setKeepAlive(boolean on)
```

The following methods determine whether and for how long the socket should stick around after being closed. These calls expose the IP SO_LINGER socket option.

```
getSoLinger()
setSoLinger(boolean on, int linger)
```

The next code enables or disables the Nagle algorithm that waits for the network to deliver a packet before sending the next packet. These calls expose the TCP_NODELAY socket option.

```
getTcpNoDelay()
setTcpNoDelay(boolean on)
```

Java Multicast-Specific Configurations

This section lists the options you can set on a MulticastSocket object. These functions determine how many router hops the socket allows before a packet should die.

The following methods expose the IP_MULTICAST_TTL socket option. (Strangely, Java does not let you specify the TTL for the other socket types.)

```
getTimeToLive()
setTimeToLive(int ttl)
```

The next methods set the primary network interface for multicast transmissions by exposing the IP_MULTICAST_IF socket option.

```
getInterface()
setInterface(InetAddress inf)
```

Multitasking the Programs

Java has made several programming techniques easy and direct. Along with the networking and I/O packages, which dramatically reduce programming and complexity, it has an integrated multithreading structure. Java threads are as simple as declaring an interface.

While doing network programming, you definitely need to take advantage of all the multitasking capabilities that the system affords you. This section summarizes a few things you need to know if you want to use threading in your Java programs.

Threading a Class

To create a threadable class, you can either derive from the `Thread` class or implement the `Runnable` interface. In both cases, you must define the `run()` method where the thread actually begins running. In the first case, you can simply write the following:

```
public class TestThread extends Thread
{
  public void run()
  {
   /*** thread runs here ***/
  }
```

Extending `Thread` lets you create the thread based on the class. The `run()` method determines where the thread begins to run. When the method exits, the thread terminates. The next few lines create the thread and run it.

```
  public static void main(String[] args)
  {
   start(); // <-- start the thread and call run()
   /*** do something while the thread runs ***/
  }
}
```

If you want to create several threads, call `start()` each time. As the name implies, all threads share all the data. To create a separate workspace for a thread, you can create a new object:

```
Thread t = new TestThread();
t.start();
```

Any part of your program, including event and exception handlers, can create and start a thread. However, remember that you want to hold on to the reference to any created object. Otherwise, when a random garbage collection occurs, your dangling thread may suddenly terminate.

Adding Threads to a Class

Sometimes, however, inheriting from Thread is not possible. The typical example is when you are writing a class that derives from Frame. Java does not allow multiple inheritance, so inheriting from both Frame and Thread is impossible. In this case, you can use the second technique of implementing the Runnable interface. The results are the same, and the program changes only slightly.

```
public class TestFrameThread extends Frame
  implements Runnable
{
  public void run()
  {
   /*** child thread ***/
  }
  public void someMethod()
  {
   Thread t = new Thread(this);
   t.start();
  }
}
```

The bold text indicates two changes to the source. The first is the inheritance of Frame and the implementation of Runnable. This declares the relationships we need to get the right program behavior. The second change is the creation of a thread. The Thread class has an additional constructor that accepts any object that implements the Runnable interface and makes a Thread object out of it. Calling start() does the same thing as if the class were derived from Thread.

All threads that run in a class can actually be unrelated to the class's base functionality. You really don't have any restriction. But if you encounter different groups of responsibilities, be certain that in reality you don't have two different classes. Two ways to determine whether you really have disparate classes include how much the separate threads (parent and child) share and whether the child-thread could exist without the parent's data or features.

Creating a separate class for each primary responsibility is good object design, and it really helps in a multiprogramming environment. If you need access to each object's methods or resources, create property control methods (set()/get()). By centralizing all the attribute control through methods, you really build on encapsulation and make thread synchronization easier.

Synchronizing Methods

One primary advantage of threads is the capability to share resources. This causes the same mutual exclusion problems that Chapter 7 describes. Java solves this problem by using synchronized methods.

The synchronized method replaces the semaphores used in pthreads. The declaration is

```
public synchronized changeSomething()
{
  /*** Manage contended resource ***/
}
```

The synchronized keyword forces all entries in the method to happen one at a time. Before another thread can enter the method, the first has to complete its call.

Sometimes you need a little more control. For example, suppose you have three threads (parent and two children) that control the incoming and outgoing of buffers through a socket. You don't want to send a buffer until it is full, and the child threads control the outgoing buffers. A synchronized method grabs control of a buffer, but it is not full enough. The method could return a fail-value, forcing the child to retry the call. Alternatively, the method could hold on to the resource and force the thread to yield control temporarily.

Stepping back for a minute, when threads contend for a controlled resource, they enter a waiting queue. When the current resource owner exits the synchronized method, the next thread in the queue grabs control of the resource. This continues as long as the threads contend.

During the times you need more control, the thread grabs control only to discover that it does not have enough of the resource to do anything. In this case, it can yield control and automatically move to the end of the waiting queue. The tools it uses are wait() and notifyAll().

```
public synchronized changeSomething()
{
  while ( buffer_not_full )     // Is there enough data?
  {
    try { wait()}        // No, move to the queue's end
    catch (Exception err)
    { System.err.println(err); }
  }

  /* Send the message */     // Do processing on the data

  notifyAll();             // Tell all waiting threads
}
```

The wait() method places the current thread back on the waiting queue. The scheduler wakes up the next thread in the queue. If it can proceed, it drops out of the loop and sends the message. When done, the notifyAll() method tells all the waiting threads that they can have a shot now at the resource.

Implementation Limitations

Java's implementation of network programming is a great model for quick and simple development. It is easy to create sockets and send messages and manage exceptions. However, it does have a few limitations.

- *Confusing I/O*—The I/O package is not as intuitive as it could be. The possible reason is the use of verbs as the classnames. The separation of the different types of I/O is great, but the result was a *class explosion* (the classes are permuted between I/O types and the base classes), not something that makes deployment really direct.

- *IPv4 Only*—Java apparently supports only the TCP/IPv4 network. At the time of writing, the java.sun.com Web site indicates a project named Merlin that defines support for IPX and IPv6. But that's down the road, and some class methods need to change to support other networks.

- *No Raw Sockets*—Java does not support raw sockets.

- *Incomplete Socket Options*—Some socket option configurations are missing. These include TTL for TCP and UDP, retransmit times, and so on.

- *No Direct Forking*—Process creation (forking) is limited to external calls. You can simulate a process by instantiating a new threaded object, but you have no guarantee of resource corruption because the threads still share the same virtual space.

- *No Broadcasting*—Java's package does not include broadcasting. The probable reason is broadcasting's dwindling popularity. You can probably expect broadcasting to completely drop out of existence relatively soon.

Even with all these limitations, Java is a good, solid programming environment. You can do quite a lot with all the features it has.

Summary: Java-Style Network Programming

Java includes a large library that can help you write network programs. The Network packet includes classes for streaming (TCP), datagram (UDP), and multicasting (UDP) sockets. It also includes classes for managing the addresses and conversions.

When used with the I/O package, the sockets package increases its capabilities. The I/O package offers several ways to interact with the communications between sockets, memory, and threads. The library, while a little confusing, has tremendous power to make network programming very quick.

Java's capacity for threading simplifies socket programming and eases server development. You can create threads one of two ways: inheriting Thread or implementing Runnable. With that, calling the start() method creates a new execution thread and starts the task at your custom implementation of run(). Synchronizing a multithreaded class is fairly easy with two tools: synchronized methods and execution yielding.

Analyzing and using Java as a programming base helps you to see how you can deploy sockets in an object-enabled language. The next chapter proposes and lays out an implementation in C++.

Designing and Using a C++ Socket Framework

IN THIS CHAPTER

The last chapter showed you how to program sockets in Java. Java is a very powerful language and has many advantages, such as platform independence, JIT (Just In Time) compiling, and even native compilers/converters. However, not everyone wants to use Java, claiming lack of stability or needed performance, and some may be more inclined to use a C++ version instead.

Writing a socket *framework* (or class library) takes in all technologies described in this book. In fact, this chapter offers a few additional socket features that are covered in Part IV, "Advanced Sockets—Adding Value."

To use this chapter, you must be familiar with C++ and object programming. As in earlier chapters, it is assumed that you know how to write in C++ and compile and link the files. Tutorials for these procedures are easy to find on the Internet.

This chapter steps you through the process of analyzing, designing, and creating a class framework. This particular framework only provides a wrapper (an interface with little added functionality) around the Socket API. You can still use these principles to define other frameworks, not just wrappers.

Why Use C++ for Sockets Programming?

A C++ framework that wrappers the Socket API offers several advantages over making the individual system calls manually. As you may have noticed, the process of creating, configuring, and using a socket varies very little from application type to application type.

Simplifying Sockets Interfacing

Writing a class that matches the application type lets you focus more on the programming and less on the network. The sockets interfacing is not difficult but requires specific steps to get the communication channels to work consistently.

The C++ language is more powerful than C, and is a complete superset of C's feature set. In fact, you can compile C++ programs with the same tool as with C (cc). (In reality this is not 100% accurate. When cc discovers a .c or .cpp extension, it calls g++ instead of gcc.) Along with this additional power, the C++ language is quite a bit more complicated as well. Nevertheless, the advantages outweigh the drawbacks.

Writing a Sockets Framework lets you define simpler interfaces for others to use. Program simplicity is imperative for testability and defect fixing. Additionally, the simpler the interface, the easier it is to use. Similarly, the easier something is to use, the more likely it is used correctly and frequently.

A properly designed and written C++ framework offers very easy and direct interfaces that let the programmer really focus on the job at hand.

Hiding Implementation Details

Interfaces promote the simplicity or complexity of a product. As the interface's complexity increases, the ease of use diminishes. Hiding implementation details is very important for ensuring simplicity. The design and implementation—particularly in a wrapper—attempt to hide details from the user-programmer.

Of course, the user-programmer may want to know how you did certain things, but that information can hurt you and him or her. Encapsulation, one of the foundations of objects identified in Chapter 11, "Saving Time with Objects," protects both the framework writer and the user-programmer. By hiding how you implement certain steps, you protect the programmer from changes in those implementations. This also protects the framework by allowing the system to evolve internally without affecting the interfaces to the outside world.

As with all other object-enabled languages, C++ enforces the rules of ownership so that the program can only access what it can see and own. If planned well, one framework can support all forms of socket networks.

Deploying Reusable Components with Easy to Use Interfaces

Interfaces and hiding implementation details creates a very thin membrane between the program and the framework. The program must pass all requests through this membrane. The operations inside the class accept and work on the data and requests.

Keeping the interfaces simple is very important. The result is clear: a set of program tools that many programs can use. In fact, several implementations can exist for the same interface. You simply choose the one that behaves the best for the circumstances.

As you write these tools, the clear advantage of reuse becomes apparent to the user-programmers. They in turn promote your work by releasing programs based on these tools. (An excellent example is Qt.)

Demonstrating the Framework Design Processes

Framework tools exist on the Internet. You can find various flavors' forms. Finding a sockets framework, on the other hand, is a little more difficult. Writing one here lets you configure it in whatever form you would like and has an added bonus of showing the process of writing tools.

Unlike the UML-style of OOA/D, writing libraries or frameworks works more from the bottom than entirely from the top. OOA/D states that you must start with the requirements and eventually build a product—similar to peeling an onion. The whole idea is to minimize feature-creep and implement only what is needed.

Framework creation takes a different perspective: the features that the user-programmer desires are not yet known, so the framework implements as many features as the user-programmer might use. This approach, of course, just shouts: "We want features!" which can raise a concern of dead code (linked-in unused/unreachable code). Dead code does not occur much in programs anymore. Newer, smarter linkers excise all code that appears to be unneeded.

Laying Out the Framework

Creating an object framework is similar to framing a wall: You begin with set dimensions and nail everything together in a specific order. This section lays out the steps for creating a framework by identifying the features, grouping into components, organizing the hierarchy, and so on.

Defining the General Features

The framework must depend on some kind of related requirements. A program that has too few requirements is uninteresting (and not worth implementing), and a program that has too disparate requirements yields an awkward result. The requirements define the parameters in which the framework must operate.

Often, when you get a list of wanna-haves, the list is not detailed enough for analysis. Be prepared to ask questions. The sockets framework must support most of the major capabilities described in this book.

Supporting the Different Types of Sockets

The primary feature of an Internet sockets framework is access to the protocols. The first protocol that this book mentions is a TCP connection. This style of programming always has a client and a server. The server awaits a client's request for a connection, creates a distinct connection to it, and then interacts with the client.

Another communication capability connects one host to another as peers. This style does not really have a client or server exactly, but it does have an initiator and a replier. Also, it uses a UDP connection.

Two additional types of communications are broadcasting and multicasting, discussed later in the book. Both allow you to send messages to several destinations at the same time. For more information on these protocols, please refer to Chapter 15, "Network Encapsulation with Remote Procedure Calls (RPCs)."

The last two types of sockets are far too low-level for this framework: raw and promiscuous sockets. These types could be integrated in the framework but, because of the level of detail and management required, these are best left to direct API use. Feel free to revise the framework to include these features as you desire.

Sending Simple Messages

The second major feature is crucial for effective functionality—the framework must be able to send and receive messages. The message has three parts: addresses, the channel, and the message body.

Earlier chapters describe two methods each for sending and receiving messages. These calls assume certain socket states. For example, you must have a connected socket to use the `send()` system call. The primary goal for getting and receiving messages includes simplifying these interfaces.

What would simplify communications is to get the message to ship itself. One of the extended features described in Chapter 11 was data streaming—the automatic packaging and unpackaging of data. The class would know its internals rather well; it should assume that role.

The C++ language does not lend itself to providing data streaming. It has a significant limitation—it must know the data before it uses it. Compare with Java—Java lets you define a class and attach a `Serializable` interface. From there, the class packages/unpackages itself automatically. Very easy. It can do this because it uses interpreted byte code. It assumes no machine-specific information.

A C++ program must provide the packaging and unpackaging procedures. And, because C++ does not support interfaces, you must inherit from a common class that describes those procedures.

Managing Exceptions

The third major feature must control the various exceptions and errors that the network introduces to programming. While you create and configure your sockets and while sending and receiving messages, any number of asynchronous errors can occur.

All errors originate from the socket, the connection, the route, or the other host. Quickly and efficiently collecting the errors helps the user-programmer to isolate the problem and recover appropriately.

The framework uses the C++ exception management construct `try...catch()`, similar to that found in Java. The user-programmer must catch all exceptions that the framework throws; otherwise, the program terminates with an uncaught exception error. You can catch all unexpected exceptions at the root of the program and return some meaningful message to improve debugging.

Configuring the Socket and Connections

The last major feature is configuring the socket or connection you created. All of the socket types have different settings that allow you to tune them. The different tunable settings change the behavior of the socket or the send and receive channels.

Grouping into Major Components

The next step in creating a framework is identifying all of the major pieces or components. *Components* are networks of objects that work together to solve a particular problem or provide a service. Just as with objects, components have responsibilities and interfaces, so you can treat them like objects as well.

Typically, these components are heterogeneous objects contained in a single interface. Some object analysts call these groups *packages*, due to the method of distribution, or *patterns*, and because the systems of objects often fit in generalized ways. But, they can also be hierarchies with abstract objects as the primary interface.

This section describes the four basic components of the Socket Framework. Each of these components is a hierarchy as previously described.

Exceptions: Handling Problems

All frameworks should identify and use exceptions. The kinds of exceptions you may want to capture include networking, I/O, boundary, and so on. The exception hierarchy depends on the Exception class for basic functionality. Figure 13.1 displays the exception component.

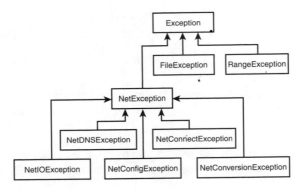

FIGURE 13.1
All exception classes derive from Exception, *which captures only a string and the error code.*

An exception class hierarchy infrequently defines any startling or ingenious design. In fact, if you employ a class hierarchy for exceptions, be very careful that you do not create a potential for recursive exceptions. For example, if you allocate memory and have mapped the memory handler to an exception, you could crash the program from one bad new() call. Leave the design of exceptions to the simplest form with little more than values and a brief message.

Messages: Packaging and Shipping the Data

To send and receive messages through the I/O subsystem, you need blocks of data and buffers. The Message virtual class provides the basic interface to package (Wrap()) and unpackage, (Unwrap()) itself. This interface helps approximate the serialization Java's I/O offers.

Another class, TextMessage, supplies an example of how to use this interface. For example, the Wrap() method creates a block of contiguous memory and copies the text into it. (The responsibility of freeing up the block is left to the caller.) The message of TextMessage is a variable-length C-style string.

The unpackaging method, Unwrap(), does the reverse. It takes the block of data from the caller and begins to reassemble the internal information. Sometimes, the message may be incomplete, so Unwrap() must get more data to finish the reassembly. For example, the TextMessage may be larger than 64KB (the buffer limit), so the TextMessage class must be smart enough to ask for more data. The Unwrap() method returns a Boolean to indicate whether it's done.

Addressing: Identifying the Source and Destination

Each message comes from and goes to some host. The addressing of these hosts is important for getting the message to the rightful owner. Another simple component is HostAddress. Using the struct sockaddr addressing names, this component manages the name and resolution to an IP level.

The framework translates all addresses into this component. And, the component can support several addressing types.

Sockets: Establishing, Configuring, and Connecting

The last component has the most functionality. It is based on the Socket class and derives all basic connections. It uses the other components to get the job done. The hierarchy places the basic functionality in the Socket class and all specializations in the inherited classes.

All protocols listed in the requirements list have a dedicated class: SocketServer, SocketClient, Datagram, Broadcast, and MessageGroup (multicast). All protocol-specific configurations reside in the appropriate protocol-class. When you need to change a setting, look at the protocol you are using. If you do not find it, look in the parent.

The classes also assume you are following proper rules. From the earlier send() example, the classes do not check for a connected socket. Instead, the program throws an exception.

Creating the Framework Hierarchy

The components ease the transition into connecting the objects together. The components provide the interface for the outside world and may hint at the features of the top-most parent (*superclass*). Before working on the framework hierarchy, you need to have defined the non-abstract classes within each component.

At this point, you should have several classes, such as those listed in the last section. From there, you find the relationships and inheritances. Don't be surprised to see features disappear and reappear from parent to child. This is normal, and often is still implementable.

Relationships

The first step is to identify the relationships between the components and the classes. Use general terms, such as uses, is-a, has-a, and throws, to label the connections between component or class.

In Figure 13.2, the different components are connected to show how they interact with each other. Some diagram systems use special line ends (such as arrows). Use whatever you are most comfortable with. The most important factor is clarity.

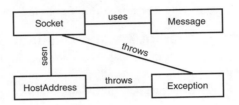

FIGURE 13.2
Each component uses a resource from the other.

The Socket component is connected with all other components, as expected. The classes may not all have these connections, but that is not important. Drilling down shows you more of the detail and which class really uses what.

Mining Natural Inheritances

The second step looks in the components and tries to see special relationships called *inheritance*. As described in Chapter 11, inheritance lets you create a related class from some other class (base class) and only change a few features (specialization) without rewriting the whole class. This is the primary power of object technology.

The only component that has any interesting classes is Socket. It has five classes that are clearly related. See Figure 13.3. The Broadcast and MessageGroup (multicast) classes use UDP sockets and have similar functionality, so they must derive from Datagram. However, while SocketClient and SocketServer use TCP, they don't operate the same. The client actively connects while the server waits for the connections.

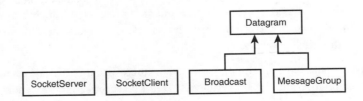

FIGURE 13.3
The Datagram, MessageGroup, *and* Broadcast *classes appear to be related. The* SocketServer *and* SocketClient *are not close enough.*

The `Exception` and `Message` components could have many classes and several levels of inheritance. As implemented, however, the hierarchies are very simple. (Please note that in UML, the arrows point to the parent class.)

Identifying Abstractions

Going back to the Socket hierarchy, the classes do fit together, but it requires some additional classes. Clearly, the `Socket` class must be the superclass, the mother of all sockets. It does not really have any function other than to provide a common set of features for all child classes.

The `Socket` superclass provides all the `get` and `set` functions. It also includes the `creation`, `send`, `receive`, and `close` functions. But, it cannot honestly exist in real time and space. The reason is that it has no protocol. The protocol is defined elsewhere.

Adapting the Hierarchy for Raw Sockets

You could revise the hierarchy so that Socket, by itself, creates a raw or promiscuous socket. However, you can run into problems. First, the function of these low-level sockets are closer to UDP than TCP. You would have to *turn off* functionality for the SocketClient and SocketServer classes. That's ugly. Or, you could abstract that functionality more, adding a new layer to the UDP half of the hierarchy. Either way, the component becomes more complicated. This is a real, persistent problem in writing frameworks; the more features you add, the more complicated it becomes and the less easy it is to use.

The `SocketClient` and `SocketServer` remain different enough that joining them directly to `Socket` does not provide the TCP commonality. Additionally, they have more functional differences that keep them from being directly related.

You can resolve the close relationship between `SocketClient` and `SocketServer` with an intermediate class (`SocketStream`) that defines the features of a TCP socket without losing the identity of the superclass. Figure 13.4 shows the completed diagram.

The two classes, `Datagram` and `SocketStream`, provide the configuration and features their protocols require. Separating the protocols like this makes it easy and clean to add other protocols, such as `SOCK_RAW`, or even new protocols, such as RDM (reliably delivered messages).

Defining Each Class's Capabilities

The last step in the design differs from the standard OOA/D reiterative processing. The main reason is that OOA/D focuses primarily on projects, not libraries. Looking at a library, you cannot precisely know what the user wants or needs. Often, the designer must consider the question, "What could the library be used for?"

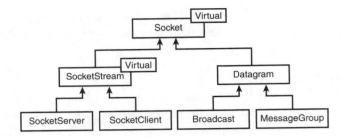

FIGURE 13.4

The completed Socket *class hierarchy includes two virtual classes:* Socket *and* SocketStream.

The Project-Yields-the-Library Fallacy

Many programmers and designers consider the project to be the ultimate source for designing a library. Their logic has merit: Write the tools as we write the project. However, this logic has two major flaws: Why do most libraries or frameworks built this way lack scalability? and Why do the libraries begin to look like a crazy quilt filled with swatches of different program snippets? The problem is simple; projects never have the big picture to help define the philosophy of a library. The best example of an *over*-overloaded class is MFC's CString class. To start a good, flexible, and clean library, the philosophy has to be defined first. Then you consider the possibilities for each class.

This section takes you through the process of fleshing-out the details of each class. The first and second steps are reversed when compared to normal object-project development.

Attributes: Adding What It Knows

In most cases, the next step places the functions or methods in each class. However, when creating a library, especially a wrapper for the sockets API, you identify all the available features or attributes.

The socket's features are mostly built into the socket options. Chapter 9, "Breaking Performance Barriers," and Appendix A, "Data Tables," list the standard and Linux-dependent socket options. These are good candidates for the Socket class's attributes. In reality, the class does not keep the attributes as separate entries in the class. Instead, the socket descriptor holds each setting. Every get/set pair that normally accompanies the CRUD (Create/Read/Update/Delete) methods really calls getsockopt()/setsockopt().

Figure 13.5 shows the get/set function calls for each exposed attribute. Some attributes only turn on or off a feature, so the design does not include a get() function. A class may not expose all attributes; typically, the attributes that it exposes are those that change the behavior of the class. Other internal attributes may change only the state of the class, so they tend to remain hidden from view.

A last special attribute requires a little more than changing a value. These are true properties that look like attributes but, in reality, they perform several operations. For example, the `MinimizeDelay()`, `MaximizeThroughput()`, `MaximizeReliability()`, and `MinimizeCost()` calls in `Datagram` all interface with a single `setsockopt()`. But to simplify the interface, they calculate and set the right bit values so you don't have to.

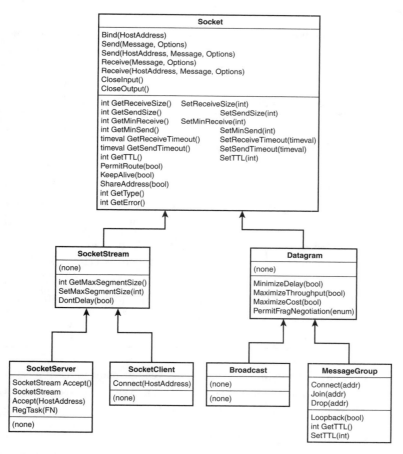

FIGURE 13.5

Each attribute in a class may have an associated `get...()`/`set...()` *function.*

The classes in the socket component can include other attributes that are particular to the specific implementation of the class. For example, SocketServer can store the registered callback routine for accepted connections. Also, the multicasting socket does not have a way of cleanly dropping the groups, so MessageGroup includes an array of joined groups.

Methods: Adding What It Does

As with the join group function available for multicasting sockets, some classes have specific method implementations that extend the CRUD methods. The normal OOA/D methodology identifies what each class must do to fulfill its responsibilities. These responsibilities are related to functions mentioned in the use-cases (as described in Chapter 11).

However, a library does not have any solid use-cases from which to work, so the methods often reflect functions found in socket API. Of course, not every function is appropriate for every class. Table 13.1 lists by class the specific implementations defined in the socket component.

TABLE 13.1   Special Methods Implemented in the Socket Component

Class	Method	Description
Socket	Bind	Offers the bind() call
	Send	Offers the send() and sendto() calls
	Receive	Offers the recv() and recvfrom() calls
	CloseInput	Closes the input channel using shutdown()
	CloseOutput	Closes the output channel using shutdown()
SocketServer	Accept	Offers the accept() call
SocketClient	Connect	Offers the connect() call
MessageGroup	Connect	Offers the connect() call
	Join	Joins connection to multicast group using socket option
	Drop	Drops multicast connection

A class may not have any specific implementation or even attributes to merit a new class; it only needs a different behavior. The Broadcast class is an example of this; it differs enough in behavior from the base class (Datagram) to merit its existence.

Constructors: What Ways to Create Object

Each class usually has a set of configuration parameters that define some of the initial behaviors. Again, the Broadcast class does not have any additional methods or attributes to offer, but it must be configured to send and receive broadcast messages. This configuration would go in the constructor.

Constructors differ very slightly from regular methods; you can do most operations as you would in a regular method—create objects, allocate space, perform calculations, and so on. For example, the following is the declaration of the `Socket` class constructor:

```
//****************************************************************
//*** Default Socket constructor
//*** Using the Network (PF_INET) and Protocol (SOCK_STREAM),
//*** create a socket and place the reference in the SD
//*** attribute.
Socket::Socket(ENetwork Network, EProtocol Protocol)
{
  SD = socket(Network, Protocol, 0);
  if ( SD < 0 )
    throw NetException("Could not create socket");
}
```

If anything goes wrong in the creation, you do not have a way of sending back an error with conventional methods. Instead, the framework uses exceptions to send the error directly to the handler. If everything goes well, the construction finishes and returns to the caller.

Not all operations are available to a constructor. You cannot call methods to the class you are creating unless they are declared `static`. Each class carries with it a context or its state. Every method assumes the context to be complete and stable. While in the constructor, the compiler considers the context to be incomplete or unstable.

Static methods of a class do not depend on a context, so you can use them basically anytime and anywhere. In fact, you don't even need an instantiated object to use them. So, the relationship between the static methods and class is very loose, almost ancillary. Classes rarely use static methods because of this loose relationship. However, they are useful on certain occasions. Some system calls, such as signal handlers, do not support the contexts that standard methods require. So if, for example, you want to capture various signals in a class, you must declare the signal handlers as static methods.

Destructors: What Requires Cleanup

Just as constructors initialize the object and get it ready for use, destructors reverse some of the steps and get the object ready for the free heap. Unlike Java, which uses a garbage collector to free up space, C++ requires you to manually clean up objects.

Often, the objects are self-contained and require little more than freeing the space. However, some classes (such as `SimpleString` and `TextMessage`) use some of the heap. The compiler cannot tell if the pointers in these classes really point to anything more than one element. Destructors let you specify what needs to be cleaned up and when.

Other typical cleanup steps include closing files and unhooking handlers. The following is the destructor for the Socket class:

```
//***********************************************************
//*** Socket destructor
Socket::~Socket(void)
{
  if ( close(SD) != 0 )
    throw FileException("Can't close socket");
}
```

You should declare all destructors as virtual so that all destructors in the inheritance hierarchy get executed. A non-virtual destructor indicates that you do not want the parents' destructors to fire when you delete an object. You can just specify the superclass's destructor as virtual—this makes all inherited destructors virtual as well. However, for clarity, you may want to explicitly declare them as virtual.

Testing the Socket Framework

The Socket Framework is a custom implementation based on the criteria that the previous sections described. The following sections show you how to use it by stepping you through a couple of examples. The Web site that accompanies this text has a few other examples that show you how to implement datagram, broadcast, and multicast sockets.

The Echo Client/Server

The first example (and the most cited throughout the text) is the echo client/server. The real reason for using an echo client/server is to test that the communications work correctly. After you have that part down, the rest is easy.

Listing 13.1 presents the basic client.

LISTING 13.1   Echo-Client.cpp

```
//***********************************************************
// Client main body
HostAddress addr(strings[1]);   // <address:port> format
try
{
  SocketClient client(addr);   // Create the socket & connect
  TextMessage msg(1024);       // Set aside the message space
  do               // Repeat until "bye"
  {
    char line[100];
    client.Receive(msg);    // Get the welcome or reply
```

LISTING 13.1   Continued

```
    printf("msg=%s", msg.GetBuffer()); // Display it
    fgets(line, sizeof(line), stdin);  // Get line
    msg = line;           // Place in message space
    client.Send(msg);        // Send message to server
  }
  while ( strcmp(msg.GetBuffer(), "bye\n") != 0 );
}
catch (Exception& err)
{
  err.PrintException();
}
```

All the programs use the same try...catch() format. You want to use that to capture and recover from an exception that the system might encounter. The following is one catch() omitted in Listing 13.1 that you should always have at the of the calling tree:

```
//*************************************************************
// Exception Catchall
catch(...)
{
  fprintf(stderr,"Unknown exception!\n");
}
```

This definition captures everything that you did not anticipate.

The server could be a built-in echo server, mail server, or HTTP server. The TextMessage class is compatible to each of these. Still, Listing 13.2 shows you the object version of the echo server.

LISTING 13.2   Echo-Server.cpp

```
//*************************************************************
// Server's main body
try
{
  SocketServer server(port);  // Create & config the socket
  do                // Repeat forever
   server.Accept(Echoer);  // Connect & serve a client
  while ( 1 );
}
```

As you can see, the body of the server is very simple. The SocketServer does all of the configuration and setup for you. The variable, Echoer, is the other half of the process (see Listing 13.3).

13

DESIGNING AND
USING A C++
SOCKET FRAMEWORK

LISTING 13.3   Echo-Server.cpp, Part 2

```
//*************************************************************
// Server's client service routine (Echoer)
try
{
  TextMessage msg(1024);   // Get a message buffer
  client.Send(welcome);    // Send "welcome" message
  do               // Repeat until "bye"
  {
   client.Receive(msg);  // Get message
   client.Send(msg);     // Echo it back
  }
  while ( msg.GetSize() > 0 &&
    strcmp(msg.GetBuffer(), "bye\n") != 0 );
}
```

Again the algorithm is simple: accept a message and send it back until the client sends a bye message. You may notice that this program excerpt has its own try...catch() block. This is a good idea. If an error occurs with this connection, it is only associated with that connection and must not affect the main socket. Without the dedicated try...catch block in Listing 13.3, when the client suddenly disconnects, the whole server would crash because main's try...catch block would capture the exception.

> ### Placing Exception Handlers
>
> Plan carefully where and when to place an exception handler. Also, you may not want to handle all exception types. Instead you may want to support only specific types. Generally, different connections require their own try...catch() blocks, and catastrophic exceptions should reside only at the root of the calling tree.

The current implementation of the server does not offer multitasking. The class includes some of the hooks you need to implement it.

Multitasking Peer-to-Peer

You can still do multitasking with processes or threads. Even though the current framework does not implement it, you can create tasks in your code. The classic example is the datagram that must accept any number of messages while sending them (see Listing 13.4).

LISTING 13.4   Peer.cpp

```
//**************************************************************
// Datagram message sender
try
{
  HostAddress addr(strings[1]);     // Define own address
  Socket *channel = new Datagram(addr); // Create socket
  if ( !fork() )               // Create process
   receiver(channel);          // Call data receiver
  channel->CloseInput();            //Close input channel
  HostAddress peer(strings[2]);      // Define peer addr
  TextMessage msg(1024);             // Create msg space
  do
  {
   char line[100];
   fgets(line, sizeof(line), stdin); // Read line
   msg = line;              // Place in message
   channel->Send(peer, msg);     // Ship it.
  }
  while ( !done );
  delete channel;
}
```

The implementation for `receiver()` looks a lot like the `SocketServer`'s `Echoer` call.

If you want to use multitasking with the framework, you need to remember a couple of rules:

- *Follow Rules*—Review the notes and advice in Chapter 7, "Dividing the Load: Multitasking." In particular, be sure to capture the child-termination signals. Also, threads share their I/O channels; closing one end closes it for all threads.

- *Memory Sharing*—Be aware that memory resource contention is an almost intractable problem. Share as little as possible.

- *C++ Limitations*—Employing multithreading in C++ is hazardous. So much is going on behind the scenes that you must be very careful what thread owns what data. Creating objects on the stack before firing a new thread can cause unpredictable results.

Multitasking has its advantages, and you can still use C++, but be very careful.

Implementation Limitations

The framework is just a functional—but incomplete—example of how you could implement sockets in a C++ library. This should give you a few ideas of how to adapt it (or write your own) to meet your programming needs.

As it stands, you can create client, server, datagrams, and multicast/broadcast sockets. It allows you to configure the sockets using socket options. It includes a messaging abstraction so that you can write your own message formats. The following sections list a couple of ideas for feature enrichment.

Sending Unknown/Undefined Messages

The current framework lets you derive your own message type from `Message`. This is very handy if you work exclusively with the `Message` component or have known types. However, you may not have the flexibility to solely derive from a single class—especially if you are integrating a legacy system.

Multiple inheritance is sometimes a necessary evil, particularly when you are trying to merge different and often conflicting frameworks. Java has the advantage of interfaces, but that does not seem like an option for C++ in the near future.

Likewise, you do not always know the data itself. This often happens when you have a newer client interfacing with a legacy server. The server does not know what extensions the client may support, so the performance can suffer. Writing an abstract messaging protocol would solve this problem.

The abstract messenger would not only hold the data, it would also hold the data structure. This would be similar to sending the files with the directory structure. An abstract messenger can make the communications between hosts more useful and extensible.

Adding Multitasking

Another limitation, as mentioned earlier, is the lack of multitasking support. Most programs that work with the network do several tasks at the same time to improve performance. Offering processes and threads as an intrinsic feature of the framework would make that programming much simpler.

The problem stems from the mere definition of a class: something that does and knows something. So, if you define a socket class, would you have a multitasking socket and a multithreading one? Furthermore, is a task an object? If so, there are really two derivable classes: `Socket` and `Process`/`Thread`. The result is a multiple-inheritance problem (which most object-fundamentalists would scowl at).

Perhaps the problem is simpler than it appears. But the idea of combining client, server, datagram, broadcast, and multicast with non-multitask, thread, and process into 15 classes is not optimal.

Summary: A C++ Socket Framework Simplifies Programming

Using an object-oriented language, such as C++, can help simplify socket development. You have seen how much of socket programming is very similar with only a few variations, but you need to follow certain rules to write a library or framework for sockets. These rules differ slightly from the standard OOA/D practices.

A framework coordinates the interfaces between components, and components define the job or primary functionality of a set of networked classes. Every class in the component works toward completing this job.

The Sockets Framework includes four components: exception, message, address, and socket. The exception component remains separate from the other components to reduce the likelihood of internal failure. The address and message components provide support to the socket component.

This chapter demonstrates for you the process of creating a framework for sockets and shows you how you can do it for your own programs. The extensibility of C++ and the framework may help you try out these features in your own C++ jobs.

Limits to Objects

IN THIS CHAPTER

Object Technology does not solve everything. Yes, that is true. It is simply a new tool to wield at the right time. If you try to use it everywhere, you lose out on the simplicity of alternative programming methods.

When you choose to use objects, you may want to be aware of some of the problems. The problems include getting people to think in objects, realizing that objects still can't do some things, being prepared for additional complexity, and managing a new paradigm.

The power of Object Technology is alluring, but this chapter lets you know of the few limitations it has.

Mind Over Objects

The first problem programmers, designers, and analysts encounter when they begin an object project is trying to take a look at the objects themselves. If you forget to do this, you can fall into the same pitfalls that many have before you. Each step through the object analysis focuses on what the system is supposed to do, what the object contributes to the effort, and when you know it's done.

This section presents several pitfalls that you can face during the development. Remember, this is only a sampling of what can go wrong.

Beginning on the Right Foot

The Beguin is a Spanish dance that predates the Tango. Like this dance, if you don't start on the right foot in an object project, you might as well dance with Death. Understanding what the user wants is the most important step you take. The interaction with your user is much like a dance—and the user leads.

The user is the person or system that will interact with your program. If you do not identify and solidify the interfaces, the dance can turn on you—you may end up leading. This is not a good position; the result will inevitably be something other than what the user wants.

You can use four essential tools to define the wants and needs of the user: the context, the function list, the use-cases/scenarios, and the system flow. Get a good book on requirements gathering and management for a detailed how-to. These tools will help you prove the program works according to the user's expectations.

The context simply defines what your program does *not* do. It identifies all the users, the information flowing in and out, and the functions for which the users are responsible. This is very crucial for a successful project. If you do not identify what you're going to omit, the user may assume the program will have it.

The context leads you directly to a list of functions that the program will do. Each function is in a verb-object pair. For instance, a good function would be "Prints statistical report for user." The implied subject is the program.

The functional list logically leads to use-cases. The use-case describes generally how the program is to perform the function. The use-case always starts and ends with the outside; the steps in between describe the transformation required. You can subdivide the use-cases into individual scenarios. Remember that the use-case is the function, and the scenario addresses the differences in the data. Consider the follow examples:

Use-Case #9: "Send a message to person on the network"

[User types message and clicks Send]

Open connection to destination

Contact recipient

[Recipient accepts interruption]

Send message

Return confirmation to user

[User receives status]

Scenario #9.1: "Send a message; message denied"

[User types message and clicks Send]

Open connection to destination

Contact recipient

[Recipient rejects interruption]

Return rejection to user

[User receives status]

Scenario #9.2: "Send lengthy message to person on the network"

[User types message and clicks Send]

Open connection to destination

Contact recipient

[Recipient accepts interruption]

Send message in parts

Return confirmation to user

[User receives status]

The scenarios in this example are simple mutations of the original use-case. The use-cases often include negative or *exception-cases*. An exception-case is one that demonstrates how the program will respond to a problem with the data or transaction.

The last step takes the use-cases and shows graphically how the program will work functionally. It is important that you include each use-case and show how the data changes until it reaches the final destination.

A Blender Is Not an Object

Another problem designers face is proper naming. After you have an understanding of what the user wants, you can begin the process of analyzing the "things" in the program's system. This system of things has responsibilities ("What it knows" and "What it does") that determine its behavior.

Naming the object with something representative determines its current behavior and its evolution. A good name is always a noun. For example, naming an object Socket is better than NetIO because you can do much more to the network than just I/O. But, if you name the object with a verb (NetIO is short for Network Input/Output—both verbs), you have limited the effectiveness and evolution of the object. With Socket, you don't have to stop at reading and writing messages; you can include network control, subscribing to multicast networks, and so on.

Most nouns work very well. However, the English language has a problem with certain words: you can name an object with a false or misleading name. Typical misleading names are verbal nouns (words that acts like nouns but are really verbs). For example, a blender is not an object.

What does a blender do? It blends. So what methods would a blender have? blend()? That's not enough to be a good object. Coming up with a good name is very difficult. When you base a name on what it does, it's very hard to take your mind off what it could do in the future.

Sometimes, you can't identify a name that fits the bill. An oversimplified (and often effective) solution is to give it an unrelated name like bob. Then let the responsibilities drive the object.

Separating Analysis from Design

Naming is very important, but making sure that you don't get too far into the details is more important. Companies commonly define that a project requires a database long before they define the whole problem. What does that do? Is that bad?

Designing before analyzing places the technology in the center of the process while everything else revolves around it. No good home architect would define the timber width before identifying the load on it. Similarly, if the analysis concludes with "It must be written in Java" before the entire problem is known can cause harm to health and life (note the disclaimer Sun places on Java).

Analysis is the time to look at the world through rose-colored glasses. When you enter the analysis phase, you only look at what needs to be done at the macro level. Anytime someone mentions a specific implementation detail, the detail goes directly to the design *parking lot* (a list of items to be reviewed later).

> **System Constraints**
>
> Sometimes the requirements have constraints that include specific hardware and software materials. If in moderation and part of the business requirements, you must consider them. However, you often can ignore most of them until the design. Still, if the requirement states that it must be written in COBOL, you must consider how that impacts your inheritances.

Analysis also assumes that you have all the tools and container types you may ever need. Don't worry yet about how certain things get done; just focus on the major things in the system and how they interact to implement the use-cases.

The Right Level of Detail

The use-cases are very important for leading you through the process of analysis. However, just like your analysis, if you get too bogged down in the details, you won't rise high enough to prove that the design meets the requirements.

As you walk through the requirements, you begin to flesh out the superficial "how" of the system. Work directly with the business people and show them how your high-level solution works to do what they ask. Inevitably, they discover that what you did is exactly what they asked for and not what they intended. If you go too far in the detail, the listeners either become lost or lose focus on the use-cases.

If your customers (the business people) want to know more about how you intend to implement the product, that may be a good sign that your work is good. You can assure them that they can review the work again after you complete the design. At that point, they can see all the details they want.

The Inheritance Explosion

During the design phase, you take the classes you defined and provide the details. You must be very careful at this point; the temptation is to merely inherit all the classes to a design-level detail. The rationale is "We have a pristine and portable analysis. Let's keep that pure during the design." In fact some object-technologists strongly encourage this object explosion. However, that is rarely needed.

Most implementations do nothing more than fleshing out the container classes and adding a user interface. The analysis is still pristine and the work you did is not diluted. Just proceed to add the needed pieces to map the analysis to the system architecture.

Also, if you permit an object explosion, the result is inevitable—object anarchy and a maintenance nightmare. You should only inherit a class if you need to mutate a behavior or add functionality. If the functionality is not part of the analysis but in the design, be sure that that was not an oversight.

Object anarchy really demonstrates a lack of responsibility modeling. Inheriting each class increases the likelihood of a tangled web as each class tries to establish the appropriate association.

Maintaining this nest of connections is very difficult, even with the documentation. And when you try to revise one object in the inheritance tree, it may affect another, thus defeating the purpose of encapsulation.

Reuse-Misuse

A common myth that object-aficionados hold to is their claim that they can reuse everything. This belief is very unrealistic. Just as converting a hammer into a dentist drill is at best a mismatch, some classes are best suited in one place—their intended design.

If you want to reuse a class, make sure that the intent along with the interface closely match your needs. If you have to refit much of the interface, you may not have a good fit, or the original design is flawed. The following are a few issues to consider:

Does the class's intended function approximate your own?

Would you have to refit only one or two interfaces?

Do the parent classes and superclass meet your needs?

Do you use the existing data as intended?

If you say "no" to any of these, you may have a problem with reuse-misuse. One solution is to find a different parent class that more closely resembles what you are looking for. Another solution is to completely break away from the hierarchy and start a new development path.

Using C++'s `friend` Correctly

Inheritance is a dangerous feature—especially when you are inheriting from a foreign class. Another dangerous practice is the use of `friend`. The `friend` directive lets other classes peer into and use the private parts of your class (breaking encapsulation). It also lets you insert your class into a set of working functions (such as operator overloads).

Almost all object experts disavow the `friend` directive. Only in the use of operator overloading is this directive accepted as a necessary evil. Some have equated this directive to a `goto`. Don't use it unless you can't in all other ways avoid it.

The Overloaded Operator

Even operator overloading is now deemed unneeded and unwanted. It doesn't break any cardinal rule of objects, but it does make code less readable and maintainable. The whole purpose of improving the software engineering technology is to increase reuse and pluggability. Overloaded operators often do exactly the opposite. They are confusing to use and maintain.

Still, if you want to use overload operators, keep the following rules in mind:

- *Don't pass data by value or pointer*—Instead, pass by reference (&) wherever possible. If you don't, you can end up with dangling pointers or degraded performance as you call the constructor and destructor over and over.

- *Always overload the equals operator*—You must do this to do type conversions properly.

- *Choose the operator that best fits your operation*—For example, <string>+<string> is clear, but *<queue> does not necessarily mean Queue->Pop().

- *Consider overloading the* `new()` *and* `delete()` *operators*—Some authors suggest this is a good idea, but this advice is dubious.

- *Never overload the strange operators*—Function call ("()") and field accessors ("." and "->") rarely result in clear interface usage.

Overall, try to use meaningful programming. If you want people to use your good work, make it intelligible to them.

Objects Don't Solve Everything

Some people claim that objects are the end-all and be-all of programming. You can do a lot by using objects and Object Technology, but some tasks are simpler in other paradigms. Like the plumber that has only a hammer, a strict object programmer may see everything as an object problem.

This section presents the problems with Object Technology.

Fads Come and Evolve

Object Technology actually was the latest technology fad. The new one is patterns, which look at common systems of objects. The lesson is clear: Good fads evolve into something better. Just as you begin to learn one technology, another comes up to take its place in the limelight.

Inheritance Infection

Objects introduced the concept of inheritance, reusing the behaviors of established classes. Unfortunately, some programmers believe that this is the panacea of programming—so they inherit everything. These programmers try to place everything into one hierarchy, even though individual things are completely unrelated.

A typical-size program has between three and five primary components, and each component may have between two and seven objects. Having all the classes related logistically is extremely rare, and forcing this relationship is unnecessary. (Please note that this does not apply to Java, which inherits all classes from Object.)

Unreachable Code

Object Technology can answer many problems in a particular domain of programming. Many of the problems thrown at it are general and probably may not change. This is why reuse is so important. Someone once said that it is probable that most of the programs have already been written. The work that is now done is in human interfaces and new technology.

Object Technology cannot solve a small set of problems, however. These problems get closer to nature than the current definition of objects does. This section introduces these limitations and possible ways around them.

Partial Class

The first limitation is the partial class. In nature, if you remove all but one of the legs from a chair, it still would be a chair. However, if a class loses some of its functionality, it would no longer qualify as the original class. While it has the original interface, it is not an inheritance of the original form.

Null Functions

The partial class also extends into null functions. The *null function* allows you to turn off a method so that it no longer offers the service. While inheriting from a parent class, you may find that a particular service is now obsolete or even destructive to the new class. A null function or method prunes the method completely out of the new class and from there is forgotten.

If you want this feature, some programmers override the method and attach no behavior to it. While this effectively accomplishes the same goal, the method is still there, occupying definition space.

Object Mutation

Another limitation is *object mutation*, which lets the programmer change one object into another without casting. Casting types is very dangerous, even in the strongly typed world of object-enabled languages such as C++ and Java. Mutation is a kinder form of casting that has certain rules to ensure you get from A to B without too much trouble.

Mutation is a tool that lets you create a generic object and, while discovering more about it, you can change or mutate it little by little—even coming up with a whole new, previously unknown class. A perfect place for this kind of tool would be object streaming, where you can get a general blob of data and have to decipher it. You can, in part, create a translator constructor that takes the other form and creates a new class from it, but you would have to write a translator constructor for every other related class—a combinatorial problem.

The mutation engine requires the following criteria:

- *The blob must remain intact*—The engine does not create a copy or translate any information. Instead, it changes the interpretation of the information.

- *The blob can only mutate within the inheritance hierarchy*—To change an object into another, the two classes must have a common thread of identity.

- *The discovery engine must be able to create an instance of an abstract class*—You may find this difficult to accept, but during the discovery process (just as when playing Twenty Questions) you may have to start with the abstract.

- *The result must always be an instance of a concrete class*—The reason is obvious: No object can exist on an incomplete class.

- *The discovery engine must have access to private elements*—This does appear to fly in the face of encapsulation, but to discover the true nature of the blob, you need to know the intimate parts of the destination class.

- *The process must be able to nullify methods and support partial classes*—Sometimes, you may need to turn off methods of defined classes dynamically so that the resulting mutated object behaves correctly. A mutated thing in nature may have abilities and limitations beyond those defined by the genus.

The mutated object has great power in dealing with instances the program code did not anticipate. It provides a little more intelligence to the system and more closely resembles nature.

Heuristic Algorithms

Object Technology does not directly support heuristic algorithms. *Heuristic algorithms* are goal-based problems in which the user describes the problem, and the computer resolves to the goal. Much can be simulated, but a whole premise of nondeterministic resolution is computationally unreachable.

You can create heuristic algorithms and use a pseudo-random number generator to approximate the resolution nondeterminism. However, this simulation is bound by the effectiveness of the random numbers.

Massively Parallel Algorithms

The last algorithmic problem involves massively parallel problems, such as true neural networks. Again, like heuristic algorithms, it can only simulate the results. True compliance to a massively parallel system would require dedicated goal-based processors. Even the highly integrated parallel Fortran program would struggle to meet those requirements.

Complexity Give and Take

Object Technology has other limitations beyond just the technology itself. Professionals have discovered that as they work with large frameworks (library hierarchies) or maintain existing implementations, the promises of objects are not panning out. This section expands the issues with objects and what history has shown.

Simplifying Programs with Established Interfaces

Over the years that object programming has flourished, professionals have discovered several learning points. One learning point is the importance of established interfaces. The interface of a class is critical for its longevity. However, programmers rarely put the time into designing the best interface.

The interfaces of hacked code often are too specialized or too functional to really take advantage of the power of objects. So, when others open up the code to maintain it, they find that the methods and even the entire behavior of the class has devolved over time. It is very common to encounter a paintball-approach to programming in these classes: "It works here—why not copy and paste the code here and here?"

The interface is the most important part of modular programming—that cannot be said enough. However, the interface must be simple and intuitive. Another problem is the frameworks themselves and their multi-class interfaces. It is very common to find that you have to instantiate several classes in a particular order as you program with these systems of classes. This order and complexity are very evident in GUI programming, perhaps because of the features and options GUIs offer.

As you create your objects, consider how simple and clear the method interfaces are. More importantly, make sure that this is the way the programmer works with your classes. If you need class interdependencies, make them as easy to assemble as possible.

Multiple Inheritance Conundrum

Another complexity stems from the features of inheritance. The C++ language lets you create classes that inherit from multiple parent classes. Managing an inheritance hierarchy is difficult enough. Chapter 11, "Saving Time with Objects," mentions the concept of coupling. Inheriting from multiple sources introduces unhealthy coupling between classes.

This coupling forms a dependency on the parent classes. If these classes change, the designer has to verify the interfaces between them and the subclass. The changes sometimes are very subtle but may require special name resolutions in the subclass. This is pretty messy.

From a theoretical view, multiple inheritance is viable but impractical. A design that has multiple inheritances is typically broken. Most of the reasons stem from improper responsibility delegation or class naming. The most common cause is improper abstraction and delegation. Often, the two parent classes have a common set of behaviors that should be extracted and placed above them as a superclass.

Another common cause of multiple inheritance is naming a class with a verb. For example, if you have `StreamReader` and `StreamWriter`, you must merge the two to get a random access `Stream`. The names `-Reader` and `-Writer` are the problem.

You can solve the majority of multiple inheritance problems either by pulling out the common features into an abstract superclass or by using containers. Usually, the new class is more similar to one parent class than to the other. Inherit from the more similar class, and contain the other one.

Task-classes prove to be a small exception to that rule. If you have a class that is related to one parent class and is also a task (process or thread), you may be stuck using multiple inheritance. The reason is that the class cannot contain a task-class: The programming just does not work very well. Your subclass is usually more related to the other class.

To solve the task-class problem without multiple inheritance, you may have to force the subclass to inherit from the task and contain the other class. It's doable but can be cumbersome.

Code Bloat

The inheritances, abstractions, overloads, and templates are tremendous helps in getting your job done quickly. However, you can run into another problem: source- and object-code bloat. The increases in object size may not be important if you have plenty of memory. But the more lines of code you write, the more likely the program has defects.

Depending on the complexity of your classes, you can see a 20% to 50% increase in the number of lines of code you have to write compared to a modular design. This is largely due to the language syntax and support. With the sacrifice of increased source complexity, you do get more capability and stronger typing.

The first object programmers were surprised by object-code bloat. In some instances, for identical functionality, converting C to C++ yielded a 10× increase in the resulting program. This is an extreme example, but you can expect a typical 2 to 5× increase in program size.

You can reduce these increases by doing the following:

- Don't overload operators.
- Don't try to unify all classes into single inheritance hierarchies.
- Don't use virtual inheritance.
- Don't go overboard on virtual methods.
- Never use multiple inheritance.
- Limit inline functions. (Some say that you should always avoid explicit inline functions and let the compiler choose that feature.)

These hints can help you a great deal to minimize the size of your source and object code. Still, expect an increase nonetheless; the name resolution engine and support libraries are larger than those of functional or modular languages.

Project Management Dilemma

An object program presents a new and unusual set of problems for the manager. He has to coordinate more people at once and prove that work is moving forward. Especially when multiple teams are involved and unless the project has a technology manager, the project manager has to coordinate with many more people than those who are working on the project.

The Object-Project Manager has to be all things to all people. Having skills in delegation, coordination, organization, and even negotiation are critical for the project's success. Keep in mind that a successful project means much more than getting a product out on time and under budget. If the team disintegrates after completion or if the documentation does not represent the product or if the customer is unsatisfied or feels beaten up, the project was a failure.

This section merely touches on some of these issues. You may want to remember that this is a much bigger problem than what a few pages can outline. Every manager must face the reality that the success of the project is the team—not the product.

Getting the Right People at the Right Time

The best project has the best people moving in and out of the picture. Training is an ancillary issue and must be coordinated with mentors. The reason the product is not the determining fact of success is that the product was requested and approved by those who would use it. Its acceptance is a given if the result matches what the users had in mind.

The team's success is more important, and the manager has more people than programmers on the team. The following is a list of those on the team and when they are needed:

- *Project Sponsor*—Provides money to the project. He needs to lead the major milestones of the project.
- *Customer Advocate*—Interfaces with and checkpoints the customer. The advocate must be very familiar with the way the customers think and how they work. He drives the requirements of the product and is involved all the way through the project.
- *Business Analysts*—Collect and distill the requirements documentation. They are involved during requirements gathering and analysis and must checkpoint with the customer advocates. Later, they are very helpful during testing.
- *Technical Analysts*—Take the analyses through the design process. They map the modeled form of the analysis to the real world, and they must checkpoint regularly with the business analysts.
- *Quality Representative*—Collects and archives documentation and drives the testing process. After the business analysts solidify the requirements, the quality representative begins to generate the acceptance tests. When the design is done, he can begin to work on the boundary and stress tests.
- *Programmers*—Take the design and codify it in the selected language.
- *Legacy Systems* (if needed)—Stand as a resource to the technical analysts to ensure that the interfaces match up.

This is a much larger team than most managers think about. If the project manager runs the process smoothly, each person moves in and out of the picture and places a stamp of approval on the product.

WISCY ("Whiskey") Phenomenon

With all the people that need to be involved, the manager often faces the "Why Isn't Sam Coding Yet?" (WISCY) problem. Both the Project Sponsor and the Customer Advocate often raise this issue. That's natural: One wants to see the results of his money, and the other wants to see the product.

According to the industry's best practices, only 20% of the total project time is coding. The other 80% of the time is equally divided to analysis/design and testing (40% analysis and design, 20% coding, and 40% testing). Typically, the American software industry ends up following more closely to 33% analysis and design, 34% coding, and 33% testing. So at most, 33% of the time is really spent in coding. Why not spend the time up front ironing out all the requirements and definitions and design?

To appease the Project Sponsor and the Customer Advocate, let them know what the schedule looks like and keep them apprised of the progress. Involve them with presentations and show them the documentation. Let them know how important their project is to you, the manager.

If that doesn't work, you can use Just-In-Time (JIT) design. JIT Design gets you coding quickly but can introduce holes. When that occurs, plug them. As you run into problems that need clarification, work with the Customer Advocate and even the customers themselves because a JIT design requires a much stronger interfacing.

However, do not fall into the trap of creating a throwaway prototype to show your customers. That never works. If you create a prototype (especially during JIT design), expect to use it and never have the time to "do it right later."

Testing (Dis-)Integration

The whole software development cycle depends on a sequence of deriving and validating needs. The first part of the process describes the needs, and a supervisory process ensures that the project codifies the needs. This supervisory process is often called *testing* or *quality assurance*.

In reality, validation does much more than just test features. It gathers and archives work products; it checks and verifies product deliverables; and it assures business and product-line compliance. Of all the responsibilities of a project, the Quality Representative has the most difficult.

Object Technology does not help matters. In fact, it doubles to quadruples the level's complexity. First, white- and black-box (defined in the next section) testing and validation were sufficient. The modules introduced gray-box testing. Objects add inheritance, polymorphic, framework, reuse-compliance, and interface testing. The sheer complexity that Object Technology adds to the field of software quality has caused many to rethink testing entirely.

The first mistake many make is to have the designer or coder alone test his work. This problem should be obvious: The same blind spots that caused the defect may possibly interfere with discovering them. The probability of this coincidence is too high to overlook. Get good experienced testing engineers to crosscheck the programmers' work.

When creating an object project, you and your customer must identify how much testing is to be done. Be aware that validation costs resources and time. Expect the number of man-hours spent on a regular project to double or triple as you transition to an object project.

Shades of Gray

The last section mentions white-, gray-, and black-box testing. Software testing uses techniques similar to those found in objects, one being encapsulation. Defining the *grayness* of the system exposes the amount of visible internals. In full light (white-box), the tester explores every function, path, decision, and statement. Often, the programmer or designer can do that fairly safely.

Black-box testing perceives the system from the user's point of view. Black-box is similar to acceptance testing where the use-cases decide compliance.

The last is gray-box testing, which meets in the middle. It has more knowledge of the implementation (down to the module or function level, but goes no further), and it depends on the use-cases for the validation paths.

Objects blur these definitions quite a bit. For example, where do you fit inheritance, overrides, and polymorphic testing? What about reuse testing? The result is clear; everyone has to test everything.

Define "System Integration"

As the project builds the product, it composes and assembles the pieces one by one. The last definition that objects muddy a little is when the pieces really fit together as a system. When working with internal or off-the-shelf frameworks, you could consider any assembly as a system. On the other hand, some projects are split into programs that work together locally or distributed on the network. So, when do you really integrate the system?

Actually, true system integration died a long time ago. It has become apparent only within the last several *Internet years* (3-month product lifecycles). Companies that still use that term mean something entirely different that the original meaning. For objects, integration is whenever you deliver a snap or freeze.

Summary: Walk Carefully on Shale

Object Technology provides a great deal of power, but this power does have incremental costs. The increased costs arise from theory, technology, and personnel. Like climbing a mountain of shale, you have to step carefully and expect a little backsliding.

Some backsliding comes from trying to do too much at once. Try to control that urge. Educate and share the learning process. The most important task you may ever do is involve your customers. If the customers feel like they are involved and important, they will be happy with what they get.

14

LIMITS TO
OBJECTS

Working with the extended team is next in importance. Try to look out for the pitfalls of Object Technology and let each person know how he can be important. In the way a director brings actors in and out of a scene, you can give the participants the heads-up when they are needed.

The success of the team supercedes the success of the product because the product is a known want or desire. The rest is getting done on time with satisfaction. A satisfied customer wants more, and a satisfied team works more closely—like a well-oiled machine.

Advanced Sockets—Adding Value

PART
IV

IN THIS PART

Network Encapsulation with Remote Procedure Calls (RPCs)

IN THIS CHAPTER

Looking from a developer-user perspective, knowing all the eccentricities of network programming may be more laborious than you want. Sometimes, you or your peers (the developer-users) simply want to focus on the development of the programs at hand and leave the network details to established libraries or tools. Remote Procedure Calls (RPCs) fit that bill perfectly.

RPCs handle all the connection and data translation for your developer-users. From the perspective of the developer-users, the networking piece is a small part of the program's feature set. For them to dedicate more than a small portion of their time to the writing and testing of the network interfaces would be very costly and inefficient.

In turn, you could write tools (service calls) that provide their programs robust ways of communicating. These tools would interface with the client, server, and peer. Depending on the protocol, your service calls can be complex—requiring your tools to provide large amounts of checking and retransmission (UDP)—or simple (TCP).

This chapter shows you how to write RPCs from two different approaches. The first approach demonstrates how to write them with your own bare hands, without any tools. The second introduces the rpcgen tool. Before all of this, the next section revisits the concepts of the network model to show how RPCs fit.

Revisiting the OSI Model

Back in Chapter 5, "Understanding the Network Layering Model," you read that the network model layers all features and operations, hiding information from the user *and* the program. The operation includes information about how the network actually passes data from one program to another. The network layering model also increases the likelihood that the destination gets the message. According to networking theory, no user actually interfaces with anything other than the Application layer (layer 7).

The IP protocol stack, however, effectively stops at layer 4 (the Networking layer). TCP is the last protocol and has the highest reliability of the IP protocol stack. You can create a socket that acts a lot like a file stream. This gives you a lot of power and flexibility. The protocol leaves the responsibility of implementing the higher layers to the applications.

This does present a small problem. Without defining the higher layers, many applications have emerged that essentially duplicate effort. Consider the FTP and Telnet protocols. Each provides a authentication phase—user login. While the login interfaces may be small and minor, they duplicate the procedure. Furthermore, this complicates methods for you as a professional programmer. If you want to incorporate authentication in a client program, you basically have to write your own.

You can provide some of this functionality using your own interfaces. Other programs can then use these functions. As with the various networking models, you may want to make the interfaces *network-transparent*. Network-transparent programs never force the user (or programmer) to interact with the network. The whole idea is to make the network connection as effortless as possible.

Comparing Network and Procedural Programming

Whenever you start considering network interfacing, you open a whole side of programming that software engineers rarely touch. The challenge of it is clearly very interesting, but that is not enough to simply begin programming it. You must think ahead to how the client and server (the system) are to work together.

Network programming is not at all like procedural programming. Procedural programming is very forgiving. If you write a program that two people use (a client and a server), these people expect a higher quality and better recovery from errors.

To create a library of network-ready tools, you face several hurdles. The hurdles involve performance and reliability; they also involve simple limitations in the technology.

Language Limits

The first problem you face is the language interface itself. The C programming language allows you to do several things that are not meaningful in a network interface.

First, information that you send must be in a *value* form. Pointers are not meaningful in a network environment for obvious reasons; one computer's address is not the same as another's address. Your program must pass all data as values. This goes against some programmers' grain. No one likes to pass a structure or array by value; the data-copy chews up memory and CPU time.

C-Style Data Copying

The C language assumes that you do *not* want to copy large data types because of the potential to chew up performance merely moving data around. So it tries to pass information by pointer or reference as much as possible. All complex languages support scalars (simple types like int and char) and vectors (arrays and structures). By default, C passes scalars by value. However, some compilers complain when you try to pass a structure by value. To pass an array by value, you have to declare a new type or use a structure. In all cases, the program uses the hardware stack to store your data, and you must ensure that you have enough stack space to accommodate the data.

This does result in the problem of getting information back unless you let the return value be the result. You can get around passing everything by value, but at some point *the program does have to send the data.* With this approach, you still pass your parameters by reference, but the program does copy the data at least at the very last stage.

The following example shows a prototype of an interface of the getphoto() service call. The types image_t and host_t are custom types that you create. If you are adventurous, you can return the result by value as well. Still, you might want to leave the return value open to indicate an error; if you return a structure or type by value, you can't effectively detect errors.

```
/************************************************************/
/*** Pass-by-value example – call a camera server to get  ***/
/*** recent snapshot.                                     ***/
/************************************************************/
image_t *getphoto(host_t host);
```

Returning Vectors by Value

The C language permits you to return a vector by value. However, the implementation is compiler-specific and may surprise you. Because of the way some processors handle the hardware stack, the compiler may *not* actually copy the result to the stack. Instead, it may create a local or static variable and pass back the variable reference. Upon returning, the caller then copies the value into the appropriate destination. This may have a significant side effect in multithreaded programs. Alternatively, some compilers may even be "smart" and note the destination before calling the function. As the function populates the vector, it's really revising the actual destination.

The parameters themselves are a particular problem. Most programmers do not designate which parameters are input only, output only, or input/output. But, because the interface has to determine which parameters to send and which to fill, you need to indicate that in the interface somehow. Often the documentation *is* the interface. Consider the following example:

```
/************************************************************/
/*** Network interface example                            ***/
/************************************************************/
/**/
/*-----------------------------------------------------------*/
/*              ***PUBLICATION NOTES***                    */
/* getuserinfo – get the finger information from a host     */
/*    user – (input) user's login id                       */
/*    host – (input) the external host name                */
/*    data – (output) the results of the call              */
/* RETURN VALUE: success or failure (check errno)           */
int getuserinfo(char* user, char* host, userinfo_t *data);
```

This example is more typical. You organize the parameters in the following order: input only, input/output, and output only. Each parameter is passed by reference, and the call assumes that the user reads the publication notes.

Holding Connected Sessions

The communication between client and server at a service-call level assumes seamless channels. You don't want your user to log in more than once or even be aware that the client program makes multiple connections. This is part of the concept of holding network sessions.

The simplest form of a service call is *stateless*, requiring no more from the server than to do some tasks. But if you want to create a session, you have to do additional work on both the client and server sides.

The network session includes implicit guarantees that most people understand and expect. Chapter 5 introduces some of these guarantees. In RPC service calls, you have to deploy them.

Establishing a Dialog

The first step in providing the Session layer's functionality is determining the communication order and keeping it. Most RPC connections require some form of authentication, but the client drives the communication.

The initial connection between the client and your server usually requires a login process. The client must provide some level of verification (like username and password). For security, you must ensure that this interchange is secured through some form of encryption, because anyone on the same subnet can see the messages between client and server. After logging in, the client and server establish which communicates first.

Sometimes losing a message can confuse the connection. Both the client and server end up waiting for each other. As noted in Chapter 5 and described in Chapter 10, "Designing Robust Linux Sockets," you can keep track of whose turn it is to talk. The easiest method is to periodically send a message indicating each other's state using the OOB data protocols.

Checkpointing

Some service-directed connections can have critical transactions. The transactions cannot permit data loss (for example, bank transactions). After the client and server have established a dialog, you might want to periodically force a checkpoint.

Checkpointing is like the `commit` command in some databases. During the session, you may have several transactions. These transactions change the server's state (such as transferring funds or paying bills). Both the client and server keep track of the transactions and the expected results. The checkpoint is like checking the balance after several transfers.

15

NETWORK
ENCAPSULATION
WITH RPCs

You may experience another twist in checkpointing. Clients sometimes have to log the transactions locally to a file for auditing. If this is the case, you might want to encrypt each transaction.

Recoverable Connections

A session requires a single connection that apparently remains open at all times. That requirement may not always be possible; the network can drop a connection at any time. Also, the Socket API does not directly tell you when it has lost a connection.

Having a recoverable connection means that you not only attempt to reconnect, but it also means that your program must determine the *liveness* of the connection (the channel is clear and active). Chapter 10 describes a few ways to check for connection liveness.

Recovering a connection is easy if you have designed the requirement into your program. Part of the problem with losing a session is trying to keep track of where you were. Somewhat like using a bookmark, you need to mark the place where you left off. Both the client and server must support the bookmark, or *Session ID*. Without the Session ID, you may find that recovering the connection becomes very difficult if not impossible.

After your program finds that the connection was dropped, it can simply reconnect to the server. Doing it with the minimal amount of user interaction is part of seamless connections.

Seamless Connections

The target here is to provide the user an easy-to-use interface with the minimum amount of user awareness. In contrast, some applications have an *in-your-face* approach that requires the user to re-enter passwords or to establish the network connection manually.

You need to provide the user only as much interaction with the network as he desires. This may mean that you keep track of login information during a defined session. For example, if you define a session to be the duration of your client-program's execution, you could watch all the user logins, remembering them for future use.

However, you must be fully aware of security issues. Keeping passwords in a file for automatic login is often an unnecessary security risk. (It is surprising that some professional applications offer this feature—by default!) Likewise, you may want to drop the connection and forget the login information after a certain time period of inactivity. In the extreme, if the connection must be ultra-secure, you may have to force a login upon each reconnection. Use your best judgment and consult with your end users.

Supplying Middleware Methods

You can write a set of service calls that interface with a server. The service calls provide a passive (or active) interface between the network, hiding the implementation of the network connection. More often than not, the interface, or *middleware*, is passive, doing no computation—only copying and translating information from one place to another.

Middleware is an important process for modern products. Most applications interface with it from various levels and requirements. Making your middleware components very robust is critical.

The first step in creating good, solid middleware service calls is to define the interface for longevity. You cannot expect to write an interface for others to use that you intend to revise within six months. The short-term interface for a foundational technology like networking is likely to be unpopular.

You can create long-lasting interfaces—critical for all serious projects—by identifying the *brainchild* (a set of goals, intents, philosophies, and theories) for the services. After you have solidified your brainchild, you can work on the network stubs.

Stubbing Network Calls

If you are writing a passive interface, the interface between your client program and the network support functions only needs to be a set of simple procedure calls. These procedure calls implement different parts of the brainchild. The procedures can also be routines that do more than repackage the parameters.

The getphoto() and getuserinfo() examples, discussed earlier, are examples of interfaces that do nothing more than retrieve data. These calls could easily be part of a security desk brainchild; when the security officer needs to identify someone by face and credentials, he or she uses a tool that retrieves and displays that information.

The network stubs identify what the caller expects and what the server needs to fulfill the request. The interface must be simple as well; the more information your user-developer has to provide, the more difficult it becomes to use.

Adding the Service Call Implementation

After your client-side service call accepts the request, the call has to package up data and ship it to the server. The server, in turn, implements the server-side service calls that accept and unpackage the data and request. This is the heart of middleware.

Defining Client-Side Services

Client-side services often are based on on-demand processing; the network interaction is only active during the request. The *service requestor's* basic needs are destination, request, and data. Most requests are transactional, so the middleware does not have to support any more than packaging and shipping the information. The service call module is inactive between requests. UDP fits this case well because a single message passes between client and server.

You may find occasions that require an open connection—a conversation instead of a simple request. TCP fits better in this circumstance. In fact, the client-side services' role changes slightly because the channel has to be held open, and you may have the potential of holding more than one conversation with more than one server. Along with the basic needs of an on-demand connection, your module must keep track of the session and connection. Network modules that support this level of connectivity usually add two more interfaces, an open- and close-session service call.

Answering with Server-Side Services

The server-side services act in the same way as the client-side. Just as you can create network modules for the client-side program, you can write network modules for the server. Servers usually do much more than serve up data. However, the similarities between client and server network service modules abruptly end there.

The first big issue you face as you begin to write the server's *service provider* is the potential that several requests will arrive at the same time. You could accept and process each one sequentially (remember that the kernel enqueues all messages until the recv() system call reads it). However, you cannot be sure how long the request may have to wait in the queue. That can be a very long time.

Multitasking the server reduces the delays from a transactional system. Linux runs more efficiently when the programs are multitasked (using threads and processes). Each new request creates a task to serve it. The organization differs little from the program hierarchy that Chapter 6, " A Server Primer," demonstrates.

1. The client program calls the client-side network module.
2. The client-side network module (service requestor) packages the request and data and ships them through the network. It waits for a reply.
3. The server-side network module (service provider) accepts the request and passes it to the server program.
4. The server program (request processor) processes the request and returns the results.
5. The server-side network module accepts the results, packages it, and pushes it through the network.
6. The client-side network module accepts the results message, unpackages it, and returns it to the client program.
7. The client program accepts the results.

You may note that the hierarchical placement of the network services module differs between the client side and the server side. Often, the client-side network module is a leaf (the very bottom) in the program hierarchy. The server program, on the other hand, places the network module at the apex of the hierarchy, after all initialization is done. Writing reusable modules for this upside-down interface can be problematic.

To solve the upside-down interface problem, you can use one of two methods. The first method is to define an external procedure that the server-side module calls. The server program must define that procedure as an entry point into its request processor. The problem with this approach is the inflexibility of using predefined procedure names. As your programs evolve, the interface name can lose its meaning.

Another approach is to offer a registration service. As part of initialization, before the server is up and awaiting connections, the server program could register all of its request processor routines. This is the preferred way to overcome the upside-down interface problem. It ensures the longevity of the interfaces.

Implementing the Presentation Layer

During the process of accepting and passing on the data, you often just have to copy the data into messages and pass them on. However, you cannot be sure that all clients can talk the same way as your server. One obvious example is endianness. Intel-based programs talking with Alpha-based programs have different byte orders for binary data. Another example is ASCII versus EBCDC.

The Presentation layer of the OSI model creates a way to convert the information from one form to another. As you create your brainchild, you need to consider what types of clients and servers your program may run on. As with the first step, byte-order independence is very important.

Creating RPCs with `rpcgen`

Linux distributions often include a tool, `rpcgen`, to help you write your own RPCs. This tool vastly simplifies RPC programming and offers ways to help you build your program. This section shows you how to use this tool and describes some of the syntaxes involved.

`rpcgen`'s Interface Language

The `rpcgen` tool is yet another language translator that proliferates the UNIX world. This language lets you define the interface and data that the programs use and transmit through the network. The file, by convention, uses a `.x` as the extension to the filename. Its format is very similar to C, with a few exceptions.

> ## Microsoft's COM and COM+
>
> Using and learning how to manipulate the RPC definitions is useful in other areas. Microsoft's "new" definition of COM and COM+ essentially uses the RPC protocols. In fact, you can read the X file format in one of the COM project files. It is slightly different and has a few extensions, but it follows the same basic flow.

Generating the Basic Interface

For example, if you wanted to get the server's time in UTC (number of seconds from Jan 1, 1970) format, you could define the interface as follows:

```
/*************************************************************/
/*--- Define the interface to get the server's time     ---*/
/*************************************************************/
program RPCTIME
{
    version RPCTIMEVERSION
    {
        long GETTIME() = 1;
    } = 1;
} = 2000001;
```

The first line of the declaration defines the name of the program (RPCTIME). Declaring it in uppercase is a standard convention; however, rpcgen converts all names to lowercase. You can have several versions of the same interface, so the next declaration defines the first interface version. Within it, you find the actual procedure interface.

Each section in the declaration is assigned a numeric ID. This ID is important for the client-to-server communication. You can use any number for the version and procedure name, but some program IDs are reserved. You can safely experiment with numbers between 2,000,000 and 3,000,000.

You may notice in the example that the call returns long instead of time_t. The rpcgen tool accepts any type (ignores it, actually) syntactically and leaves the semantic checking (type declaration and meaning) to the C compiler. However, rpcgen assumes it knows something about the type to translate it correctly. You could define a type (just like C) so that the program uses the standard definition:

```
typedef long time_t;
```

The rpcgen's XDR (data translation) interface handles all the conversion for you.

The next step is to run rpcgen:

```
rpcgen -a rpctime.x
```

The -a option creates all the files that you may need to create and run the client and server. Without the -a, you get only the client (rpctime_clnt.c) and server (rpctime_svc.c) interface files. If you defined any types, you get the XDR file (rpctime_xdr.c). Do not revise any of these files—they are dynamically generated from the *.x file. With the -a option, rpcgen generates sample client (rpctime_client.c) and server (rpctime_server.c) files and a Makefile.rpctime for compiling everything. This makes development very easy.

> ## Use Care when Executing make clean
> If you plan to use the sample files for your development, do not call make with the standard clean option. The Makefile erroneously deletes these files.

Looking at the files, you may notice that the GETTIME procedure call is now named gettime_1(). The _1 is the version number of this procedure. When calling these procedures, you need to specify the interface version number. While it would be nice to simply call gettime() and let the system choose the right one based on parameters or even just the latest version, that's not how rpcgen works.

The next step is to add the time-related code to the example after running rpcgen -a (to generate the sample client and server files). Open the rpctime_client.c file and add the following code:

```
/*******************************************************/
/*** RPC Time Client code snippet                   ***/
/*******************************************************/
/*---This is automatically generated                ---*/
result_1 = gettime_1((void*)&gettime_1_arg, clnt);
if (result_1 == (long *) NULL) {
    clnt_perror (clnt, "call failed");
}
/*---Add the following code                          ---*/
else
    printf("%d |%s", *result_1, ctime(result_1));
```

The added code simply prints out the result of the call. The server code is similar:

```
/*******************************************************/
/*** RPC Time Server code snippet                   ***/
/*******************************************************/
static long  result;
time(&result);  /*---Custom code---*/
return &result;
```

The rpcgen tool adds a commented section indicating to insert the server code between the variable declaration and the return statement. When done, you compile and test with the following:

```
make -f Makefile.rpctime
./rpctime_server &
./rpctime_client 127.0.0.1
```

The result is the time in seconds and in standard ASCII format. The tool is very simple to use and develop with.

Using More Complicated X Files

After you have had some success with rpcgen, you may want to try to use some of its types. The rpcgen tool adds two new types—string and bool_t. The bool_t fills C's oversight of a Boolean value. Only 1 and zero are allowed, even though the actual size may be larger.

The string type requires a little more explanation. The C language allows you to use char* to mean a pointer to a char, an array of char, or a NULL-terminated string. That's too ambiguous. So, it created a type, string, to reduce the ambiguity. The format looks as follows:

```
string filename<100>; /*---Up to 100 chars long---*/
string myname<>;      /*---Any length---*/
```

All strings are of variable length. If you know that the string has a maximum length, you may want to define it with that length. This ensures that the XDR transmits only the specified number of bytes.

Additionally, you can include unions in the X file. These unions look more like a cross between Pascal and C's switch statement:

```
/***********************************************************/
/*** RPC union code snippet                            ***/
/***********************************************************/
union proc_res switch (int Err)
{
   case 0:
      string Data<>;   /*---If Err is 0, Data is value---*/
   default:
      void;            /*---If Err is anything else, no data---*/
};
```

In this example, the union can either return a string or nothing, depending on the key variable Err. The rpcgen tool converts this into structure with a union:

```
/***********************************************************/
/*** RPC genrpc code snippet result                    ***/
/***********************************************************/
```

```
struct proc_res
{
    int Err;
    union
    {
        char *Data;
    } proc_res_u;
};
```

The union is very useful if you want to send back a specific error code without tripping up the XDR routines. The server-side code always returns a pointer to the result, not the result itself. If the server fails, it returns a NULL. First, a NULL is not very descriptive, and second, the lower-level calls may intercept a NULL return.

The next example uses the union structure to either return the information from a file in /proc or an error code. The full X file is as follows:

```
/*************************************************************/
/*** RPC RPCProc X File declaration                    ***/
/*************************************************************/
union proc_res switch (int Err)
{
    case 0:             /*---no error, return string---*/
        string Data<>; /*---no limit---*/
    default:            /*---if error, return nothing---*/
        void;
};

program RPCPROC
{
    version RPCPROCVERSION
    {
        proc_res READPROC(string) = 1; /*---/proc filename---*/
    } = 1;
} = 2000025;
```

The server accepts the filename that points in the /proc virtual file system and opens the file. If no error occurs, the server reads the contents, closes the file, and returns the result. You can run into a little problem here. First, the server returns the reference to the result, so the data must not be on the stack. All return values are made static to ensure that the data is still around. However, strings are always converted into char*.

When you fill your return record, you must allocate memory to insert strings. This means that you must somehow free up the memory; otherwise, your program develops memory leaks. The XDR routines offer a way to clean up from the previous call:

```
xdr_free((xdrproc_t)xdr_proc_res, (void*)&result);
```

The only parameter that changes is the xdr_<return-type> (xdr_proc_res, in this case). You always call this function before doing anything else. It is smart enough not to do anything if called the first time. (For a complete listing of the algorithm and files for this program, please refer to the Sams Publishing Web site.)

Adding Records and Pointers to the Fray

The last type should be very familiar. The struct is identical to C's record declaration and fills the same purpose. But, the struct serves an additional purpose. Using the rpcgen toolset has a significant (but not intractable) limitation: You cannot pass more than one parameter through a service call. All multiple parameter calls must use records to pass in and out the data.

A structure definition is as follows:

```
/************************************************************/
/*** RPC RPCList X File snippet                          ***/
/************************************************************/
typedef struct NodeStruct *TNode;
struct NodeStruct
{
    string Name<>;
    TNode Next;
};
```

You may notice that the structure has a pointer type (TNode) in the body. If you recall, the earlier part of the chapter stated that you cannot send pointers over the network—the memory spaces are not the same, so a pointer reference is meaningless. The rpcgen XDR is very smart; it copies and translates all pointer references in a complex structure so that the client or server can understand the results. You can send trees, linked lists, and any non-looping dynamic memory storage.

The only strangeness is the syntax in the X file. A pointer type must be declared as a typedef:

```
/************************************************************/
/*** RPC syntax example                                  ***/
/************************************************************/
typedef struct NodeStruct TNode;
struct NodeStruct
{
    string Name<>;
    TNode *Next;        /*--- This is not legal ---*/
};
```

The Sams Web site has several examples, including a RPC ps command that ships the information back in a dynamically allocated table with rows and fields.

Creating Non-Stateless Calls with Open Connections

Passing information back and forth from the client to the server involves much more than the data. Each program often has to keep track of the machine state in order to respond correctly to a request. The previous sections focused on programs that assume nothing about other calls; they also refer to another type of call. Each call is typically independent from every other (a *stateless connection*). This is not very useful if you have to maintain some kind of information from call to call.

For lack of a better term, a *stateful* (or non-stateless) connection must retain some kind of information so that proper communications can occur. A couple examples of this are logins (the person must be logged in before he gets any data) and database transactions (the server may not transmit the entire table all at once).

The first course of action is to answer these questions: "Why are stateless connections common?" and "Why are stateful connections a burden?"

Diagnosing the State Problem

The stateless connection is simple. The client sends information, and the server replies with the answer. If the question is lost, the client simply asks again. That approach falls very short of the needs of a stateful connection.

The stateful connection has to maintain a relationship. As noted in earlier sections and chapters, a server and client must make sure that the handshake is deterministic and recoverable. The problems with stateful connection include the following:

- *Current State*—The session must keep track of the actions already performed. No one likes to answer questions or jump through the same hoops over and over.

- *State Path or Route*—The session must clearly have a particular path or route. The steps forward and back must be deterministic and clear. If not, state recovery or next steps become uncertain or confused.

- *State Recovery*—If a state is lost the system may need to roll back to a previously known state. Even if connections drop, the client and server must pick up where they left off. As a last resort, both systems must be able to completely undo the transactions up to the point of disconnection.

The state problem must address each of these issues. In some cases, recovery is moot. But, overall, the client and server must uniquely identify each other's current session.

Remembering Where You Are

The simplest stateful connection is one that keeps track of the current state. You can do this with a session ID. This ID must be encoded so that only the client and server understand the significance of it. As a simple example, the client requests the first row of a database query result. To get the next row, the server must be able to associate the next call with the initial query.

A simple way to address this problem is to divide up the calls into at least three phases: initialize, transact, and terminate. The sole purpose of the initialization state would be to establish the session and begin the processing. The transaction-based calls manipulate the state that the initialization started. And, the termination state flushes any pending transactions, closes the connection, and secures the data.

After the session is closed, the session ID is no longer valid.

Following a Specific Route

The three primary states—initialize, transact, and terminate—are the beginnings of providing a state route map. The state route map shows all the states and how to get between them. Given the current information about the session, the server and client know exactly what they can do and how to get to the next state.

Determinism in a state map means that you must have unique states and unique transitions. Specifically

- *No single transition leads to disparate states*—Example: If the server changes directory, the client must reflect the change.

- *No two states can have the same transition*—Example: A transaction cannot result in both the client and the server waiting for a message.

Without the predictability that determinism provides, you cannot recover from any state failure.

Recovering from a State Failure

Of the three different problems that stateful connections face, recovering from state failure is the most difficult. The network particularly introduces many different ways to lose state. Some state loss causes include hardware, routing, connectivity, program defects, and so on. The first problem is recognition.

State loss can be a nasty problem if you do not plan for it. First, both programs must check each other's session ID. The session ID must also include some level of security, expiration, and state identification. You can even include the last state and potential next states. If any of these keys gets out of sync, your program can determine that state has been lost.

Recovery from state loss brings its own set of difficulties. After you have determined that state is lost, you then face the challenge of what to do next. The following are a few ideas:

- *Connection Reset*—Force the client to start the session over again. The server rolls back all transactions from the previous session.

- *State Rollback*—Both the client and the server roll back to a known state. Intermediate transactions are dropped. If the known state interferes with the either the client or the server, they choose a different state. If all else fails, they reset the connection.

- *State Force*—The server tells the client what the correct state is. The client replies whether that is acceptable. If not, both execute a state rollback.

Depending on how critical the transactions are, you may choose one idea over the other. However, each idea depends on the previous. You cannot easily choose one without selecting the simpler one(s) as well.

Summary: Creating an RPC Toolset

You can use your sockets programming experience to help other user-developers who want the benefits of network programming without having to worry about the implementation details. RPCs come in two forms: creating home-grown interfaces or using standard tools like rpcgen.

Creating home-grown tools lets you define how the interface works and lets you customize the transport policies. The interfaces are unrestricted, allowing you send as many parameters you want and in any form or order that seems best. However, you cannot send pointers, and you must copy all data manually.

The rpcgen toolset lets you focus on the program instead of the transport. You can choose between TCP or UDP protocols, but the transport is off limits. It provides you with a wealth of automatic conversions including the capability of sending pointers. The tools are very easy to use and make programming simple.

Finally, most RPC connections are stateless—a simple ask-and-reply scheme. However, some connections require more complex stateful interactions—the current call is dependent on previous calls. To achieve this level of interfacing, you must implement the states, sessions, and recovery yourself.

Secure Sockets Layer (SSL), which has many states embedded in its protocol, depends heavily on RPCs. The next chapter discusses security and SSL.

Adding Security to Network Programs and SSL

16

IN THIS CHAPTER

- Giving Permission to Work   340
- The Problem with the Internet   342
- Securing a Network Node   344
- Encrypting the Messages   351
- Secure Sockets Layer (SSL)   352
- Summary: The Secure Server   357

A secure system provides no more functionality than an insecure system—the data it provides is more reliable. An insecure system provides services and information sharing, but it is prone to attacks and becomes unreliable. This unreliability casts a shadow on the value of the services and can even harm the company's reputation or brand.

In most cases, security is assumed as you build the product. Rarely do business requirements say, "The server must be impervious to Denial of Service attacks." Security is a foundational requirement that the customer assumes to be part of the product. You must incorporate the needed security into your program. The most difficult decision you face is, "How much security is necessary?"

This chapter discusses many issues of network programming security: concepts and terms, Internet impact, methods and implementation, and the Secure Sockets Layer (SSL).

Giving Permission to Work

Network programming revolves around the idea of sharing information and distributing work. To share information, you need to know who is interacting with your server; is this a friend or a foe? The increased number of attacks on current systems indicates that the number of foes is on the rise, so designing in security has more priority than implementing the product features.

Interaction implies recognition and trust. Security places the onus of identification on both the client and the server. After identification has been established, the client can ship or retrieve information or can even collaborate calculations.

To manage the scope of security, you need to know what the levels of security are and where security needs to be enforced.

Levels of Identification

Establishing levels of user identification is an important part of creating a secure system. The simplest form of security, *authentication*, simply identifies the client. This is the first door of a secure system that the user passes through. An example of a program that authenticates a connection is a remote login. The login procedure just checks your username and password.

The next level of security, *authorization*, permits or denies access to features in the system. Linux's remote login couples the authentication with the authorization by attaching the user's roles and group permissions. Some operating systems either do not distinguish one remote person from another or provide very limited authorization. For example, if you share files in Microsoft Windows 95 and 98 with more than read-only access, it only checks the client's authentication. Once authenticated, the client can do anything he or she wants to your files and printer.

The problem with authentication and authorization is that the client cannot determine whether the server is a Trojan horse. *Certification* offers the most secure level of authentication. It requires a trusted third party to prove both the client and the server. The third party is a trusted certificate server that proves that both client and server are who they claim to be.

Forms of Interchange

After you have established the client's identity, you need to look at the information that the computers pass between each other. Data interchange comes in two forms: *scrutiny* and *intrusion*. Data scrutiny can be a problem only if the communication is restricted. Revealing restricted data like usernames and passwords can lead to intrusions. Data intrusion is a bigger problem because the intruder can add or even revise the data.

Often, the communication is public because the data in the channel would not compromise the client or the server. Web servers and other simple services work at this level.

A public interchange does not mean that everyone sees the data. Instead, it means that the two programs take no precautions for privacy. Any computer on the same physical LAN connection can see the interchanged messages. This form of communication is very prone to network scrutiny and intrusion.

Another form of data interchange is within groups. Shared messages depend on the TCP/IP protocols for broadcasting messages or isolating traffic. All computers in the same network segment can see these messages. Because routers do not pass foreign broadcast messages, the group messages are isolated in the destination segment. It tends to be more secure than the public form, but it is still subject to network snooping (within the same network segment). Intrusion is not as much of an issue because the segment typically assumes that you are among friends.

Private messages try to limit access to the information between the source and destination. They often have critical information to which external data prying can cause serious damage. Private messages require extra measures, both physical and logical, to ensure data security and integrity.

Another important message form that requires inclusion here is a special data form that distributes program execution to other sites. These commands include RPCs and direct commands (like those of `telnet`, `rlogin`, or `rsh`). The data's function demonstrates its difference from regular data. Regular data (or *inactive data*) only changes the meaning or its interpretation if corrupted. Distributed commands (or *active data*) change execution when corrupted and can even compromise host security. The Love Bug virus in Microsoft Outlook is an example of corrupted active data.

Of the different types of data interactions, active data presents the greatest security risk. If you are required to include remote instructions and commands, you must be careful to verify that the remote host is trusted.

The Problem with the Internet

The Internet itself presents its own unique problems. Its very nature is the heart of the problem; it was designed in anarchy to solve the anarchy problem. You can find several stories of how the Internet was created, but the most relevant fact is that it was designed to circumvent the problem of nuclear explosion blackout. That is the reason that the paths from host to host are so dynamic.

No path through the system is really exact. You cannot say to the network system: "Take this packet through these routers to the destination." Each packet may even follow a different path. Your pipe may go in and out of enemy territory on the Internet.

Everything Is Visible

When writing network programs, you must remember an important rule: The Internet cannot guarantee you a private channel. Like yelling a sell command on the New York Stock Exchange floor, everyone there can hear you. However, most of the time those who hear don't care and ignore the message. Other times, the room can have listeners that can intercept or even revise that message for ulterior motives.

Similarly, the message may move in and out of trusted zones. A *trusted zone* is a network that a company trusts to be safe. For example, two popular trusted zones are the AT&T and US Sprint backbones. Other major corporations buy into these networks through dedicated lines. They are trusted because the zones' host company provides limited guarantee of privacy.

Corporations create or buy into trusted zones as part of their own network or intranet. The intranet is the corporation's own network system. When two more corporations collaborate and share information in a special network (which often happens to be the same physical medium), they form an *extranet*. Because each company must get information quickly from host to host, the boundaries defining Internet, intranet, and extranet are beginning to blur.

Alternately, individual messages may go through the equivalent of no-man's land in the Internet, where messages are subject to snooping. Even the tools that were once restricted to the privileged root are accessible to everyone. With these tools, a less-than-benevolent super-user can access—and even revise—messages. The power of a free and powerful operating system, such as Linux, can also be its folly.

The best solution is to be aware of the risks and to protect the data you need to send. Follow good practices, such as always masking username and password information and never ship a credit card number without encrypting it.

Forms of Intrusion/Attack

You can protect your client and server by being aware of the typical forms of attack. These revolve around the basic form of communication. All forms of attack exclusively follow this nature: The client communicates with the server.

- *Line-Tapping*—An eavesdropper listens to the messages waiting for some juicy data that he can use. Network snoopers neatly fit into this category.

- *Line-Severing*—A malicious program limits the accessibility of the server or client. This act does something to the network or the host itself that delays the reply or even eliminates it. Two examples are ping-storming and Denial-of-Service (DoS).

- *Line-Hijacking*—Instead of impeding communications, a program could take over the communication interchange between host and client. Some protocol stacks, such as the one in Linux, make hijacking difficult because of how they generate the TCP sequence numbering.

More security intrusion forms may undoubtedly appear, but you can depend on the fact that all forms fit into one of these categories. (Viruses are an entirely different problem. They can cause security problems, but they are not direct data security attacks.) Security issues for network programming apply to everything connected to the network. Security is mostly independent of the operating system's implementation (see the next section for an exception).

Linux has security built into the system, and that was the fundamental design. The effect is obvious: a very secure and reliable system. Other operating systems that adopt that philosophy have a solid level of security. Similarly, those systems that are not founded on this philosophy will never be as secure. Still, security in network programs appears to be mostly independent from the system's foundational philosophy, so the degree of network security relies on the programs you write.

TCP/IP Crackability

Most computers now use the Internet protocols. Even Novell and Microsoft have begun to move away from their proprietary protocols so that they can more easily interface with the Internet. How crackable is IP?

Actually, the Internet Protocol is rather easy to crack. Network snoopers, as presented in this book, are a good example of how easy watching network messages really is. Using raw sockets (remember this is a privileged protocol), a protocol cracker can simulate all protocols, typically flooding the recipient with bogus messages. The easiest protocols to falsify are ICMP, UDP, and RDP. (Reliable Datagram Protocol (RDP) is not yet implemented on most operating systems.)

Each protocol in the TCP/IP stack has its vulnerabilities. Some security experts claim that TCP is the hardest to crack. This is true...to a point. They claim that the packet sequence number presents a level of attachment—if you cannot guess the next sequential number, you cannot hijack the communications. The hijacker must duplicate exactly the next number in order to fool the recipient into assuming that the other message is a duplicate.

The TCP/IP protocol does not restrict the numbering sequence other than to ensure that each packet is uniquely numbered (for the lifetime of the packet). If the algorithm for determining the next number is predictable, the channel is vulnerable. (Please note that the sequence number itself is not the vulnerability. Instead, the way it's generated is the weakness.) Is TCP the hardest IP protocol to hijack? Yes, but other networked computers can still eavesdrop, and hijacking is still possible.

Securing a Network Node

How do you begin to lock down a system from attack and intrusion? Network security is a very large and complicated mix of tools and rules. This section identifies a few good practices for controlling the system. Some ideas do not have direct relevance to network programming, but they are still important. You may want to be aware that this is hardly exhaustive; you must consider the ideas from multiple sources to increase your network security.

Restricting Access

You can increase your server and client program's security using the following suggestions:

- *File Permissions*—The first step in network security is to make sure that your files have the right permissions and ownership. Some network programs may require root access (raw IP, for example); be very careful what you do in these programs. In fact, some programs that require root access relinquish root privilege as soon as they successfully open the raw socket.

- *Connection Limitations*—Restrict how much a remote host can do while connected. Do not allow blanket remote commands without proper authorizations.

- *Reducing Port Holes*—Limit the number of ports available. Each port in a system increases the security risk by another level. (Don't go overboard on this suggestion. Just remember that the more ports you have, the more openings that a program can get into.)

- *Focusing on Cards*—If you have a router or gateway with more than one ethernet card (or interface), set your services to one device. Most services serve all devices unless told otherwise. Again, if you have more than one physical interface, the services are rarely needed on all interfaces. For example, you may want Telnet on one card for the intranet, but not on the card that connects to the Internet.

- *Severing Unneeded Services*—If you don't intend to use a particular service (even rarely), don't run it. When you need it, start it up at that time but, until then, leave it turned off. (This includes your own servers.)

Your server can run more efficiently if you trim out all the unnecessary features and services it offers. Looking at the server's logs, you can quickly determine what is required at all times and what you can drop.

Firewalls

Firewalls offer very specific services or interfaces between external clients and internal servers. The services are very critical to the security of the internal network. Often, firewalls are not even visible to the client and can act transparently with the servers.

The firewall's primary role is filtering. The algorithms in the firewall provide two forms of filtering: passive and active. *Passive filtering* only looks at the addressing of each message. A good firewall hides the address of each internal server and forces translation of all addresses. Additionally, if desired, the firewall can remap ports. Passive filtering acts as an initial buffer or barrier between clients and servers.

Active filtering digs deeper in the packet and tries to determine if it contains compromising commands or other discrepancies. This form of filtering needs to know about the services available on the servers. For example, FTP connections require different security measures than HTTP.

Additionally, servers inside the firewall can use non-registered IP addresses. For example, an internal server would issue these fake addresses using DHCP. The firewall then uses masquerading to translate the addresses (passive filtering). Without real addresses, clients cannot easily initiate communications.

> **NOTE**
>
> Some network administrators believe that a client cannot initiate communications with a server that has a bogus IP address. This is not completely true and can give a false sense of security. For example, FTP's protocol uses a backward session: The client makes a request to the server to download, but the server creates the channel to the client to get the file. The client may really be behind a firewall. In that case, the external server is able to initiate communications through the firewall. This can happen through a firewall event with masquerading enabled.

Demilitarized Zones (DMZs)

Firewalls help you increase security by channeling information from client to server. Some companies take the firewall concept one step further: the creation of *Demilitarized Zones* or *DMZs*. The concept is not very new; two or three encompassing walls around cities and castles in Europe and the Middle East demonstrates their effectiveness.

DMZs define a simple and effective way of slowing penetration. An attack can break through one firewall only to discover another wall. The innermost netspace would be the company's intranet, which has critical and company-private information. As the ancients proved, this increased security in their favor by slowing assaults, improving detection, and increasing protection.

Simple forms of firewalls place the hosting servers outside with no connection to the intranet (see Figure 16.1). This is thoroughly secure, because there is no path to the sensitive data. This technique presents two fundamental problems: How does the server get updates, and how does the company keep internal information in sync? One solution is to hand carry the updated information to the server. Engineers like to call this approach "sneakernet." These server islands really limit the capabilities for accessing databases, tools, and dynamic information that usually reside inside the intranet. More advanced DMZs integrate the company's access to the Internet, the services to the external customer, and the intranet.

DMZs place more than one barrier between the Internet and the intranet (see Figure 16.2).

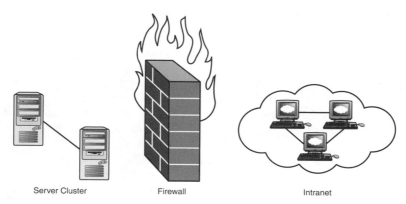

FIGURE 16.1

A basic Internet service places the servers outside the firewalls.

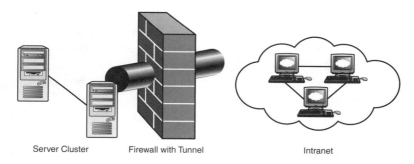

FIGURE 16.2

A DMZ requires conduits through the firewall to pass information.

To get the most out of a DMZ, you must establish rules about what goes inside it. Firewalls rarely provide many services; the servers behind the firewall do. However, if you expose too much inside the DMZ, you might as well forget DMZs and save your money. The rules of conduct become (by necessity) more relaxed as you get closer to the intranet. The following list offers several common rules:

- *Minimize ports* (exposed firewalls)—Most firewalls exposed to the outside world limit the number of ports available. These ports provide precisely what the client needs to get information offered by the company. The ports that are exposed provide more ways an attacker may gain access.

The RPC Hole

Many network programmers recognize the potential for intrusion as the number of ports rises. However, less-experienced programmers may not realize that they may use tools that create ports on-the-fly. For example, the portmap program for Remote Procedure Calls (RPCs) creates ports. Furthermore, Java's Remote Method Invocation (RMI) and Microsoft's COM/COM+ sit on top of RPCs. Webmasters who write script for servers may not realize that they are opening new security holes with each new object.

- *Minimize services* (exposed servers)—Servers closest to the Internet offer only the absolute minimum services. Typically, those services are closely linked to the ports the firewall passively filters. Some include HTTP, HTTPS, and FTP (read-only).

- *Limit databases* (inner DMZs)—Databases often house the company's most valuable information. No private database should be in any of the DMZs. Some systems often place the LDAP in one of the inner DMZs (instead of the intranet), but that practice is a security hazard as well because the database often contains unencrypted usernames and passwords. If servers in the DMZs need database access, you can easily create point-to-point messengers that hand carry requests back to the intranet. These messengers should be compiled programs to reduce cracking.

- *Use compiled services* (exposed servers)—Scripts like Perl, while easier to program in than C/C++, are in human-readable form that make them a security risk. As often as possible, try to produce tools that prevent the perpetrator from changing the behavior of your server if an intrusion occurs.

- *Separate masquerading*—Each DMZ can use a separate fake IP space with masquerading. Changing the addressing from one DMZ to another makes penetration into the intranet more difficult and complicates network maintenance.

The comparison with castles and walled cities of long ago is very appropriate to the Internet's current state. The Internet has no rules and often runs about in a state of anarchy. Establishing the needed security measures can protect you and your real customers.

Securing the Channel

The network has two distinct elements that you can tune to your needs: the physical network and the message. Protecting both against attack is important.

Physical Espionage

An obvious physical measure is a dedicated connection. Unfortunately, this is not as secure as once thought. The technology for non-intrusive snooping even in dedicated connections is

Adding Security to Network Programs and SSL

CHAPTER 16

349

16

ADDING SECURITY
TO NETWORK
PROGRAMS

simple. Nevertheless, it is a very good start. The physical medium offers several ways to hide (or expose) your data. The more esoteric the connection, the higher the cost. This section describes the four basic physical transmission forms: electrical/optical and conductor/conductorless.

Conductor-based, electrical conduits (such as twisted pair or coax) are, perhaps, the easiest to tap. The flexible wires are very forgiving of a surgical probe into the primary conductor. Also, the properties of electromagnetism permit someone to snoop undetected. Inflexible conduit is more secure and has less loss, but it is expensive and hard to work with.

Conductorless electrical (such as radio or microwave) and optical transmissions (such as infrared or directed laser) are really the easiest form to tap. You simply need an antenna in the field or in the path of transmission. Microwave is a directed transmission similar to laser. Lower frequencies and infrared, on the other hand, tend toward broadcast. These forms cannot be physically protected and have little security.

Optical conduits are the most secure. However, a few years ago, researchers found that if they bent the flexible conduit just the right amount (the critical angle), the light signal would leak out. They used this to prove that even fiber optic was not impervious to snooping. At the time, they still could not introduce a signal. If the research teams have not found a way to introduce an optical signal, they may very soon. Again, to solve this problem, you can get fiber conduits that are more rigid and do not allow the fiber to be bent near the critical angle.

To summarize, a rigid conducted conduit reduces the possibility of tapping. Optical has the added security of being impervious to electromagnetic snooping. Optical, additionally, has proven to carry very high bandwidths.

Message Espionage

Protecting the message is less obvious. The firewalls pass through and filter information exposed to the Internet. They use specific ports and services that the client expects. Changing some of the expected settings and interfaces can increase your security.

While not encouraged in the Open Source movement, using privatized protocols can discourage intrusion (on the other hand, it can also increase attention). For example, instead of using HTTP as the protocol, invent a new and specialized version. This approach does have significant drawbacks: You must write the client interface and get that to your customers.

Another method is to limit windows of availability and information sent. For example, during World War II, the Allies used Native Americans to chat with each other over the airwaves for hours on end in their own language. At specified intervals, the message would shift to a tactical or strategic instruction or status.

Using that example, you could write a financial transfer mechanism that would fire up at specific intervals or even have it open all the time with irrelevant information during off hours.

Increasing randomness is the key to message security. For example, suppose you have an ATM (Automatic Teller Machine) that is connected to the Internet (scary thought!). It needs to send and receive transaction requests to the host server. One way it could use randomness is by continuously sending and receiving fake transactions. Then, at specified intervals, both the host and the ATM would recognize that a transaction is real. (Of course, this is still too loose for actual implementation.)

Another form of randomness is data encryption. Good data security depends strongly on the amount of randomness data encryption introduces. The more random the data is, the more difficult to decrypt the data. The key sets the range of possible outcomes. The perfect encryption key has no limit in size. Unfortunately, as the key increases in size, the computation time increases exponentially. So, a good key is one that is long enough to reduce the likelihood of discovery computationally. This is why everyone wants 128-bit encryption.

Encryption Through Firewall Filters

You cannot join some technologies together to make a stronger defense against attack. For example, encryption defeats a firewall's active filtering. Again, active filtering looks into the packet for anything that might be suspicious. Unfortunately, if contents are encrypted, only the client and server know the contents (hopefully). If you have filtering enabled, you may only be able to expect passive filtering to work with encrypted messages.

128-bit encryption has a wide enough range that if a computer were to try each key in succession every nanosecond (1×10^{-9} seconds), it would require over 10^{20} years to find the key. That's a long time. In terms of randomness, 128-bit encryption appears to be a large enough range to approximate the perfect key—at least for now.

Encryption has two forms: one-way (lossy) and two-way (lossless). A one-way encryption loses information about the original data. The typical encryption used in UNIX passwords is one-way. One-way encryption does not have to recover any data; for example, the password that a user types in only has to match the encrypted form.

Requests sent to a server require a way to get the data back. Two-way encryption scrambles the data in such a way that the information is retrievable with a decryption key. The server and the client must know both the encryption algorithm and the encryption/decryption keys.

Encrypting the Messages

Encryption is far from new. The most famous encryption device was the German Enigma Machine. In fact, some of the current algorithms are based on this WWII device. The whole idea of encryption is to make sure that only the recipient understands the message. Modern encryption algorithms (*ciphers*) are as common as the computer.

When two hosts communicate with each other, the designers assume that other hosts can snoop the messages. A network snooping device can open and examine every protocol this book has defined. Of course, the snooper must be physically on the same network to get any message. Likewise, the snooper has to wade through a lot of fluff to get to the really juicy messages.

This section describes the different parts of encryption and introduces a common negotiation used in computers.

What Are the Available Encryption Types?

Networked computers use two different ciphers: public-key and symmetric-key. The public-key cipher uses two keys—one for encryption and one for decryption. A server often uses this algorithm to start the encryption process or to do single transactions.

The symmetric-key cipher uses the same key to encrypt as decrypt. The decryption simply undoes what the encryption does (somewhat like unwinding a tightened spring). Because of the nature of the symmetric-key cipher, the two hosts must keep the key secret. The algorithms are very fast and relatively simple. Likewise, you can use any random number for the key.

The public-key ciphers, on the other hand, have two keys—an encryption (public) key and a decryption (private) key. The servers share the encryption key with any client on the network. (The key is not itself critical—only the data that the algorithm translates is critical.) The server internally retains the decryption key for decrypting the incoming message.

Public-key ciphers have a few limitations. First, the keys must be related. The host cannot randomly generate the encryption key without calculating the decryption key as well. This significantly restricts the number of available keys. Because the number must be related to encrypt and then decrypt, you can only have a few key pairs available compared to the complete set of integers. For example, within a 128-bit key, you can only have 2^{32} possible key pairs. Second, because you only have a limited number of key pairs (not the whole range of numbers), these ciphers are less secure than the private key. For example, a 128-bit public cipher can be only as strong as a 64- or 32-bit symmetric cipher.

Published Encryption Algorithms

The Internet offers many different public and symmetric cipher suites (sets of different ciphers). The most common are based on the RSA (names of the authors, Rivest, Shamir, and Adleman) public-key, DES (Data Encryption Standard), and RC2/RC4 (Rivest Ciphers). Some ciphers are still patented and require royalties to use (in October 2000, RSA's patent ran out).

Most Linux distributions either include the suites with the installation or link you to a site to download them.

Problems with Encryption

Ciphers present an interesting set of problems. First, and until recently, the United States limited the export of strong encryption algorithms. In fact, that is one reason some distributions would not place the cipher suites on their CD-ROMs. Instead, the install process would try to grab the suite from a foreign country server. In 2000, the government lifted this restriction, and it is a little easier to get the ciphers.

Another problem is computational time. While the symmetric ciphers are relatively quick, all initial communications must use the slower public-key. Public-key is not very good for large blocks of data. So the added complexity of negotiating the ciphers and the keys has to be part of the protocols.

The last problem is rather strange. Encryption actually invites the very thing that it intends to avoid—cracking and snooping. Apparently, the Internet has a sector of crackers that want to appear on the headline news.

Secure Sockets Layer (SSL)

As noted earlier, two hosts must agree on a set of ciphers to communicate with some security. The Secure Sockets Layer (SSL) defines this protocol. It is a process carefully designed to severely limit the potential of cracking. SSL uses both public and symmetric ciphers to establish connections, negotiate protocols, and communicate data.

The scope of this section cannot include the details of how SSL negotiates the keys and communication channel. Instead, this section shows you how to write an SSL client and server using the OpenSSL API. Again, this chapter cannot cover the entire API—that information could easily fill another book.

Using OpenSSL

You can get a functional, although not well-documented, SSL API called OpenSSL. It is available at www.openssl.org and supports several platforms, including Linux, of course. To use the API, you need to follow a few steps to configure, compile, and install it.

Adding Security to Network Programs and SSL

CHAPTER 16

353

16

ADDING SECURITY
TO NETWORK
PROGRAMS

It is not compiled out-of-the-box, and some of the installation steps do not integrate well with Mandrake or Red Hat Linux. (Other distributions may have similar problems, so you may want to take note.) The following steps will help you get the tool installed and usable:

1. Download the tarball, open it in a secure (non-root) directory, and go into the newly created directory.

2. Run the config file (./config). If it complains, you need to specify the OS type explicitly with ./config linux-elf.

3. Run make to compile the sources.

4. Run make test to verify the algorithms.

5. Log in as root. Run make install to move the needed files into their directories (/usr/local/ssl/).

6. Create references to libraries:
   ```
   ln -s /usr/local/ssl/lib/libssl.a /usr/lib/
   ln -s /usr/local/ssl/lib/libcrypto.a /usr/lib/
   ```

7. Create the reference to include files:
   ```
   ln -s /usr/local/ssl/include/openssl/ /usr/include
   ```

8. Add MANPATH /usr/local/ssl/man to your /etc/man.config file. (You may want to run makewhatis to do topic searches.)

9. Add /usr/local/ssl/bin to your path.

One little glitch to this process is that all compilations use static libraries, so don't be surprised if your execution files start out at 600KB in size. If you want to use shared libraries, you must convert libssl.a and libcrypto.a to *.so files.

After you have all this completed, you are ready to write secure sockets. The linking stage must include the libraries in a specific order. The program link fails with unresolved externals if the two libraries are swapped:

```
cc test.c -lssl -lcrypto
```

You may note that the API includes some demo C++ source files. This is overkill. All calls to the libraries can be plain C. (In fact, if you look at the source itself, you may note that it is really C source in a C++ file.)

Creating an SSL Client

Now that you have the API installed, you can try it out by writing a simple client/server pair of programs. Creating an SSL client/server is almost as easy as creating a regular socket. In fact, OpenSSL builds on top of that framework.

The first step in the client is to set up the SSL library state:

```
/*************************************************************/
/*** Initialize Client SSL state                        ***/
/*************************************************************/
SSL_METHOD *method;
SSL_CTX *ctx;
OpenSSL_add_all_algorithms();       /* Load cryptos, et.al. */
SSL_load_error_strings();           /* Load/register error msg */
method = SSLv2_client_method(); /* Create new client-method */
ctx = SSL_CTX_new(method);          /* Create new context */
```

If the return values of the API calls are NULL or zero, you can display the error with the following:

```
ERR_print_errors_fp(stderr);        /* Print errors to stderr */
```

The next step is to create a regular socket.

```
/*************************************************************/
/*** Connect client's socket to SSL server             ***/
/*************************************************************/
struct sockaddr_in addr;
struct hostent *host = gethostbyname(hostname);
int sd = socket(PF_INET, SOCK_STREAM, 0);  /* create socket */
bzero(&addr, sizeof(addr));
addr.sin_family = AF_INET;
addr.sin_port = htons(port);                /* server port */
addr.sin_addr.s_addr = *(long*)(host->h_addr); /* server IP */
connect(sd, &addr, sizeof(addr);   /* connect to the server */
```

After connecting the sockets between client and server, you need to create an SSL instance and associate it to the connection:

```
/*************************************************************/
/*** Establish SSL protocol and create encryption link   ***/
/*************************************************************/
SSL *ssl = SSL_new(ctx); /* create new SSL connection state */
SSL_set_fd(ssl, sd);        /* attach the socket descriptor */
if ( SSL_connect(ssl) == -1 )    /* perform the connection */
    ERR_print_errors_fp(stderr);        /* report any errors */
```

From this point on, you have an SSL connection with full encryption (depending on what the client and server negotiated). You can get the cipher suite as follows:

```
char* cipher_name = SSL_get_cipher(ssl);
```

You can also read the certificates with the following calls:

```
/**************************************************************/
/*** Read certificates                                    ***/
/**************************************************************/
char line[1024];
X509 *x509 = X509_get_subject_name(cert);    /* Get subject */
X509_NAME_oneline(x509, line, sizeof[line]); /* Convert it */
printf("Subject: %s\n", line);
x509 = X509_get_issuer_name(cert);              /* get issuer */
X509_NAME_oneline(x509, line, sizeof(line));  /* convert it */
printf("Issuer: %s\n", line);
```

Lastly, the programs can send and receive data using calls similar to send() and recv(). These calls have a few differences, however. First, the flags parameter is missing; second, if an error occurs, the function returns –1. The formal definition of send() and recv() states that if an error occurs, the return value is negative.

```
/**************************************************************/
/*** Send & receive messages                              ***/
/**************************************************************/
int bytes;
bytes = SSL_read(ssl, buf, sizeof(buf));       /* get/decrypt */
bytes = SSL_write(ssl, msg, strlen(msg));    /* encrypt/send */
```

The API has many more functions available for controlling flow, changing SSL state, and configuration.

Creating an SSL Server

The client and server differ only slightly. Both must initialize the context, establish the connection, and start the SSL protocol. The server has a couple more steps it must take. First, the context initialization changes only slightly:

```
/**************************************************************/
/*** Initialize Server SSL state                          ***/
/**************************************************************/
SSL_METHOD *method;
SSL_CTX *ctx;
OpenSSL_add_all_algorithms();        /* Load cryptos, et.al. */
SSL_load_error_strings();          /* Load/register error msg */
method = SSLv2_server_method(); /* Create new server-method */
ctx = SSL_CTX_new(method);           /* Create new context */
```

You may have noticed that the program uses SSLv2, not SSLv3. You can use either. However, if you want Netscape to connect with your SSL server, it requires SSLv2. Even then, for some reason, Netscape thinks that it is connected to an SSLv3 socket.

Unlike the client, the server must load its certificate file. This comes in two parts: the certificate and the private key. You must load both as part of initialization. Both parts can reside in the same file.

```
/************************************************************/
/*** Load certificate and private key files           ***/
/************************************************************/
/* set the local certificate from CertFile */
SSL_CTX_use_certificate_file(ctx, CertFile, SSL_FILETYPE_PEM);
/* set private key from KeyFile */
SSL_CTX_use_PrivateKey_file(ctx, KeyFile, SSL_FILETYPE_PEM);
/* verify private key */
if ( !SSL_CTX_check_private_key(ctx) )
    fprintf(stderr, "Key & certificate don't match");
```

Clients have the option of loading certificate files as well, but it is not required. You may want your client to have certificates if the data security requires it.

> **NOTE**
>
> Normally, if you are going live on the Internet, you can purchase a certificate from various places, such as VeriSign. However, if you are just doing some testing, you can create your own certificates using the tools in OpenSSL. (Don't use the certificate supplied with OpenSSL.) The Perl tool CA.pl that creates certificates resides in the build directory /usr/local/ssl/misc. If it does not ask you a series of questions, you have not set your path to point to /usr/local/ssl/bin.

The server socket is essentially the same as a regular socket server:

```
/************************************************************/
/*** Establish socket server port                     ***/
/************************************************************/
struct sockaddr_in addr;
int sd, client;
sd = socket(PF_INET, SOCK_STREAM, 0);      /* Create socket */
bzero(&addr, sizeof(addr));
addr.sin_family = AF_INET;
addr.sin_port = htons(port);
addr.sin_addr.s_addr = INADDR_ANY;    /* permit any network */
bind(sd, &addr, sizeof(addr));             /* bind to a port */
listen(sd, 10);                /* convert to listening socket */
client = accept(server, &addr, &len);  /* accept connection */
```

Adding Security to Network Programs and SSL

CHAPTER 16

357

16

ADDING SECURITY
TO NETWORK
PROGRAMS

As with the client, the server must create an SSL session state and associate it with the client's connection.

```
/****************************************************************/
/*** Create SSL session state based on context & SSL_accept ***/
/****************************************************************/
ssl = SSL_new(ctx);          /* get new SSL state with context */
SSL_set_fd(ssl, client); /* associate socket with SSL state */
if ( SSL_accept(ssl) == FAIL )    /* do SSL-protocol accept */
   ERR_print_errors_fp(stderr);
else
{  int bytes;
   bytes = SSL_read(ssl, buf, sizeof(buf));  /* get request */
   SSL_write(ssl, reply, strlen(reply));       /* send reply */
}
```

The steps are really that simple. Try out the code on the Sams Web site and connect with Netscape. Because Netscape does not recognize your custom-made certificate, the program presents a warning message along with several setup dialogs to temporarily register the certificate.

Summary: The Secure Server

The network socket connects you with many possible opportunities to increase productivity and distribute processing. However, the information that you share between hosts is not hidden from other hosts connected on the same network. Placing vital or secret information on the Internet is an invitation for loss, espionage, corruption, and so on. The very nature of the Internet can be your liability.

You can cut your losses by planning ahead and establishing security around your vital products. Most companies cannot ignore the fact that they must have a presence on the Internet to survive. Firewalls, policies, and encryption are typical ways to lock down a site and blockade against attack.

When two or more hosts communicate in a public setting, such as the Internet, you can require certain protocols and algorithms to reduce the possibility of snooping. Encryption comes in various forms and provides different levels of security. Two standard encryption forms are symmetric- and public-key. Both are used today for communications such as SSL.

Writing programs in an SSL API depends strongly on the API implementation. No standard API for SSL exists at the time of this writing. However, you can get a taste of what it is like to use SSL in C with an Open Source version called OpenSSL. OpenSSL is a very rich implementation with over 200 API calls.

With good planning, foresight, and standard tools such as OpenSSL, you can create an effective, reliable, and secure resource for the Internet.

The next chapter takes you to the other extreme of information sharing with multicasting and broadcasting. Security attempts to ensure privacy. Multicasting and broadcasting attempt to share as much as possible and as efficiently as possible.

Sharing Messages with Multicast, Broadcast, and Mbone

IN THIS CHAPTER

A network is a very good medium for getting a message from one place to another. It has a wide range of technologies and bandwidths that let you try different things. One advantage that you may not consider as a plus is the fact that all the computers are typically connected to a backbone of some kind. Now, how would having a computer connected on the same backbone be advantageous? Normally, the traffic would be greater and a dedicated connection from host to host would be best.

Some services can go to several destinations simultaneously. Instead of sending the same message to each host, you could send one message and have all hosts simply pick it up. The pluses to this are obvious—less redundant traffic.

The Internet Protocol offers two forms of distribution messaging: broadcasting and the newer multicasting. This chapter discusses the different types of distribution messaging and how to implement them.

Broadcasting Messages to a Domain

The first form of distribution messaging, broadcasting [RFC919, RFC922], uses the nature of subnets and network masks to determine the destination. A broadcast is a mandatory messaging distribution form; both the subnet and the hosts have to receive the message. (In reality, if a host has not enabled broadcasting, the hardware does not accept the message. Still, the message does occupy bandwidth, and every host can read it.)

Revisiting IP Structure

The subnet is very important to sending and receiving broadcast messages. As described in Chapter 2, "TCP/IP Network Language Fluency," when you define an interface with `ifconfig`, you also define a broadcast address and a netmask. The broadcast address is a special address to which the host listens to get messages.

The subnet is typically the same as the netmask and broadcast address. For example, if you have about 250 hosts in your `198.2.56.XXX` subnet, your netmask and broadcast would be `255.255.255.0` and `198.2.56.255`. So, if you want to send a message to everyone in your subnet, you would use the `198.2.56.255` address. (As noted in Chapter 2, you can get very creative with the netmasks—just remember that the last significant bit is the end of the mask.)

The subnet is really a wrapper of the hardware implementation. The real work takes place in the lower levels of the hardware and the kernel. To understand what is happening, you need to start with the physical connection.

Beyond the physical connection, sending a broadcast message is easier than receiving one. To send any message, you only need the IP address (as described in Chapter 2, the network eventually converts that address to the destination's Ethernet MAC address). To get a message, the interface card has to be listening for the matching MAC address. The problem is that broadcast messages cannot assume a different MAC address from that of the host. In fact, as noted in Chapter 2, no two hosts in the same subnet are likely to have similar MAC addresses. So broadcasting cannot depend on any specialized MAC to conduct broadcast messages.

Instead, when a program sends a broadcast message, the kernel automatically assigns a MAC address of all ones (FF:FF:FF:FF:FF:FF). This MAC is a flag to all NICs to pick it up—even if no program is listening for a broadcast message.

The NIC opens the gates and lets the message fill its internal buffers. When complete, it notifies the kernel with an interrupt. The kernel retrieves the packet and looks at the destination IP. If the address matches the broadcast address, it passes the packet up to the network subsystem's queues.

The network subsystem (typically UDP) inspects the message and, if it finds a broadcast socket with a matching port number, it moves the packet into the socket's I/O channel. If not, it drops the packet. You may want to specify a port number to tell the kernel to filter out unwanted messages for you. Otherwise, you can cause a storm of unwanted replies.

Programming to Enable Broadcasting

You can enable broadcasting using the SO_BROADCAST socket option. The rest of the program looks like a normal datagram-messaging program.

```
/*************************************************************/
/*** Create a broadcast datagram socket                 ***/
/*************************************************************/
const int on=1;
sd = socket(PF_INET, SOCK_DGRAM, 0);
if ( setsockopt(sd, SOL_SOCKET, SO_BROADCAST, &on, sizeof(on))
      != 0 )
   panic("set broadcast failed");
bzero(&addr, sizeof(addr));
addr.sin_family = AF_INET;
addr.sin_port = htons(port);
addr.sin_addr.s_addr = INADDR_ANY;
if ( bind(sd, &addr, sizeof(addr)) != 0 )
   panic("bind failed");
addr.sin_port = htons(atoi(strings[2]));
if ( inet_aton(strings[1], &addr.sin_addr) == 0 )
   panic("inet_aton failed (%s)", strings[1]);
```

After enabling broadcast, you can send messages to the broadcast address. You may want to create a process or thread for the receiver and the sender. Unlike other transmissions where you can expect a single reply for a single transmission, broadcasting can yield many replies for each message sent. If you do this, be sure to turn off the incoming queue on one of the channels.

```
/***********************************************************/
/*** Split the responsibilities into sender and listener ***/
/*** Close the sender's listening channel.               ***/
/***********************************************************/
if ( fork() )
   Receiver(sd);
else
{
   shutdown(sd, SHUT_RD);    /* close the input channel */
   Sender(sd);
}
wait(0);
```

Broadcasting Limitations

Broadcast messages have a few problems. While you may be able to reach many computers at once with a single message, you can only reach those within your subnet. Still, you can increase your range of influence by changing your broadcast address. Unfortunately, you cannot use broadcasting on the WAN because the address 255.255.255.255 is no longer legal on the Internet. (You may even find that most routers do not allow broadcast messages to pass through at all. So, even if you have the right broadcast address, say 198.2.255.255, the router at 198.2.1.0 may ignore the packet.)

Additionally, everyone on the subnet hears your message. Because of the way the hardware implements broadcasting, all network cards pick up broadcast messages. This can place a lot of unnecessary burden on the hosts that don't want the message.

Another problem is the protocol. IPv4 only supports broadcasting on datagrams (TCP is excluded). If you want reliability and streaming, you must implement your own. Datagrams serve well in many circumstances and, with a little beefing up, you can provide a good interface to which clients can connect.

Multicasting Messages to a Group

Multicasting [RFC1112] answers some of the problems with broadcasting. The primary idea of broadcasting is sending a message to everyone within an address range. Multicasting uses agreed-upon addresses that hosts can join to listen for messages.

Multicasting uses a single IP address to send messages to several recipients. It has the following advantages over broadcasting:

- *All Protocols*—It supports datagram and streaming protocols (UDP and TCP). Datagrams support multicasting right now, but streams have no immediate implementations. You can find free (not Open Source) implementations of reliably delivered multicasts.
- *WAN Accessible*—You can join global multicasting groups. However, at the time of this writing, there are sections of the WAN that do not support or pass multicast messages.
- *Limited Listeners*—A multicast message does not *necessarily* force all NICs to pick it up (see the "How the Network Provides Multicasting" section later in this chapter).
- *IPv6 Support*—IPv6 dropped support for broadcasting, but it has adopted and extended multicasting.

Turning On Multicasting Support

Most distributions include kernels that have multicasting turned on. (You can look in /proc/net/dev_mcast to check your currently running kernel.) However, multicast routing may not be enabled, or if you are using a downloaded kernel, you might not have the option set. If you want to use multicasting or you manage a router for others who want to use multicasting, you may need to reconfigure and recompile the kernel. The configurations are in the Networking part of the configuration.

Joining Multicast Groups

Using multicasting is a simple as joining a list service. Like a list service, you get as many messages as others send, so it's easy to overrun a constricted network connection. If you join a group, be careful that you have the bandwidth to support the data flow. Most likely, you may drop packets and make the connection less than useful.

Broadcast addresses follow a specific pattern so that the routers can recognize them. These addresses come directly from the IP allocation (first introduced in Chapter 2). The range is 224.0.0.0–239.255.255.255. These addresses are reserved for broadcasting. This range of addresses is subdivided into smaller ranges to indicate the *address scope* or how far the message can go before a router blocks it. Table 17.1 shows these divisions.

TABLE 27.1   Multicasting Address Allocation and Scope

Scope	Typical TTL	Address Range
Cluster	0	224.0.0.0–224.0.0.255
Site	< 32	239.255.0.0–239.255.255.255
Organization	< 128	239.192.0.0–239.195.255.255
Global	<= 255	224.0.1.0–238.255.255.255

To join a group, you use the `setsockopt()` kernel service call with a new parameter. The new parameter is the `ip_mreq` structure:

```
/***********************************************************/
/*** The ip_mreq structure for selecting a multicast addr ***/
/***********************************************************/
struct ip_mreq
{
    struct in_addr imr_multiaddr;   /* known multicast group */
    struct in_addr imr_interface;   /* network interface */
};
```

The `imr_multiaddr` field specifies the multicast group you want to join. It is the same format as the `sin_addr` field in the `sockaddr_in` structure. The `imr_interface` field lets you choose a particular host interface. This is similar to a `bind()`, which lets you specify the host interface (or leave the host option wide open with an `INADDR_ANY` value). However, it may not work the way you expect it.

Defaulting a Multicast Interface

When you select `INADDR_ANY` for `imr_interface`, the kernel selects the interface for you. At least with the 2.2.XX Linux kernel, it does not mean "listen on all interfaces." So if you have multiple interfaces, you may have to join on all the interfaces on which you want to listen.

The following code snippet shows you how to join a group using the `ip_mreq` structure. It sets the `imr_interface` field to `INADDR_ANY` merely for demonstration. Do not use it unless you have only one interface on your host; the results can be unpredictable (see the box above).

```
/***********************************************************/
/*** Join a multicast group                            ***/
/***********************************************************/
const char *GroupID = "224.0.0.10";
```

```
struct ip_mreq mreq;
if ( inet_aton(GroupID, &mreq.imr_multiaddr) == 0 )
   panic("address (%s) bad", GroupID);
mreq.imr_interface.s_addr = INADDR_ANY;
if ( setsockopt(sd, SOL_IP, IP_ADD_MEMBERSHIP, &mreq, sizeof(mreq)) != 0 )
   panic("Join multicast failed");
```

If you expect to connect another program to that same address/port, you must use the
SO_REUSEADDR option on the socket. At this time, Linux does not support address/port sharing
(SO_REUSEPORT). To turn on address sharing, use the following code snippet:

```
/***********************************************************/
/*** Enable address sharing                             ***/
/***********************************************************/
if ( setsockopt(sd, SOL_SOCKET, SO_REUSEADDR, &on, sizeof(on)) != 0 )
   panic("Can't reuse address/ports");
```

The number of groups you can join depends on the hardware and the kernel's limits. Many
UNIX operating systems limit connections to 16 per host. That's right—not per program. See
"How the Network Provides Multicasting," later in this chapter, for more information.

When you are done listening on the port, you can drop the membership:

```
/***********************************************************/
/*** Drop a multicast group                             ***/
/***********************************************************/
if ( setsockopt(sd, SOL_IP, IP_DROP_MEMBERSHIP, &mreq, sizeof(mreq)) != 0 )
   panic("Drop multicast failed");
```

You can also simply end the program, and the program cleans up the connections for you.

Multicast Cleanup

You may want to drop the multicast group manually. This is one of the few times that
automatic process cleanup is not a good idea. If the kernel has any problems, no
errors appear if you simply terminate the program. Also, you could be receiving messages after your program terminates. This would leave the ports unavailable or garbled for new program instances. Closing manually lets the program see any errors on
the connection, helping you debug.

Joining a multicasting group is relatively easy. In fact, creating a local multicast group simply
requires selecting an unused IP address. Global addresses are a different matter. If you want

to publish an Internet multicast service, you may have to request an address (and port) from the IAB.

Sending a Multicast Message

Sending a message to a multicast group is as easy as sending a datagram message. Remember, UDP lets you connect to that address, simplifying the multicast send and receive.

Owning Multicast Addresses

Even though you can set up an address for a specific service, you cannot guarantee ownership of that address. Others can send messages on that address as well. If your service requires a certain amount of continuity, you may want to provide a way to distinguish your messages from others. The client still picks up all the messages sent on the network. It's left to the kernel and your program to sort out the real messages.

An interesting side effect in the making of multicasting has great potential: you do not have to be a member of a multicast group to send a message. A program can simply send the message to the broadcast address/port. A streaming multicast server may, in fact, never really join the multicast group. To receive messages, you must join the group.

For legitimate purposes, being able to serve up messages without joining is a real plus. This way, your server can avoid being hit by the traffic associated with multicasting.

How the Network Provides Multicasting

The way operating systems (such as Linux) implement multicasting can lead to a barrage of messages. Knowing how it works can help you with performance considerations and how to filter messages quickly.

Many NICs support a form of MAC aliasing (taking on an additional identification for a short time). All NICs have assigned MAC addresses. Unlike broadcasting, which uses a broadcast address (FF:FF:FF:FF:FF:FF), multicasting creates a temporary MAC address using the multicast address as the key. The standard prefix for multicast MACs is 01:00:5E, and the last three bytes (actually 23 bits) come from the multicast address. For example, a multicast address 224.138.63.10 (E0:8A:3F:0A) morphs into a MAC address 01:00:5E:0A:3F:0A (note that the 8 in 8A is dropped).

The operating system takes this address and programs the NIC to accept that address. NIC accepts this programming in three ways:

- *Tag Table*—The NIC holds the entire address verbatim. It checks every message on the network against its own MAC and all the MACs in this table. This is 100% reliable.
- *Hash Key* (*imperfect filtering*)—The NIC hashes the MAC into a 64- to 512-bit hash array. When a message passes through the network, the NIC hashes that MAC address. If the corresponding bit is on in the array, the NIC accepts the message. This approach can accept messages not intended for the host. The next layer is then responsible for filtering out unwanted messages.
- *Promiscuous Mode*—Some cards cannot support multicasting. The alternative is placing the card in promiscuous mode and receiving all messages. The next layer must drop all unwanted messages. This is least desirable.

The network cards have no concept of ports, so the higher layers in the IP stack must move messages to their appropriate queues or drop them. Remember that, even though you are not listening to a port, your host gets all messages multicast on the address you joined. If you select UDP or TCP, the kernel filters the ports for you. If you select a raw socket, you must do the filtering in the program.

Getting Out the Multicast Message

The first step in getting multicast messages is writing the program and enabling the host's hardware and kernel for multicasting. The next step is telling the routers that you want the message. This is not all. Your multicast messages face several obstacles before getting out to the WAN's baseband.

You may have to perform other tasks to get the messages out. This section discusses these issues and ways to solve them.

Letting the Routers Know

The Internet tries to get a message from originator to destination using two addresses—the IP address and the MAC. The MAC is rarely known before the message is sent out, and the IP address has built-in routing. But the routers expect but one destination for a given message—having two destinations for a single address is typically an error.

Multicasting requires a couple of unusual network features. These unusual features influence the configuration of supporting routers. First, the routers must accept the generated MACs. This is actually a change in the responsibilities of the router and can require additional router configurations.

17

SHARING
MESSAGES

With the creation of multicasting protocol, the Internet standards proposed Internet Group Management Protocol (IGMP) [RFC1112, RFC2236] to pass on multicasting group advertisements. IGMP carries the group IDs and MACs that the hosts in the subdomains desire to join or drop. The join message passes only as far as the scope allows. Even if no host behind a router joins the group, the router still has to keep track of the groups available. (If the router goes down, the information is not lost. When the internal host joins a group, the router begins to rebuild the group list.)

Another burden placed on the routers defines the uniqueness of the new protocol. Even though all subscribers to the group see each message, all subscribers may not see exactly the same message (see "Multicasting Limitations"). The router must pass all broadcast and multicast messages to all subdomains that have joined. This may require implicitly or explicitly copying the message.

A router explicitly copies a message to two or more different connections. Routers often are connected to several networks, and they route traffic between them. An explicit copy places the packet on more than one of those networks.

The implicit copy is due to the nature of the network. Everyone can see everything else (on the same subdomain) because they are physically connected to the same wire. An implicit copy happens when more than one host picks up a message as they see it on the network.

Tunneling Through the Firewalls (Mbone)

Some routers or firewalls do not have the needed implementation support for multicast groups, so a host inside the subdomain would not be able to see any messages from the outside. A router that only supports directed (or unicast) messages is a *unicast router*.

Shortly before 1992, programmers wanted to take advantage of the newer features of multicasting. Unfortunately, the network was full of unicast routers. The answer was to encapsulate the new protocol in an IP wrapper and send it directly to a receiver that would unwrap and pass it on. This virtual network backbone for multicasting (Mbone) can be used today for firewalls as well.

How does it work? Mbone uses a multicast router (`mrouted`) to accept and pass messages through the external domain to another `mrouted` server. The `mrouted` server accepts each complete message packet and places it in another packet with its own header. The result is a message with two IP headers. On the other end, the receiving `mrouted` server unwraps the message and places the result in its subdomain.

Multicasting Limitations

Multicasting answers a lot of issues from broadcasting, but it has its own issues. Some issues are hardware support, performance/bandwidth bottlenecks, accountability, and uniqueness.

Getting Hardware Support

The last section described how the operating system and hardware supports multicasting. Unfortunately, some NICs (like the Ethernet Express) do not support multicasting and promiscuous mode at all. To get a multicast message, the hardware must support promiscuous mode—at the bare minimum. While testing some of the algorithms for this chapter, this very problem hampered development for a short time.

You can see the list of supporting NICs in `/.../linux/Documentation/networking/multicast.txt`. If your programming attempts do not work, make sure you card has full support.

Bottlenecking Performance

You face another problem with getting broadcast or multicast messages (especially for those NICs that use promiscuous mode for multicasting). The program has to filter a lot of unwanted messages. Broadcasting has that problem as well, and multicasting reduced its effect a lot. But the problem is still there.

Similarly, the connection from client to the network may not be able to handle all the messages that the multicast group sends (for example, a video feed on a 56Kbps modem). What happens? The router enqueues the messages until they expire. Knowing the bottlenecks between your server and the client can help you maintain high reliability and usability.

A potential solution to the bottleneck problem might require some stronger control from routers.

Accounting for Every Message

The last issue is accountability; anyone can send any message whether or not he owns or is part of a multicast group. This can result in interference from those who want to harm the effectiveness of the Internet.

Message Uniqueness

Another form of accounting appears as you work with the multicasting protocols. You may be familiar with the potential message mirroring datagrams have. In multicasting, the problem is more pronounced because of the requirement to copy the message for different paths.

An example of this duplication is when a host connects to the Internet and has to pass through several routers. At one point, the message goes through a couple routers in the same subdomain. This should not happen because a proper network would only have one router per domain, but it does happen.

When a host joins a group, the two routers see the request and pass the message to the parent router. Later, a multicast message arrives to the parent. The parent recognizes the message as one that the routers advertised using IGMP. It passes the message on, and the two routers pass it to their subdomain. Because of the implicit copy (by each router), the host gets two identical messages.

To get around this problem, first, make sure that you tag all your messages and, second, try to keep the network topology clean.

Summary: Efficient Message Sharing

If you need to share messages between multiple hosts without sending to each one directly, you can use broadcasting or multicasting. Broadcasting, the older form, uses the IP addressing with the netmask to create and send a message. It uses the network resources more efficiently but forces every host on the subnet to hear the message. Also, broadcasting on the WAN is not permitted.

Multicasting solves many of broadcast's limitations and has greater extensibility. Even though routers may need to send different copies of the same message, it is a better method for sharing messages on the LAN and WAN. Listening to multicast messages is voluntary, unlike broadcasting.

Multicasting is a growing technology with more and more multicast routers in place to get over the unicast routers. However, you may not see broadcasting disappear entirely because it has a place in some low-level protocols.

The Power of Raw Sockets

IN THIS CHAPTER

Sometimes the materials available do not fit the intent and needs of your project. When this happens, you have to start with very raw materials. TCP and UDP do not give you access to the raw guts of the IP packets. You have to delve deeper and do more foundational work.

The raw socket offers you a lot of flexibility. Also, the programs that use raw sockets tend to be very simple and fast. This chapter details the use and intent of raw sockets and gives you tips on how to construct the packets.

When Would You Use Raw Sockets?

The raw material of IP programming is only one layer above the actual network frame. When you use a raw socket, you don't have the overhead of the higher-level protocols that can erode your network throughput. But, at the same time, you lose the features of the higher-level protocols. You must choose carefully when to use raw sockets.

Exposing the ICMP

Using raw socket opens up the messaging (error) protocols. The higher-level protocols, such as TCP and UDP, lock you out of sending ICMP packets. Additionally, the IP API does not provide a SOCK_MSG (compared to the names SOCK_STREAM or SOCK_DGRAM). To send SOCK_MSG-style packets, you would have to create a raw packet, create and populate the ICMP header, and send it out.

The ICMP subcommands offer several services as listed in Appendix A, "Data Tables." Some of the useful subcommands include echo (used in ping), time stamping, router request, and address masking. Of course, these functions are all very low level. ICMP is not designed to manage more than the simplest messaging tasks.

Controlling the IP Header

Also, if you want to manage the IP header itself, you must use raw sockets with the appropriate socket option (IP_HDRINCL). Referring back to Chapter 3, "Different Types of Internet Packets," the IP header has several fields that you can normally set with setsockopt(). Also, the IP header has fields that you cannot set.

For example, if you want (for whatever reason) to test the fragmentation fields, you would have to use a raw socket with IP_HDRINCL enabled. Another use for this feature is programming some of the alternative IP versions listed in Chapter 3, Table 3.1.

Speeding Through the Physical Network

As noted earlier, the lower-level protocols are very fast. Raw sockets are only one level of abstraction above the network frame. Essentially, your raw packets fly through the network at physical network speed.

Most network frames are 1–2KB for 10Mbps networks. Faster networks offer larger frame sizes. If you need speed, try to match the network frame size. This reduces the need to carve up your message. This is actually harder to do than it sounds; you cannot directly get the frame size. You could ask the user or query the hardware for the configuration, but that would require much more work (and less payback).

If you need to work at the very low level of the IP stack, the raw socket is the answer. Alternatively, if data communication is important and accuracy is a must, most programs use the higher-level protocols to provide most of the communication.

What Are the Limitations?

Raw sockets provide you with a lot of flexibility, but they are not a panacea. Choosing when to use raw sockets requires knowing what the limitations are.

- *Reliability loss*—You lose a lot of features from the higher-level protocols. For example, TCP offers reliable connections—data sent is data received. (Of course, raw sockets and UDP share the same level of unreliability.)

- *No ports*—You lose ports (virtual network connections). This actually can be a problem. Because you have no ports, the kernel passes a raw packet to all matching raw sockets. In other words, the kernel cannot determine the actual destination if more than one raw socket has the same protocol number. The MyPing example, later in this chapter, demonstrates this problem.

- *Nonstandard communication*—Sender and receiver must understand what you're doing. You cannot simply write a raw socket transmitter without writing a companion receiver. ICMP has its own receiver in the IP stack.

- *No automatic ICMP*—As noted earlier, ICMP does not have an interface like TCP (SOCK_STREAM) or UDP (SOCK_DGRAM). Instead, you have to create a raw socket, set aside a header that looks like Listing 3.2 (see Chapter 3), populate it, calculate the checksum, attach any data, and ship it.

- *No raw TCP and UDP*—You cannot expect a raw TCP or UDP to work. You can set the protocol parameter to whatever you want, even to TCP (6) or UDP (17), but not all operating systems honor the receiver-socket. In other words, you may be able to create a UDP-raw socket, build and initialize the UDP header, and send the message, but don't expect any reply.

- root *privilege*—Unlike the other protocols, the program must run with root privileges.

If you can live with these limitations, raw sockets can be a real bonus to speed up your programs.

18

THE POWER OF
RAW SOCKETS

Putting Raw Sockets to Work

After you have chosen to use raw sockets, you need to know how to work with them. Unfortunately, one needed tool is not available. This section presents missing algorithms and introduces a new system call.

Selecting the Right Protocol

The first step to creating a raw socket is selecting the right protocol. The /etc/protocol file (see Appendix A, Table A.7) lists the protocol numbers, names, and synonyms. You can use this file to get the correct protocol number from the standard alphabetic name without having to define any constants. The system call to use is getprotobyname():

```
#include <netdb.h>
struct protoent* getprotobyname(const char* name);
```

This call, if successful, returns a structure (struct protoent*). This structure holds a field (p_proto) that you would use to make your socket() system call:

```
struct protoent* proto;
int sd;
proto = getprotobyname("ICMP");
sd = socket(PF_SOCKET, SOCK_RAW, proto->p_proto);
```

As previously mentioned, ICMP does not have its own constant for socket()'s second parameter, so you use SOCK_RAW with the appropriate protocol value.

Creating an ICMP Packet

After creating the raw socket, you need to initialize a message packet. Each packet is going to have some kind of header information (even your own proprietary packet is likely to have a header). As far as the low-level IP layer is concerned, this is all data. Whether you choose to include a header means little to the sendto() command, so you need to manage the header in your program.

The ICMP packet has a header and a body of data. To ease your programming (and architecture independence), Linux includes the header definition in the libraries:

```
#include <netinet/ip_icmp.h>
struct icmphdr *icmp_header;
```

Because you are likely to include more information in the packet than just the header, you might want to define your own structure as follows:

```
#define PACKETSIZE    64    /* bytes */
struct packet_struct
{
```

```
    struct icmphdr header;
    char message[PACKETSIZE-sizeof(struct icmphdr)];
} packet;
```

You can use this structure for sending and receiving messages.

Calculating a Checksum

The next step, at least for the ICMP packet, is to calculate the checksum. The checksum is a one's-complement sum of the entire packet. Unfortunately, this algorithm is not part of the standard libraries in Linux distributions (even though it is used time and again in the kernel). Listing 18.1 presents the missing subroutine.

LISTING 18.1   The ICMP Checksum

```
unsigned short checksum(void *b, int len)
{   unsigned short *buf = b, result;
    unsigned int sum=0;

    for ( sum = 0; len > 1; len -= 2 )  /* Sum all 16b words */
        sum += *buf++;
    if ( len == 1 )                     /* If any stray bytes, */
        sum += *(unsigned char*)buf;       /* add to sum */
    sum = (sum >> 16) + (sum & 0xFFFF);  /* Add the carry */
    sum += (sum >> 16);                       /* (again) */
    result = ~sum;              /* Take the one's complement */
    return result;                      /* Return 16b value */
}
```

The receiver validates the packet by reversing the algorithm—it sums the entire contents of the packet. The result should be zero (because of the one's-complement checksum). This is a very slick way to check packets, but it has limitations.

The main limitation is the fact that the algorithm can only detect unique bit errors in the 16-bit words. It cannot detect like defects from word to word. For example, if the packet has two words each with a bit flipped in the same position, the checksum would compute the same.

Controlling the IP Header

The IP header uses the same checksum algorithm for its own checksum field. This becomes an issue when you choose to create your own IP header. Unlike the ICMP protocol, the IP header does a couple of jobs for you. For example, it always calculates the checksum, and the checksum only encompasses the IP header. (Recall that the ICMP calculates the sum for the entire packet.) If you want to calculate the checksum, go right ahead—it will just be redone.

The IP layer leaves all raw IP fields (as shown in Table 3.4) alone except for the IP network version number and the checksum. If you set the version number to zero, `sendto()` sets the value to whatever the current network is (for example, 4 for `PF_INET` or 6 for `PF_INET6`). If you set it to another value, the IP layer leaves it as is.

Unless you're doing something very unusual, `setsockopt()` touches most of the functional fields in the IP header.

Third-Party Traffic

Direct manipulation of the IP header permits you some very unusual abilities. One is low-level third-party traffic. Suppose you had a network of three servers—the source, the destination, and an intermediary. The intermediary accepts messages from the source, does some processing, and then passes the result to the destination. This is called third-party traffic. In most instances, the packet sent to the intermediary would include the source and final destination (along with its own address).

Now you have to interface with a legacy system that does not understand that the reply must be sent to a different host other than your source. Most non-TCP protocols reply to the Source-IP field in the IP header. Using IP header manipulation you can set the Source-IP field to the third-party's address instead of the source's.

Third-Party Traffic May Test Ethics

The ability to set the Source-IP field to whatever you would like is very powerful—and unusual and rarely necessary. More often than not, programmers who use this feature are really trying to *spoof* the network, fooling the hosts into concluding the message came from somewhere else. Those who try network spoofing put themselves at risk of breaking local, national, and international laws.

First, ISPs can (and should) easily detect if a packet is spoofed by tracking messages and verifying Source-IP fields. Second, Linux does not allow spoofed packets to be sent: It fills the IP source field. And third, ISPs typically drop these "source-routed" packets.

How Does Ping Work?

When creating your first raw socket program, you typically start off with ping, a standard "Are you there?" client. When you send a request like that, the IP stack almost always replies—there is no application or server waiting for that message.

Because the user may want to test the roundtrip time, the program often has two processes running—one for sending and the other for receiving. The sender process typically waits one second between each transmission, and the receiver keeps track of the messages and their times.

The MyPing Receiver

The receiver is simple. After creating the raw socket, it repeatedly calls `recvfrom()`, as shown in Listing 18.2.

LISTING 18.2 MyPing Receiver Loop

```
/********************************************************/
/*** MyPing Receiver - Get pending message and display it.***/
/*** From MyPing.c on Web site.                        ***/
/********************************************************/
for (;;)
{   int bytes, len=sizeof(addr);

    bzero(buf, sizeof(buf));        /* Clear buffer & Get msg */
    bytes = recvfrom(sd, buf, sizeof(buf), 0, &addr, &len);
    if ( bytes > 0 )                        /* If no error, */
        display(buf, bytes);            /* check ID & display */
    else
        perror("recvfrom");
}
```

The `display()` call converts the `buf` to a `packet_struct` and checks for the ID. If the ID matches, the packet really does belong to the process.

The ID is needed because of how the kernel delivers messages to raw sockets. As noted earlier, the kernel has no way to determine the correct destination of a raw packet without ports, so it delivers all raw packets to all raw sockets of a particular protocol.

The protocol is a key for the kernel. If your program registers a raw socket with an ICMP protocol, the program gets all ICMP messages (even those meant for other processes). How do you tell the difference? ICMP includes an ID field into which most programs place their PID (process ID). The responding host echoes back everything that it receives, including the ID. If the ID does not match the PID, the receiver drops it.

The MyPing Sender

The sender has a little more work to do. Along with preparing and shipping the message, it has to accept any spurious messages the kernel chooses to place in its queue (see Listing 18.3).

18

THE POWER OF
RAW SOCKETS

LISTING 18.3   MyPing Sender Loop

```
/***************************************************************/
/*** MyPing Sender - Get & toss any pending messages,     ***/
/*** compose message, send message, and pause.           ***/
/*** From MyPing.c on Web site.                           ***/
/***************************************************************/
for (;;)
{   int len=sizeof(r_addr);

    /*---Get any message that the kernel may have sent---*/
    if ( recvfrom(sd, &pckt, sizeof(pckt), 0, &r_addr,
            &len) > 0 )
        printf("***Got message!***\n");

    /*---Initialize outgoing packet---*/
    bzero(&pckt, sizeof(pckt));              /* Zero contents */
    pckt.hdr.type = ICMP_ECHO;               /* Request echo */
    pckt.hdr.un.echo.id = pid;                 /* Set ID */
    for ( i = 0; i < sizeof(pckt.msg)-1; i++ )
        pckt.msg[i] = i+'0';                 /* Fill buffer */
    pckt.msg[i] = 0;              /* Make C-string compatible */
    pckt.hdr.un.echo.sequence = cnt++;       /* Set counter */
    pckt.hdr.checksum =                  /* Compute checksum */
        checksum(&pckt, sizeof(pckt));
    if ( sendto(sd, &pckt, sizeof(pckt), 0, addr,  /* SEND! */
            sizeof(*addr)) <= 0 )
        perror("sendto");
    sleep(1);                          /* Wait for 1 second */
}
```

Resetting the message to the same values is not completely necessary but is precautionary. When the destination replies, the sender will get a copy of the message. If you don't get the message (and any other ICMP messages), the kernel ends up setting aside more and more memory for unwanted messages.

For the algorithm to work correctly, the program has to change some of the socket's default settings. First, most ping programs set the TTL (time to live) to the highest hop value (255). Also, the sender's socket must have nonblocking enabled to call recvfrom() without stalling.

The MyPing program is a good starting point for most ICMP-style packet messaging. After you are comfortable with this algorithm, other raw socket programs are similar to datagram programming.

How Does Traceroute Work?

Another type of ICMP-style raw socket program is traceroute. You probably have used trace-route for figuring out the path of a host-visitor or a spam message. The program builds on top of the MyPing program because it uses ICMP messages.

The basic algorithm is to send a ping message to the destination with an insufficient TTL. The intercepting router expires the packet and spits back an error. Repeat with a larger TTL until the message arrives at the destination. The result is actually pretty clever: The router between the source and the destination discovers that the TTL has expired, so it sends back an error (ICMP message) to the source. The router places its address in the error message. Only a raw ICMP socket works here because you may not get the error messages from the routers.

The loop is similar to the MyPing's sender process. The program needs a little extra logic to interpret the replies:

```
TTL = 0;
do
{   int len=sizeof(r_addr);
    struct iphdr *ip;

    TTL++;
    if ( setsockopt(sd, SOL_IP, IP_TTL, &TTL,     /* Set TTL */
            sizeof(TTL)) != 0)
        perror("Set TTL option");

    /***Initialize the message (see MyPing's sender)***/

    if ( sendto(sd, &pckt, sizeof(pckt), 0, addr,  /* SEND! */
            sizeof(*addr)) <= 0 )
        perror("sendto");
    if ( recvfrom(sd, buf, sizeof(buf), 0,      /* Get reply */
            &r_addr, &len) > 0 )
    {   struct hostent *hname;
        ip = (void*)buf;
        printf("Host #%d: %s \n", cnt-1, /* Print router IP */
            inet_ntoa(ip->saddr));
        hname = gethostbyaddr(          /* Try getting name */
            (void*)&r_addr.s_addr, sizeof(r.addr.s_addr),
            r_addr.sin_family);
        if ( hname != NULL )
            printf("(%s)\n", hname->h_name);
        else
            perror("Name");
    }
```

18

THE POWER OF
RAW SOCKETS

```
    else
        perror("recvfrom");
}
/*---Repeat until the destination is the same as the reply---*/
while ( r_addr.sin_addr.s_addr != addr->sin_addr.s_addr );
```

When you run this program a few times, you may notice that the path seems to change a lot. This is normal and not a bug. Refer to Chapter 2, "TCP/IP Network Language Fluency," for an explanation of the network's dynamics.

Summary: Making the Raw Decisions

The raw socket gives you the capability of working with the error messaging protocols (ICMP) that the IP subsystem uses. It also allows you to create your own protocols. The primary advantage of raw sockets is its sheer speed, being only one abstraction layer above the physical network frame.

The most common introductory raw socket programs are ping and traceroute. When you understand how these work and the risks involved in datagram messaging, you can choose the best approach to meet the requirements of your program.

IPv6: The Next Generation to IP

IN THIS CHAPTER

The Internet contains much of the network traffic in today's world. It has a great deal of power and flexibility. It bases its power and flexibility on the IP packet. This packet eases getting messages from here to there. However it has certain limitations, limitations based primarily in growth and extensibility.

This chapter digs deeply into the next generation of IP: IPng (yes, "IP Next Generation") or IPv6. Throughout this book, you have worked entirely in the IPv4 arena, and most of that knowledge is applicable in IPv6. You only need to know few extra tips and tricks to ensure longevity in your creative projects.

Current Addressing Problems

The IPv4 primarily focuses on addressing a set of computers within a subnet. As described in Chapter 2, "TCP/IP Network Language Fluency," the number is composed of 4-byte values (or a 32-bit number). Furthermore, the addresses are grouped into network classes. When companies buy blocks of addresses, they get them in these classes. These classes range from a few hundred to a few million addresses.

The number of addresses being assigned and used has alarmed the Internet Activities Board (IAB). The board has discovered that less than 1% of the numbers assigned are really associated with a node on the network. The result: a dwindling supply of available addresses.

The IAB expects the number of computers connected to the Internet to increase as much as a hundredfold within the next few years. IPv4 simply does not have enough available addresses to meet the demand.

Solving the Dwindling IPv4 Address Space

The IAB has taken some measures to solve the dwindling address problem. The cost of owning real IP addresses has risen, so companies now use masquerading and DHCP to limit the number of allocated addresses.

Additionally, the Internet could adopt a wider addressing scheme than merely 32 bits. IPv6 [RFC2460] answers that exact request. The IPv6 is 128-bits long (or 16-bytes wide). This opens the possibilities well into the next century—at least. The effective number of addresses in IPv4 is about two billion network nodes (taking out the special addresses). The effective address space for IPv6 is 1×10^{38}!

What Does IPv6 Look Like?

An IPv6 address looks a little different from IPv4 because of the large number of digits a programmer now has to manage. Each address is eight hexadecimal numbers separated with colons. For example, one legal address is 2FFF:80:0:0:0:0:94:1. For shorthand, you can replace the repeating zeros with two colons (2FFF:80::94:1).

Ports can still be tacked on to the end of the address using a period and port number in decimal. For example, port 80 for the previous address would be 2FFF:80::94:1.80. You can't use the colon separator because it makes the shorthand ambiguous.

The IPv6 address space (like that of IPv4) has already been divided up into specific regions or groups [RFC1897, RFC2471]. The groups attempt to merge different addresses (like IPX). As of the writing of this book, the definition is still in flux, many groupings remaining undefined.

Of the different groupings, the numeric address value that starts with 001 as the first three bits specifically replaces the IPv4 addressing. Figure 19.1 shows what this address contains.

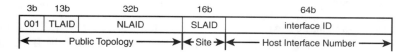

FIGURE 19.1

The IPv6 address is divided into five main parts. These parts identify the nature of the address, the routing, and the host.

Figure 19.1 has five parts: allocation ID, TLA ID, NLA ID, SLA ID, and interface ID. Table 19.1 defines the purpose of each part.

TABLE 19.1   IPv6 Address Parts

Field	Description
Allocation ID	This is the 3-bit flag (001) that indicates that this is a public Internet address. (3 bits)
TLA ID	Top-Level Aggregation. This represents the highest level of the worldwide Internet. (13 bits)
NLA ID	Next-Level Aggregation. Subdivided group within the TLA. (32 bits)
SLA ID	Site-Level Aggregation. This could be a large corporation or conglomerate. (16 bits)
Interface ID	The specific machine ID. (64 bits)

One of the problems networks had to solve was the "everybody knows everybody" problem first discussed in Chapter 2. This problem forces all the routers to know every address available so that it routes a message correctly. That is why machines could not use the MAC address.

IPv4 solved that problem using classes built into the network IP address. IPv6 uses a more diluted form. It still has to resolve addresses in the TLA, NLA, and SLA regions, but it does not have to resolve them at the same time. Instead, the routers move the message from one group to the next, based on only the address part it has to.

How Do IPv4 and IPv6 Work Together?

The promised routing mechanisms do add some attraction to the proposed change. But the Internet, of course, has yet to convert completely over to IPv6. In fact, it may always keep IPv4 around. So, how do servers and clients mix the two?

Nearly all systems that now support the IPv6 protocol stack also support the IPv4 protocol stack. These *dual stack* systems may exist for quite a while, or until most applications migrate completely over to IPv6. The main problem is how to get them to work together.

In reality, the increase in address width has little effect on the protocol stack. The primary protocols that the Internet uses are UDP and TCP, and these are embedded in the IP packet anyway. When you send a message from an IPv4 client to a dual stack server, the IPv4 stack would respond accordingly. But, after being stripped of the IP wrapper, it would appear like a TCP or UDP message. If you are careful about programming your applications, you can move from IPv4 to IPv6 very easily.

Essentially, IPv6 is a superset of IPv4. It adopts all the good features of IPv4 and drops the out-of-date ones. IPv4 addresses are remapped to an IPv6 address. To map the address, all the upper bits of the IPv6 address are set to zero and the last 48 bits become 0xFFFF plus the IPv4 address. For example, converting 128.10.48.6 to an IPv6 address, you would get ::FFFF:128.10.48.6 or ::FFFF:800A:3006 (again, the :: is the shorthand for all zeros).

Of course, the only limitation is you can't go backwards: an IPv4 application cannot directly accept an IPv6 message. (Some systems allow *address mutilation*, which converts the 128-bit address into a temporary 32-bit address. When the IPv4 application accepts the IPv6 message, it only sees the mutilated address. When it replies with the address, the kernel converts the message back to the 128-bit address.)

Trying Out IPv6

To try out IPv6, not only do you have to change your programs slightly, but the kernel and the networking tools must support it also. Some distributions omit its support to reduce installation complexity or security risks. This section describes the process to enable support and shows you how to convert your programs to IPv6.

Configuring the Kernel

You can find out quickly whether your kernel version supports IPv6. If you have /proc support, look in /proc/net. If you see igmp6 or if_inet6, you have IPv6. If you don't see these files, you may need to load the ipv6.o module.

Ifconfig Defect

The ifconfig tool found in net_tools has a defect and does not load the ipv6.o module automatically. If you have this problem, you may want to recompile the kernel's ipv6 as a non-module.

If you need to reconfigure the kernel, go to the source directory. (Some distributions do not automatically install the kernel source for some reason, so you may need to download and install it. The Web site www.kernel.org is a good source.) Be sure that all your settings are correct in all the options, and select Experimental Drivers. Next select IPv6 in the Network Settings menu. You can find it in the It Is Safe to Leave These Untouched section. Some kernel configurations permit you to select exclusive IPv6. Don't do it. Again, you may want to include the IPv6 in the kernel and *not* compile it as a module. That can save you some debugging time.

Be sure to keep a backup of your old kernel. If you have a problem, you can use it to get back to a sane state.

Configuring the Tools

The next test needed is the tools. If you have confirmed kernel support, run ifconfig without any arguments. It displays the current configurations of each network interface. If it supports IPv6, the list includes an IPv6 address in the second or third line of each interface.

If you do not see the addresses, run it again with a --help option. The command then lists for you all the supported protocols. You probably won't see IPv6 in this case. If it's omitted, you need to get the net_tools RPM and reconfigure it and compile it. After installation, configure it using configure.sh and enable IPv6. You can include IPv6 over IPv4, if you would like, but that may be unnecessary. Compile the package and copy all the executables to their typical homes (this is often /sbin).

Again, keeping a backup of your tools is a very good idea. (You may note that the default settings of configure.sh are the same as your old install. So if your backup does not work, you could simply recompile.)

After you compile and install your tools and kernel, reboot the host. When the system is ready again, running ifconfig shows you the mapped addresses for its assigned IPv4 address. You can even add an IPv6 alias with the following:

```
ifconfig eth0 add <IPv6 Address>
```

For example

```
ifconfig eth0 add 2FFF::80:453A:2348
```

After you have your system all set up, you can begin to write a few IPv6 programs.

Converting IPv4 Calls to IPv6

With a computer properly set up for supporting IPv6, you can write a few programs. You only need to change a few parameters to make the conversion. Essentially, everything continues to work as you might expect, if you have followed the formula rules defined in the first chapters.

The first change is the socket structure. Instead of using sockaddr_in, you use sockaddr_in6:

```
struct sockaddr_in6 addr;
bzero(&addr, sizeof(addr));
```

Use this structure for the bind(), connect(), and accept() system calls. Similarly, the socket option to get the address of your socket or the peer's socket needs this new structure. The second change is the socket type. You cannot receive different protocols from the same socket. Even though IPv6 is almost a complete superset of IPv4, you must choose a different socket type:

```
sd = socket(PF_INET6, SOCK_STREAM, 0);   /* TCP6 */
/*---OR---*/
sd = socket(PF_INET6, SOCK_DGRAM, 0);   /* UDP6 */
/*---OR---*/
sd = socket(PF_INET6, SOCK_RAW, 0);     /* Raw-6 or ICMP6 */
```

In each of these examples, you may notice that everything stays the same except for the socket type. This is the intent of the common socket() interface. The next few steps change slightly too:

```
addr.sin6_family = AF_INET6;
addr.sin6_port = htons(MY_PORT);
if ( inet_pton(AF_INET6, "2FFF::80:9AC0:351", &addr.sin6_addr) == 0 )
    perror("inet_pton failed");
```

The sockaddr_in6 has other fields that you can ignore in your program. Just set them to zero (using bzero() or memset()), and everything should work fine. Also, you don't have to do anything more in your program.

The previous code fragment uses a new call, inet_pton(). It and its companion call, inet_ntop(), are new and help with the various forms of address calculation. The n, of course, represents network, and the p represents presentation. This call supports many address formats including IPv4, IPv6, Rose, IPX, and HAM radio. The current version that the GNU library offers is undocumented and only supports INET and INET6.

The full prototype looks as follows:

```
#include <arpa/inet.h>
int inet_pton(int domain, const char* prsnt, void* buf);
char *inet_ntop(int domain, void* buf, char* prsnt, int len);
```

The inet_pton() call converts the alphanumeric address in prsnt into the network byte-ordered binary form and places the result in buf. The inet_ntop() call does the reverse. Parameters domain and len define the network (AF_INET or AF_INET6) and prsnt array length, respectively.

Converting Raw Sockets to IPv6

If you are using a UDP or TCP socket, that's all you have to do. However, if you are programming a raw or ICMP socket, you have to use special new record formats. Raw-6 and ICMP6 include new or revised fields to support the extra capabilities.

The IPv6 header is much simpler than the IPv4 header and only doubles the overhead (40 bytes versus 20 bytes). The header is also a fixed size because no options are allowed (please note that this is not quite true, as the next section describes). The IP (for raw sockets) can be defined as follows in network byte order:

```
/*********************************************************/
/*** IPv6 Packet definition                          ***/
/*********************************************************/
union IPv6_Address
{
    unsigned char u8[16];
    unsigned short int u16[8];
    unsigned long int u32[4];
    unsigned long long int u64[2];
};

struct IPv6_Header
{
    unsigned int version:4;      /* The IP version (6) */
    unsigned int priority:4;
    unsigned int flow_label:24;
    unsigned int payload_len:16; /* bytes following header */
```

```
    unsigned int next_header:8;   /* protocol (6 for TCP) */
    unsigned int hop_limit:8;     /* same as TTL */
    union IPv6_Address source;
    union IPv6_Address dest;
};
```

Only three of the fields require more explanation. The `priority` field is an experimental field that sets the priority of the packet. If the network becomes congested, routers may hold or drop lower-priority packets. By default, all packets are `priority` zero.

The `flow_label` field is also experimental and works with `priority`. The flow is a sequence of packets that move from source to destination through a series of routers. `flow_label` helps the routers determine any special handling. A message has only one `flow_label`; after it is selected, the flow value does not change for all packets in the flow. You can set the `priority` and `flow_label` when you bind the socket address using the optional `sin6_flowinfo` field in `sockaddr_in6`.

The last field, `payload_len`, can be zero to indicate a huge packet. A one gigabit (or even 100Mbit) network sending small packets (less than 100KB) is a waste of bandwidth. Set this field to zero and include an additional record between the header and the payload. The following is the definition as it would appear in network-byte order:

```
/****************************************************************/
/*** Jumbo (extra large) packet option definition        ***/
/****************************************************************/
struct Jumbo_Payload
{
    unsigned char option;     /* equals 194 */
    unsigned char length;     /* equals 4 (bytes) */
    unsigned long bytes;      /* payload length */
};
```

With this option, you can send up to a 4GB packet. Not too bad for a little while.

Converting ICMPv6 Sockets to IPv6

The physical layout of an ICMPv6 header [RFC2463] is the same as for an ICMPv4, but the `type` and `code` fields have changed considerably. For example, echo request and echo reply have new numbers (`128` and `129`, respectively). Several codes are no longer supported. For a complete list of codes, refer to Appendix A, "Data Tables."

The New Multicast Protocol

Another architectural change is in the way IPv6 manages multicasting. It has to work with three aspects: hardware, addressing, and routing.

As Chapter 17, "Sharing Messages with Multicast, Broadcast, and Mbone," describes, multicasting has to work with the hardware to tell it to pick up packets that are not its own ethernet or MAC address. These addresses depend on the requested multicast address—IPv6 takes the last four bytes of the address and creates a MAC address with the prefix of `33:33`. For example, if the requested multicast address is `FF02::725:6832:D012`, the resulting MAC would be `33:33:68:32:D0:12` (ignoring the `725`).

IPv6's addressing for multicasting differs slightly from that of IPv4. The first byte, FF, indicates that it is a multicast address, but the next byte contains additional information about the type of multicast group and routing details, each four bits wide.

The first subfield has four bit-flags each representing a feature. The least significant bit (bit #0) is zero (`0`) to indicate a well-known multicast address. It is one (`1`) to indicate a transient address. The other three bits are currently reserved.

The other subfield likewise has four bits and indicates the scope of the address (a local or global address). The higher the number, the wider the scope. On the other hand, IPv4 uses just the TTL to determine the scope (lower numbers would expire before reaching global addresses). Also, as stated in Chapter 17, IPv4 has allocated certain address blocks to local, site, or global scopes. Table 19.2 defines the different scopes.

TABLE 19.2   IPv6 Multicast's Scope Subfield

Scope	Range	Description
1	Node	Local on the same host (like `127.0.0.1`).
2	Link	Messages stay within the router's group. The routers never let these messages pass through.
5	Site	As defined by the network administrators, the messages stay within the site's locality.
8	Organization	As defined by the network administrators, the messages stay within the organization's locality.
14	Global	All routers permit messages to pass through the global network (until they expire).

Lastly, the rules for routing (as described in Chapter 17) remain the same. IPv6 uses IPv4's optional IGMP to pass on the request to join or drop a multicast group. Because both use the MAC address to get multicast messages, IPv6 did not have to define anything beyond IPv4's implementation.

The procedure for joining an IPv6 multicast group is almost the same as the IPv4, but you need to use a different structure for selecting the address:

```
/*************************************************************/
/*** IPv6 multicast structure definition                ***/
/*************************************************************/
struct ipv6_mreq
{
    struct in6_addr ipv6mr_multiaddr; /* IPv6 multicast addr */
    unsigned int ipv6mr_interface;         /* interface number */
};
```

The first field, ipv6mr_multiaddr, is the broadcast message address. You place the IPv6 address in this field (for example, FF02::10). The next field is the interface number: 0 means all interfaces, 1 for the first interface (eth0), and so on.

To enable IPv6 multicasting, use the following code snippet:

```
/*************************************************************/
/*** Join a IPv6 multicast group                         ***/
/*************************************************************/
const char *GroupID = "FF02::4590:3A0";
struct ipv6_mreq mreq;
if ( inet_pton(GroupID, &mreq.ipv6mr_multiaddr) == 0 )
    panic("address (%s) bad", GroupID);
mreq.ipv6mr_interface = 0;                     /* any interface */
if ( setsockopt(sd, SOL_IPV6, IPV6_ADD_MEMBERSHIP, &mreq, sizeof(mreq)) != 0 )
    panic("Join multicast failed");
if ( setsockopt(sd, SOL_SOCKET, SO_REUSEADDR, &on, sizeof(on)) != 0 )
    panic("Can't reuse address/ports");
```

As you can see, the code is very similar to the IPv4 multicasting code.

IPv6 Pros and Cons

As a protocol, IPv6 cleans up some of the antiquated features in IPv4 and moves the protocol into higher-performance networks. First, and the most obvious, is the wider addressing range that the 128-bit address offers. Networks are a lot more sophisticated today than they were when IPv4 was first introduced. Routers can more easily and quickly resolve these addresses.

Another great feature is the larger packet size that increases its usefulness in gigabit environments. IPv4 was limited to 64KB packets. IPv6's support of the Jumbo payload makes it more economical (not as taxing on the network). This payload supports 4GB packets.

Multicasting is another plus to the protocol. However, many of the new features in multicasting have been retrofitted into IPv4, so you may not notice much of a difference.

IPv6 has three limitations. First, it doubles the overhead. A typical IPv4 message header is about 20 bytes wide. If your messages are 1500 bytes wide, about 1% of your message is IP overhead. IPv6 doubles that to 40 bytes, increasing the typical message overhead to about 2%. However, unlike the IPv4, the length of the packet is not included in IPv6's payload length. This recovers a few bytes—IPv4's maximum packet size is 65,535 bytes, and IPv6's non-Jumbo packet's maximum is 65,535+40 bytes.

IPv6 has dropped IPv4's broadcasting support. In reality, this is not a problem. Multicasting has greater flexibility and control than broadcasting, and broadcasting is not really used in modern projects anymore.

Lastly, the IPv6 no longer includes the checksum field in the header. In simplifying the IP header, they have dropped some out of data fields. However, this can cause problems with older interfaces that do not include a checksum or CRC in the physical frame. The newer hardware interfaces do all the data integrity for the operating system. If you have old hardware, you may want to check into this.

Expected Linux Incorporation

The Linux developer community has been on top of the IPv6. All versions from 2.2.0 incorporate complete support for the current version of IPv6. Unfortunately, IPv6 has a major drawback: It is not fully accepted as a standard, and much of it is still undefined.

Linux supports as much as it can with the limited definitions. You can still use it in your development, but keep in mind that IPv6 is a moving target, so no operating system is 100% compliant yet. You can expect it to remain in the experimental options section of the kernel.

Internet Support and 6bone

Just as the initial support for multicasting presented problems and led to Mbone, many routers do not support IPv6. Like Mbone, IPv6 enthusiasts created 6bone, an IPv6-over-IPv4 (IP-in-IP) messaging subsystem. 6bone places the IPv6 packet inside an IPv4 packet that one routing server passes to another. While not as prevalent as Mbone servers, the support is growing (particularly in Europe and the Far East).

19

One last note: Be aware that due to its experimental nature, IPv6 may cause some security holes in your system. You may not want to work on it in a network that connects the Internet to an intranet.

Summary: Moving Your Code into the Future

IPv6 answers the limitations currently found in the IPv4's addressing structure. By extending the addressing range several orders of magnitude, IPv6 appears to be the clear future for the Internet. Still in its infancy, the addressing allocation has adopted standard networks, such as IPX. It already has support in European and Far Eastern networks.

With the extended addresses, the physical appearance has changed and has included some shorthand notation for ease of representation and programming. Porting programs from IPv4 to IPv6 is straightforward as long as you follow the guidelines and examples in this text. The `socket()` system call really helps network programming to adapt to different networks.

The IPv6 network encompasses the IPv4 network, so all IPv4 addresses still work. Most operating systems that support IPv6 may likely use a dual stack to support and translate between the two networks. The addressing scheme and translation inside these dual stacks permit some implicit collaboration—requiring little reprogramming for support.

The Linux kernel, as of 2.2.0, supports IPv6, but not all operating system distributions install a compiled kernel with this feature enabled. In fact, if your distribution does not include a kernel compiled with IPv6, the distribution does not likely have the updated tools either. This chapter describes how to get IPv6 working on your Linux host.

Additionally, this chapter demonstrated by example how to translate IPv4 programs. It also introduced two new tools to help in address conversion. Supporting IPv6 in your programs increases the likelihood of the future use of your work.

Appendixes

PART

V

IN THIS PART

Data Tables

IN THIS APPENDIX

This appendix identifies and lists all the tables and data formats relevant to sockets programming.

Domains: First Parameter to `socket()`

Table A.1 lists the values for the first parameter of the `socket()` system call. You can use these types as well in a `bind()` system call. While most programs use the AF style for both `socket()` and `bind()`, the correct form is to use the PF style for `socket()` and the AF style for `bind()`. If you are uncomfortable using the PF style, you can safely use the AF style because the C header files define the AF style as the PF style. The structure definitions are located in `<bits/socket.h>`.

TABLE A.1 Protocol Family Values for the Domain Parameter of socket()

Type	Description and Example	Affiliated Data

PF_UNSPEC	Unspecified	```struct sockaddr {```
		 ``` unsigned short int sa_family;```
		 ``` unsigned char sa_data[14];```
		 ```};```

PF_LOCAL
PF_UNIX
PF_FILE
	BSD method for
	accessing local
	named pipes
		```#define UNIX_PATH_MAX 108```
		
		 ```struct sockaddr_un {```
		 ``` sa_family_t sun_family;```
		 ``` char sun_path[UNIX_PATH_MAX];```
		 ```};```

	```#include <linux/un.h>```
	 ```struct sockaddr_un addr;```
	 ```addr.sun_family = AF_UNIX;```
	 ```strcpy(addr.sun_path,```
	 ``` "/tmp/mysocket");```	

PF_INET	Internet IPv4
	protocol family
		```struct sockaddr_in {```
		 ``` sa_family_t sin_family;```
		 ``` unsigned short int sin_port;```
		 ``` struct in_addr sin_addr;```
		 ``` unsigned char pad[];```
		 ```};```

	```#include <linux/in.h>```
	 ```struct sockaddr_in addr;```
	 ```bzero(&addr, sizeof(addr));```
	 ```addr.sin_family = AF_INET;```
	 ```addr.sin_port = htons(9999);```
	 ```if (inet_aton("127.0.0.1",```
	 ``` &addr.sin_addr) == 0)```
	 ``` perror("Addr conversion");```	

A

DATA TABLES

TABLE A.1 Continued

Type	Description and Example	Affiliated Data
AF_AX25	Amateur Radio AX.25 #include <linux/AX25.h>	```typedef struct {
char ax25_call[7];
} ax25_address;```
PF_IPX	Novell Internet Protocol #include <linux/ipx.h>	```struct sockaddr_ipx
{
sa_family_t   sipx_family;
__u16   sipx_port;
__u32   sipx_network;
unsigned char
sipx_node[IPX_NODE_LEN];
__u8   sipx_type;
/* padding */
unsigned char sipx_zero;
};```
PF_APPLETALK	Appletalk DDP #include <linux/atalk.h>	```struct sockaddr_at {
sa_family_t sat_family;
u8   sat_port;
struct at_addr {
u16 s_net;
u8 s_node;
}   sat_addr;
char   sat_zero[];
};```

TABLE A.1 Continued

Type	Description and Example	Affiliated Data
PF_NETROM	Amateur Radio NetROM	
PF_BRIDGE	Multiprotocol Bridge	
PF_ATMPVC	ATM PVCs	
PF_X25	(Reserved for X.25 project)	typedef struct { char x25_addr[16]; } x25_address;

	#include <linux/x25.h>	struct sockaddr_x25 {
		    sa_family_t sx25_family;
		    /* X.121 Address */
		    x25_address sx25_addr;
		};

PF_INET6	IPv6 protocol family	struct in6_addr
		{
		    union {
		        u8 u6_addr8[16];
		        __u16 u6_addr16[8];
		        __u32 u6_addr32[4];
		#if (~0UL) > 0xffffffff
		#ifndef __RELAX_IN6_ADDR_ALIGNMENT
		/* Alas, protocols do not respect
		64bit alignment. rsvp/pim/... are
		broken. However, it is good idea to
		force correct alignment, when
		    it is possible. */
		        __u64 u6_addr64[2];
		#endif
		#endif

	#include <linux/in6.h>	

TABLE A.1 Continued

Type	Description and Example	Affiliated Data
| | | ```c
} in6_u;
#define s6_addr    in6_u.u6_addr8
#define s6_addr16  in6_u.u6_addr16
#define s6_addr32  in6_u.u6_addr32
#define s6_addr64  in6_u.u6_addr64
};

struct sockaddr_in6 {
    unsigned short int sin6_family;
    __u16              sin6_port;
    __u32              sin6_flowinfo;
    struct in6_addr    sin6_addr;
};

typedef struct {
    char rose_addr[5];
} rose_address;
``` |
| PF_ROSE | Amateur Radio X.25 PLP | |
| | ```c
#include <linux/rose.h>
struct sockaddr_rose {
    sa_family_t  srose_family;
    rose_address srose_addr;
    ax25_address srose_call;
    int          srose_ndigis;
    ax25_address srose_digi;
};

struct full_sockaddr_rose {
    sa_family_t  srose_family;
    rose_address srose_addr;
    ax25_address srose_call;
``` | |

TABLE A.1 Continued

Type	Description and Example	Affiliated Data
| | | ```
unsigned int srose_ndigis;
ax25_address
srose_digis[ROSE_MAX_DIGIS];
};
``` |
| PF_DECnet | (Reserved for DECnet project) | |
| PF_NETBEUI | (Reserved for 802.2LLC project) | `#define NB_NAME_LEN    20` |
| | `#include <linux/netbeui.h>` | ```
struct sockaddr_netbeui
{
    sa_family  snb_family;
    char       snb_name[NB_NAME_LEN];
    char       snb_devhint[IFNAMSIZ];
};
``` |
| PF_SECURITY | Security callback pseudo AF | |
| PF_KEY | PF_KEY key management API | |
| PF_NETLINK<br>PF_ROUTE | Aliases to emulate 4.4 BSD | ```
struct sockaddr_nl
{
    sa_family_t    nl_family;
    unsigned short nl_pad;
    __u32          nl_pid;
    __u32          nl_groups;
};
``` |
| | `#include <linux/netlink.h>` | |
| PF_PACKET | Packet family | ```
struct sockaddr_pkt
{
``` |

A

DATA TABLES

TABLE A.1 Continued

Type	Description and Example	Affiliated Data
| | `#include <linux/if_packet.h>` | ```
unsigned short    spkt_family;
unsigned char     spkt_device[14];
unsigned short    spkt_protocol;
};

struct sockaddr_ll
{
unsigned short    sll_family;v
unsigned short    sll_protocol;
int               sll_ifindex;
unsigned short    sll_hatype;
unsigned char     sll_pkttype;
unsigned char     sll_halen;
unsigned char     sll_addr[8];
};
``` |
| PF_ASH | Ash | |
| PF_ECONET | Acorn Econet | ```
#include <linux/if_ec.h>
struct ec_addr
{
/* Station number.  */
unsigned char station;
/* Network number.  */
unsigned char net;
};

struct sockaddr_ec
{
unsigned short sec_family;
unsigned char port;
``` |

TABLE A.1 Continued

Type	Description and Example	Affiliated Data

		`/* Control/flag byte. */`
		`unsigned char cb;`
		`/* Type of message. */`
		`unsigned char type;`
		`struct ec_addr addr;`
		`unsigned long cookie;`
		
		`};`

PF_ATMSVC	ATM SVCs	
PF_SNA	Linux SNA project	
PF_IRDA	IRDA sockets	

	`#include <linux/irda.h>`	`struct sockaddr_irda {`
		`    sa_family_t  sir_family;`
		`/* LSAP/TSAP selector */`
		`    unsigned char sir_lsap_sel;`
		`/* Device address */`
		`    unsigned int  sir_addr;`
		`/* Usually <service>:IrDA:TinyTP */`
		`    char          sir_name[25];`
		
		`};`

Types: Second Parameter to `socket()`

The second parameter (`type`) selects the protocol layer. Some constants defined in Table A.2 are mere placeholders for when the kernel supports the protocol.

TABLE A.2 Protocol Values for the `type` Parameter in `socket()` Call

Protocol Type	Description
SOCK_STREAM	(TCP) Reliable, two-way communication in a stream. You can use this kind of socket in higher-level I/O function calls that involve the FILE* type. This protocol offers you a virtual connection to the network using ports and a dedicated client channel. After connection, the `accept()` call returns a new socket descriptor specifically for the new client.
SOCK_DGRAM	(UDP) Unreliable connectionless communication. Each message is independent and can be lost during transmission. This protocol virtualizes the network with ports and allows you to send and receive messages from many peers without reconnection.
SOCK_RAW	(IP) Accesses the internal network interfaces and fields. If you want to create ICMP messages, you need to create a raw socket. Root access only.
SOCK_RDM	(RDM—Reliably Delivered Messages) Makes sure that each packet arrives safely to the destination, but does not guarantee correct packet order. (Not yet implemented in Linux and other UNIX operating systems.)
SOCK_SEQPACKET	Sequenced, reliable, connection-based datagrams of fixed length. (Not yet implemented in Linux.)
SOCK_PACKET	(Physical Layer) Places the socket in promiscuous mode (if available) where it will receive any and all packets on the network. This is a Linux-only tool. Root-access only. (Deprecated—use PF_PACKET instead.)

Protocol Definitions

Listing A.1 is an excerpt from the `/etc/protocols` file [RFC2292] on your distribution. It contains the common and standard protocol standards used in the network packet. Revising this file is *not* a good idea.

LISTING A.1   /etc/protocols File

```
ip          0 IP        # internet protocol, pseudo number
icmp        1 ICMP      # internet control message protocol
igmp        2 IGMP      # Internet Group Management
ggp         3 GGP       # gateway-gateway protocol
ipencap     4 IP-ENCAP  # IP encapsulated in IP
st          5 ST        # ST datagram mode
tcp         6 TCP       # transmission control protocol
egp         8 EGP       # exterior gateway protocol
pup        12 PUP       # PARC universal packet protocol
udp        17 UDP       # user datagram protocol
hmp        20 HMP       # host monitoring protocol
xns-idp    22 XNS-IDP   # Xerox NS IDP
rdp        27 RDP       # "reliable datagram" protocol
iso-tp4    29 ISO-TP4   # ISO Transport Protocol class 4
xtp        36 XTP       # Xpress Tranfer Protocol
ddp        37 DDP       # Datagram Delivery Protocol
idpr-cmtp  39 IDPR-CMTP # IDPR Control Message Transport
rspf       73 RSPF      # Radio Shortest Path First
vmtp       81 VMTP      # Versatile Message Transport
ospf       89 OSPFIGP   # Open Shortest Path First IGP
ipip       94 IPIP      # Yet Another IP encapsulation
encap      98 ENCAP     # Yet Another IP encapsulation
```

Standard Internet Port Assignments (First 100 Ports)

Listing A.2 shows the standard ports (up to port #100) defined in the /etc/services file. You can change many of these to suit your needs, but be sure to notify the clients if you do so.

LISTING A.2   /etc/services File

```
tcpmux    1/tcp                  # TCP port service multiplexer
rtmp      1/ddp                  # Routing Table Maintenance Protocol
nbp       2/ddp                  # Name Binding Protocol
echo      4/ddp                  # AppleTalk Echo Protocol
zip       6/ddp                  # Zone Information Protocol
echo      7/tcp
echo      7/udp
discard   9/tcp    sink null
discard   9/udp    sink null
systat   11/tcp    users
daytime  13/tcp
```

A

DATA TABLES

LISTING A.2   Continued

```
daytime      13/udp
netstat      15/tcp
qotd         17/tcp    quote
msp          18/tcp                        # message send protocol
msp          18/udp                        # message send protocol
chargen      19/tcp    ttytst source
chargen      19/udp    ttytst source
ftp-data     20/tcp
ftp          21/tcp
fsp          21/udp    fspd
ssh          22/tcp                        # SSH Remote Login Protocol
ssh          22/udp                        # SSH Remote Login Protocol
telnet       23/tcp
# 24 - private
smtp         25/tcp    mail
# 26 - unassigned
time         37/tcp    timserver
time         37/udp    timserver
rlp          39/udp    resource            # resource location
nameserver   42/tcp    name                # IEN 116
whois        43/tcp    nicname
re-mail-ck   50/tcp                         # Remote Mail Checking Protocol
re-mail-ck   50/udp                         # Remote Mail Checking Protocol
domain       53/tcp    nameserver          # name-domain server
domain       53/udp    nameserver
mtp          57/tcp                         # deprecated
bootps       67/tcp                         # BOOTP server
bootps       67/udp
bootpc       68/tcp                         # BOOTP client
bootpc       68/udp
tftp         69/udp
gopher       70/tcp                         # Internet Gopher
gopher       70/udp
rje          77/tcp    netrjs
finger       79/tcp
www          80/tcp    http                # WorldWideWeb HTTP
www          80/udp                         # HyperText Transfer Protocol
link         87/tcp    ttylink
kerberos     88/tcp    kerberos5 krb5      # Kerberos v5
kerberos     88/udp    kerberos5 krb5      # Kerberos v5
supdup       95/tcp
linuxconf    98/tcp
# 100 - reserved
```

HTTP 1.1 Status Codes

If you want to write your own Web server, you need to understand and use the standard status codes of HTTP 1.1 [RFC2616, RFC2817]. Table A.3 lists these codes.

TABLE A.3 HTTP Result Codes

Code Class Value	Class Name	Specific Code and Description
1xx	Informational	100 Continue
		101 Switching Protocols
2xx	Successful	200 OK
		201 Created
		202 Accepted
		203 Non-Authoritative Information
		204 No Content
		205 Reset Content
		206 Partial Content
3xx	Redirection	300 Multiple Choices
		301 Moved Permanently
		302 Moved Temporarily
		303 See Other
		304 Not Modified
		305 Use Proxy
4xx	Client Error	400 Bad Request
		401 Unauthorized
		402 Payment Required
		403 Forbidden
		404 Not Found
		405 Method Not Allowed
		406 Not Acceptable
		407 Proxy Authentication Required
		408 Request Timeout
		409 Conflict
		410 Gone
		411 Length Required

A

DATA TABLES

TABLE A.3   Continued

Code Class Value	Class Name	Specific Code and Description
		412 Precondition Failed
		413 Request Entity Too Large
		414 Request-URI Too Long
		415 Unsupported Media Type
5xx	Server Error	500 Internal Server Error
		501 Not Implemented
		502 Bad Gateway
		503 Service Unavailable
		504 Gateway Timeout
		505 HTTP Version Not Supported

Socket Options (`get`/`setsockopt()`)

Tables A.4 through A.7 list the various socket options and the required parameters. Not all options are size compatible between UNIX types. For example, `IP_TTL` in Linux allows a type `int`, but only fills the first byte. IBM's AIX restricts the same option to a `char` instead.

TABLE A.4   General Socket Options

Level	Option	Description	*	R	W	Value	Type
SOL_SOCKET	SO_ATTACH_ FILTER	Attach filter	?	?	?	Integer	int
SOL_SOCKET	SO_ BINDTODEVICE	Bind to device	?	?	?	String	char*
SOL_SOCKET	SO_BROADCAST	Enable broadcast	Y	Y	Y	Boolean	int
SOL_SOCKET	SO_BSDCOMPAT	Request BSD bug-for-bug compatibility	Y	Y	Y	Boolean	int
SOL_SOCKET	SO_DEBUG	Enable socket debugging	Y	Y	Y	Boolean	int
SOL_SOCKET	SO_DETACH_ FILTER	Detach filter	?	?	?	Integer	int
SOL_SOCKET	SO_DONTROUTE	Forbid routing	Y	Y	Y	Boolean	int
SOL_SOCKET	SO_ERROR	Last error	Y	Y	Y	Integer	int

TABLE A.4   Continued

Level	Option	Description	*	R	W	Value	Type
SOL_SOCKET	SO_KEEPALIVE	Enable keeping connection alive	Y	Y	Y	Boolean	`int`
SOL_SOCKET	SO_LINGER	Linger until data sent	Y	Y	Y	Linger	`struct linger`
SOL_SOCKET	SO_NO_CHECK	No checking	Y	Y	Y	Boolean	`int`
SOL_SOCKET	SO_OOBINLINE	Place out-of-band inline	Y	Y	Y	Boolean	`int`
SOL_SOCKET	SO_PASSCRED	Enable passing user credentials	Y	Y	Y	Boolean	`int`
SOL_SOCKET	SO_PEERCRED	Peer Credentials	Y	Y	Y	Credentials	`struct ucred`
SOL_SOCKET	SO_PRIORITY	Set the queue priority	Y	Y	Y	Integer	`int`
SOL_SOCKET	SO_RCVBUF	Receive buffer size	Y	Y	Y	Integer	`int`
SOL_SOCKET	SO_RCVLOWAT	Receive low water mark	Y	Y	N	Integer	`int`
SOL_SOCKET	SO_RCVTIMEO	Receive Timeout	Y	Y	Y	Time	`struct timeval`
SOL_SOCKET	SO_REUSEADDR	Reuse Address	Y	Y	Y	Boolean	`int`
SOL_SOCKET	SO_REUSEPORT	Reuse Address (multicasting)	N	-	-	Boolean	`int`
SOL_SOCKET	SO_SECURITY_ AUTHENTICATION	Security authentication	N	-	-	Integer	`int`
SOL_SOCKET	SO_SECURITY_ ENCRYPTION_ NETWORK	Security encryption network	N	-	-	Integer	`int`
SOL_SOCKET	SO_SECURITY_ ENCRYPTION_ TRANSPORT	Security encryption transport	N	-	-	Integer	`int`
SOL_SOCKET	SO_SNDBUF	Send buffer size	Y	Y	Y	Integer	`int`
SOL_SOCKET	SO_SNDLOWAT	Send low water mark	Y	Y	Y	Integer	`int`
SOL_SOCKET	SO_SNDTIMEO	Send Timeout	Y	Y	Y	Time	`struct timeval`
SOL_SOCKET	SO_TYPE	Socket Type	Y	Y	Y	Integer	`int`

A

DATA TABLES

TABLE A.5   IP-Level Socket Options

Level	Option	Description	*	R	W	Value	Type
SOL_IP	IP_ADD_MEMBERSHIP	Add multicast membership	Y	Y	Y	IPv4 Multicast Address	struct ip_mreq
SOL_IP	IP_DROP_MEMBERSHIP	Drop multicast membership	Y	Y	Y	IPv4 Multicast Address	struct ip_mreq
SOL_IP	IP_HDRINCL	Enable manual IP header creation	Y	Y	Y	Boolean	int
SOL_IP	IP_MTU_DISCOVER	MTU discover	Y	Y	Y	Integer	int
SOL_IP	IP_MULTICAST_IF	Outgoing multicast interface	Y	Y	Y	IPv4 Address	struct in_addr
SOL_IP	IP_MULTICAST_LOOP	Enable multicast loopback	Y	Y	Y	Boolean	int
SOL_IP	IP_MULTICAST_TTL	Multicast TTL	Y	Y	Y	Integer	int
SOL_IP	IP_OPTIONS	IP options	Y	Y	Y	Options	int[ ]
SOL_IP	IP_PKTINFO	Enable getting packet info	Y	Y	Y	Boolean	int
SOL_IP	IP_PKTOPTIONS	Packet options	N	-	-	Options	int[ ]
SOL_IP	IP_RECVERR	Enable receive error packets	Y	Y	Y	Boolean	int
SOL_IP	IP_RECVOPTS	Enable receive options	Y	Y	Y	Boolean	int
SOL_IP	IP_RECVTOS	Get received TOS	Y	Y	Y	Integer	int

TABLE A.5 Continued

Level	Option	Description	*	R	W	Value	Type
SOL_IP	IP_RECVTTL	Get received TTL	Y	Y	Y	Integer	int
SOL_IP	IP_RETOPTS	RETOPTS	Y	Y	Y	Boolean	int
SOL_IP	IP_ROUTER_ALERT	Enable router alerts	N	-	-	Boolean	int
SOL_IP	IP_TOS	Type of Service (TOS)	Y	Y	Y	Integer	int
SOL_IP	IP_TTL	Time to Live (TTL)	Y	Y	Y	Integer	int

TABLE A.6 IPv6-Level Socket Options

Level	Option	Description	*	R	W	Value	Type
SOL_IPV6	IPV6_ADD_MEMBERSHIP	Join multicast membership	?	?	?	IPv6 Multicast Address	struct ip_mreq6
SOL_IPV6	IPV6_ADDRFORM	Change address for socket	?	?	?	Integer	int
SOL_IPV6	IPV6_AUTHHDR	AUTHHDR	?	?	?	Integer	int
SOL_IPV6	IPV6_CHECKSUM	Offset of checksum for raw sockets	?	?	?	Integer	int
SOL_IPV6	IPV6_DROP_MEMBERSHIP	Drop multicast membership	?	?	?	IPv6 Multicast Address	struct ip_mreq6

TABLE A.6   Continued

Level	Option	Description	*	R	W	Value	Type
SOL_IPV6	IPV6_DSTOPTS	Enable getting destination options	?	?	?	Boolean	int
SOL_IPV6	IPV6_HOPLIMIT	Enable getting hop limit	?	?	?	Boolean	int
SOL_IPV6	IPV6_HOPOPTS	Enable getting hop-by-hop options	?	?	?	Boolean	int
SOL_IPV6	IPV6_MULTICAST_HOPS	Specify number of multicast hops	?	?	?	Integer	int
SOL_IPV6	IPV6_MULTICAST_IF	Specify outgoing multicast interface	?	?	?	IPv6 Address	struct in6_addr
SOL_IPV6	IPV6_MULTICAST_LOOP	Enable multicast loopback	?	?	?	Integer	int
SOL_IPV6	IPV6_NEXTHOP	Enable specifying next hop	?	?	?	Boolean	int
SOL_IPV6	IPV6_PKTINFO	Receive packet information	?	?	?	Integer	int
SOL_IPV6	IPV6_PKTOPTIONS	Specify packet options	?	?	?	Options	int []
SOL_IPV6	IPV6_ROUTER_ALERT	Enable router alerts	?	?	?	Boolean	int
SOL_IPV6	IPV6_RXSRCRT	Receive source route	?	?	?	Boolean	int
SOL_IPV6	IPV6_UNICAST_HOPS	Specify hop limit	?	?	?	Integer	int

TABLE A.7   TCP-Level Socket Options

Level	Option	Description	*	R	W	Value	Type
SOL_TCP	TCP_KEEPALIVE	Keep alive delay (replaced with sysctl call)	N	-	-	Integer	int
SOL_TCP	TCP_MAXRT	Maximum retransmit time	N	-	-	Integer	int
SOL_TCP	TCP_MAXSEG	Set max segment (transmission buffer) size	Y	Y	Y	Integer	int
SOL_TCP	TCP_NODELAY	Enable Nagle algorithm	Y	Y	Y	Boolean	int
SOL_TCP	TCP_STDURG	Specifies location of urgent byte (replaced with sysctl call)	N	-	-	Boolean	int
SOL_TCP	TCP_CORK	Never send partially complete segments	Y	Y	Y	Boolean	int
SOL_TCP	TCP_KEEPIDLE	Start keep-alives after this period	Y	Y	Y		int
SOL_TCP	TCP_KEEPINTVL	Interval between keep-alives	Y	Y	Y		int
SOL_TCP	TCP_KEEPCNT	Number of keep-alives before death	Y	Y	Y		int
SOL_TCP	TCP_SYNCNT	Number of SYN retransmits	Y	Y	Y		int
SOL_TCP	TCP_LINGER2	Lifetime of orphaned FIN-WAIT-2 state	Y	Y	Y		int
SOL_TCP	TCP_DEFER_ACCEPT	Wake up listener only when data arrive	Y	Y	Y		int
SOL_TCP	TCP_WINDOW_CLAMP	Bound advertised window	Y	Y	Y		int

A

DATA TABLES

Signal Definitions

Table A.8 lists the standard signals and their meanings.

TABLE A.8   Standard Linux Signal Codes

Signal	Value	Action	Comment
SIGHUP	1	A	Hangup detected on controlling terminal or death of controlling process
SIGINT	2	A	Interrupt from keyboard
SIGQUIT	3	A	Quit from keyboard
SIGILL	4	A	Illegal instruction
SIGABRT	6	C	Abort signal from abort(3)
SIGFPE	8	C	Floating point exception
SIGKILL	9	AEF	Kill signal
SIGSEGV	11	C	Invalid memory reference
SIGPIPE	13	A	Broken pipe: write to pipe with no readers
SIGALRM	14	A	Timer signal from alarm(2)
SIGTERM	15	A	Termination signal
SIGUSR1	30,10,16	A	User-defined signal 1
SIGUSR2	31,12,17	A	User-defined signal 2
SIGCHLD	20,17,18	B	Child stopped or terminated
SIGCONT	19,18,25		Continue if stopped
SIGSTOP	17,19,23	DEF	Stop process
SIGTSTP	18,20,24	D	Stop typed at tty
SIGTTIN	21,21,26	D	tty input for background process
SIGTTOU	22,22,27	D	tty output for background process
SIGIOT	6	CG	IOT trap; A synonym for SIGABRT
SIGEMT	7,-,7	G	
SIGBUS	10,7,10	AG	Bus error
SIGSYS	12,-,12	G	Bad argument to routine (SVID)
SIGSTKFLT	-,16,-	AG	Stack fault on coprocessor
SIGURG	16,23,21	BG	Urgent condition on socket (4.2 BSD)
SIGIO	23,29,22	AG	I/O now possible (4.2 BSD)
SIGPOLL		AG	A synonym for SIGIO (System V)

TABLE A.8　Continued

Signal	Value	Action	Comment
SIGCLD	-,-,18	G	A synonym for SIGCHLD
SIGXCPU	24,24,30	AG	CPU time limit exceeded (4.2 BSD)
SIGXFSZ	25,25,31	AG	File size limit exceeded (4.2 BSD)
SIGVTALRM	26,26,28	AG	Virtual alarm clock (4.2 BSD)
SIGPROF	27,27,29	AG	Profile alarm clock
SIGPWR	29,30,19	AG	Power failure (System V)
SIGINFO	29,-,-	G	A synonym for SIGPWR
SIGLOST	-,-,-	AG	File lock lost
SIGWINCH	28,28,20	BG	Window resize signal (4.3 BSD, Sun)
SIGUNUSED	-,31,-	AG	Unused signal

A—Default action is to terminate the process.
B—Default action is to ignore the signal.
C—Default action is to dump core.
D—Default action is to stop the process.
E—Signal cannot be caught.
F—Signal cannot be ignored.
G—Not a POSIX.1-conformant signal.

ICMP Codes

Table A.9 shows the different types of ICMP [RFC792] packets and what they mean.

TABLE A.9　ICMP Code Descriptions

Type	Code	Description
0	0	Echo reply
3		Destination unreachable
	0	Network unreachable
	1	Host unreachable
	2	Protocol unreachable
	3	Port unreachable
	4	Fragmentation needed but DF bit set
	5	Source route failed
	6	Destination network unknown

A

DATA TABLES

TABLE A.9   Continued

Type	Code	Description
	7	Destination host unknown
	8	Source host isolated (obsolete)
	9	Destination network administratively prohibited
	10	Destination host administratively prohibited
	11	Network unreachable to TOS
	12	Host unreachable for TOS
	13	Communication administratively prohibited
	14	Host precedence violation
	15	Precedence cutoff in effect
4	0	Source quench—gateway requesting the host to reduce transfer rate
5		Redirect
	0	Redirect for network
	1	Redirect for host
	2	Redirect for type-of-service and network
	3	Redirect for type-of-service and host
8	0	Echo request
9	0	Router advertisement
10	0	Router solicitation
11		Time exceeded
	0	TTL equals 0 during transit
	1	TTL equals 0 during fragment reassembly
12		Parameter problem
	0	IP header bad
	1	Required option missing
13	0	Timestamp request
14	0	Timestamp reply
15	0	Information request
16	0	Information reply
17	0	Address mask request
18	0	Address mask reply

IPv4 Multicast Allocation

Table A.10 defines the current multicast address allocation [RFC2365] in spectrum order.

TABLE A.10   Proposed Multicast Allocation

Address Range	Scope	Typical TTL
224.0.0.0–224.0.0.255	Cluster	0
224.0.1.0–238.255.255.255	Global	<= 255
239.0.0.0–239.191.255.255	(undefined)	
239.192.0.0–239.195.255.255	Organization	< 128
239.196.0.0–239.254.255.255	(undefined)	
239.255.0.0–239.255.255.255	Site	< 32

Proposed IPv6 Address Allocation

Table A.11 lists the proposed IPv6 address allocation in bits.

TABLE A.11   Proposed IPv6 Address Allocation

Allocation	Address Prefix
(reserved)	0000 0000
(unassigned)	0000 0001
NSAP	0000 001
IPX	0000 010
(unassigned)	0000 011
(unassigned)	0000 1
(unassigned)	0001
Aggregate global unicast addresses	001
(unassigned)	010
(unassigned)	011
(unassigned)	100
(unassigned)	101
(unassigned)	110
(unassigned)	1110
(unassigned)	1111 0

TABLE A.11   Continued

Allocation	Address Prefix
(unassigned)	1111 10
(unassigned)	1111 110
(unassigned)	1111 1110 0
Link-local unicast address	1111 1110 10
Site-local unicast address	1111 1110 11
Multicast address	1111 1111

ICMPv6 Codes

Table A.12 shows the new ICMPv6 [RFC2463] for IPv6.

TABLE A.12   ICMPv6 Code Descriptions

Type	Code	Description
1		Destination unreachable
	0	No route to destination
	1	Administratively prohibited (firewall filter)
	2	Not a neighbor (incorrect strict source route)
	3	Address unreachable (general)
	4	Port unreachable
2	0	Packet too big
3		Time exceeded
	0	Hop limit exceeded during transit
	1	Fragment reassembly time exceeded
4		Parameter problem
	0	Erroneous header field
	1	Unrecognized next header
	2	Unrecognized option
128	0	Echo request (ping)
129	0	Echo reply (ping)
130	0	Group membership query
131	0	Group membership report

TABLE A.12   Continued

Type	Code	Description
132	0	Group membership reduction
133	0	Router solicitation
134	0	Router advertisement
135	0	Neighbor solicitation
136	0	Neighbor advertisement
137	0	Redirect

IPv6 Multicast Scope Field

Table A.13 defines the different values for the scope field in the multicast IPv6 addresses.

TABLE A.13   IPv6 Multicast Scope Field Descriptions

Scope	Range	Description
0	(undefined)	
1	Node	Local on the same host (like 127.0.0.1).
2	Link	Messages stay within the router's group. The routers never let these messages pass through.
3–4	(undefined)	
5	Site	As defined by the network administrators, the messages stay within the site's locality.
6–7	(undefined)	
8	Organization	As defined by the network administrators, the messages stay within the organization's locality.
9–13	(reserved)	
14	Global	All routers permit messages to pass through the global network until they expire.
15	(reserved)	

IPv6 Multicast Flags Field

Table A.14 shows the currently defined flag fields for IPv6 multicast addresses.

TABLE A.14   IPv6 Multicast Flags Field Descriptions

Bit #	Description
0	Transience
	0= well known address
	1= transient address
1	(reserved)
2	(reserved)
3	(reserved)

Networking API

IN THIS APPENDIX

This appendix groups all the networking library and system calls.

Connecting to the Network

The Sockets API provides tools to help you create sockets and connect to other hosts. This section describes the API relevant to socket creation and connection.

socket()

socket() creates a bidirectional channel that typically connects with the network. You can use this channel with network-specific system calls or general file I/O.

Prototype

```
#include <resolv.h>
#include <sys/socket.h>
#include <sys/types.h>int socket(int domain, int type, int protocol);
```

Return Value

If successful, the call returns a valid socket descriptor. Otherwise, the result is less than zero. Check errno for more information about the error.

Parameters

domain	Selects the network protocol for socket (see Appendix A, "Data Tables").
type	Selects the network layer (see Appendix A).
protocol	Usually zero (see Appendix A).

Possible Errors

EPROTONOSUPPORT	The protocol type or the specified protocol is not supported within this domain.
ENFILE	Not enough kernel memory to allocate a new socket structure.
EMFILE	Process file table overflow.
EACCES and ENOBUFS	Permission to create a socket of the specified type or protocol is denied.
ENOMEM	Insufficient memory is available. The socket cannot be created until sufficient resources are freed.
EINVAL	Unknown protocol or protocol family not available.

Examples

```
/*** Create a TCP socket ***/
int sd;
sd = socket(PF_INET, SOCK_STREAM, 0);
```

```
/*** Create an ICMP socket **/
int sd;
sd = socket(PF_INET, SOCK_RAW, htons(IPPROTO_ICMP));
```

bind()

bind() defines a port or name to a socket. If you want a consistent port for an incoming connection, you have to bind your socket to a port. In most instances, the kernel automatically calls bind() for the socket if you do not call it explicitly. The kernel-generated port assignment can be different from execution to execution.

Prototype

```
#include <sys/socket.h>
#include <resolv.h>
int bind(int sockfd, struct sockaddr* addr,
    int addrlen);
```

Return Value

Zero if everything goes well. If an error occurs, you can find the cause in errno.

Parameters

sockfd	The socket descriptor to bind.
Addr	The port assignment or name.
Addrlen	The length of addr because addr can be different sizes.

Possible Errors

EBADF	sockfd is not a valid descriptor.
EINVAL	The socket is already bound to an address. This may change in the future; see .../linux/unix/socket.c for details.
EACCES	The address is protected, and the user is not the superuser.
ENOTSOCK	Argument is a descriptor for a file, not a socket.

Example

```
/*** Bind port #9999 to socket from any Internet Address ***/
int sockfd;
struct sockaddr_in addr;
sockfd = socket(PF_INET, SOCKET_STREAM, 0);
bzero(&addr, sizeof(addr));
addr.sin_family = AF_INET;
addr.sin_port = htons(9999);  /* or whatever port you want */
/* to bind any network interface */
addr.sin_addr.s_addr = INADDR_ANY;
/* -or- to bind a specific interface, use this: */
/* inet_aton("128.1.1.1", &addr.sin_addr); */
if ( bind(sockfd, &addr, sizeof(addr)) != 0 )
    perror("bind");
```

listen()

listen() converts the socket into a listening socket. This option is available only to SOCK_STREAM protocols. The call creates a queue of incoming connections.

Prototype

```
#include <sys/socket.h>
#include <resolv.h>
int listen(int sockfd, int queue_len);
```

Return Value

Zero if everything goes well. If an error occurs, you can find the cause in errno.

Parameters

sockfd	A SOCK_STREAM socket that has been bound to a port
queue_len	The maximum number of pending connections

Possible Errors

EBADF	The argument sockfd is not a valid descriptor.
ENOTSOCK	The argument sockfd is not a socket.
EOPNOTSUPP	The socket is not of a type that supports the listen() operation. If you supply any socket that is not SOCK_STREAM, you get this error.

Example

```
/*** Convert a socket to a listening socket with 10 slots ***/
int sockfd;
sockfd = socket(PF_INET, SOCK_STREAM, 0);
/*---set up address with bind()---*/
listen(sockfd, 10);  /* create a 10-pending queue */
```

accept()

Wait for a connection. When a connection arrives, return a new socket descriptor (independent of sockfd) for that specific connection. This call is available only to SOCK_STREAM sockets.

Prototype

```
#include <sys/socket.h>
#include <resolv.h>
int accept(int sockfd, struct sockaddr *addr, int *addr_len);
```

Return value

If >= 0	A new socket descriptor.
If < 0	Error; errno has details.

Parameters

sockfd	The bound and listening socket descriptor.
addr	If nonzero, the call places the address definition in this region. While it should match the sockfd's family (AF_INET), do not assume it.
addr_len	You pass the length by reference so that the call can tell you exactly how much of addr's data block it used. This means that you need to reset the value for each call.

Possible Errors

EBADF	The socket descriptor is invalid.
ENOTSOCK	The descriptor references a file, not a socket.
EOPNOTSUPP	The referenced socket is not of type SOCK_STREAM.
EFAULT	The *addr* parameter is not in a writeable part of the user address space.
EAGAIN	The socket is marked non-blocking and no connections are present to be accepted.
EPERM	Firewall rules forbid connection.
ENOBUFS, ENOMEM	Not enough free memory.

Examples

```
/*** Accept a connection, ignoring the origin ***/
int sockfd = socket(PF_INET, SOCK_STREAM, 0);
/*---bind address to socket with bind()---*/
/*---convert it to a listening socket with listen()---*/
for (;;)
{   int client;
    client = accept(sockfd, 0, 0);
    /*---interact with client---*/
    close(client);
}

/*** Accept a connection, capturing the origin in a log ***/
int sockfd = socket(PF_INET, SOCK_STREAM, 0);
/*---bind address to socket with bind()---*/
/*---convert it to a listening socket with listen()---*/
for (;;)
{   struct sockaddr_in addr;
    int client, addr_len = addr;
    client = accept(sockfd, &addr, &addr_len);
    printf("Connected: %s:%d\n", inet_ntoa(addr.sin_addr),
        ntohs(addr.sin_port));
    /*---interact with client---*/
    close(client);
}
```

connect()

Connect to a peer or server. You can use this function for either SOCK_DGRAM or SOCK_STREAM protocols. For UDP, it merely remembers the port to which you connected. This allows you to use send() and recv(). For TCP (SOCK_STREAM), this call starts the three-way handshake for stream communications.

Prototype

```
#include <sys/socket.h>
#include <resolv.h>
int connect(int sockfd, struct sockaddr *addr, int addr_len);
```

Return Value

Zero (0) if everything goes well. If an error occurs, you can find the cause in errno.

Parameters

sockfd	The freshly created socket. You could optionally call bind() before this to assign the local port. If you do not, the kernel assigns the next available port slot.
addr	The address and port of the destination address.
addr_len	The length of addr data block.

Possible Errors

EBADF	Bad descriptor.
EFAULT	The socket structure address is outside the user's address space. This is caused by a bad addr structure reference.
ENOTSOCK	The descriptor is not associated with a socket.
EISCONN	The socket is already connected. You cannot reconnect a connected socket. Instead, you have to close the socket and create a new one.
ECONNREFUSED	Connection refused at server.
ETIMEDOUT	Timeout while attempting connection.
ENETUNREACH	Network is unreachable.
EADDRINUSE	Address is already in use.
EINPROGRESS	The socket is non-blocking, and the connection cannot be completed immediately. It is possible to select() or poll() for completion by selecting the socket for writing. After select() indicates writeability, use getsockopt() to read the SO_ERROR option at level SOL_SOCKET to determine whether the connection was successful (SO_ERROR is zero) or unsuccessful (SO_ERROR is one of the usual error codes previously listed, explaining the reason for the failure).

EALREADY	The socket is non-blocking, and a previous connection attempt has not yet been completed.
EAFNOSUPPORT	The passed address didn't have the correct address family in its sa_family field.
EACCES	The user tried to connect to a broadcast address without having the socket broadcast flag enabled.

Example

```
/*** Connect to a TCP server ***/
int sockfd;
struct sockaddr_in addr;
sockfd = socket(PF_INET, SOCK_STREAM, 0);
bzero(&addr, sizeof(addr));
addr.sin_family = AF_INET;
addr.sin_port = 13; /* current time */
inet_atoi("127.0.0.1", &addr.sin_addr);
if ( connect(sockfd, &addr, sizeof(addr)) != 0 )
    perror("connect");
```

socketpair()

Creates a pair of sockets that are linked together like a pipe but uses the socket subsystem. It is nearly identical to a pipe() system call but gives you the added functionality of the Socket API. socketpair() supports PF_UNIX or PF_LOCAL sockets only. You do not need to bind() this socket to a file system filename.

Prototype

```
#include <sys/socket.h>
#include <resolv.h>
int socketpair(int domain, int type, int protocol,
    int sockfds[2]);
```

Return Value

Zero (0) if everything goes well. If an error occurs, you can find the cause in errno.

Parameters

domain	Must be PF_LOCAL or PF_UNIX.
type	SOCK_STREAM; This creates a socket like a pipe(). On some UNIX systems the pipe is bidirectional. Posix 1, however, does not require bidirectionality.
protocol	Must be zero (0).
sockfds[2]	An array of integers into which the call stores the new socket descriptors if successful.

Possible Errors

EMFILE	Too many descriptors are in use by this process.
EAFNOSUPPORT	The specified address family is not supported on this machine.
EPROTONOSUPPORT	The specified protocol is not supported on this machine.
EOPNOSUPPORT	The specified protocol does not support creation of socket pairs.
EFAULT	The address sockfds does not specify a valid part of the process address space.

Example

```
/*** Create a socket pair ***/
int sockfd[2];
struct sockaddr_ux addr;
if ( socketpair(PF_LOCAL, SOCK_STREAM, 0, sockfd) != 0 )
    perror("socketpair");
```

Communicating on a Channel

After establishing the socket and connection, you can use the API for sending and receiving messages. This section defines the calling API for all socket I/O.

send()

Send a message to the connected peer, client, or server. This call is like the write() system call, but send() permits you to define additional options for channel control.

Prototype

```
#include <sys/socket.h>
#include <resolv.h>
int send(int sockfd, void *buffer, int msg_len,
    int options);
```

Return Value

Like write(), the call returns the number of bytes written. The byte count can be less that msg_len. If the call does not succeed in writing all required bytes, you can use a loop for successive writes. If negative, the call stores the error detail in errno.

Parameters

sockfd	The socket channel. This can be a connected SOCK_DGRAM or SOCK_STREAM socket.
buffer	The data to send.

msg_len	The number of bytes to send.
options	A set of flags to enable special message handling:

- MSG_OOB   Send message out-of-band (urgent).
- MSG_DONTROUTE   Send the message bypassing all routers. If unsuccessful, the network sends an error back.
- MSG_DONTWAIT   Don't allow blocking. Similar to the fcntl() option call, but only applies to this call. If the call would block, the call returns with EWOULDBLOCK in errno.
- MSG_NOSIGNAL   If the peer severs the connection, don't raise a SIGPIPE signal locally.

Possible Errors

EBADF	An invalid descriptor was specified.
ENOTSOCK	The argument sockfd is not a socket.
EFAULT	An invalid user space address was specified for buffer.
EMSGSIZE	The call can't complete because the socket requires that the message be sent atomically, and the size of the message to be sent has made this impossible.
EAGAIN	The socket is marked non-blocking and the requested operation would block.
ENOBUFS	The system was unable to allocate an internal memory block. The operation may succeed when buffers become available.
EINTR	A signal occurred.
ENOMEM	No memory available.
EINVAL	Invalid argument passed.
EPIPE	The local end has been shut down on a connected socket. In this case, the process will also receive a SIGPIPE unless MSG_NOSIGNAL is set.

Example

```
/*** Send a message (TCP, UDP) to a connected destination ***/
int sockfd;
int bytes, bytes_wrote=0;
/*--- Create socket, connect to server/peer ---*/
while ( (bytes = send(sockfd, buffer, msg_len, 0)) > 0 )
    if ( (bytes_wrote += bytes) >= msg_len )
        break;
if ( bytes < 0 )
    perror("send");
```

```
/*** Send an URGENT message (TCP) to a connected destination ***/
int sockfd;
int bytes, bytes_wrote=0;
/*--- Create socket, connect to server ---*/
if ( send(sockfd, buffer, 1, MSG_OOB) != 1 )
    perror("Urgent message");
```

sendto()
Send a message to a specific destination without connecting. Typically, you use this system call for UDP and raw sockets. Using this call for TCP sockets is Transaction TCP (T/TCP). (Linux, however, does not yet support T/TCP.)

Prototype
```
#include <sys/socket.h>
#include <resolv.h>
int sendto(int sockfd, void* msg, int len, int options,
    struct sockaddr *addr, int addr_len);
```

Return Value
Returns the number of bytes sent or –1 if an error occurred.

Parameters
sockfd	The socket descriptor
msg	The data to send
len	The number of bytes to send
options	Message-controlling flags (same as send())
addr	The address of the destination
addr_len	The size of the destination data body

Possible Errors
(Same as send())

Example
```
/*** Send a message (TCP, UDP) to an UNconnected destination ***/
int sockfd;
struct sockaddr_in addr;
if ( (sd = socket(PF_INET, SOCK_DGRAM, 0)) < 0 )
    perror("socket");
bzero(&addr, sizeof(addr));
addr.sin_family = AF_INET;
addr.sin_port = htons(DEST_PORT);
inet_aton(DEST_ADDR, &addr.sin_addr);
if ( send(sockfd, buffer, msg_len, 0, &addr, sizeof(addr)) < 0 )
    perror("sendto");
```

sendmsg()

Assemble a message from several blocks of data. This routine takes the data the `iovec` structure and creates a single message. If the `msg_name` points to a real `sockaddr`, the routine sends the message connectionless. If `NULL`, the routine assumes that the socket is connected.

Prototype

```
#include <sys/socket.h>
#include <resolv.h>
#include <sys/uio.h>
int sendmsg(int sockfd, const struct msghdr *msg,
    unsigned int options);
```

Return Value

This call returns the total number of bytes sent or –1 if error (check `errno` for more information).

Parameters

sockfd	The open socket descriptor.
msg	This is a reference to a `msghdr` structure that holds destination, flags, and messages. The structure definitions are as follows:

```
struct iovec
{
    void *iov_base;          /* Buffer start */
    __kernel_size_t iov_len; /* Buffer length */
};

struct msghdr
{
    __ptr_t msg_name;         /* Dest address */
    socklen_t msg_namelen;    /* Address length */
    struct iovec *msg_iov;    /* Buffers vector */
    size_t msg_iovlen;        /* Vector length */
    __ptr_t msg_control;      /* Ancillary data */
    size_t msg_controllen;    /* Ancillary data len */
    int msg_flags;            /* Received msg flags */
};
```

The ancillary data allows the program to transfer special data like file descriptors.

options	Message-controlling flags (same as `send()`).

Possible Errors

(Same as `send()`)

Example
```
int i, sd, len, bytes;
char buffer[MSGS][100];
struct iovec io[MSGS];
struct msghdr msg;
struct sockaddr_in addr;

sd = socket(PF_INET, SOCK_DGRAM, 0);
bzero(&addr, sizeof(addr));
addr.sin_family = AF_INET;
addr.sin_port = htons(8080);
inet_aton(&addr.sin_addr, "127.0.0.1");
bzero(&msg, sizeof(msf));
msg.msg_name = &addr;
msg.msg_namelen = sizeof(addr);
for ( i = 0; i < MSGS; i++ )
{
    io[i].iov_base = buffer[i];
    sprintf(buffer[i], "Buffer #%d: this is a test\n", i);
    io[i].iov_len = strlen(buffer[i]);
}
msg.msg_iov = io;
msg.msg_iovlen = MSGS;
if ( (bytes = sendmsg(sd, &msg, 0)) < 0 )
    perror("sendmsg");
```

sendfile()
A fast way to transmit a file through a socket. The call reads the data from in_fd and writes it out to out_fd. The call does not change the file pointer in in_fd, but out_fd's file pointer is changed. The call begins reading from *offset for count bytes. When done, *offset points to the byte after the last byte read. If you need to add header information, refer to the TCP_CORK option in TCP(4) to improve performance.

Prototype
```
#include <unistd>
int sendfile(int out_fd, int in_fd, off_t *offset,
    size_t count);
```

Return Value
If successful, the call returns the total number of bytes copied. If error, the call returns –1 and sets errno to the error code.

Parameters

out_fd	The destination descriptor (file pointer modified)
in_fd	The source descriptor (file pointer not modified)
offset	A pointer to a variable that holds the starting offset
count	The number of bytes to send

Possible Errors

EBADF	Input file was not opened for reading or output file was not opened for writing.
EINVAL	Descriptor is not valid or locked.
ENOMEM	Insufficient memory for reading from in_fd.
EIO	Unspecified error while reading from in_fd.

Example

```
#include <unistd.h>
...
struct stat fdstat;
int client = accept(sd, 0, 0);
int fd = open("filename.gif", O_RDONLY);
fstat(fd, &fdstat);
sendfile(client, fd, 0, fdstat.st_size);
close(fd);
close(client);
```

recv()

Wait for and accept a message from a connected peer, client, or server. The system call behaves similarly to read() but adds control flags. UDP can use this call if connected to a peer.

Prototype

```
#include <sys/socket.h>
#include <resolv.h>
int recv(int sockfd, void* buf, int maxbuf,
    int options);
```

Return Value

The number of bytes read or –1 if an error occurred.

Parameters

sockfd	The open socket descriptor
buf	The byte array to accept the incoming message

maxbuf	The size of the array
options	A set of flags that can be arithmetically ORed together:

- MSG_OOB   This flag requests receipt of out-of-band data that would not be received in the normal data stream. Some protocols place expedited data at the head of the normal data queue, and so this flag cannot be used with such protocols.

- MSG_PEEK   This flag causes the receive operation to return data from the beginning of the receive queue without removing that data from the queue. Thus, a subsequent receive call will return the same data.

- MSG_WAITALL   This flag requests that the operation block until the full request is satisfied. However, the call may still return less data than requested if a signal is caught, an error or disconnect occurs, or the next data to be received is of a different type than that returned.

- MSG_ERRQUEUE   Receive packet from the error queue.

- MSG_NOSIGNAL   This flag turns off raising of SIGPIPE on stream sockets when the other end disappears.

- MSG_ERRQUEUE   This flag specifies that queued errors should be received from the socket error queue. The error is passed in an ancillary message with a type dependent on the protocol (for IP, IP_RECVERR). The error is supplied in a sock_extended_error structure.

Possible Errors

EBADF	The argument s is an invalid descriptor.
ENOTCONN	The socket is associated with a connection-oriented protocol and has not been connected (see connect() and accept()).
ENOTSOCK	The argument sockfd does not refer to a socket.
EAGAIN	The socket is marked as non-blocking, and the receive operation would block, or a receive timeout had been set and the timeout expired before data was received.
EINTR	A signal interrupted the receive operation before any data was available.
EFAULT	The receive buffer pointer points outside the process's address space.
EINVAL	An invalid argument was passed.

Example

```
/*** Recv a message (TCP, UDP) from a connected destination ***/
int sockfd;
int bytes, bytes_wrote=0;
/*--- Create socket, connect to server/peer ---*/
if ( (bytes = recv(sockfd, buffer, msg_len, 0)) < 0 )
    perror("send");

/*** Recv an URGENT message (TCP) from a connected destination ***/
/*** This code is typically in a SIGURG signal handler ***/
int sockfd;
int bytes, bytes_wrote=0;
/*--- Create socket, connect to server ---*/
if ( (bytes = recv(sockfd, buffer, msg_len, 0)) < 0 )
    perror("Urgent message");
```

recvfrom()

Wait for and receive a message from an unconnected peer (UDP and raw sockets). Please note that T/TCP never uses this call. Instead, the receiver uses accept().

Prototype

```
#include <sys/socket.h>
#include <resolv.h>
int recvfrom(int sockfd, void *buf, int buf_len, int options,
    struct sockaddr *addr, int *addr_len);
```

Return Value

If successful, the number of bytes read. If an error occurred, the return value is -1, and errno holds the error code.

Parameters

sockfd	The open socket descriptor.
buf	The byte array to receive the data.
buf_len	The maximum size of the buffer (message truncated and dropped if buffer too small).
options	Channel controlling options (same as recv()).
addr	The sending peer's address and port.
addr_len	The maximum size of addr (address truncated if too small). Upon return, this value changes to match the number of bytes used.

Possible Errors

(Same as recv())

Example
```
struct sockaddr_in addr;
int addr_len=sizeof(addr), bytes_read;
char buf[1024];
int sockfd = socket(PF_INET, SOCK_DGRAM, 0);
/***Bind socket to specific port***/
bytes_read = recvfrom(sockfd, buf, sizeof(buf), 0, &addr, &add_len);
if ( bytes_read < 0 )
    perror("recvfrom failed");
```

recvmsg()

Receive several messages at once from the same source. This call is customarily used with SOCK_DGRAM sockets (same reasoning as sendmsg()). The operation does not have the flexibility to accept from different sources.

Prototype
```
#include <sys/socket.h>
#include <resolv.h>
#include <sys/uio.h>
int recvmsg(int sockfd, struct msghdr *msg,
    unsigned int options);
```

Return Value

Total number of bytes received if no error occurred; otherwise, returns -1.

Parameters

sockfd	The socket descriptor waiting for a message
msg	The data received
options	Channel controlling options (same as recv())

Possible Errors

(Same as recv())

Example
```
char buffer[MSGS][1000];
struct sockaddr_in addr;
struct iovec io[MSGS];
struct msghdr msg;
...
bzero(&addr, sizeof(addr));
msg.msg_name = &addr;
msg.msg_namelen = sizeof(addr);
for ( i = 0; i < MSGS; i++ )
{
```

```
        io[i].iov_base = buffer[i];
        io[i].iov_len = sizeof(buffer[i]);
}
msg.msg_iov = io;
msg.msg_iovlen = MSGS;
if ( (bytes = recvmsg(sd, &msg, 0)) < 0 )
    perror("recvmsg");
```

Terminating Connections

The last step a solid program performs after communicating with the external host is to close the connection. This section describes the API for socket termination.

shutdown()

Closes specific paths or directions of data flow. Socket connections, by default, are bidirectional. If you want to limit the flow to be read-only or write-only, shutdown closes the other half of the channel.

Prototype

```
#include <sys/socket.h>
int shutdown(int sockfd, int how);
```

Return Value

Zero if everything goes well. If an error occurs, you can find the cause in errno.

Parameters

sockfd	The open socket descriptor.
how	A flag indicating which half (or both) of channel to close:
	SHUT_RD (0)—Make the channel output only.
	SHUT_WR (1)—Make the channel input only.
	SHUT_RDWR (2)—Close both halves, functionally same as close().
	This operates only on connected sockets.

Possible Errors

EBADF	sockfd is not a valid descriptor.
ENOTSOCK	sockfd is a file, not a socket.
ENOTCONN	The specified socket is not connected.

Example

```
int sockfd;
struct sockaddr_in addr;
```

```
sockfd = socket(PF_INET, SOCK_STREAM, 0);
bzero(&addr, sizeof(addr));
addr.sin_family = AF_INET;
addr.sin_port = htons(DEST_PORT);
inet_aton(DEST_ADDR, &addr.sin_addr);
connect(sockfd, &addr, sizeof(addr));
if ( shutdown(sockfd, SHUT_WR) != 0 )
    PANIC("Can't make socket input-only");
```

Network Data Conversions

While working with data on the network, you must consider the data byte-ordering, converting addresses, and so on. The Socket API includes a sizeable list of tools to help you get the information you need. This section describes the tools that the book has used (and a few others).

htons() or htonl()

Convert host-byte order binary data to network-byte order. On a little-endian processor, the call swaps the bytes around. A big-endian host does nothing but return the value.

Prototype

```
#include <netinet/in.h>
unsigned short int htons(unsigned short int host_short);
unsigned long int htonl(unsigned long int host_lonf);
```

Return Value

(none)

Parameters

host_short	The 16-bit host value
host_long	The 32-bit host value

Possible Errors

(none)

Example

```
/*** Assign #1023 to socket ***/
struct sockaddr_in addr;
addr.sin_port = htons(1023);

/*** Assign 128.1.32.10 to the destination address ***/
struct sockaddr_in addr;
addr.sin_addr.s_addr = hton(0x8001200A);
```

ntohs() or ntohl()

Converts the network byte order to the host's byte order.

Prototype
```
#include <netinet/in.h>
unsigned short int ntohs(unsigned short int network_short);
unsigned long int ntohl(unsigned long int network_lonf);
```

Return Value
The converted value (16 bits or 32 bits).

Parameters

network_short	The 16-bit value to convert
network_long	The 32-bit value to convert

Possible Errors
(none)

Example
```
struct sockaddr_in addr;
int client, addrlen=sizeof(addr);
client = accept(sockfd, &addr, &addrlen);
if ( client > 0 )
    printf("Connected %lX:%d\n", ntohl(addr.sin_addr),
        ntohs(addr.sin_port));
```

inet_addr()
A deprecated conversion tool for converting numeric, dot-notation addresses into the network-byte-order binary form. If it fails, the return value (-1 or 255.255.255.255) is still a legal address. The inet_aton() tool has better error handling.

Prototype
```
#include <netinet/in.h>
unsigned long int inet_addr(const char *ip_address);
```

Return Value

Non-zero	If everything goes well, the value is the converted IP address.
INADDR_NONE(-1)	The parameter is not valid. (This is the call's defect—there is no negative value, and 255.255.255.255 is the general broadcast address.)

Parameters

ip_address	The human-readable, dot-notation form (for example, 128.187.34.2)

Possible Errors
(errno not set)

Example
```
if ( (addr.sin_addr.s_addr = inet_addr("128.187.34.2")) == -1 )
    perror("Couldn't convert address");
```

inet_aton()
Converts a human-readable IP address from the dot-notation to the binary, network-byte ordered form. This call replaces inet_addr().

Prototype
```
#include <netinet/in.h>
int inet_aton(const char* ip_addr, struct in_addr *addr);
```

Return Value
Non-zero if everything goes well. If an error occurs, the call returns a zero.

Parameters

ip_addr	The ASCII string of the IP address (for example, 187.34.2.1).
addr	The destination. Typically, you would populate the sin_addr field from the sockaddr_in structure.

Possible Errors
(errno not set)

Example
```
Struct sockaddr_in addr;
if ( inet_aton("187.43.32.1", &addr.sin_addr) == 0 )
    perror("inet_aton() failed");
```

inet_ntoa()
This call converts the network-byte order binary to a human-readable form. Note that this call uses a static memory region; subsequent calls overwrite the older results.

Prototype
```
#include <netinet/in.h>
const char* inet_ntoa(struct in_addr *addr);
```

Return Value
The address is in the returned string.

Parameters

addr	The binary address (typically the address field of struct sockaddr_in)

Possible Errors

(errno not set)

Example

```
Clientfd = accept(serverfd, &addr, &addr_size);
if ( clientfd > 0 )
    printf("Connected %s:%d\n",
        inet_ntoa(addr.sin_addr), ntohs(addr.sin_port));
```

inet_pton()

Converts a human-readable IPv4 or IPv6 address from the dot/colon-notation to the binary, network-byte ordered form.

Prototype

```
#include <netinet/in.h>
int inet_pton(int domain, const char* prsnt, void *addr);
```

Return Value

Non-zero if everything goes well. If an error occurs, the call returns zero.

Parameters

domain	The network type (AF_INET or AF_INET6).
prsnt	The ASCII string of the IP address (for example, 187.34.2.1 or FFFF::8090:A03:3245).
addr	The destination. Typically, you would populate the sin_addr field from the sockaddr_in structure or sin6_addr field from the sockaddr_in6 structure.

Possible Errors

(errno not set)

Example

```
struct sockaddr_in addr;
if ( inet_pton(AF_INET6, "187.43.32.1", &addr.sin6_addr) == 0 )
    perror("inet_pton() failed");
```

inet_ntop()

This call converts the network-byte order binary to a human-readable form. Unlike the inet_ntoa, you need to supply it a scratchpad string. This function supports both AF_INET and AF_INET6.

Prototype

```
#include <arpa/inet.h>
char* inet_ntop(int domain, struct in_addr *addr, char* str, int len);
```

Return value
The call returns the parameter `str`.

Parameters

domain	The network type (`AF_INET` or `AF_INET6`)
addr	The binary address (typically the address field of `struct sockaddr_in`)
str	The string buffer
len	The number of bytes available in `str`

Possible Errors
(errno not set)

Example
```
char str[100];
clientfd = accept(serverfd, &addr, &addr_size);
if ( clientfd > 0 )
    printf("Connected %s:%d\n",
        inet_ntop(AF_INET, addr.sin_addr, str, sizeof(str)),
        ntohs(addr.sin_port));
```

Network Addressing Tools

Like the data and addressing tools, the API gives you access to the naming services. These services include domain name services (DNS), the protocols, and so on. This section describes the calls for converting human-readable names.

getpeername()
This routine gets the bound address or name of connected peer at the other end of the `sockfd` channel. The call places the results in `buf`. The `buf_len` is the number of bytes available in `buf`. If too small, the information gets truncated. This is the same information you get with the `accept()` call.

Prototype
```
#include <sys/socket.h>
int getpeername(int sockfd, struct sockaddr *addr,
    socklen_t *addr_len);
```

Return Value
Zero if everything goes well. If an error occurs, you can find the cause in `errno`.

Parameters

sockfd	The connected socket channel.
addr	A buffer that holds the address structure.
addr_len	The number of bytes available in addr. This is passed by reference (the call changes this field).

Possible Errors

EBADF	The argument sockfd is not a valid descriptor.
ENOTSOCK	The argument sockfd is a file, not a socket.
ENOTCONN	The socket is not connected.
ENOBUFS	Insufficient resources were available in the system to perform the operation.
EFAULT	The addr parameter points to memory that is not in a valid part of the process address space.

Example

```
struct sockaddr_in addr;
int add_len = sizeof(addr);
if ( getpeername(client, &addr, &addr_len) != 0 )
    perror("getpeername() failed");
printf("Peer: %s:%d\n", inet_ntoa(addr.sin_addr),
    ntohs(addr.sin_port));
```

gethostname()

Gets the localhost's name. The call places the result in the name parameter up to len bytes.

Prototype

```
#include <unistd.h>
int gethostname(char *name, size_t len);
```

Return Value

Zero if everything goes well. If an error occurs, you can find the cause in errno.

Parameters

name	The buffer to accept the name of the localhost
len	The number of bytes available in name

Possible Errors

EINVAL	len is negative or, for gethostname() on Linux/i386, len is smaller than the actual size.
EFAULT	name is an invalid address.

Example
```
char name[50];
if ( getpeername(name, sizeof(name)) != 0 )
    perror("getpeername() failed");
printf("My host is: %s\n", name);
```

gethostbyname()
Search for and translate the hostname to an IP address. The name can be a hostname or an address. If it is an address, the call does no searches; instead, it returns the address in the h_name and h_addr_list[0] fields of the hostent structure.

If the hostname ends with a period, the call treats the name as an absolute name with no abbreviation. Otherwise, the call searches the local subnetwork names. If you have HOSTALIASES defined in your environment, the call searches the file to which HOSTALIASES points.

Prototype
```
#include <netdb.h>
struct hostent *gethostbyname(const char *name);
```

Return Value
The call returns a pointer struct hostent; if it fails, the return value is NULL. The structure lists all the names and addresses the host owns. The macro h_addr provides backward compatibility.

```
#define h_addr h_addr_list[0]
struct hostent {
    char *h_name;        /* official name of host */
    char **h_aliases;    /* alias list */
    int h_addrtype;      /* host address type */
    int h_length;        /* length of address */
    char **h_addr_list;  /* list of addresses; 0th is the primary */
};
```

Parameters
name   The hostname to search or the IP address

Possible Errors

ENOTFOUND	The specified host is unknown.
NO_ADDRESS, NO_DATA	The requested name is valid but does not have an IP address.
NO_RECOVERY	A non-recoverable name server error occurred.
EAGAIN	A temporary error occurred on an authoritative name server. Try again later.

Example
```
int i;
struct hostent *host;
host = gethostbyname("sunsite.unc.edu");
if ( host != NULL )
{
    printf("Official name: %s\n", host->h_name);
    for ( i = 0; host->h_aliases[i] != 0; i++ )
        printf("   alias[%d]: %s\n", i+1,
            host->h_aliases[i]);
    printf("Address type=%d\n", host->h_addrtype);
    for ( i = 0; i < host->h_length; i++ )
        printf("Addr[%d]: %s\n", i+1,
            inet_ntoa(host->h_addr_list[i]));
}
else
    perror("sunsite.unc.edu");
```

getprotobyname()
This function reads the /etc/protocol file to get the protocol that matches pname. You use this call to translate names such as HTTP, FTP, and Telnet into their default port numbers.

Prototype
```
#include <netdb.h>
struct protoent *getprotobyname(const char *pname);
```

Return Value
The call returns a pointer to protoent (defined later in this appendix) if successful. Otherwise, it returns NULL.

```
struct protoent {
    char    *p_name;        /* official protocol name */
    char    **p_aliases;    /* alias list */
    int     p_proto;        /* protocol number */
};
```

The field p_proto is the port number.

Parameters
pname   Protocol name. This can be any of the recognized protocol names or aliases.

Possible Errors
(errno not set)

Example

```
#include <netdb.h>
...
int i;
struct protoent *proto = getprotobyname("http");
if ( proto != NULL )
{
    printf("Official name: %s\n", proto->name);
    printf("Port#: %d\n", proto->p_proto);
    for ( i = 0; proto->p_aliases[i] != 0; i++ )
        printf("Alias[%d]: %s\n", i+1,
            proto->p_aliases[i]);
}
else
    perror("http");
```

Socket Controls

While the socket is open, you can configure it to behave in various ways. This section describes the API calls.

setsockopt()

Change the behavior of socket sd. Every option has a value (some options are read- or write-only). You can set each option through optval and optlen. For a complete list of options, see Appendix A.

Prototype

```
#include <sys/types.h>
#include <sys/socket.h>
int setsockopt(int sd, int level, int optname,
    const void *optval, socklen_t optlen);
```

Return Value

Zero if everything goes well. If an error occurs, you can find the cause in errno.

Parameters

sd	The socket to modify
level	The feature level (SOL_SOCKET, SOL_IP, SOL_TCP, SOL_IPV6)
optname	The option to revise
optval	A pointer to the new value
optlen	The length of value in bytes

Possible Errors

EBADF	The argument sd is not a valid descriptor.
ENOTSOCK	The argument sd is a file, not a socket.
ENOPROTOOPT	The option is unknown at the level indicated.
EFAULT	The address pointed to by optval is not in a valid part of the process address space.

Example

```
const int TTL=128;
/*---Change the time-to-live to 128 hops---*/
if ( setsockopt(sd, SOL_IP, SO_TTL, &TTL, sizeof(TTL)) != 0 )
    perror("setsockopt() failed");
```

getsockopt()

Get the socket configuration.

Prototype

```
#include <sys/types.h>
#include <sys/socket.h>
int getsockopt(int sd, int level, int optname, void *optval,
    socklen_t *optlen);
```

Return Value

Zero if everything goes well. If an error occurs, you can find the cause in errno.

Parameters

sd	The socket to read.
level	The feature level (SOL_SOCKET, SOL_IP, SOL_TCP, SOL_IPV6).
optname	The option to revise.
optval	Place for value.
optlen	The length of value in bytes. This field is passed by reference.

Possible Errors

EBADF	The argument sd is not a valid descriptor.
ENOTSOCK	The argument sd is a file, not a socket.
ENOPROTOOPT	The option is unknown at the level indicated.
EFAULT	The address pointed to by optval or optlen is not in a valid part of the process address space.

Example

```
int error, size=sizeof(error);
if ( getsockopt(sd, SOL_SOCKET, SO_ERROR, &error,
        &size) != 0 )
    perror("getsockopt() failed");
printf("socket error=%d\n", error);
```

Kernel API Subset

IN THIS APPENDIX

This appendix lists all the manual pages of the kernel library and system calls that are not directly related to sockets but are typically used in conjunction with sockets.

Tasks

Tasks include both processes and threads. Threads (pThreads) are defined in the next section; this section covers processes and low-level tasks (clones).

fork()

Create a new process (independent task) at this call. This call creates a child process to run with the parent. You must be careful that you capture the child and direct it to its assigned task; otherwise, the child runs each statement the parent does (they run together).

Prototype

```
#include <unistd.h>
pid_t fork(void);
```

Return Value

0	The task that gets this is the child.
>0	The task that gets this is the parent.
<0	The parent failed to create a new child; check errno.

Parameters

(none)

Possible Errors

EAGAIN	The fork() cannot allocate sufficient memory to copy the parent's page tables and allocate a task structure for the child.
ENOMEM	The fork() failed to allocate the necessary kernel structures because memory is tight.

Example

```
int PID;
if ( (PID = fork()) == 0 )
{ /*--- CHILD ---*/
    /**** Run the child's assignment ***/
    exit();
}
else if ( PID > 0 )
{ /*--- PARENT ---*/
    int status;
    /**** Do parent's work ****/
```

```
    wait(status); /* may be done in SIGCHLD signal handler */
}
else /*--- ERROR ---*/
    perror("fork() failed");
```

__clone()

This is a low-level system call for creating tasks. You can directly control what is shared between the parent and the child. This is not for amateur programmers; you can create very unpredictable programs. (See Chapter 7, "Dividing the Load: Multitasking," for a complete description of this call.)

Prototype
```
#include <sched.h>
int __clone(int (*fn)(void* arg), void* stacktop, int flags, void* arg);
```

Return Value

process ID   If negative, errno has the exact error code.

Parameters

fn

The home for the child task. Create a function (or procedure) that accepts a void* parameter argument. When the routine attempts to return, the operating system terminates the task for you.

stacktop

You must create a stack for the child task. This parameter points to the top of that stack (the highest address of the data block). Because you provide the stack, the stack is fixed in size and cannot grow like a normal task's stacks.

flags

Two types of information arithmetically ORed together; the VM spaces to share and the termination signal. This flag supports all signal types and, when the task terminates, the operating system raises the signal you define.

The available VM spaces are as follows:

- CLONE_VM   Share the data space between tasks. Use this flag to share all static data, preinitialized data, and the allocation heap. Otherwise, copy data space.

- CLONE_FS   Share the file system information: current working directory, root file system, and default file creation permissions. Otherwise, copy settings.

- CLONE_FILES   Share open files. When one task changes the file pointer, the other tasks see the change. Likewise, if the task closes the file, the other tasks are not able to access the file any longer. Otherwise, create new references to open inodes.

- CLONE_SIGHAND   Share signal tables. Individual tasks may choose to ignore open signals (using sigprocmask()) without affecting peers. Otherwise, copy tables.
- CLONE_PID   Share Process ID. Use this flag carefully; not all the existing tools support this feature. The PThreads library does not use this option. Otherwise, allocate new PID.

arg   You can pass a pointer reference to any data value using this parameter. When the operating system finishes creating the child task, it calls the routine fn with the arg parameter. If you use this feature, be sure to place the value arg points to in the shared data region (CLONE_VM).

Possible Errors

EAGAIN   The __clone() cannot allocate sufficient memory to copy the parent's page tables and allocate a task structure for the child.

ENOMEM   The __clone() failed to allocate the necessary kernel structures because memory is tight.

Example

```
#define STACKSIZE    1024

void Child(void* arg)
{
    /*---child's responsibility---*/
    exit(0);
}

...
int main(void)
{   int cchild;
    char *stack=malloc(STACKSIZE);

    if ( (cchild = __clone(&Child, stack+STACKSIZE-1,
        SIGCHLD,  0) == 0 )
```

exec()

Run an external program (either a binary or an executable script with #! <interpreter> [arg] in the first line). This call replaces the currently running task with the external program's context. The new program keeps the caller's PID and open files.

The calls execl(), execlp(), execle(), execv(), and execvp() are all front ends to execve().

Prototype

```
#include <unistd.h>
int execve(const char* path, char* const argv[], char* const envp[]);
int execl(const char* path, const char* arg, ...);
int execlp(const char* file, const char* arg, ...);
int execle(const char* path, const char* arg, ..., char* const envp[]);
int execv(const char* path, char* const argv[]);
int execvp(const char* file, char* const argv[]);
```

Return Value

This call does not return if successful. If it fails, the return value is -1.

Parameters

file	The program to execute. The call searches for the name in this variable using the defined PATH.
path	The absolute path and filename of the program to execute.
argv	The string array of command-line parameters. The first array element value must be arg0 (or the name of the program). The last array element is always zero (0).
arg	A command-line parameter. This is followed by an ellipsis (...) to indicate that there are several arguments. The first arg is always the name of the program, and the last arg is always zero (0).
envp	The string array of environment parameters. Each parameter is in the form <param>=<value> (for example, TERM=vt100). The last array element is always zero (0).

Possible Errors

EACCES	The file or a script interpreter is not a regular file, or execute permission is denied for the file or a script interpreter, or the file system is mounted noexec.
EPERM	The file system is mounted nosuid, the user is not the superuser, and the file has an SUID or SGID bit set.
EPERM	The process is being traced, the user is not the superuser, and the file has an SUID or SGID bit set.
E2BIG	The argument list is too big.
ENOEXEC	An executable is not in a recognized format, is for the wrong architecture, or has some other format error that means it cannot be executed.
EFAULT	The filename points outside your accessible address space.
ENAMETOOLONG	The filename is too long.

C

KERNEL API
SUBSET

ENOENT	The filename or a script or ELF interpreter does not exist.
ENOMEM	Insufficient kernel memory was available.
ENOTDIR	A component of the path prefix of filename, script, or ELF interpreter is not a directory.
EACCES	Search permission is denied on a component of the path prefix of filename or the name of a script interpreter.
ELOOP	Too many symbolic links were encountered in resolving filename, the name of a script, or ELF interpreter.
ETXTBUSY	Executable was open for writing by one or more processes.
EIO	An I/O error occurred.
ENFILE	The limit on the total number of files open on the system has been reached.
EMFILE	The process has the maximum number of files open.
EINVAL	An ELF executable had more than one PT_INTERP segment.
EISDIR	An ELF interpreter was a directory.
ELIBBAD	An ELF interpreter was not in a recognized format.

Example

```
execl("/bin/ls", "/bin/ls", "-al", "/home", "/boot", 0);
perror("execl() failed"); /* No IF needed here: if successful, no return */

char *args[]={"ls", "-al", "/home", "/boot", 0};
execvp(args[0], args);
perror("execvp() failed");
```

sched_yield()

Relinquish control of the CPU without blocking. This routine tells the scheduler that the currently running task wants to give up the remains of its current timeslice. The call returns on the next timeslice.

Prototype

```
#include <sched.h>
int sched_yield(void);
```

Return Value

Zero if all goes okay and control is transferred; otherwise, -1.

Parameters

(none)

Possible Errors

(none defined)

Example
```
#include <sched.h>
sched_yield();
```

wait(), waitPID()

Wait for and acknowledge the termination of a child process. This is important to keep zombie processes from lingering in the process table and to free up valuable resources. The `wait()` call waits for any process to terminate, and the `waitPID()` call permits you to specify a specific process or group. You can use the following macros to get the meaning from the status:

- `WIFEXITED(status)` is non-zero if the child exited normally.
- `WEXITSTATUS(status)` evaluates to the least significant eight bits of the return code of the child that terminated, which may have been set as the argument to a call to `exit()` or as the argument for a return statement in the main program. This macro can only be evaluated if `WIFEXITED` returned non-zero.
- `WIFSIGNALED(status)` returns `true` if the child process exited because of a signal that was not caught.
- `WTERMSIG(status)` returns the number of the signal that caused the child process to terminate. This macro can only be evaluated if `WIFSIGNALED` returned non-zero.
- `WIFSTOPPED(status)` returns `true` if the child process that caused the return is currently stopped; this is only possible if the call was done using `WUNTRACED`.
- `WSTOPSIG(status)` returns the number of the signal that caused the child to stop. This macro can only be evaluated if `WIFSTOPPED` returned non-zero.

Prototype
```
#include <sys/types.h>
#include <sys/wait.h>
PID_t wait(int *status);
PID_t waitpid(PID_t PID, int *status, int options);
```

Return Value
Both calls return the PID of the child that terminated.

Parameters

status   Returns the ending status of the child. If not zero or NULL, this parameter picks up the child's termination code and `exit()` value.

PID   Indicates which process to wait for:

                < -1 Wait for any child process whose process group ID is equal to the absolute value of PID.

== -1   Wait for any child process; this is the same behavior that
wait() exhibits.

== 0   Wait for any child process whose process group ID is
equal to that of the calling process.

> 0   Wait for the child whose process ID is equal to the value
of PID.

options   WNOHANG   Return immediately if no child has exited.

WUNTRACED   Return for children who are stopped and whose status has not been reported.

Possible Errors

ECHILD   If the process specified in PID does not exist or is not a child of the calling process. (This can happen for one's own child if the action for SIGCHLD is set to SIG_IGN.)

EINVAL   If the options argument was invalid.

EINTR   If WNOHANG was not set and an unblocked signal or a SIGCHLD was caught. Just try again.

Example

```
void sig_child(int signum) /* This handler only gets one waiting zombie */
{   int status;
    wait(&status);
    if ( WIFEXITED(status) )
        printf("Child exited with the value of %d\n", WEXITSTATUS(status));
    if ( WIFSIGNALED(status) )
        printf("Child aborted due to signal #%d\n", WTERMSIG(status));
    if ( WIFSTOPPED(status) )
        printf("Child stopped on signal #%d\n", WSTOPSIG(signal));
}

void sig_child(int signum)  /* This handler removes all waiting zombies */
{
    while ( waitpid(-1, 0, WNOHANG) > 0 );
}
```

Threads

Threads are another kind of task. This section defines a few library calls from the pThreads library.

pthread_create()

This call creates a lightweight kernel process (thread). The thread starts in the function that start_fn points to using arg as the function's parameter. When the function returns, the thread terminates. The function should return a `void*` value, but if it doesn't, the thread still terminates and the result is set to `NULL`.

Prototype
```
#include <pthread.h>
int pthread_create(pthread_t *tchild, pthread_attr_t *attr,
void (*start_fn)(void *), void *arg);
```

Return Value
This is a positive value if successful. If the thread-create call encountered any errors, the call returns a negative value and sets `errno` to the error.

Parameters

thread	The thread handle (passed by reference). If successful, the call places the thread handle in this parameter.
attr	The thread's starting attributes. See `pthread_attr_init` for more information.
start_fn	The routine in which the thread is to start. This function should return a `void*` value.
arg	The parameter passed to `start_fn`. You should make this parameter a nonshared (unless you plan on locking it), nonstack memory reference.

Possible Errors

EAGAIN	Not enough system resources to create a process for the new thread.
EAGAIN	More than `PTHREAD_THREADS_MAX` threads are already active.

Example
```
void* child(void *arg)
{
    /**** Do something! ****/
    pthread_exit(arg); /* terminate and return arg */
}

int main()
{   pthread_t tchild;

    if ( pthread_create(&tchild, 0, child, 0) < 0 )
        perror("Can't create thread!");
    /**** Do something! ****/
    if ( pthread_join(tchild, 0) != 0 )
        perror("Join failed");
}
```

pthread_join()

Similar to the wait() system call, this call waits for and accepts the return value of the child thread.

Prototype
```
#include <pthread.h>
int pthread_join(pthread_t tchild, void **retval);
```

Return Value
A positive value if successful. If the thread-create call encountered any errors, the call returns a negative value and sets errno to the error.

Parameters

thread	The thread handle to wait on
retval	The pointer to the value passed back (passed by reference)

Possible Errors

ESRCH	No thread could be found corresponding to that specified by tchild.
EINVAL	The tchild thread has been detached.
EINVAL	Another thread is already waiting on termination of tchild.
EDEADLK	The tchild argument refers to the calling thread.

Example
(see pthread_create())

pthread_exit()

Explicitly terminates the current thread, returning retval. You can use a simple return statement as well.

Prototype
```
#include <pthread.h>
void pthread_exit(void *retval);
```

Return Value
(none)

Parameter

retval	The void* value to return. Make sure that this value is non-stack memory.

Possible Errors

(none)

Example

(see pthread_create())

pthread_detach()

Detaches tchild thread from the parent. Normally, you need to join or wait for every process and thread. This call lets you create several threads and ignore them. This is the same as setting the thread's attribute upon creation.

Prototype
```
#include <pthread.h>
int pthread_detach(thread_t tchild);
```

Return Value

A zero if successful. If the thread-create call encountered any errors, the call returns a negative value and sets errno to the error.

Parameter

tchild   The child thread to detach

Possible Errors

ESRCH	No thread could be found corresponding to that specified by tchild.
EINVAL	The tchild thread has been detached.
EINVAL	Another thread is already waiting on termination of tchild.
EDEADLK	The tchild argument refers to the calling thread.

Example
```
void* child(void *arg)
{
    /**** Do something! ****/
    pthread_exit(arg); /* terminate and return arg */
}

int main()
{   pthread_t tchild;

    if ( pthread_create(&tchild, 0, child, 0) < 0 )
        perror("Can't create thread!");
    else
        pthread_detach(tchild);
    /**** Do something! ****/
}
```

Locking

The primary advantage of using threads is sharing data memory. Because the threads may try to revise the memory at the same time, you need to lock the memory for exclusive access. This section describes pThread calls that you can use (even with clones) to lock memory.

pthread_mutex_init(), pthread_mutex_destroy()

These calls create and destroy mutex semaphore variables. You may not need the initializer because the defined variables are easier and faster to use. The destroy call normally frees up any resources. However, the Linux implementation uses no allocated resources, so the call does nothing more than check whether the resource is unlocked.

Prototype

```
#include <pthread.h>

/*---Predefined mutex settings---*/
pthread_mutex_t fastmutex = PTHREAD_MUTEX_INITIALIZER;
pthread_mutex_t recmutex = PTHREAD_RECURSIVE_MUTEX_INITIALIZER_NP;
pthread_mutex_t errchkmutex = PTHREAD_ERRORCHECK_MUTEX_INITIALIZER_NP;

int pthread_mutex_init(pthread_mutex_t *mutex,
          const pthread_mutexattr_t *mutexattr);
int pthread_mutex_destroy(pthread_mutex_t *mutex);
```

Return Value

Always zero.

Parameters

mutex	The mutex to create or destroy.
mutexattr	Any attributes to set. If NULL, the call uses the default setting (PTHREAD_MUTEX_INITIALIZER).

Possible Errors

(none)

pthread_mutex_lock(), pthread_mutex_trylock()

Lock or try to lock a semaphore for entering a critical section. The parameter is simply a variable that acts like a reservation ticket. If another thread tries to lock a reserved spot, it blocks until the reserving thread releases the semaphore.

Prototype

```
#include <pthread.h>
int pthread_mutex_lock(pthread_mutex_t *mutex);
int pthread_mutex_trylock(pthread_mutex_t *mutex);
```

Return Value

The call returns zero on success and nonzero on error. You can find the exact code in errno.

Parameter

mutex   The semaphore variable

Possible Errors

EINVAL   The mutex has not been properly initialized.

EDEADLK   (pthread_mutex_try_lock) The calling thread has already
                         locked the mutex (error-checking mutexes only).

EBUSY   (pthread_mutex_lock) The calling thread can't acquire because
                         it is currently locked.

Example

```
pthread_mutex_t mutex = fastmutex;
...
if ( pthread_mutex_lock(&mutex) == 0 )
{
    /**** work on critical data ****/
    pthread_mutex_unlock(&mutex);
}

pthread_mutex_t mutex = fastmutex;
...
/*---Do other processing while waiting for semaphore---*/
while ( pthread_mutex_trylock(&mutex) != 0  &&  errno == EBUSY )
{
    /**** Work on something else while waiting ****/
}
/*---Got the semaphore!  Now work on the critical section---*/
if ( errno != ENOERROR )
{
    /**** work on critical data ****/
    pthread_mutex_unlock(&mutex);
}
```

pthread_mutex_unlock()

Unlock a mutex semaphore.

Prototype

```
#include <pthread.h>
int pthread_mutex_unlock(pthread_mutex_t *mutex);
```

Return Value

The call returns zero on success and nonzero on error. You can find the exact code in errno.

Parameter

mutex   The semaphore variable

Possible Errors

EINVAL   The mutex has not been properly initialized.

EPERM   The calling thread does not own the mutex (error-checking
                             mutexes only).

Example

(see pthread_mutex_lock())

Signals

When working with tasks, your program may get signals (or asynchronous notifications). This
section describes system calls that let you capture and process them.

signal()

Register the sig_fn routine to answer the signum signal. The default behavior is a single shot;
the signal handler reverts to the default after getting the first signal. Use sigaction() instead
if you want to control the behavior more.

Prototype

```
#include <signal.h>
void (*signal(int signum, void (*sig_fn)(int signum)))(int signum);
-or-
typedef void (*TSigFn)(int signum);
TSigFn signal(int signum, TSigFn sig_fn);
```

Return Value

A positive value if successful. If the thread-create call encountered any errors, the call returns a
negative value and sets errno to the error.

Parameters

signum   The signal number to capture

sig_fn   The program routine that the schedule calls

Possible Error

(errno not set)

Example

```
void sig_handler(int signum)
{
    switch ( signum )
    {
        case SIGFPE:
...
    }
}


...
if ( signal(SIGFPE, sig_handler) == 0 )
    perror("signal() failed");
```

sigaction()

Similar to `signal()`, `sigaction()` establishes the receiver of certain signals. Unlike `signal()`, however, this call gives you a lot more control over how the signaling notification behaves. It is also a little more complicated to use.

Prototype

```
#include <signal.h>
int sigaction(int signum, const struct sigaction *sigact,
        struct sigaction *oldsigact);
```

Return Value

Zero upon success; otherwise, nonzero.

Parameters

signum	The signal to capture.
sigact	The desired behavior and signal handler, using the following structure:

```
struct sigaction
{
    void (*sa_handler)(int);
    sigset_t sa_mask;
    int sa_flags;
    void (*sa_restorer)(void);
};
```

sa_handler	Signal handler function pointer.
sa_mask	The set of signals to block while servicing a signal in the signal handler.

| sa_restorer | Obsolete; do not use. |
| sa_flags | How to handle the signals. You can use the following flags: |

- SA_NOCLDSTOP   If the signal is SIGCHLD, ignore cases when the child stops or pauses.
- SA_ONESHOT or SA_RESETHAND   Reset the handler to the default after getting the first signal.
- SA_RESTART   Try to restart an interrupted system call. Normally, system calls that are interrupted return an EINTR error. This option tries to restart the call and avoid EINTR errors.
- SA_NOMASK or SA_NODEFER   Allow like signals to interrupt the handler. Normally, if your handler is responding to a particular signal like SIGCHLD, the kernel suspends other SIGCHLD signals. This can lead to lost signals. Using this option permits your handler to be interrupted. Be careful using this option.

| oldsigact | A repository of the old behaviors. You can copy the old settings here. |

Possible Errors

EINVAL	An invalid signal was specified. This will also be generated if an attempt is made to change the action for SIGKILL or SIGSTOP that cannot be caught.
EFAULT	The sigact or oldsigact parameter points to memory that is not a valid part of the process address space.
EINTR	System call was interrupted.

Example

```
void sig_handler(int signum)
{
    switch ( signum )
    {
        case SIGCHLD:
...
    }
}


...
struct sigaction sigact;
bzero(&sigact, sizeof(sigact));
sigact.sa_handler = sig_handler;  /* set the handler */
sigact.sa_flags = SA_NOCLDSTOP | SA_RESTART; /* set options */
if ( sigaction(SIGCHLD, &sigact, 0) == 0 )
    perror("sigaction() failed");
```

sigprocmask()

Sets which signals are permitted to interrupt while servicing a signal.

Prototype
```
#include <signal.h>
int sigprocmask(int how, const sigset_t *sigset, sigset_t *oldsigset);
```

Return Value

Nonzero upon error; otherwise, zero.

Parameters

how   The following are how the interrupting signals are treated while servicing a signal:

- SIG_BLOCK   The set of blocked signals is the union of the current set and the sigset argument.
- SIG_UNBLOCK   The signals in sigset are removed from the current set of blocked signals. It is legal to attempt to unblock a signal that is not blocked.
- SIG_SETMASK   The set of blocked signals is set to the argument sigset.

sigset   The destination signal-set.

Oldsigset   If non-NULL, the call places a copy of the old values in here.

Possible Errors

EFAULT   The sigset or oldsigset parameter points to memory that is not a valid part of the process address space.

EINTR   System call was interrupted.

Files and So On

This section describes a few library and system calls for file management.

bzero(), memset()

bzero() initializes the specified block to zeros. This call is deprecated, so you might want to use memset() instead.

memset() sets the specified block to val.

Prototype
```
#include <string.h>
void bzero(void *mem, int bytes);
void* memset(void *mem, int val, size_t bytes);
```

Return Value

`bzero()` returns no value.

`memset()` returns the reference mem.

Parameters

`mem`	The memory segment to initialize
`val`	The value to fill the segment with
`bytes`	The number of bytes to write (the size of the memory segment)

Possible Errors

(none)

Example

```
bzero(&addr, sizeof(addr));

memset(&addr, 0, sizeof(addr));
```

fcntl()

Manipulate the file or socket handle.

Prototype

```
#include <unistd.h>
#include <fcntl.h>

int fcntl(int fd, int cmd);
int fcntl(int fd, int cmd, long arg);
int fcntl(int fd, int cmd, struct flock *flock);
```

Return Value

On error, `-1` is returned and `errno` is set appropriately. For a successful call, the return value depends on the operation:

`F_DUPFD`	The new descriptor
`F_GETFD`	Value of flag
`F_GETFL`	Value of flags
`F_GETOWN`	Value of descriptor owner
`F_GETSIG`	Value of signal sent when read or write becomes possible, or zero for traditional `SIGIO` behavior

All other commands return zero.

Parameters

fd

The descriptor to manipulate.

cmd

The operation to perform. Some operations are duplicates of existing functions. Some operations require an operand (arg or flock). Each operation is grouped into specific functions:

- *Duplicate descriptor* (F_DUPFD) Same as dup2(arg, fd), this operation replaces fd with a copy of the descriptor in arg.

- *Manipulate close-on-exec* (F_GETFD, F_SETFD) The kernel does not pass all file descriptors to the exec-child process. With this parameter, you can test or set the close-on-exec.

- *Manipulate descriptor flags* (F_GETFL, F_SETFL) Using these commands, you can get the flags (set by the open() system call) of the descriptor. You can only set O_APPEND, O_NONBLOCK, and O_ASYNC.

- *Manipulate file locks* (F_GETLK, F_SETLK, F_SETLKW) GETLK retrieves the lock structure that currently holds the file. If the file is not locked

  - *Determine who owns I/O signals* (F_GETOWN, F_SETOWN)—Return or set the PID of the current owner of the SIGIO signal.

  - *Determine the kind of signal to send* (F_GETSIG, F_SETSIG)—Gets or sets the signal type when more I/O operations can be performed. Default is SIGIO.

arg

The value to set.

flock

The locking key.

Possible errors

EACCES

Operation is prohibited by locks held by other processes.

EAGAIN

Operation is prohibited because the file has been memory-mapped by another process.

EBADF

fd is not an open file descriptor.

EDEADLK

It was detected that the specified F_SETLKW command would cause a deadlock.

EFAULT

lock is outside your accessible address space.

EINTR	For F_SETLKW, the command was interrupted by a signal. For F_GETLK and F_SETLK, the command was interrupted by a signal before the lock was checked or acquired—most likely when locking a remote file (locking over NFS), but it can sometimes happen locally.
EINVAL	For F_DUPFD, arg is negative or is greater than the maximum allowable value. For F_SETSIG, arg is not an allowable signal number.
EMFILE	For F_DUPFD, the process already has the maximum number of file descriptors open.
ENOLCK	Too many segment locks open, lock table is full, or a remote locking protocol failed (locking over NFS, for example).
EPERM	Attempted to clear the O_APPEND flag on a file that has the append-only attribute set.

Example

```
#include <unistd.h>
#include <fnctl.h>
...
printf("PID which owns SIGIO: %d",
    fnctl(fd, F_GETOWN));

#include <unistd.h>
#include <fnctl.h>
...
if ( fnctl(fd, F_SETSIG, SIGKILL) != 0 )
    perror("Can't set signal");

#include <unistd.h>
#include <fnctl.h>
...
if ( (fd_copy = fcntl(fd, F_DUPFD)) < 0 )
    perror("Can't dup fd");
```

pipe()

Creates a pipe that points to itself. Each file descriptor in fd[] coincides with input (fd[0]) and output (fd[1]). If you write to fd[1], you can read the data on fd[0]. Used mostly with fork().

Prototype

```
#include <unistd.h>
int pipe(fd[2]);
```

Return Value

Zero if okay; -1 on error.

Parameter

fd   An array of two integers to receive the new file descriptor values

Possible Errors

EMFILE   Too many file descriptors are already in use by the current process.

ENFILE   The system's file table is full.

EFAULT   The process does not own the memory that fd points to (invalid memory reference).

Example

```
int fd[2];
pipe(fd); /* create pipe */
```

poll()

Similar to select(), this call waits on any one of several I/O channels for changes. Instead of using macros for managing and controlling the descriptor list, the programmer uses structure entries.

Prototype

```
#include <sys/poll.h>
int poll(struct pollfd *ufds, unsigned int nfds, int timeout);
```

Return Value

If less than zero, an error occurred; a zero returned means that the call timed out. Otherwise, the call returns the number of descriptor records that changed.

Parameters

ufds   The following is an array of pollfd structures. Each record tracks a different file descriptor.

```
struct pollfd
{
    int fd;            /* file descriptor */
    short events;      /* requested events */
    short revents;     /* returned events */
};
```

The fd field is the file descriptor to check. The events and revents fields indicate the events to check and the events that occurred, respectively. The bit-values available are as follows:

POLLIN   There is data to read.

POLLPRI   There is urgent data to read.

POLLOUT   Writing now will not block.

POLLERR	Error condition.	
POLLHUP	Hung up.	
POLLNVAL	Invalid request; fd not open.	
POLLRDNORM	Normal read (Linux only).	
POLLRDBAND	Read out-of-band (Linux only).	
POLLWRNORM	Normal write (Linux only).	
POLLWRBAND	Write out-of-band (Linux only).	

nfds   The number of records to check during the call.

timeout   The timeout in milliseconds. If timeout is negative, the call waits
                forever.

Possible Errors

ENOMEM   There was no space to allocate file descriptor tables.

EFAULT   The array given as argument was not contained in the calling
                program's address space.

EINTR   A signal occurred before any requested event.

Example

```
int fd_count=0;
struct pollfd fds[MAXFDs];
fds[fd_count].fd = socket(PF_INET, SOCK_STREAM, 0);
/*** bind() and listen() socket ***/
fds[fd_count++].events = POLLIN;
for (;;)
{
    if ( poll(fds, fd_count, TIMEOUT_MS) > 0 )
    {   int i;
        if ( (fds[0].revents & POLLIN) != 0 )
        {
            fds[fd_count].events = POLLIN | POLLHUP;
            fds[fd_count++].fd = accept(fds[0].fd, 0, 0);
        }
        for ( i = 1; i < fd_count; i++ )
        {
            if ( (fds[i].revents & POLLHUP) != 0 )
            {
                close(fds[i].fd);
                /*** Move up FDs to fill empty slot ***/
                fd_count--;
            }
            else if ( (fds[i].revents & POLLIN) != 0 )
```

```
                    /*** Read and process data ***/
            }
        }
    }
```

read()

Read `buf_len` bytes from the `fd` file descriptor into the buffer. You can use this system call for sockets as well as files, but this call does not provide as much control as the `recv()` system call.

Prototype
```
#include <unistd.h>
int read(int fd, char *buffer, size_t buf_len);
```

Return Value
The number of bytes actually read.

Parameters

fd	File (or socket) descriptor
buffer	The memory buffer to accept the read data
buf_len	The number of bytes to read and the number of legal bytes in the buffer

Possible Errors

EINTR	The call was interrupted by a signal before any data was read.
EAGAIN	Non-blocking I/O has been selected using O_NONBLOCK and no data was immediately available for reading.
EIO	I/O error. This will happen when the process is in a background process group, tries to read from its controlling tty, is either ignoring or blocking SIGTTIN, or its process group is orphaned. It can also occur when there is a low-level I/O error while reading from a disk or tape.
EISDIR	fd refers to a directory.
EBADF	fd is not a valid file descriptor or is not open for reading.
EINVAL	fd is attached to an object that is unsuitable for reading.
EFAULT	buf is outside your accessible address space.

Example
```
int sockfd;
int bytes_read;
char buffer[1024];
/*---create socket & connect to server---*/
if ( (bytes_read = read(sockfd, buffer, sizeof(buffer))) < 0 )
    perror("read");
```

select()

Wait for any I/O status changes from the file descriptor sets. When any of the specified sets changes, the call returns. You have four macros to help construct and manage the file descriptor sets:

- FD_CLR   Remove a descriptor from the set.
- FD_SET   Add a descriptor to a set.
- FD_ISSET   Test if specified descriptor is ready for I/O.
- FD_ZERO   Initialize the set to empty.

Prototype

```
#include <sys/time.h>
#include <sys/types.h>
#include <unistd.h>
int select(int hi_fd, fd_set *readfds, fd_set *writefds,
fd_set *exceptfds, struct timeval *timeout);
FD_CLR(int fd, fd_set *set);
FD_ISSET(int fd, fd_set *set);
FD_SET(int fd, fd_set *set);
FD_ZERO(fd_set *set);
```

Return Value

The number of descriptors that have changed states. If an error occurred, the return value is negative. If the timeout expired, the return value is zero.

Parameters

hi_fd	This is the highest file descriptor number + 1. For example, if you have four files open plus the stdio, your descriptors could be 0, 1, 2, 3, 5, 6, and 8. The highest is 8. If you include fd(8) in your select statement, hi_fd would equal 9. If the highest fd were 5, this parameter would be 6.
readfds	The set of descriptors to test for readability.
writefds	The set of descriptors to test for writing.
exceptfds	The set of descriptors to test for out-of-band data.
timeout	The maximum time to wait for data to arrive in microseconds. This is a pointer to a number. If the number is zero (not the pointer), the call returns immediately after checking all the descriptors. If the pointer is NULL (zero), the select's timeout feature is disabled.
fd	The file descriptor to add, remove, or test.
set	The file descriptor set.

Possible Errors

EBADF	An invalid file descriptor was given in one of the sets.
EINTR	A non-blocked signal was caught.
EINVAL	n is negative.
ENOMEM	select was unable to allocate memory for internal tables.

Example

```
int i, ports[]={9001, 9002, 9004, -1};
int sockfd, max=0;
fd_set set;
struct sockaddr_in addr;
struct timeval timeout={2,500000}; /* 2.5 sec. */

FD_ZERO(&set);
bzero(&addr, sizeof(addr));
addr.sin_family = AF_INET;
addr.sin_addr.s_addr = INADDR_ANY;
for ( i = 0; ports[i] > 0; i++ )
{
    sockfd = socket(PF_INET, SOCK_STREAM, 0);
    addr.sin_port = htons(ports[i]);
    if ( bind(sockfd, &addr, sizeof(addr)) != 0)
        perror("bind() failed");
    else
    {
        FD_SET(sockfd, &set);
        if ( max < sockfd )
            max = sockfd;
    }
}
if ( select(max+1, &set, 0, &set, &timeout) > 0 )
{
    for ( i = 0; i <= max; i++ )
        if ( FD_ISSET(i, &set) )
        {   int client = accept(i, 0, 0);
            /**** process the client's requests ****/
        }
}
```

C

KERNEL API
SUBSET

write()

Write msg_len bytes to fd field descriptor from buffer. You can use a socket descriptor as well, but it does not provide you with as much control as the send() system call.

Prototype
```
#include <unistd.h>
int write(int fd, const void *buffer, size_t msg_len);
```

Return Value
Number of bytes written. The byte count can be less than msg_len. If the call does not succeed in writing all required bytes, you can use a loop for successive writes. If negative, the call stores the error detail in errno.

Parameters

fd	File descriptor (can be a socket descriptor)
buffer	The message to write
msg_len	The length of the message

Possible Errors

EBADF	fd is not a valid file descriptor or is not open for writing.
EINVAL	fd is attached to an object that is unsuitable for writing.
EFAULT	buf is outside your accessible address space.
EPIPE	fd is connected to a pipe or socket whose reading end is closed. When this happens, the writing process will receive a SIGPIPE signal; if it catches, blocks, or ignores the error, EPIPE is returned.
EAGAIN	Non-blocking I/O has been selected using O_NONBLOCK and there was no room in the pipe or socket connected to fd to write the data immediately.
EINTR	The call was interrupted by a signal before any data was written.
ENOSPC	The device containing the file referred to by fd has no room for the data.
EIO	A low-level I/O error occurred while modifying the inode.

Example
```
/*** Write a message (TCP, UDP or Raw) ***/
int sockfd;
int bytes, bytes_wrote=0;
/*--- Create socket, connect to server ---*/
while ( (bytes = write(sockfd, buffer, msg_len)) > 0 )
    if ( (bytes_wrote += bytes) >= msg_len )
        break;
if ( bytes < 0 )
    perror("write");
```

close()

Closes all descriptors (file or socket). If the socket is connected to a server or client, it requests a close(). The channel actually remains active after the close until the channel empties or times out. Every process has a limit to the number of open descriptors it can have. getdtablesize() returns 1024 in Linux 2.2.14, and the /usr/include/linux/limits.h file defines this limit with NR_OPEN. Also, the first three descriptors default to stdin (0), stdout (1), and stderr (2).

Prototype

```
#include <unistd.h>
int close(int fd);
```

Return Value

Zero if everything goes well. If an error occurs, you can find the cause in errno.

Parameter

fd	The file or socket descriptor

Possible Error

EBADF	fd isn't a valid open file descriptor.

Example

```
int sockfd;
sockfd = socket(PF_INET, SOCK_RAW, htons(99));
if ( sockfd < 0 )
    PANIC("Raw socket create failed");
...
if ( close(sockfd) != 0 )
    PANIC("Raw socket close failed");
```

Object Classes

IN THIS APPENDIX

This appendix lists the classes defined in the Java API and the custom C++ library described in the book and on this book's Web site. Each class has one of three designations: *Class* (a normal class that you can instantiate), *Abstract Class* (a class that defines a skeleton for derived classes), and *Superclass* (an instantiable parent class).

C++ Exceptions

This section describes the classes for exception classes defined in the book. The hierarchy holds to the philosophy of doing as little as possible so as to minimize the potential of catastrophic class creations.

```
Exception <- RangeException
          <- FileException
          <- NetException    <- NetConversionException
                             <- NetDNSException
                             <- NetIOException
                             <- NetConnectException
                             <- NetConfigException
```

FIGURE D.1
The C++ exceptions class hierarchy.

Exception (Superclass)

Constructor:

Exception(SimpleString s);

General Description: Generic exception message with SimpleString type.

Method:

    const char* GetString()   Retrieve the string message.

Child Exceptions:

    RangeException   Any range exception. Used by MessageGroup class.
    FileException   Any file exception. Used by Socket class.

NetException (Class)

Constructor:

NetException(SimpleString s);

General Description: Generic network exception.

Parent Class: `Exception`

Child Exceptions:

`NetConversionException`	Host (`inet_ntop`/`inet_pton`) address conversion exception. Used by `HostAddress` class.
`NetDNSException`	Could not resolve hostname exception. Used by `HostAddress`.
`NetIOException`	`send()`/`recv()` exception. Used by `Socket`.
`NetConnectException`	Exception when trying to use `bind()`, `connect()`, `listen()`, or `accept()`. Used by `ServerSocket`, `ClientSocket`, and `MessageGroup`.
`NetConfigException`	Exception when trying to set or get socket option. Used by all `Socket` classes.

C++ Support Classes

This section describes several classes that are related to the framework but are simpler than those of other class libraries. Feel free to replace these as desired with the standard C++ class libraries.

SimpleString (Class)

Constructor:

```
SimpleString(const char* s);
SimpleString(const SimpleString& s);
```

General Description: Very simple and lightweight string type.

Methods:

`+(char *)+(Simplestring& )`	Append string to current instance.
`const char* GetString()`	Retrieve the string message.

Exceptions Thrown: (none)

HostAddress (Class)

Constructor:

```
HostAddress(const char* Name=0, ENetwork Network=eIPv4);
HostAddress(HostAddress& Address);
```

General Description: Class to manage host identification.

Methods:

`void SetPort(int Port);`	Set the port number.
`int GetPort(void) const;`	Get the port number.
`ENetwork GetNetwork(void) const;`	Get the network type.
`struct sockaddr* GetAddress(void) const;`	Get the actual socket address.
`int GetSize(void) const;`	Get socket address size.
`int ==(HostAddress& Address) const;`	Compare if equal.
`int !=(HostAddress& Address) const;`	Compare if not equal.
`const char* GetHost(bool byName=1);`	Retrieve the hostname.

Exceptions Thrown:

```
Exception
NetConversionException
NetDNSException
```

C++ Messaging Classes

This class hierarchy lets you define classes that self-package and self-unpackage the internal data. While not as simple or direct as the hierarchy in Java, it's simple and direct.

Message (Abstract Class)

Constructor: (none)

General Description: Message pattern for creating a specific message to send and receive.

Methods:

`virtual char* Wrap(int& Bytes) const;`	Interface for packaging object.
`bool Unwrap(char* package, int Bytes, int MsgNum);`	Interface for unpackaging object.

Exceptions Thrown: (none)

TextMessage (Class)

Constructor: (none)

General Description: Message pattern for creating a specific message to send and receive.

Parent Class: `Message`

Methods:

`=(const char* str);` `=(const TextMessage& s);`	Assign a new string to object.
`+=(const char* str);` `+=(const TextMessage& s);`	Append string to object.
`const char* GetBuffer(void) const;`	Get the text.
`char* Wrap(int& Bytes) const;`	Wrap object to send.
`bool Unwrap(char* package, int Bytes, int MsgNum);`	Unwrap received object.
`GetSize(void) const;`	Get length of string.
`void SetSize(int Bytes);`	Set string length.
`int GetAvailable(void) const;`	Get available bytes in buffer.

Exceptions Thrown: (none)

C++ Socket Classes

This hierarchy defines the classes that make up the socket interfaces. It contains effectively five different classes that you can instantiate: `SocketServer`, `SocketClient`, `Datagram`, `Broadcast`, and `MessageGroup`. You can easily expand this hierarchy with OpenSSL classes (`SSLServer` and `SSLClient`).

```
Socket    <- SocketStream    <- SocketServer
                             <- SocketClient
          <- Datagram        <- Broadcast
                             <- MessageGroup
```

FIGURE D.2
The C++ Socket class hierarchy.

Socket (Superclass)

Constructor:

```
Socket(void);
Socket(int sd);
Socket(ENetwork Network, EProtocol Protocol);
Socket(Socket& sock);
```

General Description: General socket class, not intended for direct instantiation.

Methods:

`void Bind(HostAddress& Addr);`	Bind socket to port/interface.
`void CloseInput(void) const;`	Close input stream.
`void CloseOutput(void) const;`	Close output stream.
`int Send(Message& Msg, int Options=0) const;`	Send message to connected site.
`int Send(HostAddress& Addr,` `  Message& Msg, int Options=0) const;`	Send directed message.
`int Receive(Message& Msg, int Options=0) const;`	Receive message from connection.
`int Receive(HostAddress& Addr,` `    Message& Msg, int Options=0) const;`	Receive directed message.
`void PermitRoute(bool Setting);`	Allow routable packets.
`void KeepAlive(bool Setting);`	Keep connection alive.
`void ShareAddress(bool Setting);`	Share port/interface address.
`int GetReceiveSize(void);` `void SetReceiveSize(int Bytes);`	Get/set receive buffer size.
`int GetSendSize(void);` `void SetSendSize(int Bytes);`	Get/set send buffer size.
`int GetMinReceive(void);` `void SetMinReceive(int Bytes);`	Get/set minimum watermark for SIGIO receive signal.
`int GetMinSend(void);` `void SetMinSend(int Bytes);`	Get/set minimum watermark for SIGIO send signal.
`struct timeval GetReceiveTimeout(void);` `void SetReceiveTimeout(struct timeval& val);`	Get/set time before aborting a receive.
`struct timeval GetSendTimeout(void);` `void SetSendTimeout(struct timeval& val);`	Get/set time before aborting a send.
`ENetwork GetType(void);`	Get the socket type (network).
`virtual int  GetTTL(void);` `virtual void SetTTL(int Hops);`	Get/set the time-to-live.
`int GetError(void);`	Get any pending errors.

Exceptions Thrown:

    NetException

    FileException

```
NetConnectException

NetIOException

NetConfigException
```

SocketStream (Class)

Constructor:

```
SocketStream(void);
SocketStream(int sd);
SocketStream(ENetwork Network);
SocketStream(SocketStream& sock);
```

General Description: Streaming (SOCK_STREAM) socket.

Parent Class: Socket

Methods:

`int  GetMaxSegmentSize(void);`	Get/set the segment size
`void SetMaxSegmentSize(short Bytes);`	(MSS).
`void DontDelay(bool Setting);`	Enable/disable Nagle algorithm.

Exception Thrown:

```
NetConfigException
```

D

OBJECT CLASSES

SocketServer (Class)

Constructor:

```
SocketServer(int port, ENetwork Network=eIPv4, int QLen=15);
SocketServer(HostAddress& Addr, int QLen=15);
```

General Description: TCP server.

Parent Class: SocketStream

Methods:

`void Accept(void (*Servlet)`	Accept a connection and call `Servlet`
`(const Socket& Client));`	with `Socket` handle.
`void Accept(HostAddress& Addr,`	Accept connection and capture host ID.
`void (*Server)(const Socket& Client));`	

Exceptions Thrown:

```
Exception

NetConnectException
```

SocketClient (Class)

Constructor:

```
SocketClient(ENetwork Network=eIPv4);
SocketClient(HostAddress& Host, ENetwork Network=eIPv4); //auto-connect
```

General Description: TCP client.

Parent Class: `SocketStream`

Method:

    `void Connect(HostAddress& Addr);`   Connect to host at `Addr`.

Exception Thrown:

    `NetConnectException`

Datagram (Class)

Constructor:

```
Datagram(HostAddress& Me, ENetwork Network=eIPv4,
    EProtocol Protocol=eDatagram);
Datagram(ENetwork Network=eIPv4, EProtocol
    Protocol=eDatagram);
```

General Description: General datagram (UDP) socket.

Parent Class: `Socket`

Methods:

    `void MinimizeDelay(bool Setting);`   Request minimal packet delay.

    `void MaximizeThroughput(bool Setting);`   Request maximum network throughput.

    `void MaximizeReliability(bool Setting);`   Request maximum reliability.

    `void MinimizeCost(bool Setting);`   Request minimal cost.

    `void PermitFragNegotiation(EFrag Setting);`   Set fragmentation negotiation.

Exception Thrown:

    `NetConfigException`

Broadcast (Class)

Constructor:

```
Broadcast(HostAddress& Me);
```

General Description: Broadcast socket for subnets.

Parent Class: `Datagram`

Methods: (none)

Exception Thrown:

> `NetConfigException`

MessageGroup (Class)

Constructor:

`MessageGroup(HostAddress& Me, ENetwork Network=eIPv4);`

General Description: Multicast socket.

Parent Class: `Datagram`

Methods:

`Connect(HostAddress& Address);`	Connect to multicast group address.
`void Join(HostAddress& Address, int IFIndex=0);`	Join multicast group.
`void Drop(HostAddress& Address);`	Drop multicast group.

Exceptions Thrown:

> `NetConfigException`
> `NetConnectException`
> `RangeException`

Java Exceptions

This section describes all the relevant exceptions that a Java program may generate while working with its sockets.

```
IOException   <- ProtocolException
              <- UnknownHostException
              <- UnknownServiceException
              <- SocketException  <- BindException
                                  <- ConnectException
                                  <- NoRouteToHostException
```

FIGURE D.3

The Java exceptions class hierarchy.

java.io.IOException (Class)

Constructor:

```
IOException();
IOException(String msg);
```

General Description: General exceptions during input and output.

Parent Class: Exception

Child Exceptions:

java.net.ProtocolException	Protocol error in Socket.
java.net.UnknownHostException	Hostname not found in DNS.
java.net.UnknownServiceException	Unsupported service attempted.

java.net.SocketException (Class)

Constructor:

```
SocketException();
SocketException(String msg);
```

General Description: Exception when trying to use bind(), connect(), listen(), or accept(). Used by ServerSocket, ClientSocket, and MessageGroup.

Parent Class: IOException

Child Exceptions:

java.net.BindException	Could not bind to address/port (often because it is already in use by another process).
java.net.ConnectException	Host unavailable, not found, not responding, or not process listening on designated port.
java.net.NoRouteToHostException	Route to the destination could not be established.

Java Support Classes

Like the C++ framework, Java uses several support classes to interface with its socket API. This section describes only those that are directly relevant to sockets.

java.net.DatagramPacket (Class)

Constructor:

```
DatagramPacket(byte[] buf, int len);
DatagramPacket(byte[] buf, int len, InetAddress addr, int port);
```

```
DatagramPacket(byte[] buf, int Offset, int len);
DatagramPacket(byte[] buf, int Offset, int len, InetAddress addr, int port);
```

General Description: Basic message carriers for receiving and sending messages.

Methods:

`InetAddress getAddress();` `void setAddress(InetAddress addr);`	Get or set the source or destination address of the packet.

`byte[] getData();`
`void setData(byte[] buf);`
`void setData(byte[] buf, int offset, int len);`
	Get or set the message data.

`int getLength();` `void setLength(int length);`	Get or set the message data length.
`int getOffset();`	Get the offset of the data to be sent or received.
`int getPort();` `void setPort(int port);`	Get or set the source or destination port of the packet.

Exceptions Thrown: (none)

java.net.InetAddress (Class)

Constructor: (none)

General Description: Internet address socket. This class does not have a constructor. Instead, use one of the static methods.

Static Methods:

`InetAddress getByName(String host);`	Return an InetAddress for host.
`InetAddress getAllByName(String host);`	Return all InetAddresses for host.
`InetAddress getLocalHost();`	Get the localhost IP address.

Methods:

`String getHostAddress();`	Get the numeric address.
`byte[] getAddress();`	Get the binary address.
`boolean isMulticastAddress();`	Check to see if the address is in the multicast range.
`String getHostName();`	Get the host's actual name.

Exception Thrown:

```
UnknownHostException
```

Java I/O Classes

Java has an outstanding set of classes that work with various I/O. Unfortunately, they are not very intuitive, and connecting them together is similar to working with a puzzle. Please read Chapter 12, "Using Java's Networking API," for more information on how to interlock these pieces into useful streams.

```
Object    <- InputStream     <- ByteArrayInputStream
                             <- ObjectInputStream
          <- OutputStream     <- ByteArrayOutputStream
                             <- ObjectOutputStream
          <- Reader   <- BufferedReader
          <- Writer   <- PrintWriter
```

FIGURE D.4
The Java I/O class hierarchy.

java.io.InputStream (Abstract Class)

Constructor:

`InputStream();`

General Description: A general class for basic stream input.

Parent Class: `Object`

Methods:

`int available();`	Return the number of bytes you can read without blocking.
`void close();`	Close the channel.
`void mark(int readlimit);`	Set the maximum number of bytes to buffer for `mark()` and `reset()`.
`boolean markSupported();`	Check to see if stream supports `mark()`/`reset()`.
`int read();`	Read a single byte from the stream.
`int read(byte[] arr);`	Read an array of bytes into `arr`.
`int read(byte[] arr, int offset, int length);`	Read an array of bytes into `arr` beginning at `offset` for `length` bytes.
`void reset();`	Return to last `marked` place.
`long skip(long n);`	Skip n bytes forward in the stream.

Exceptions Thrown:

    IOException

`java.io.ByteArrayInputStream` (Class)

Constructor:

```
ByteArrayInputStream(byte[] buf);
ByteArrayInputStream(byte[] buf, int offset, int length);
```

General Description: Allows you to create a virtual input stream from an array of bytes. Sometimes you get a block of data (such as from `DatagramSocket`); this class takes the role of streaming that information.

Parent Class: `InputStream`

Methods: (none; many overridden methods from `InputStream`)

Exceptions Thrown: (none)

`java.io.ObjectInputStream` (Class)

Constructor:

```
ObjectInputStream(InputStream o);
```

General Description: Using this class, you read transmitted or stored objects. You create this object with an `InputStream` (available in the `Socket` class).

Parent Class: `InputStream`

Methods:

`int available();`	Return the number of bytes you can read without blocking.
`void close();`	Close this channel.
`void defaultReadObject();`	Read the current class's non-static and non-transient fields from this stream.

`int read();`
`int read(byte[] arr,`
`    int offset, int len);`
`readFully(byte[] arr);`
`readFully(byte[] arr,`
`    int offset, int len);`
	Read a byte or an array of bytes beginning at `offset` for `len` bytes. `readFully()` reads all the bytes to fill the array, blocking as needed.

```
boolean readboolean();
byte readByte();
char readChar();
double readDouble();
float readFloat();
int readInt();
long readLong();
short readShort();
int readUnsignedByte();
int readUnsignedShort();
```
Read the designated type.

```
String readUTF();
Object
readObject();
```
Read `Object` instance. You can discover the type and then convert it later with the casting operators.

Exceptions Thrown:

```
IOException
ClassNotFoundException
NotActiveException
OptionalDataException
InvalidObjectException
SecurityException
StreamCorruptedException
```

java.io.OutputStream (Abstract Class)

Constructor:

```
OutputStream();
```

General Description: A general class for basic stream input.

Parent Class: `Object`

Methods:

```
void close();
void flush();
void write(byte b);
int write(byte[] arr);
int write(byte[] arr,
 int offset, int len);
```
Close the channel.
Flush written data from buffers.
Write a single byte to the stream.
Write an array of bytes (arr) to the stream.
Write an array of bytes (arr)
beginning at offset for len bytes.

Exception Thrown:

```
IOException
```

java.io.ByteArrayOutputStream (Class)

Constructor:

```
ByteArrayOutputStream();
ByteArrayOutputStream(int size);
```

General Description: Allows you to stream data into an array of bytes. Classes like DatagramSocket work only with blocks of data; this class takes the role of streaming information.

Parent Class: OutputStream

Methods:

void reset();	Clear buffers and empty array.
int write(byte[] arr, int offset, int len);	Write an array of bytes (arr) beginning at offset for len bytes.
byte[] toByteArray();	Return the array of streamed data.
int size();	Return the current size of the buffer.
String toString(String encoder);	Create string, translating chars with encoder.
void write(int b);	Write a single byte to the stream.
void write(OutputStream o);	Send the array of data through OutputStream.

Exceptions Thrown: (none)

java.io.ObjectOutputStream (Class)

Constructor:

```
ObjectOutputStream(OutputStream o);
```

General Description: Using this class, you transmit or store objects. You create this object with an OutputStream (available in the Socket class).

Parent Class: OutputStream

Methods:

void close();	Close this channel.
void defaultWriteObject();	Write the current class's non-static and non-transient fields to this stream. You can call this only while in the writeObject() method during serialization.
int flush();	Flush written data from buffers.

```
int reset();
```
Toss the information written to the stream.

```
void useProtocolVersion(int version);
```
Force earlier serialization version.

```
void write(byte b);
int write(byte[] arr);
int write(byte[] arr,
  int offset, int len);
```
Write a byte or an array of bytes beginning at offset for len bytes.

```
void writeboolean(boolean b);
void writeByte(byte b);
void writeBytes(String s);
void writeChar(int c);
void writeChars(String s);
void writeDouble(double d);
void writeFloat(float f);
void writeInt(int i);
void writeLong(long l);
void writeShort(int us);
```
Write the designated type.

```
void writeUTF(String s);
int writeFields();
```
Write buffered fields to stream.

```
void writeObject(Object o);
```
Write Object instance.

Exceptions Thrown:

```
IOException
SecurityException
```

java.io.BufferedReader (Class)

Constructor:

```
BufferedReader(Reader i);
BufferedReader(Reader i, int size);
```

General Description: Keeps buffers for improved performance. Does some translation of types for line recognition. size specifies the size of the input buffers.

Parent Class: Reader

Methods:

```
void close();
```
Close the channel.

```
void mark(int readlimit);
```
Set the maximum number of bytes to buffer for mark() and reset().

`boolean markSupported();`	Check to see if stream supports `mark()`/`reset()`.
`int read();`	Read a single byte from the stream.
`int read(byte[] arr, int offset, int length);`	Read an array of bytes into `arr` beginning at `offset` for `length` bytes.
`String readLine();`	Read up to newline and return `String`.
`boolean ready();`	Return true if ready to read.
`void reset();`	Return to last `mark`ed place.
`long skip(long n);`	Skip n bytes forward in the stream.

Exception Thrown:

    IOException

`java.io.PrintWriter` (Class)

Constructor:

```
PrintWriter(Writer o);
PrintWriter(Writer o, boolean autoFlush);
PrintWriter(OutputStream o);
PrintWriter(OutputStream o, boolean autoFlush);
```

General Description: does some translation from data types into readable text. The `autoFlush` flag forces a flush when the program calls `println()`.

Parent Class: `Writer`

Methods:

`boolean checkError();`	Flush stream and check for any errors.
`void close();`	Close this channel.
`void defaultWriteObject();`	Write the current class's non-static and non-transient fields to this stream. You can only call this while in the `writeObject()` method during serialization.
`int flush();`	Flush written data from buffers.
`int reset();`	Toss the information written to the stream.

`void write(byte b);`
`int write(byte[] arr);`
`int write(byte[] arr, int offset, int len);`
	Write a byte or an array of bytes beginning at `offset` for `len` bytes.

```void print(boolean b);```
```void print(char c);```
```void print(char[] s);```
```void print(double d);```
```void print(float f);```
```void print(int i);```
```void print(long l);```
```void print(Object obj);```
```void print(String s);```
	Print the designated type. The `Object` type uses the `String.valueOf()` method to convert data.

```void println();```
```void println(boolean b);```
```void println(char c);```
```void println(char[]s);```
```void println(double d);```
```void println(float f);```
```void println(int i);```
```void println(long l);```
```void println(Object obj);```
```void println(String s);```
	Print the designated type and terminate line with newline. If `autoFlush` is enabled, flush the stream.

```void write(int b);```	Write a single byte to the stream.
```int write(char[] arr);```	Write an array of chars (`arr`) to stream.
```int write(char[] arr,``` ``` int offset, int len);```	Write an array of chars (`arr`) beginning at `offset` for `len` bytes.
```int write(String s);```	Write string to stream.
```int write(String s,``` ```int offset, int len);```	Write string to stream beginning at `offset` for `len` bytes.

Exceptions Thrown:

```
IOException

SecurityException
```

Java Socket Classes

The Java Socket API supports four basic IPv4 classes: `Socket`, `ServerSocket`, `DatagramSocket`, and `MulticastSocket`. This section describes the interface for each of these classes.

```
Object    <- Socket
          <- ServerSocket
          <- DatagramSocket   <- MulticastSocket
```

FIGURE D.5

The Java socket class hierarchy.

java.net.Socket (Class)

Constructor:

```
Socket(String host, int port);
Socket(InetAddress addr, int port);
Socket(String host, int port, InetAddress lAddr, int lPort);
Socket(InetAddress addr, int port, InetAddress lAddr, int lPort);
```

General Description: This is the basic communication interface (TCP) for all network traffic.

Parent Class: `Object`

Methods:

`void close();`	Close the socket.
`InetAddress getInetAddress();`	Get the host address of the peer.
`InputStream getInputStream();`	Get the `InputStream` for receiving messages.
`boolean getKeepAlive();` `void setKeepAlive(boolean on);`	Keep the connection alive.
`InetAddress getLocalAddress();`	Get the local address the socket is connected to.
`int getLocalPort();`	Get the local port.
`OutputStream getOutputStream();`	Get the `OutputStream` for sending messages.
`int getPort();`	Get the peer's port number.
`int getReceiveBufferSize();` `void setReceiveBufferSize(int size);`	Get/set receive buffer's size.
`int getSendBufferSize();` `void setSendBufferSize(int size);`	Get/set send buffer's size.
`int getSoLinger();` `void setSoLinger(boolean on, int linger);`	Get/set the socket linger time (in seconds).
`int getSoTimeout();` `void setSoTimeout(int timeout);`	Get/set the timeout for I/O. If enabled, reading the pipe aborts after specified time.

D

OBJECT CLASSES

```
boolean getTcpNoDelay();
void setTcpNoDelay(boolean on);
```
Enable/disable the Nagle algorithm, which determines the process for sending information. If disabled, the computer sends the data before it receives any confirmation.

```
void shutdownInput();
```
Close the input channel.
```
void shutdownOutput();
```
Close the output channel.

Exceptions Thrown:

```
IOException
SocketException
```

java.net.ServerSocket (Class)

Constructor:

```
ServerSocket(int port);
ServerSocket(int port, int backLog);
ServerSocket(int port, int backLog, InetAddress bindAddr);
```

General Description: This specialized TCP socket creates a listening server socket.

Parent Class: Object

Static Method:

```
setSocketFactory(SocketImplFactory fac);
```
Set the Socket implementation factory.

Methods:

```
Socket accept();
```
Accept a client connection and return a Socket.
```
void close();
```
Close the socket.
```
InetAddress getInetAddress();
```
Get the local address the socket is connected to.
```
int getLocalPort();
```
Get the local port.
```
int getSoTimeout();
void setSoTimeout(int timeout);
```
Get/set the timeout for I/O. If enabled, reading the pipe aborts after specified time.

Exceptions Thrown:

```
IOException
SocketException
```

java.net.DatagramSocket (Class)

Constructor:

```
DatagramSocket();
DatagramSocket(int port);
DatagramSocket(int port, InetAddress bindAddr);
```

General Description: This is the general datagram (UDP) socket for message passing.

Parent Class: Object

Methods:

`void close();`	Close the socket.
`void connect(InetAddress addr, int port);`	Connect peers for implicit sending.
`void disconnect();`	Disconnect connected peers.
`InetAddress getInetAddress();`	Get the host address of the peer.
`InetAddress getLocalAddress();`	Get the local address the socket is connected to.
`int getLocalPort();`	Get the local port.
`int getPort();`	Get the peer's port number.
`int getReceiveBufferSize();` `void setReceiveBufferSize(int size);`	Get/set receive buffer's size.
`int getSendBufferSize();` `void setSendBufferSize(int size);`	Get/set send buffer's size.
`int getSoTimeout();` `void setSoTimeout(int timeout);`	Get/set the timeout for I/O. If enabled, reading the pipe aborts after specified time.
`void receive(DatagramPacket p);`	Receive message.
`void send(DatagramPacket p);`	Send message.

Exceptions Thrown:

```
IOException
SocketException
```

java.net.MulticastSocket (Class)

Constructor:

```
MulticastSocket();
MulticastSocket(int port);
```

General Description: This is the general datagram (UDP) socket for unconnected messages.

Parent Class: DatagramSocket

Methods:

```
InetAddress getInterface();           Get/set the local address the socket is
void setInterface(InetAddress addr);  connected to.

int getTimeToLive();                  Get/set the time-to-live for each message.
void setTimeToLive(int TTL);

void joinGroup(InetAddress addr);     Leave multicast group.
void leaveGroup(InetAddress addr);    Join multicast group.
void send(DatagramPacket p, int TTL); Send message with specific TTL.
```

Exceptions Thrown:

```
IOException
SocketException
```

INDEX

SYMBOLS

A

build and test paradigm,
118
business analysts, 315
byte ordering, 37
bzero() system call, 19,
465

C

C programming language
C++ (comparison), 284
compiling programs with
threads, 142
network programming, 323
passing data, 323
returning vectors by value,
324
string types, 332
C++ programming language
C comparison, 284
exception classes, 478
friend directive, 309
limitations, data streaming,
287
messaging classes, 480
socket classes, 481
socket programming, 284
support classes, 479
-c <count> command, 68
calculating checksums,
375
calling external programs
with exec server,
168-170
calloc() system call, 230
calls, 223. *See also* system
calls
IPv4, converting to IPv6,
386-387
non-stateless, creating with
open connections, 335

phases, 336
Socket API calls, return
values, 223-225
UNIX library calls,
222-223
capturing
SIGFPE handler, 158
signals, 462
cards
Ethernet cards
LAN cards, 98
security, 345
network cards, promiscu-
ous mode, 99
**casting sockaddr types,
18**
**certificates, creating with
OpenSSL, 356**
**certification, 126, 235,
341**
**CGI (Common Gateway
Interface), 168**
channels, 8, 428
checkpointing, 104, 325
checksums
calculating, 375
TCP, 90
UDP, 90
child exceptions
Exception superclass, 478
java.io.IOException class,
486
java.net.SocketException
class, 486
NetException class, 479
children
bi-lateral connections with
parents, 155
controlling, 165
creating, 199
creating pipes in, 152
detaching, 167
getpid() system call, 139

return values, 167
setting state, 149
unilateral connections with
parents, 154
terminating, 455
zombies, 165
**CIDR (Classless Internet
Domain Routing), 31**
ciphers, 351-352
public-key ciphers, 351
symmetric-key ciphers,
351
classes, 291, 478. *See also*
components
abstract
*java.io.InputStream,
488*
*java.io.OutputStream,
490*
Message, 480
adding functions, 292-294
attributes, 293
Broadcast, 484
constructors, 294
coupling, 313
Datagram, 484
DatagramPacket class
(Java), 269
DatagramSocket class
(Java), 269
defining capabilities, 291
destructors, 295
Exception, 288
friend directive (C++), 309
HostAddress, 479
I/O classes (Java), 272-275
inheritance, 290
foreign classes, 309
*program development,
308*
Internet addressing, 30
java.io.BufferedReader,
492

passive interfaces, 327
reusable modules for
   upside down interfaces,
   329
Sockets Frameworks, 284
**WSTOPSIG(status) macro,
455**
**WTERMSIG(status) macro,
455**

X – Z

.x file extension, 329
X files, 332
XDR interface
   pointer references, 334
   rpcgen tool, 330
   strings, 332

zeroth addresses, 32
zombies
   creating, 165
   exec(), 167
   killing, 165, 455
zone locking, 163

Hey, you've got enough worries.

Don't let IT training be one of them.

Get on the fast track to IT training at InformIT,
your total Information Technology training network.

 | **www.informit.com** | **SAMS**